SIR JAMES GRAHAM

By the same author

The Factory Movement, 1830–1855

Sir James Graham

SIR
JAMES
GRAHAM

J. T. WARD

MACMILLAN
London · Melbourne · Toronto

ST MARTIN'S PRESS
New York
1 9 6 7

© J. T. Ward 1967

MACMILLAN AND COMPANY LIMITED
Little Essex Street London WC2
also Bombay Calcutta Madras Melbourne

THE MACMILLAN COMPANY OF CANADA LIMITED
70 Bond Street Toronto 2

ST MARTIN'S PRESS INC
175 Fifth Avenue New York NY 10010

Library of Congress catalog card no 67–18374

PRINTED IN GREAT BRITAIN

TO KAY

Contents

Contents

List of Illustrations

List of Illustrations

Preface

Sir James Graham has never been popular. Throughout a long and varied political career he incurred the suspicion and hostility of journalists, and his changes in party allegiance provoked attacks from assorted groups. To Cobbett, in 1826, he seemed 'stupid . . . empty-headed . . . [and] insolent'; to the *Manchester Guardian* in 1837 he was a 'turn-coat', to the *Morning Chronicle* in 1841 'a busybody', to *Blackwood's Magazine* in 1855 'wicked and shameless'. As his nominal affiliations altered so contemporaries adjusted their views. For instance, Disraeli, who had known him socially, found him 'eloquent and patriotic' in 1837 and 'bitter' in 1844. Graham obviously lacked the hack partisanship of a Tadpole and Taper, but he agreed with too many of their attitudes for Disraeli's taste. In 1834 Taper had suggested a party cry:

'Ancient institutions and modern improvements, I suppose, Mr. Tadpole?'

'Ameliorations is the better word; ameliorations. Nobody knows exactly what it means.'

'. . . The time has gone by for Tory governments. What the country requires is a sound Conservative government.'

'A sound Conservative government,' said Taper, musingly. 'I understand: Tory men and Whig measures.'

Suspicions of Graham were heightened by his often vague and sometimes ambiguous support of 'amelioration', as well as by his party shortcomings. In 1852 Marx dismissed him and his allies as 'perambulant Peel monuments . . . nothing but [a] staff of bureaucrats which Robert Peel had schooled for himself'.[1]

Later historians — making at best imperfect use of his private papers — tended to accept the verdicts of contemporary critics.

Graham appears in many books as a cold, calculating man, ruthlessly efficient but devoid of humanity and perhaps of principle. He changed parties, disdained potential allies, haughtily offended opponents and lost some of his closest friends. He never sought popular acclaim and rarely obtained it. He appeared to fear the future and the responsibility of shaping it. His career lacked the dramatic attractions and even glamour of some of his colleagues. Historians, like contemporaries, have observed the contrast between his ability to predict long-term strategic dispositions and his weakness on immediate tactics. Recognition of his talents, however, has always been qualified by other considerations. 'I begin to be interested for Aberdeen,' Croker told Herries in August 1853,[2]

> for I see not who is to succeed him. Graham seems to me to stand the most forward for the succession, but what between his boldness of language and timidity in action, I should be afraid, for him and for us, of some great catastrophe; but he is, I think, the cleverest administrator in the Cabinet . . .

Such feelings sometimes prevented even ostensible friends from expressing sympathy during difficult periods; indeed, the sight of Graham in trouble must have brought vindictive pleasure to many who had suffered his verbal lashings in the House of Commons. In February 1845, when Graham was under bitter attack over the secret opening of letters, a young Yorkshire Conservative, Gathorne Hardy, recorded that[3]

> The personality is extreme and the unfairness to Sir James Graham most abominable. However, there are exceptions on the Opposition side who do him justice. Charles Buller rightly enough said that he seemed to have a love for unpopularity, and certainly there is nothing conciliatory about him.

Personal unpopularity dogged Graham through his life and after it.

In recent years historians have been increasingly interested in the Victorian administrative revolution, the politics of the mid-century party desert and the manœuvres of clique and Cabinet now more fully documented with the opening of many family muniments. It may now be possible to see Graham in a new light, as a statesman who made a considerable contribution to the politics of the age of transformation, the period between Lord Liverpool's post-Napoleonic War régime and the era of Lord Palmerston's dominance. As a young Whig he opposed Liverpool's tired Ministry, and as an elder statesman (and 'a man of peace') he condemned what he regarded as Palmerston's warlike proclivities. On both occasions, his views were probably unfair.[4] But in virtually every political event for four decades Graham played some part, often an important part.

Born into a well-connected but not particularly affluent landowning family, Graham never enjoyed the vast wealth of an Earl of Durham or Derby. He earned neither popularity nor notoriety by lavish hospitality or costly excesses. Youthful wild oats were sown rapidly; at 21 Graham regaled Lord William Bentinck with confessions about his romantic life. Thereafter, Graham did not even have the quality of providing scandalous material for the inquisitive, 'liberal-minded' gossips of London society. His neglect of 'Society' played some part in creating his unpopular public image; the hostesses of the party salons were disappointed at the absence of a handsome politician. The family finances rarely allowed Graham to cut a great figure even in his native county. He was nevertheless prominent in public life, at a time when major changes in both political and constitutional arrangements were being made. As a member of the four-man planning committee, he helped to shape the first Reform Act. His role was at least controversial; Durham's first biographer commented that[5]

> Graham was not exactly a man after Durham's heart, and it was probably in deference to Grey that he was appointed. He was certainly the least progressive member of the quartette, a fact which the political caricaturists of the hour were quick to seize, since they represented him as the man in charge of the brake on the new Reform Coach.

The brakeman was, however, highly discriminating in his application of pressure.

Despite periodic 'radical' outbursts, however, Graham was generally conservative. He supported the Church, as a patron, as a politician, as a member of the Church estates committee and as a practising Anglican. And he often dreaded the possibility of social revolution and subsequent anarchy. Consequently, working-class agitations aroused his immediate concern. During the 1842 riots, for instance, he told the Lord Chancellor that 'treason was stalking abroad'; and he believed that 'force alone could subdue this rebellious spirit'. He bitterly resented what he considered to be the cowardly inaction of some magistrates and even considered taking action against them.[6] 'I am glad that you are residing on your property,' he told Kay-Shuttleworth at this time,[7]

> and I am willing to hope that your influence, good advice and good example may contribute in your neighbourhood to win back the poor deluded workmen from the error of their ways . . . I am sure that you will point out to your neighbours the madness of concessions made to threats and open violence.

The vision of the squire firmly administering his ancestral estate still attracted Graham; but the country gentry must, of course, be backed up during major troubles by soldiers, yeomanry and policemen. Graham introduced the first plain-clothes section in the Metropolitan Police.[8] He supported decorum, tradition and moderation in Church and State, but was prepared strongly to oppose any factor disturbing them. Political Radicalism and religious Tractarianism were both anathema. 'The Protestants, weary of abusing the Papists, are disposed to turn semi-Papists themselves,' he complained to Croker in 1844, '. . . and the Church, which has overcome her Enemies from without, is now in imminent danger from the Feuds within her Pale'.[9]

Graham was inclined to regret the signs, which he only too often suspected, of major changes in society. He tended to see a deep-laid conspiracy behind spontaneous, ill-organised protests against social grievances. The campaigns for legislative reform of factory conditions, symbolic as they were of a wide range of operative opinion, failed to rouse his sympathy; and he never professed to accept the varied panaceas for proletarian misery. In a negative way, Graham's view on some industrial problems thus accord with those of some 'liberal' historians. But Graham would not deny (as some later commentators did) the existence of widespread wretchedness and poverty: he accepted them as sadly natural and inevitable. Such features of society could no more be abolished than could sin; but Christians and the State had some duty in the line of 'ameliorations'.

While fearing and hating the possibility of revolutionary change — and despite his long, morose study of Burke — Graham sought no dramatic role in the Counter-Revolution. Indeed, he always disliked the Tory Right as much as the Radical Left. His answer to 'extremist' demands through most of his life was moderate concession: he would lead no Vendée. In a sense, his whole career was a long rearguard action, consisting of sometimes hasty tactical retreats and of carefully-planned strategic withdrawals to prepared positions. To this eventually consistent but seemingly opportunist and certainly unheroic philosophy, Graham brought the service of brilliant administrative talents. He was allowed to demonstrate his ability most obviously as a Whig First Lord of the Admiralty in the early 1830s, a Conservative Home Secretary in the 1840s and a Peelite First Lord during the Crimean War.

The political situations which allowed Graham to play his unique part were often strange and novel. From 1828 the time-honoured elements of the constitution were being shaken and modified. Reform of parliamentary representation, the 'enactment' of religious toleration and the development of party organisation and tactics proceeded together with the dismantling of old Mercantilist controls on aspects of the economy and the growth of new administrative 'interference'. The rural Britain from which most prominent politicians hailed was already paling before the industrial expansion of the world's workshop. During Graham's life, the 'age of improvement' described by Professor Briggs gradually created the 'age of equipoise' described by Professor Burn. Politically, a long Tory domination was followed from 1830 by a long period of liberal rule, which was only temporarily reversed by Peel in 1841. But the liberal age saw the decline of historic Whiggism and the growth of a new Liberalism compounded of many competing interests: the aristocratic hegemony was under challenge and eventually decayed. Simultaneously, the other traditional grouping was undergoing at least equally important transformation. The Toryism of Mr. Pitt, of the new peerage, of the close mercantile corporations, of backwoods squires and boozy 'Church and King' mobs sacking 'Jacobin' houses or toasting intolerance at annual dinners could not last. And, in the new political and economic setting, a Toryism centred primarily on agricultural Protection could scarcely hope to achieve real power. Thus, at differing speeds, both party traditions were gradually reshaped.

Such changes in party philosophies and attitudes were slow to develop. A division of seats which gave Thetford equal representation with Leeds and which left intact the power of the Grosvenors at Chester and the Lawrences at Ripon to some extent hid the relative decline in the importance of the agricultural interests in politics. 'This will clip the aristocracy, but a good deal must be sacrificed to save the rest,' wrote the Whig Lady Belgrave of the 1831 Reform Bill, which cost her father-in-law (Lord Grosvenor) £150,000.[10] The great national institutions soon emerged safely from their dangers. Perhaps the Monarchy changed with monarchs: while George IV 'stood by and let the country govern itself',[11] William IV came to dislike his Ministers strongly enough to exercise his prerogative to dismiss them and the young Whiggish Victoria liked them too well to accept their opponents. Under the Prince Consort's influence, however, the Court turned increasingly towards the conception of a constitutional monarchy in a roughly modern sense. Again, the transition was slow. No Bagehot could yet venture to define the Monarch's powers and rights. But ostensibly there was little change in the strength of the Crown. Indeed, when Queen and Prince aided the workings of the developing party system, their political influence increased. They were undoubtedly aided by a change in social *mores*: the 'bourgeois' virtue of their family life was more attractive to much of society than the Royal dukes' siring of progenies of Fitzgeorges and Fitzclarences, collections of debts and rash political ventures.

The House of Lords, hated by the Radical mob and humbled by
Government coercion over Reform in 1832, was soon busily
reasserting its powers and its hostility to continuing reform.
Though subsequently the peers were quieter and more reserved —
the Orange leader Cumberland became King of Hanover on
Victoria's accession, and many partisan creations were inherited
by moderate second-generation peers — the long-threatened
'reform' of their House never occurred in the nineteenth century.
Indeed, while retaining its reserve of political power and
continuing to provide politicians often of the first rank, the
aristocracy was becoming more powerful socially. The attacks of
old-fashioned urban Radicals on what they imagined to be
semi-feudal landed tyrants were increasingly anachronistic; many
landed proprietors prospered enormously as urban rents, mineral
royalties and industrial profits were added to agricultural
incomes. Even the Church emerged from the bitter attacks of
Radical Dissent, organisationally reformed and theologically
divided but still established, wealthy and powerful.

The moderation of Reform in its ultimate result was largely due
to the restraining influence of conservatives in all political groups.
Among such conservatives Graham was prominent. He loyally
supported the Church, even at the risk of strong Nonconformist
Protestant opposition. The education clauses of his Factory Bill
of 1843 seemed to one Dissenting publicist to be 'a Declaration of
War against all the Dissenters of the kingdom' and 'the greatest
outrage on Civil and Religious Liberty attempted in modern
times'.[12] Graham himself bluntly declared that 'the dissenting
bodies were not, it appeared, satisfied with toleration, contending
that the principle should be one of equality; but as long as there was
an established Church in this country he was of opinion that that
Church should enjoy the preference'. He thus earned some
Anglican gratitude.[13] A heated Nonconformist insisted that 'he
knew that Graham took Lord Sidmouth for his model'.[14] But in
fact Graham was moderate on most theological and political
subjects. Like Peel, he recognised that the Church must be aided
with great caution; and he always distrusted Oxford Catholicism.

Even after his most liberal days in politics, he insisted that he had been elected to Parliament 'as a member of the old Whig party, pledged to Parliamentary Reform, but the avowed friend of the Protestant Church Establishment and the enemy of Ballot, short Parliaments and all the nostrums by which the regal and aristocratic power is assailed'. While far from 'exclusive', his conservatism was at least socially selective, resting (as he explained) on that section of society 'which claimed to itself a great preponderance of property, of learning, of decent manners and of pure religion'.[15]

Graham's many critics were not always wrong, but they were often unfair. He certainly and inevitably made mistakes, strategic, tactical and psychological. Privately, he was capable of great kindness to friends and relations and would on occasion take great care in helping even political opponents.[16] But the difficulty in penetrating the haughty public mask led to suspicion. Closer acquaintance with Graham did not, in any case, cause approval or liking. His age produced too many attractive, immediately appealing public men — 'sentimental' reformers, brave decision-makers, debonair gamblers in politics — for Graham, at his greatest an excellent adjutant and a supreme forecaster of consequences, to exert any magnetic draw. The coolly calculating politician, who might claim some political consistency of principle but who had been loyal to few individuals and to no party, remained unattractive. Yet, as the relationship develops, the most antagonistic cynic must surely come to admire the honest toil, the often sacrificial devotion to duty, the clear and often well-applied intellect and the real loyalty to principle which together constituted one part of Graham's complex character and varied achievement. Certainly, his career was not admirable, exciting, brave or even generally pleasing in the sense in which nineteenth-century semi-hagiographers painted their subjects. Indeed, no one ever pictured Graham without including his warts — and many artists highlighted them. But the hues and contours of the portraits of some of his contemporaries have subsequently been changed, by both extra knowledge and amended taste. And whatever shapes and colours may emerge, Graham deserves a new portrait.

Acknowledgements

Many people helped, in a variety of ways, to write this book. My obligation to Sir Fergus Graham, Bt., K.B.E., who kindly allowed me to use the papers of Sir James Graham (largely reproduced on microfilm in Cambridge University Library) is primary. I am also very greatly indebted to Professor S. G. E. Lythe of the University of Strathclyde and Professor Asa Briggs of the University of Sussex, who read and greatly improved the script.

With many other historians, I am under great obligations to a great teacher and a great librarian. Mr. F. R. Salter, O.B.E., of Magdalene College, Cambridge, from whom I first heard of Graham, gave me both valuable advice and liberal hospitality. Mr. Frank Beckwith of the Leeds Library allowed me to benefit from his erudite conversation and kindly loan of books.

For help, suggestions, advice and comments on various problems I am indebted to Dr. D. G. Southgate of Queen's College, Dundee (who originally suggested the subject to me), Mr. Kenneth Carter of the Dorset County Library, Mr. F. C. Mather of the University of Southampton, Mr. R. G. Garnett of the Manchester College of Commerce, Mr. P. R. C. Ward, Miss G. Towers, Mr. Derick Mirfin, Mr. Godfrey Meynell, M.B.E., the late Colonel G. W. Ferrand, O.B.E., Mr. R. F. Drewery of the Hull Library, Mr. R. J. Marriott of the St. Ives Library, Miss D. Wood of the Ripon Library, Mr. H. J. P. Pafford of the Goldsmiths' Library in the University of London, Mr. Kenneth Smith of Carlisle Library and Mr. A. N. Cass of Queen's College, Dundee, Library. Access to library collections has been very important during the preparation of this book, and I must acknowledge with gratitude the courteous service provided by the Glasgow University Library and the Mitchell Library, Glasgow.

Miss Ann Marie McEleney, who typed the script, often at considerable inconvenience, played a vital role. My wife helped to check the text and compile the index. And our son, born during the writing of this book, permitted it to be completed. Neither he nor any of the people who have so generously aided me shares any responsibility for the following pages.

1

The Formative Years

On the evening of 12 June 1812 a handsome, rather arrogant young man left Falmouth for Lisbon. He was James Robert George Graham, the son and heir of a Cumbrian baronet, and he was newly released from two wasted years at Oxford. In the spring his reluctant father and the more willing Dean of Christ Church had agreed that he should leave the University and travel abroad. Eleven days after his twentieth birthday, supported by an allowance of £1,000 a year , he set off to see the lands where the new Earl of Wellington was fighting the French. After 'a tedious passage' across the Bay of Biscay, he arrived in Portugal on 24 June.

The Braganza kingdom, Britain's last, hesitant friend, had been invaded by General Junot in 1807, a day after the Regent, Court and Treasury had sailed for Brazil. French ineptitude and misbehaviour had soon provoked patriotic risings, and by 1808 Imperial control was confined to Lisbon and the major garrison towns. The British Cabinet, urgently needing a victory on land, then sent its only army to Oporto, under Sir Arthur Wellesley, to bolster the ragged and doubtfully-loyal local levies. But early victories were lost by subsequent negotiations, and in 1809 Napoleon's Grand Army fell upon Sir John Moore's ill-equipped troops. When Wellesley returned to Lisbon in the same year he had to restart his work.

As young Graham arrived in the battle-scarred country, armed with introductions to the British Minister, Sir Charles Stuart, and to Admiral George Berkeley, Wellesley (created Viscount Wellington in 1809) had greatly improved his situation. In June British regiments were bombarding Marshal Marmont at Salamanca, after victories which had earned their general his

earldom. Spanish guerrilla activity was aroused, and the war-
weary British public was at last savouring the pleasures of military
success.

I

Lisbon, with its streets littered with dunghills and dead animals,
seemed a shabby place to the dandified product of 'The House'.
But Graham secured 'a very nice small lodging with a beautiful
prospect of the Tagus and the hills on the opposite shore'. And
while Lisbon itself was 'dirty to a degree surpassing description',
the situation and climate 'compensated for many grievous
inconveniences', and Graham met 'most of the English and the
best Portuguese families'. There were many summer parties, and
Stuart (an experienced diplomat who became Lord Stuart de
Rothesay in 1828) and Berkeley (Lord High Admiral of Portugal
and brother of the notorious 5th Earl of Berkeley) were generous
hosts. Graham sampled the pleasures of Lisbon society for some
time, while waiting for the arrival of English saddles (the local
products being fit only for 'the sun-burnt skins of the natives').
He rode through the countryside to the scenes of Wellington's
victories and generally had a pleasant holiday. But, when Berkeley
left the capital, society 'lost all its charms', and Graham decided
to move; local hostesses, he complained, 'made all unhappy
Englishmen dance without ceasing'.[1]

In August Graham thought that Wellington's victory at
Salamanca would 'raise the siege of Cadiz, or, at all events, clear
both the Northern and Eastern coasts of Spain entirely of French
troops'. The young civilian had postponed a visit to Cadiz,
because 'even as a quiet spectator, to be blown up with a shell
would be at once absurd and unpleasant'. However, a Naval
tender now took him to the city, where he presented Stuart's
report of the victory to Wellington's youngest brother, Sir Henry
Wellesley (created Lord Cowley in 1828), who had succeeded the
eldest (Richard, 3rd Earl of Mornington and 1st Marquess
Wellesley) as Ambassador to Spain in 1809. Wellesley had been an
associate of Graham's distant relative, Thomas Graham, a leading

Peninsular general who became Lord Lynedoch in 1814, and quickly befriended his visitor, who was regularly invited to the Embassy.

Graham had another 'delightful lodging' near Cadiz harbour and was an interested spectator of the closing stages of the French bombardment. It was still possible for young men to remain civilians during a war, to tour the battlefronts and even to criticise a war-time Government, and youths with means and Whiggish sympathies availed themselves of such freedom throughout the long wars with France. While Graham missed his Cumbrian sports, he enjoyed the exciting life in 'beautiful and pleasant Cadiz'. But he never forgot his developing Whiggism. 'The battle of Salamanca', he told his father,

> has raised the drooping spirits of the Spaniards, increased their confidence in the English and added more vigour to their own paralysed exertions. But we, on the other hand, should abandon our half-measures, strain every nerve to reinforce Lord Wellington, and put a happy end to the Spanish war before Bonaparte can conclude the Russian. This, alas!, is now out of the question, for promptitude and energy are requisite; and can we hope to find these necessary qualities in a 'Household Administration'?

Almost inevitably, the 20-year-old 'expert' was unfair. On the very day when he thus complained of Ministerial lethargy Wellington was entering Madrid. Graham saw the French evacuate their lines; 'it was at moments like these that one was justly proud of being born an Englishman'. Furthermore, Cadiz provided a pleasant social life and Wellesley was 'the kindest and best friend he ever met with'. Graham also enjoyed attending the rather frothy debates of the liberal Cortes, then seeking to exercise a shadowy authority unhampered by the Church, the Bourbons or the French, and in particular he came to admire the patriot Agustín Argüelles.

During October Graham rode through the Spanish countryside with Henry Watkin Williams-Wynn (later knighted and Minister in Denmark), the 29-year-old brother of Sir Watkin, a great Welsh landowner. From Seville they moved to Aranjuez, where

General Hill entertained them at his headquarters and, 'for the first time, [Graham] saw a large army in the field'. On the 23rd, 'after a very long but pleasant journey', they reached Madrid, where Graham stayed with a cousin, the Marquess of Worcester, 'enjoyed the society of the flower of the British army, and was perfectly delighted with the splendour of the most beautiful city he ever saw'. But the autumn campaign was unsuccessful, and Marshal Soult's forces moved in on the capital as the British left it on the 31st. Ordered out 'at a moment's notice', Graham and Williams-Wynn 'by the kind aid of Worcester found their way through various hardships to Salamanca'.

Graham reported his journey to his anxious father: he

> determined to forgo the pleasure of seeing Lord Wellington, although I was then within six leagues of him, knowing almost all his personal staff, an uncle at headquarters, and a letter — the best possible — for Wellington from his brother in my pocket. But my horror of being an amateur — a character with an army I do not like — and in a moment of danger the fear of being *de trop* combined to determine me to go on. Thus I was saved from implication in the miseries of a disastrous retreat, in which Sir Edward Paget was taken prisoner and the greatest privations were endured by the army.

Several of Graham's later characteristics were revealed in such early letters, especially his desire to associate with the great and his concern to cover himself from any possible charge.

Williams-Wynn and Graham crossed northern Portugal, reaching Oporto on 13 November. Then Graham toured the countryside, spent two weeks with Stuart at Lisbon and visited Elvas, Badajoz and Seville, with the 2nd Lord Bayning and a son of Sir Henry Dashwood. But Christmas was spent in Cadiz, amid delightful company, including Lord John Russell, Lord Fitzroy Somerset, Wellington and 'the very best of all, Sir Henry himself'.[2] Indeed, Graham had many friends in the Peninsula. There was Henry Cadogan, seventh son of the 1st Earl Cadogan, a lieutenant-colonel soon to be killed at the battle of Vittoria, at the age of 33. Somerset, Wellington's military secretary and friend, was the eleventh child of the 5th Duke of Beaufort and himself became Lord Raglan. He had preceded Graham at Westminster School and bought a cavalry commission as a 15-year-old boy in 1803. Little Russell, a civilian, was the third son of the 6th Duke of Beford and briefly a pupil at Westminster; and he was soon to commence a great political career with his election for the family borough of Tavistock.

Early in 1813 Graham planned to leave the grand society of Cadiz and visit Sicily. He asked his father to 'get me any good letters of introduction', to the Embassy secretary, Frederick James Lamb (later 1st Lord Beauvale and 3rd Viscount Melbourne). Accepting an offer from General Nugent, he set sail from Gibraltar in the frigate *Rainbow*, commanded by an old Carlisle friend, Captain Mounsey. At Port Mahon he arranged a transfer for his brother Charles, a young Naval officer. And at Cagliari he was shocked to hear of the death of the 3rd Earl of Tyrconnel, a 24-year-old volunteer in the Russian army who had died at Wilna in December: 'of all the men he ever knew he loved him best'. Finally, Graham arrived at Palermo in May, to find a curious situation and his first opportunity of political service.

Since 1811 the Commander-in-Chief and virtual ruler of Sicily had been Lord William Cavendish-Bentinck, the second son of the 3rd Duke of Portland (a friend of Graham's father). A cool general who had served in India and Europe, Bentinck ruled the remnant of the Bourbon Kingdom of the Two Sicilies with a heavy Whiggish hand, exiling Queen Mary Caroline and (with the aid of the more pliable King Ferdinand III) remodelling the decrepit constitution. He had led an Anglo-Sicilian force against Marshal Suchet in Catalonia, but was forced to return to Sicily, before again crossing to Spain in May 1813, to support Wellington's new offensive.

In Bentinck's absence, Major-General Lord Montgomerie, the ailing son of the 12th Earl of Eglinton, was in charge of British interests in Sicily. He soon appointed Graham as his private secretary. This was an interesting post for a man of 21, and Graham greatly enjoyed both the diplomatic work and the social rounds which it entailed: 'I am as happy as it is possible to conceive me,' he told his father. To his delight, he was retained by Bentinck on his return from Spain; he greatly admired both generals.[3]

The work of the British Embassy in Sicily was of some importance to the prosecution of the war. Napoleon had granted the mainland territories of the Bourbon kingdom first to his brother Joseph and in 1808 (when Joseph became King of Spain) to Marshal Joachim Murat. Now, as the Emperor's long success ebbed in Russia and Germany, Murat applied his cavalry tactics to politics. He toyed with plans to save his fragile throne from a legitimist restoration either by an alliance with the Allies (particularly the Austrians) or by leading the embryonic Italian nationalist movement — with which Bentinck also had contacts and sympathy. The British, however, supported the Bourbons.

Bentinck rejected Murat's secret approaches for an armistice and always distrusted the revolutionary monarch — who rejoined the French during the summer. But in October he heard rumours of Austro–Neapolitan negotiations, and the Austrian chargé d'affaires claimed that the Earl of Aberdeen would sign the resulting treaty, as British Ambassador in Vienna. From November Murat worked incessantly on his schemes, finally gaining an Austrian guarantee on 11 January 1814. Ten days previously Bentinck had sent Graham to Naples, on an important and delicate mission, first giving him a military commission.

Graham's task was complicated; Bentinck did not officially know of the Austrian negotiations. 'I was . . . nominally charged with a mission to the Court of Naples,' Graham later told Aberdeen:

> The object I ostensibly had in view was the renewal of a negotiation with Murat, which, though repeatedly pressed in various shapes, Lord William had as constantly declined. He was, however, induced by an extract of a despatch from Prince Metternich to the Count de Mier, which was transmitted to him by the Austrian Chargé d'Affaires at the request of the Neapolitan Govt., to send me with a design of ascertaining whether the facts alleged were true, that the allies were resolved on the negotiation of a Treaty with a Sovereign as yet unacknowledged by Great Britain. My pretext was, therefore, an armistice; but the real intention was

that, under the plea of expediting the negotiation, I might obtain a passage through the Kingdom of Naples, and thus arrive, in the shortest possible space of time, first at the headquarters of the army of Italy, and afterwards at the headquarters of the Emperor of Austria, where this projected Alliance was supposed at that period to be pending.

I was instructed to inform your Lordship and General Bellegarde that Lord William was prepared to act on the coast of Italy with 12,000 men under his command, in any manner and on any point which might be deemed most useful to the common cause. It was considered of importance that the Allies should be acquainted with the disposable force of the army in Sicily and with its probable influence on the military resources and operations of Murat. His Lordship imagined that from an erroneous supposition of the whole British disposable force in the Mediterranean being at present employed in Spain, the Allies might fear lest the whole of Murat's army would be turned against them, and, therefore, that it was necessary to avert the attack by peace on any terms.

His Lordship on the contrary, conceived that a simple demonstration on his part would of necessity compel Murat to keep the greater part of his force in the Kingdom of Naples, and thus that any hostile effort in the North of Italy could not, from this quarter, be expected, and that his troops, however imposing in point of number, would in fact be neutralized.

Had I failed in inspiring your Lordship with this persuasion, and after I had also ascertained that the intention of the British Govt. was to open a negotiation, on my return I was vested with ample powers to conclude an armistice.

Such a task, involving travels through enemy territory and polite non-commitment in the schemes of experienced Austrian diplomats until British policy became clear, gave wide scope for the exercise of Graham's personal abilities. And the temporising Murat's 30,000 troops were obviously important to both the Allies and Napoleon.

Leaving Palermo on New Year's Day, the fledgling diplomat reached Naples to find — 'to his great surprise' — that the Austrian Count Neipperg had 'considerably advanced' the negotiations. Graham was instantly under pressure, but his native caution triumphed. 'I was much pressed to become an immediate party and to conclude an armistice,' he recalled. He insisted that he must discover Allied and British policy — 'which the victory of Leipsic might have subjected to a change' — but was told that Aberdeen had approved of Metternich's orders to Neipperg. 'Yet, after all,' he wrote,

> I could discern nothing but an Austrian Treaty, full of separate interests separately negotiated by an Austrian Minister, not at the headquarters of the Allies but in a corner of Europe, and the simple dictum of no man appeared to me a rational basis on which to ground a political measure of great importance. Therefore, however high my respect for Count Neipperg's character, I could not admit his bare assertion and vague assurance of your general approbation or rather acquiescence, in the policy of the Austrian Cabinet, as evidence at all conclusive either of the views of your Lordship or of the sentiments of the Allies.

Graham rejected Austrian claims of military urgency, because they differed from 'the opinion of the distinguished individual by whom he was employed; an opinion he had learned to regard with peculiar deference; an individual whom faithfully to serve was his highest ambition'. Furthermore, he could not presume to judge military matters. Consequently, he reported the news to Bentinck and resumed his journey to Marshal Bellegarde's camp at Vicenza.

On reaching Vicenza on 17 January, Graham was again urged to sign an armistice. Bellegarde insisted that 'without the co-operation of the Neapolitans . . . his movements would at best be doubtful and certainly could not be decisive', repeated reports of Aberdeen's approval and urged Graham to report to Bentinck. 'I was at first compelled most reluctantly to refuse,' wrote Graham, now determined to accept no orders from foreigners. 'But my opinion was completely reversed by a conversation and official assurances I had from Sir Robert Wilson.' This British agent reported that Aberdeen and the Government wanted an armistice with Murat, to back up Austria's new treaty and secure Neapolitan assistance for Bellegarde's offensive on the Adige. 'The necessity [of the British armistice], I found to be not simply

rested on military speculations but on much higher grounds,'
recorded Graham. 'Some brilliant success and large occupation of
territory was desirable to be obtained in the shortest possible
space of time; and this for political reasons, with a view to an
impending peace, which will restore to Europe her ancient
demarkations — which will fix the destiny of a world.'

Now convinced, Graham promised his aid to Bellegarde and
hurried south. The dash across the French-controlled Papal
States was attended with some danger. Graham's Swiss valet and
interpreter, one Bodinet (who had previously served Sir James and
was charged by Lady Graham with the task of leaving Graham a
Bible every night), was invaluable. 'Neither in the bureau of the
police, nor under the searching eyes of gendarmes was Bodinet
moved,' recorded Graham's second biographer: 'To his coolness
and diplomacy his master was indebted for escaping an
unpleasant relationship with the high authorities at Rome.'
Graham, in fact, narrowly escaped arrest while carrying despatches and a uniform.[4] But he reached Naples on 25 January, to
find that Bentinck was expected in four days. As Mier and
Neipperg confirmed his view that further delay should be avoided,
Graham called on Murat's Minister, the Duc di Gallo, and
'happily negotiated' an armistice. 'I signed it with peculiar
satisfaction', he told Aberdeen,

> because, while it gained my main object of empowering the
> Austrian Minister to demand, in conformity with the Treaty of
> Alliance, the immediate co-operation on the Po of the Neapolitan
> army, it involves no recognition of title, no question of a political
> nature on which Lord William Bentinck might have found himself
> compromised in the negotiation of a definitive treaty. I had some
> difficulties to encounter, particularly in obtaining the specific
> mention, as a primary object of this future Treaty, to be co-opera-
> tion in the common cause. In the absence of His Majesty, who is
> at Rome on his way to join the army, my project was referred to
> the Queen; it has been considerably softened down, but time is
> precious and my principal point is secured, while I confidently hope
> that nothing has been admitted which may prejudice in the least
> the approaching negotiation.

Mier instantly demanded Murat's military support, and Bentinck soon arrived 'to fix ulterior arrangements'.

In apologising to Aberdeen for his lengthy explanations, Graham wrote of 'a measure perhaps even for a young man too daring', but hoped that he might 'receive the auspicious introduction of his Lordship's valued approval'. By any standard, a man of 22 might feel proud of such negotiations — particularly an amateur working amongst (and sometimes against) skilled and Machiavellian diplomats. Graham typically covered himself carefully; but he had worked well. Aberdeen received his report as Viscount Castlereagh arrived at Châtillon-sur-Seine for peace negotiations. 'I understand that his Lordship conveys through Lord William Bentinck the expression of his approbation of your conduct,' he wrote,[5]

and I take the liberty of adding (what you may think of much less consequence) my thanks for the very clear and satisfactory statement of your proceedings, which you have had the goodness to send me, as well as my opinion of the judgment and discretion which you have shown when placed in a situation of considerable difficulty and embarrassment.

Even a less proud man than Graham would have felt some elation over such praise for his first diplomatic venture. Perhaps his major achievement was successfully avoiding Austrian domination. Aberdeen had succumbed to Metternich's scheme to guarantee Murat's throne, while Britain officially favoured a Bourbon restoration in Naples. Graham had carefully avoided any recognition of Murat.

Now determined to use his forces in the Italian campaign, in February Bentinck sent Graham to Châtillon, primarily to tell Castlereagh of his secret hopes of retaining Sicily. 'I detailed to his Lordship your plan for the permanent occupation of Sicily as a British Territory,' Graham reported, adding that, although Castlereagh insisted on honouring treaties, a Bourbon restoration would make the plan 'feasible and worthy of consideration'. Castlereagh 'coincided most entirely' in opposing a British withdrawal. 'On the whole, his Lordship entered most cordially

into your view . . .,' Graham told Bentinck. 'I have no doubt . . . if
the present negotiations should happily terminate in a peace, that
your hopes for Sicily will not be disappointed.' He was wrong:
Castlereagh did not in fact share Bentinck's views — and was
probably bored by Graham's exposition of them.[6] On his return,
Graham met the adventurous captain of the *Euryalus*, Charles
Napier, before joining the Anglo–Sicilian army, which disem-
barked at Leghorn on 12 March amid nationalistic proclamations.
Meanwhile, Castlereagh was negotiating a general European
peace, while insisting that Napoleon's dreams of retaining an
empire should be denied; after her long struggle and Spanish
victories, Britain was in no mood to buy peace by paying any
ransom to France. The much-maligned Viscount ensured that
Napoleon could not detach his Hapsburg father-in-law from the
Allies as Graham had helped to separate Napoleon from his
brother-in-law, Murat.

In March, by the Treaty of Chaumont, Castlereagh secured the
Allies' support for the British policy of containing the French
and restoring the independence of several nations. Meanwhile,
Wellington's columns had crossed the Pyrenees into France, while
other Allies closed in on the depleted French host from the east.
By the end of the month Paris, desperately defended by worn-out
veterans and young cadets, surrendered.

The abdication of the Emperor and the restoration of the
French Bourbons to their throne seemed to mark the arrival of
peace; and Britain, whose advancing Industrial Revolution had
paid for over twenty years of almost continuous war, hailed the
news deliriously. Graham supported Bentinck in 'unpleasant
discussions' with Murat at Bologna and witnessed the fall of
Genoa in April. Both Englishmen regretted the failure to liberalise
(and perhaps federate) an Italy now to be restored to a patchwork
of sovereignties. And Graham was devoted to Bentinck, as one
who 'combined the confidence of a brother with the tender
experience and care of a father'. But his work — mainly as an
emissary between the British and Austrian staffs — was now
done, and he resumed his private travels. He moved to Verona,
Venice, Trieste and Vienna, where he saw 'all that the present

age can boast in the shape of Statesmen, conquerors and heroes' assembling for the peace conference. There followed a leisurely holiday with Lamb at Baden in July and August, travels through Germany and shooting expeditions in Moravia in September.

Graham's long continental journey ended in time for him to return to the family's Border home for Christmas. It had been very different from the orthodox, tutor-dominated Grand Tour, but was a valuable experience for a young man already keenly interested in politics. Graham had met many men of all types: the great Wellington; Bentinck, who was to become the first Governor-General of India; Murat, the first cavalry general of the age; Argüelles, the Spanish liberal; and the cold, brilliant Castlereagh (who, he feared, disapproved of his Italian work under such a radical as Bentinck). He had negotiated a treaty, witnessed several military campaigns and seen five nations. As he returned to England with a collection of exotic Latin clothes, he was a man of some experience.

II

In December 1814 Graham arrived at Netherby Hall, his father's pleasant mansion about ten miles north of Carlisle, near which he was born on 1 June 1792. At the age of 22 Sir James had inherited a large and flourishing estate in northern Cumberland from his own father, in 1782. And as a friend of Portland (then a Cumbrian landowner), he was created a baronet on 28 December 1782. The inheritance of a splendid property, with high rents created by his frugal father's investment, proved too much for the young squire. He lived a sporting life, joined the current fashion of enclosing further acres but neglected farming techniques, was robbed by his agents and joined high society. In 1785 he married Lady Catherine Stewart, daughter of the 7th Earl of Galloway and sister of the Duchess of Marlborough.

While a local writer remembered Sir James as 'short in stature, slightly built, of mediocre intellect and wanting in the energy needful to direct a large and heavily-encumbered estate', Lady Catherine was described as 'tall and of a commanding presence, active, kind to the poor, and of deep religious feeling'. Both Grahams — despite Sir James's indolence and financial rashness — were touched by Evangelical idealism: 'how amiable is the simple childlike spirit of Lady Catherine Graham!' commented William Wilberforce.[7] They were Tories, supporters of William Pitt, opponents of Negro slavery and staunch members of the Church of England, who yet favoured the removal of Dissenters' disabilities. In 1798 Sir James was elected as Member for Ripon, the pocket borough of the descendants of the Aislabie family. After he had sat ineffectively at Westminster for nine years (at first with John Heathcote and later with Lord Headley), the patrons gave the seat to one of themselves, Frederick John Robinson, second son of the 2nd Lord Grantham and, as Viscount Goderich, a Prime Minister.

The Grahams had a large family. James was followed by three brothers — William (an Anglican priest), Charles (a Naval officer) and George — and had eight sisters — Elizabeth Frances, Elizabeth Anne, Catherine, Maria, Caroline, Georgiana Susan, Harriet Anne and Charlotte. All were brought up with religious care by their beautiful mother. In particular, Lady Catherine took pains to ensure that her eldest son should come under the influence of leading churchmen; and the diocese of Carlisle then provided a notable collection of clerics.

Dr. Edward Venables-Vernon, the sixth son of the 1st Lord Vernon, had been Bishop of Carlisle since 1791. This affable, generous and inactive aristocrat (who took the name of Harcourt on inheriting some property in 1831) was a close friend of the Grahams, and there were many visits between Netherby and the episcopal palace at Rose Castle. In 1807, owing partly to Sir James's support, he was translated to the Archbishopric of York.

The Archdeacon, Dr. William Paley, was one of the most celebrated Anglican writers of his age. Born in 1743, a member of an old Yorkshire family, he had a brilliant career at Cambridge, where he became a popular lecturer. In 1785 he published his *Principles of Moral and Political Philosophy*, which was followed by *Horae Paulinae, Reasons for Contentment, View of the Evidences of Christianity* and *Natural Theology*. He became Rector of

c

Musgrave in 1776 and Archdeacon in 1782, and dropped his early latitudinarianism to become the great war-time defender of the established Church. He maintained a close connection with the Grahams until his death in 1805, and one of his daughters married Sir James's brother Fergus, the Vicar of Arthuret.

Very different from the easy-going, salmon-fishing Archdeacon was the strictly Evangelical Dean, Isaac Milner, brother of the celebrated Joseph. The Milners were self-made men from Leeds, where they received their early education at the grammar school. On his father's death Isaac became a weaver and later an assistant at Hull Grammar School. A menial sizarship at Queens' College, Cambridge, led to a famous career as senior wrangler and prizeman, tutor, F.R.S., Jacksonian Professor of Natural and Experimental Philosophy, Lucasian Professor of Mathematics, President of Queens', Vice-Chancellor, 'converter' of Wilberforce and friend of Pitt. This extraordinary clergyman, who prided himself on his mastery of both academic sciences and manual crafts and who wrote on subjects ranging from chemistry to Church history, was an energetic Dean from 1792. His puritanical condemnation of 'frivolous' entertainments was balanced by his personal charm and generosity, and he had considerable influence over Lady Catherine.

The clerical quartet was completed by the Chancellor of the Diocese, Walter Fletcher, the Vicar of Dalston, a village about fifteen miles from Netherby. In his vicarage (recently vacated by Paley), Fletcher supplemented his stipends by teaching elementary classics to children of the neighbouring gentry. And by 1797 Sir James was concerned about the education of his eldest son. 'Our wish', he told Jonathan Boucher, the Rector of Epsom,

> is to give him as good and as proper an education as he can receive and to make him a good man and useful member of society. And by the word 'good' I mean a religious man — a point I am convinced should be attended to in preference to all others.

As a first step in this Evangelical education, the little boy was sent to Dalston.

Fletcher appears to have been a successful schoolmaster. Most of his pupils were the sons of small squires, but they included the

Earl of Glamorgan, the grandson of the 5th Duke of Beaufort.
The parish contained the Bishop's castle, which the boys regularly
visited, and a cotton mill. The honest Vicar later resigned from
the bench rather than sign warrants for small village children to
work illegally in the mill. And Graham never forgot 'the care and
admirable instruction which he received in the happy parsonage
at Dalston'. He told the Vicar's widow in 1846 that Fletcher was

> one of the best and most blameless men I ever knew. I owe to him
> very great and eternal obligations. The principles which he incul-
> cated were the purest, and his own never-failing example proved
> that a sincere Christian may so live on earth as to have God and his
> duty constantly in view.

But the gentle parson's moral principles were not completely
followed by his charges. Both Graham and Glamorgan associated
with that celebrated lady of pleasure, Harriette Wilson, in their
later youth, and the latter (then Lord Worcester) became one of
her leading 'friends'.

Graham enjoyed his years at Dalston. But undoubtedly the
greatest influence on his childhood was his love for his mother.
From the Continent he told Sir James in 1814:

> Tell her that to please her — sometimes to be worthy of her — is
> my greatest joy and pride. All that is good in me, all that others
> praise, I have derived from her. All that is bad I acquired away
> from her. She made me what I am.

As a child, the heir to one of the greatest Cumbrian estates was
not popular among his fellow pupils; his dandified airs appealed
no more to the tough sons of Border squireens than did his pranks
to Mrs. Fletcher and the village folk. But he learned his Latin and
Greek, played at Rose Castle, fought the Longtown boys and made
one good friend.

Among the greater yeoman families of Cumberland the
Blamires of Hawksdale had long been prominent. William
Blamire, a Naval surgeon, had married Jane, the daughter of
John Christian of Ewanrigg Hall in Cumberland and Milntown
in the Isle of Man. Their son, William, was born at The Oaks,

Dalston, on 13 April 1790, and was educated by Paley (then the
Vicar) and the Rev. John Fawcett of Carlisle.[8] Graham and
Blamire soon became close friends as children at Dalston.

In 1806 Graham followed Blamire to Westminster School. Here,
Dr. William Carey (later Bishop of Exeter) dispensed a strict
classical education to boys largely drawn from the great landed
families. 'The teaching in the under school', recalled Lord John
Russell, a pupil in 1803–4, 'consisted entirely of Latin.' Despite
the harsh horrors of early nineteenth-century public school life,
Graham apparently prospered on the traditional curriculum. He
fagged for Charles Lennox (later 5th Duke of Richmond) and
made good academic progress. In 1809 William Cunningham
described him to Lord Grenville as

> a very fine young man indeed; finest dispositions, and clever,
> and — what will be no blemish in your eyes — loves Greek.

In an age when Parliament enjoyed — and generally understood
— classical quotations, Graham's interest in Homer and Horace
was not without potential value. And Westminster boys had
special opportunities to hear parliamentary debates, of which
Graham took advantage before leaving the school in 1809.

The next stage in the education of a country gentleman was a
few years' residence at Oxford or Cambridge (or, in the case of a
liberal Whig, perhaps at Edinburgh). Graham was destined for
Christ Church, which Blamire (having inherited an estate at
Plumpton) had already entered. For this move, he was prepared
by two private tutors, George Richards, Vicar of Bampton in
Hertfordshire, and (in mathematics) a Mr. Hellins of Potterspury
in Buckinghamshire. At Bampton he also met Sir John Courtenay
Throckmorton, a landowner in Warwickshire and Berkshire, who
first interested him in those agricultural improvements which Sir
James had so obviously neglected at Netherby. But in June 1810
Graham was entered as a gentleman commoner at Christ Church.

Graham already had strong opinions. Politically, while professing independence, he was taking a Whiggish line in letters to
his father; he was 'independent' of the Government. 'The
administration', he hopefully wrote in March, 'seems tottering to

a fall.' And he held forceful views about Oxford and against the appointment of Weller, the Archbishop of York's domestic chaplain, as his tutor. 'He expresses himself very strongly indeed,' Richards lamented:

> . . . he was quite sure that he should not work at all at Oxford. You will of course talk to him very earnestly upon the subject. May it not be advisable to give the ABP a few lines requesting his assistance in the appointment, at your *express decision*, of Mr. E.G. . . . ?

The Archbishop confirmed that he had 'a very high opinion of Mr. Edward Goodenough in *all respects*'. He was looking forward to meeting the baronet in London, and 'could not see why his coming need be delayed on James' account — a month in London would do no harm'. Graham gained his point: Goodenough became his tutor, and on 1 June Richards and his father took him to Oxford.

III

Oxford in 1810 provided most — if not all — of the temptations to young men which worried the Evangelicals. Occasionally some youth might be sent down for over-indulgence in wine, women or sport (hunting, gambling and coach-driving being perhaps the most popular varieties of the last interest). But on the whole Oxford despised the tea-drinking Puritans who had infected some Cambridge colleges and sapped the normal attributes of an English gentleman. Close, religiously-exclusive corporations dominated the University and the colleges. Drunken japes against 'the Town' were fashionable, and men who paid lavishly for their entertainment might brutally answer real or imagined insults. Later moralists could only condemn the waste and immorality of life in a university which scarcely taught or even controlled its younger members. But Oxford only represented one aspect of an England as yet unreformed by Utilitarians and Evangelicals; and rough, coarse and uncultured though it might appear later, it produced very many of the leaders of nineteenth-century Britain. Such leaders, like their university, were largely unconscious of the vast industrial changes in the iron and textile industries; but they, greater or lesser classicists, administered a nation soon to become the Workshop of the World.

Graham enjoyed an active life in the little world of Oxford, where pleasures were readily available and study was still possible. A month before his arrival, Goodenough wrote hopefully to Sir James:

> From what I personally know of James and from what I have heard of him from every quarter, I shall be very much disappointed if he does not do both himself and us very great credit at this place.

But as far as Oxford was concerned, Graham earned little respect. He had some interest in history, mathematics and the classics, but his talents were mainly employed on other pursuits. Long, bleak years at public schools inclined young men of his generation to make the most of their new freedom and of parental generosity. Almost naturally, as Graham's Cumbrian biographer recorded, 'he lived the fast life of an "Oxonian dandy", and showed Border ingenuity in outwitting proctors and beadles . . .' With a private servant, a string of horses and ample money, he had a pleasant career. Equally naturally, years later he regretted some of his undergraduate actions and inaction. In 1839 he 'solemnly stated' in the Commons that in his time at Oxford

> I was never — with the exception of the required attendance at Chapel — once called upon to attend any lectures either upon theology or divinity . . . I never received any religious instruction whatever . . . I never . . . attended a University sermon; and I am ashamed to say that, whilst I was at Oxford I never . . . heard one single sermon.

'The waste of time in a college life', he told Glasgow University students in the same year, 'was an irreparable loss, ever visited with the bitterest pang which memory inflicted.'

Regrets over wasted opportunities lay many years ahead. In the meantime, 'The House' and Oxford in general gave Graham many pleasant contacts. A particular friend was Charles Stourton, the third son of the 17th Lord Stourton. The Baron's four Roman

Catholic sons were companions on sporting expeditions in the West Riding. They were to be strangely divided: William became the 18th Baron; Edward assumed the name of Vavasour on inheriting the Hazlewood Castle estate, and was made a baronet; the barrister Charles took the name of Langdale on inheriting another property; and Philip married into the Cumbrian Howards of Corby Castle. Graham was a regular visitor to the Stourton property at Allerton Park — and was later with Charles in Spain and Sicily. The nearby estate of Goldsborough Hall was tenanted by his father's old friend, a Lancashire squire named Starkey, who regularly entertained Graham for sporting holidays. His 'dear young friend' had 'a most affectionate heart', Starkey told Sir James, and was 'the delight of us all'.

More serious colleagues — like Thomas Vowler Short, who preceded Graham at Westminster and Oxford, and later became Bishop of St. Asaph — remembered him as a moderate student with a gift for memorising quotations. In 1862 the Bishop told T. M. Torrens that Graham had appeared as 'a man who wished to work, but who was not forward in his general education'. As Graham recalled in 1823, 'the temptations to idleness were many and the restraints but few'. By 1812 even the small amount of work which Oxford life involved had dismayed him. Gradually, he persuaded his father and the college to allow him to leave the University. 'I am of the opinion that the sooner our arrangements are conveniently made the better, and me despatched to foreign climes,' he told Sir James in February. Half a century later Short wrote that 'he did not take a degree because, as far as I remember, he would not have been likely to have obtained honours, and gentlemen commoners in those days rarely took degrees, except in the hope of doing so'. The departure was postponed in deference to the baronet, but eventually — as usual — the handsome young heir followed his own desires.

IV

Apart from the idleness encouraged by large allowances and splendid opportunities for spending them, Graham had another reason for wishing to leave Oxford. Politics already attracted him. Perhaps schoolboy attendances at Parliament had encouraged the interest, but the political life was almost natural to the products of the 'smarter' colleges and, after all, Sir James had served an undistinguished stint at Westminster. But Graham was no sycophant at this or any later time. His father remained a Pittite Tory, but Graham reverted to his grandfather's Whiggism, again following Blamire.

Graham moved from Oxford to London, where there was a heady and exciting atmosphere for an embryonic politician. Napoleon was marching on Russia with half a million men. A harassed Tory Government, under Spencer Perceval, faced a French-dominated Continent, the increasingly-hostile United States and rising discontent at home. Troops urgently needed in the Peninsula were employed in putting down angry, and sometimes murderous, Northern workmen protesting against technological changes, unemployment, low wages, high prices or simple starvation. The Home Office was employing secret agents who sometimes increased their status and earnings by acting as *agents provocateurs*. And on 11 May Perceval was murdered in the Commons. The subsequent Government formed by the Earl of Liverpool was not generally composed of brilliant men; its members were mainly the tired, hard-working, unimaginative, patriotic Ministers who had guided Britain through the long years of war. They almost invited Opposition sneers — especially when the Opposition had been out of office for many years. To a young 'intellectual' with liberal ideas and sizeable finances they presented a perfect target.

There were many other political attractions in the London of 1812. The Prince Regent, gross and lecherous, was an easy object for satire by the party which he appeared to have deserted; following the traditions of his house, he had formerly allied with the Opposition to his father's Government. The Monarch who had allegedly insulted Whiggish hagiography by restoring some influence to the Crown was now periodically demented. And, despite all desertions, there were still men with historic names and large estates who saw themselves as the defenders of a classic constitution, with its foundations laid in the Civil War and its columns raised at the Revolution; men who sometimes recognised kindred spirits in the neo-classicism of Imperial France; men to whom the Parisian cries of 1789 had seemed simply demands for Whiggish–Roman liberty from despotism — demands, too, made on an appropriate centenary. They were, in general, men cushioned from contemporary economic fluctuations: their tenants fared no better than those of Tory proprietors. But they announced Liberty; they fought against three almost uninterrupted decades of opponents' rule; they pointed to many Ministerial errors; they could, on occasion, take the side of the suffering and persecuted and unfortunate. They had obvious attractions for an immature and inexperienced but honest and generous youth with snobbish but 'progressive' opinions.

Graham signified his political allegiance by joining Brooks's Club on the proposal of the 1st Lord Cawdor and Viscount Morpeth (Cawdor's brother-in-law). He was actually elected after leaving for Portugal. Political interests were restrained for two years, but Graham wrote regularly to his father about the British situation and his own political hopes, which suffered several changes during his European wanderings. In the autumn of 1812 the magic of Iberian life and scenery took precedence. Throughout his life, Graham was subject to sudden changes from high hope to the depth of depression, and his moods were reflected in his correspondence. At Madrid he was again politically-minded, worrying over the Earl of Lonsdale's domination of Cumberland and hoping for Morpeth's election to assert the county's independence of its 'Lord and master'. He was delighted when Sir James followed his advice and proposed Morpeth, the scion of the Whig Howards of Carlisle, as a candidate. 'You and I can only succeed', he told his father,

> by standing aloof from all parties, and coming forward uninfluenced, unbiased and uncorrupted, without previous concert or the connivance of Lord Lowther or any other peer.

Graham personally hoped to sit for the county.

The Lowthers had dominated politics in Cumberland and

Westmorland since the second half of the eighteenth century, largely through the activities of Sir James Lowther (who was created Earl of Lonsdale in 1784). From Lowther and Whitehaven Castles he and his agents controlled numerous electors for the four county and six borough seats. Lowther political activities were supported by the huge revenues from the mines and trade of Whitehaven, a town created and owned by the Lowthers:

> E'en by the elements his pow'r confess'd,
> Of mines and boroughs Lonsdale stands possess'd,
> And one sad servitude alike denotes
> The slave that labours and the slave that votes.

Lonsdale, in fact, controlled more seats than any other owner, with seven or eight in the north, two in Surrey and 'influence' in Wigan, Durham and Lancaster.[9] At every election in Cumberland and Westmorland the Lowthers' yellow favours were well to the fore. Largely because of his hostility to Lowther control, Graham allied with the Whiggish 'Blues'.

Diplomatic employment gave Graham 'the advantage of enlarging his present humble stock of political information', and, he told his father, 'this employment being all political, you may imagine how cheerfully and how warmly I enter into it'. By July 1814 he again hoped to enter politics — if possible, as the county Member. He advised his father not to concern himself over the Carlisle election, again insisting that the family should be independent — 'without any collusion of parties or coalition of interest, unpledged as to politics or factions'. But this independence would be exercised within a general framework of Whiggism. However, later in the summer Graham again despaired of his own career:

> To be in the House of Commons I no longer desire. I can never sit there to support men I despise, and I never shall be able to support those whom I prefer. Moreover, I begin to know my own power. The heaven-born gift of eloquence is denied me, and without it there the rest is nothing.

Yet a month later he suggested that Sir James should try to win a county seat, if there were no contest and he could maintain his independence.

With these political views, now coloured by European experiences, and vacillating personal hopes, Graham had returned home in December. He joined the 'smart' West Riding Yeomanry Cavalry and again enjoyed rural sports. The continental tour had both increased his liberalism and strengthened his belief in British constitutional methods. After the Christmas festivities, Graham moved, early in 1815, to London, to establish himself politically and socially, in the capital.

2

The Making of a Whig

London in 1815 was a city of excitements and contrasts. George III, King for fifty-five years, was mad. The Regent and his legal wife, both notoriously promiscuous (but with their promiscuities condoned by rival factions) were separated. Great aristocrats, with vast Palladian mansions in the counties, maintained town palaces of equal luxury. The City already dominated much of the world's commerce, and its leaders owned substantial villas which demonstrated the wealth behind the social challenge to the gentry. And in the great docks, markets and business houses, in small factories and back-street sweat shops — unhygienic, unknown, unpoliced — worked the astonishing range of craftsmen, clerks and labourers who made up the varied hierarchies of the London working classes.

There were many amusements available in the most free of metropolitan cities. The mob could enjoy an occasional 'good hanging'; cheap alcohol was sold in thousands of taverns and shops; and sometimes there were opportunities to abuse the Regent. Extremist fraternities plotted revolutions, and other little gangs planned varied adventures in the ancient alleys. While bankers, merchants and clerks returned to their respectable bourgeois homes, sections of the aristocracy and 'proletariat' both enjoyed — and sometimes shared — nocturnal pleasures.

I

For Graham the greatest attraction of the capital was the political life of the clubs, and Brooks's became his headquarters. He already had many useful contacts, but now made many more. There was Wilfred Lawson, the 20-year-old Cumbrian squire of

Brayton and Isel, who had succeeded his brother Thomas
Wybergh in 1812 to the estates of the old Lawson baronets, whose
name he had adopted. This radical landowner was to become a
politician, a baronet, Graham's brother-in-law and father of
another, more famous Radical. Another relation was Lord
Archibald Douglas-Hamilton, second son of the 9th Duke of
Hamilton and his wife Harriet (daughter of the 6th Earl of
Galloway and aunt of Lady Catherine Graham). At 46, Lord
Archibald was an experienced politician who favoured reform of
the close Scottish electoral system.

The leading Cumbrian landowners, apart from the *parvenu*
Lowthers, were generally Whigs, and they provided many friends
for young Graham. The celebrated John Christian Curwen,
originally a Manx landowner, had married the heiress of the
long-established Curwens of Workington, added their name in
1790 and shared their hostility to the Lowthers. He made
Workington Hall into the centre of both a sizeable colliery
district and the county's agricultural revolution. In 1790, after a
petition, he defeated the Lowther interest at Carlisle. He resigned
in 1812, but was to sit again from 1816 and in 1820 was also elected
for Cumberland, which he represented until his death eight years
later. This wise old reformer, a friend of Burke (though himself
sympathetic to the French Revolution, until horrified by Jacobin
excesses), became a close associate of Graham. George Howard,
Lord Morpeth, the 42-year-old heir of the gambler 5th Earl of
Carlisle, owner of vast estates around Naworth Castle in Cumberland and Castle Howard in Yorkshire, was already a good friend.

Through the Lords Carlisle, the Howard family provided the
leadership of Cumbrian Whig politics. Lesser branches maintained
the tradition. Charles Howard of Greystoke Castle had led the
independent Cumbrian freemen against the Lowthers at Carlisle
in 1774. His father became 10th Duke of Norfolk (and head of the
family) in 1777, but Howard represented Carlisle as Earl of
Surrey from 1780 until his succession to the dukedom in 1786. The
11th Duke earned considerable notoriety. He proved his Whiggish
honesty by proposing the famous toast of 'Our Sovereign's
health — the Majesty of the People', at a London dinner in 1798.

The then Whiggish Prince of Wales was greatly amused, during an evening at Norfolk House a week later, to hear that his father had removed the Duke from the Lord Lieutenancy of the West Riding, because of this speech. However, it was only from a distance that liberal-minded writers praised the liberal-minded premier duke. The huge, debauched Earl Marshal of England, who himself controlled several boroughs with a heavy hand, was reputed to be bathed only when his servants carried his inebriated hulk to the tub. Fortunately, he was often drunk.

The Greystoke Howards maintained their Whig interest, as did their relatives at Corby Castle. Henry Howard, 'Friend of the People', Roman Catholic apologist, archaeologist, translator and friend of Sydney Smith and Louis-Philippe of Orleans, was another of Graham's fellows. His son, Philip Henry, sat for Carlisle between 1830 and 1847, and 1848 and 1852. A lesser Cumbrian squire was Francis Aglionby (born Yates), who inherited the old Nunnery estate through his mother. He was brother-in-law of the Rev. Richard Matthews of Wigton (a friend of Graham and 'mentor of the Whigs in Cumberland') and M.P. for East Cumberland in 1837–40. His cousin and successor, Henry Aglionby Bateman (who assumed the surname of Aglionby) was a radical-minded Member for Cockermouth from 1832 to 1854. Along with such such local Whig–Liberals, Graham associated with Russell and Edward Stanley, grandson of the 12th Earl of Derby — members of two great families who were to share much of his future public career.

London life was broken by a round of country-house visits; and Graham was determined to continue his European travels. 'I propose to hasten my return to the Continent,' he told his father in March: '. . . the Command of Ld. William now becomes most important . . .'. Napoleon had escaped from Elba and Frenchmen were returning to his Imperial magic, while Murat had announced himself an Italian nationalist and started on the course which soon led to his death. However, in the summer, as Wellington and a hastily-gathered army smashed Napoleon at Waterloo, Graham was ill; he recuperated at Brighton in June.

Amid social and sporting activities, Graham still tried to advise his father on estate and political matters. In January 1816 he again urged Sir James to 'refuse to commit himself', though it would be sensible to support Lonsdale's men at Carlisle in order to gain the Earl's favour in the county. Graham currently had a special reason for not fighting the Lowthers. During his Yorkshire holidays he had visited Lonsdale's brother, John Lowther, at Swillington House, where he met the Earl's fourth daughter, Lady Elizabeth. The affair with the possessive aristocrat was not a success, and Graham soon hoped to end it. In May, as he prepared for a visit to the Lane Fox estate at Bramham Park, he wrote that he had finished with 'Liz'. But in June the situation had become so embarrassing that he moved from London to Paris. 'I have lost all patience with a certain Lady', he wrote, 'who, forgetful of what is due to herself, used every exertion to detain me in England, tho' to herself even it was evident her power over me was gone . . . my eyes are opened, all delusion is past; I am not the least in love with her.' He hoped that Lady Elizabeth would not reveal their past relationship for the sake of revenge. Presumably on the same 'scrape', Lord Galloway told Sir James that 'I wish you and my Sister sincere joy with all my heart at the determination of your son — He was manfully determined to abandon disgrace . . . I always expected much from an Enlightened mind'.

In Paris Graham formed a close friendship with Henry Brougham, the rising Whig lawyer, who was a member of another old Cumbrian and Westmorland family. Now aged 38, Brougham admired Graham's energy and good looks and hoped to encourage his renewed political career by soliciting a Cumbrian nomination from the Whig leader, Earl Grey. Lord Carlisle's periodic illnesses made it likely that Morpeth would have to give up his county seat on inheriting the earldom; and Brougham thought that Graham might assume the Whig representation. But Graham felt unable to accept a nomination in his father's district. After seeing Brougham on 30 June, he wrote:

> On consideration, I was not satisfied that I sufficiently explained to you in our conversation this morning my real position and my views. I am anxious not to be mistaken by you: and before you commit by a letter to Lord Grey both yourself and me, it is better

you should clearly comprehend the actual state. I need not inform you that it is my misfortune to differ in political opinions from most of my relations — near and dear to me and to whom in duty as well as in affection I owe considerable deference . . .

The heart of the matter was that, even if he were unopposed,

I cannot, I would not, be returned without a frank exposition of my general politics, and these would be found opposite to those of my father. I should be supported by a party with which he does not act, be reprobated by a party to which in early life he unhappily attached himself.

Consequently, out of regard for his Tory father, Graham declined his first opportunity of entering Parliament. While the great landowners' electoral influence lasted, such sacrifices were almost obligatory for sons who disagreed with fathers; later reforms liberated both popular opinions and aristocratic heirs. But Graham could not regret his decision: old Carlisle lived for nine more years, and Morpeth retained his seat until 1820.

There remained many pleasures for a handsome young man to explore. The Grahams hoped that their son's amorous inclinations would lead to a lucrative union with high society; and there were already speculations over a Lowther bride. But in 1819 'the rumour afloat that young Graham had formed an attachment to one of the "Beauties at Almack's" was received with no pleasant feeling at Netherby'. When letters had no effect, Sir James sent his steward to dissuade Graham from an unsuitable marriage. The young dandy rejected the advice, and on 8 July he was married to Fanny, the youngest daughter of Colonel James Callander, of Craigforth (who assumed the name of Campbell on inheriting Sir Alexander Campbell's Ardkinlass estate), and sister of R. B. Sheridan's daughter-in-law.

The pair were, in fact, well-matched, and Graham's parents welcomed their daughter-in-law when she settled at Croft Head on the Netherby estate. When Graham and his wife attended their first Royal 'drawing room' George IV declared that 'they were the handsomest couple he ever clapped his eyes on'. Equally expert opinion on Graham (presumably at an earlier period) was given by Harriette Wilson. She met him at a dinner with Lord Lowther, Lord Yarmouth and J. W. Croker and found him 'as attentive to me as possible'. She thought that 'Graham was a beauty; a very Apollo in form, with handsome features, particularly his teeth and eyes; sensible too, and well educated', and reported their meeting:

'I brought you two together, because I knew you would fall in love with each other,' said Lowther.

'How impossible,' thought I. [Harriette was then planning designs on Lord Ponsonby] ... I rather think Graham was pedantic.

She 'had the honour of taking Mr. Graham' to the opera, and introduced him to an associate, who also admired his 'beauty' and 'anxiously inquired whether I was sure that he had taken a fancy for me'; this experienced lady was warned that Graham 'had no money'. But a year before his marriage Graham had commenced a new career, by entering Parliament.

II

Though a Cumbrian seat remained impossible, another constituency would present Graham with only the problem of finance. On 10 June 1818 he announced that he would contest the mercantile borough of Hull. Hamilton helped to secure the nomination; Viscount Milton promised the aid of the Fitzwilliam family's influence; Langdale gave his personal support; and the Grahams' friendship with the Tory emancipationist William Wilberforce was thought to be potentially useful.[1] The two seats were held by John Staniforth, a Tory merchant and Member since 1802, and Sir George Denys, who was about to retire. Since January the burgesses had been bombarded with scores of (generally scurrilous) sheets. In March John Mitchell, a West Indies merchant, offered himself for the second seat. But there was much talk of a 'third man' representing the Opposition. An anonymous burgess promised a new candidate 'of the highest respectability' in May, and in June 'a Gentleman most unexceptionable in all respects, young, gallant, gay and rich' was

D

mentioned. Soon afterwards, electors 'desirous to support Mr. Graham, the Third Man' were requested to pledge themselves. Rival factions hastened to hire taverns wherein to refresh thirsty supporters. But Staniforth, hurt at being opposed after his long service, now withdrew; the local Alderman Joseph Egginton declined to fight; and the Radical Sir Francis Burdett refused nomination — 'he would not give one shilling to be returned for any borough in England'.

The usual formalities followed. Graham's chairman, the Rev. Richard Sykes, invited the 'worthy and independent Burgesses' to escort the candidate on 10 June from the Beverley road. The Grahamites naturally expressed confidence, and Graham issued his first address:

> I tremble almost when I consider the trust I presume to ask; but, however conscious of my weakness, I am sure of the honesty of my intentions. I am unwilling to raise expectations by empty promises or professions still more vain; nor do I wish to elevate myself by attempting to depreciate my competitors.

Thus Graham entered his first campaign with unwonted modesty. But while Staniforth announced that he could not afford 'so violent and so vexatious' a contest, Graham ceremonially entered the town and delivered his first speech. 'My principles', he declared, 'are genuine Whig principles':

> Ministerial extravagance and undue influence are objects of my entire abhorrence, and all my efforts will be used in resisting them, whether in the shape of places, sinecures or pensions . . . I love peace rather than war . . . I am a friend to religious as well as civil liberty, and see no reason why men should be put into danger or difficulty on account of their religious opinions . . . I am a friend to reform in Parliament: not that wild, enthusiastic reform which, instead of improving the Constitution, would, by producing anarchy and confusion, undermine and destroy it, but a moderate reform, which would infuse new life into the Constitution and restore it to its former health and vigour.

This statement of classic Whig doctrine, nervously delivered to cheering supporters in Lowgate, expressed principles to which Graham was to remain loyal.

Tory pamphleteers mocked the young candidate for causing 'a row in the town' with 'his guineas (or his daddy's)'. Graham, they said, 'possibly knew more of fox-hunting and Bond Street lounging than politics and commerce'; while the hard-working Staniforth had brought £500,000 to the borough, Graham was merely 'the Yorkshire Dandy', the sophisticated 'Cock of the North'. In reply, the Whigs alleged that Staniforth was 'a docile hack' who supported the Corn Law (which was untrue), the suspension of Habeas Corpus, and Lord Liverpool, and that Mitchell was a 'hard-hearted Negro Driver'. Graham himself issued regular placards, and when support rose for Staniforth (who was persuaded to stand by the close Corporation) Graham's committee insisted that their man was 'not only a MAN OF BUSINESS, but a man well known and highly esteemed amongst the first Literary Characters of the Age'. Fortunately perhaps, the Whigs did not amplify their claims: Hull electors were apparently willing to believe such details of the son of a 'rich' baronet who had been educated at Oxford.

On the hustings Graham was supported by two Roman Catholics, Langdale and Edward Haggerston. Evangelical Hull was unlikely to be impressed by such allies and the Whigs were doubtless relieved to receive (and publish) a generous testimonial from the Tory Dean Milner, who wrote that

> I have been acquainted with Mr. GRAHAM from his Childhood, and know him to be a Person of Talents and Attainments, and of an excellent Character. He has been Educated in the very best of Principles, both Moral and Religious, and I am convinced the Electors of HULL will do well to make choice of one who is so well qualified and so likely to Support and Defend the Established Constitution of this Country, both in Church and State.

Yet Tories could recall previous outsiders' desertions and insist that

> This Dandy ... is ... unfit for the Representation of this large, opulent and commercial Town ... He boasts of his extensive Estates, his ready command of large Sums of Money; I will not call in question his veracity, nor inquire where those Estates are situated, or in what Bank his Cash is deposited ... I will enquire,

Where are his Ships? Where are his Commercial Connections?
What is his knowledge of Commercial Affairs?

His initial nervousness fading, Graham delivered daily speeches
on his own virtues, poverty, toleration, Anglicanism, Whiggism
and opposition to slavery. 'Depend upon it, you will hear more of
him again, and in a way of which you will not be ashamed,'
asserted his committee, constantly recalling Andrew Marvell's
example as an Opposition representative. The excitement
produced a riot, while less violent partisans produced poetic
appeals:

> Give merit your voice,
> Let GRAHAM be your choice,
> Whom virtue and sense recommend ...

A long Whig paper described the speeches:

> Orange GRAHAM spoke next, and he spoke like a Briton,
> When he spoke of taxation, the right nail he hit on.
> By TAXES, *tea, sugar* and *salt* are made dear,
> They lessen our *bread-loaf* — they spoil our *strong beer,*
> And to raise these curs'd taxes we work half the year,
> And Graham has told us again and again
> That it is the duty of Parliament men
> To see that the money is properly spent,
> Which up from the Country in taxes is sent,
> But the greatest part of them get all they can,
> To *share* public money — not *spare* it's their plan.
> These are Graham's own words, and I really believe
> He is all truth and day-light and would not deceive.

Graham's principles were clearly shown in his propaganda.
Against the advice of some supporters, he had always favoured
religious toleration. To avoid attack, he stressed his chuchman-
ship: 'he had been most rigidly educated in [Church] principles
and loved it from the bottom of his heart; but because he loved
the Church, was that a reason why he should not be a friend to
toleration?' He was

> the enemy both of public and private oppression, the lover of peace
> and hater of war, the detester of slavery at home and abroad, the
> friend of toleration, the hater unto death of spies and informers.

On 17 June the candidates were nominated before the Mansion House in Lowgate. Sykes and T. Thompson (a former M.P.) nominated Graham, noting his commendation by the town's Lord High Steward. In 'an eloquent speech', Graham naturally praised the merchants and pointed to great politicians who had started their careers at an early age. 'For his part, he should say that he detested an idle life. Brought up to no profession, he was anxious to employ his time and abilities, such as they were, in the service of his country.' He contrived, not altogether honestly, to impress the electors with their good fortune in having him:

> He might have obtained a quiet seat for some insignificant borough in his own neighbourhood, and have slept undisturbed, in obscurity. But he was actuated by different views. He wished to represent a populous town like Hull, where there was a fair opportunity of rendering himself useful; and he was determined to shrink from no exertions should the honour of their choice fall upon him.

And he maintained his liberal, though constitutional, principles. He also condemned both the evacuation of France and the retention of a large army: 'the good old British principle was to encourage our navy as our natural security against all our enemies'.

Staniforth's nomination was opposed by the crowd, and after a wet day of polling Mitchell led with 560 votes, followed by Graham with 425 and Staniforth with 398. The real struggle would obviously be for the second seat; and much was at stake for the contenders. Staniforth and the Corporation merchants who were meeting his expenses faced a loss of traditional power and patronage; Graham, who had originally hoped for a fairly cheap contest, could not afford to waste his lavish investment. Tempers were frayed, as Graham complained of Tory clubmen and Tories alleged that Whig hirelings 'possessed every avenue to the Hustings for an hour and a half'.

The poll continued next day, when the Sheriff and Mayor condemned the violence and the candidates and party leaders (the Mayor, George Schonswar, speaking for Staniforth) delivered patriotic orations on the Waterloo anniversary. By the evening

Mitchell had 1,203 votes, Graham 936 and Staniforth 903, and party agents posted last, frenzied placards. On the 19th Schonswar, constantly heckled, again supported Staniforth, and the carnival continued. When the poll closed at 1.45 in the afternoon Mitchell and Graham led, with 1,323 and 1,074 votes to Staniforth's 1,036. Whig jubilation at the victory over the Tory Corporation was modified when a scrutiny was demanded; Schonswar alleged that 'voters' had included paupers, children, impersonators and dead men! Once again, each group explained its case (and attacked its opponents), while the ultra-Radicals excused the non-appearance of their champion, T. J. Wooler. As the scrutiny proceeded, before William Voase, Samuel Scholefield and S. W. Nicol (respectively Sheriff, Under-Sheriff and assessor), Graham delivered regular speeches. He was increasingly anxious about the mounting expense; Sir James could scarcely be expected to meet it, and finally £6,000 had to be borrowed at interest. On 13 July the court settled the affair. Staniforth lost 109 votes, Graham 143 and Mitchell 168, and of their original 327, 273 and 251 'bullets' (or 'plumpers') they lost 37, 47 and none respectively. After these illegal votes were struck off, Mitchell and Graham were confirmed as Members, with 1,155 and 931 votes to Staniforth's 927.

The victors were chaired through the town before delivering final orations to cheering supporters. 'On former occasions . . . I have taken the opportunity of expressing my sentiments on universal suffrage,' declared Graham:

> If to that extraordinary doctrine I shall ever be a convert, one thing I will pledge myself to, out of gratitude to the ladies of Hull, that I will never rest satisfied until the right of voting is granted to women. Indeed, this is not only justice, but my own best interest, for sure I am that if the present election had been carried by the votes of the ladies I should have been returned with a very great majority.

But Tory papers bitterly condemned Graham's claims to independence, his reliance on Whig aristocrats and his (alleged) appeals to the mob. And there was talk of a petition against the result. The Earl of Derby, however, found the election 'highly gratifying to his feelings' and, he told Graham, a week later,

> I trust (from your report) that the threat of petitioning will end in nothing to give you further trouble or to deprive the Town of Hull of a representative whose public Principles and private character do so much honour to their choice . . .

The petition was not effective: though two Tory electors submitted it in February 1819, it was not considered by Parliament.

III

Graham took his seat next to Hamilton, on the third Opposition bench. He soon came to admire one party leader in particular, the 36-year-old Viscount Althorp, the son and heir of the 2nd Earl Spencer. Althorp was not a man of particularly great intellectual or (as Whig aristocrats went) great landed qualifications. But his personal and political honesty and his expert enthusiasm for all things agricultural endeared him to a generation of Whigs. A recent widower, he lived quietly in the Albany, and though a poor speaker devoted himself to parliamentary affairs.

In the Commons Graham took an active part in the discussions of his first Session; and his attitudes to various problems then raised further revealed his political philosophy. For instance, he soon demonstrated his views on State intervention in industry. In February 1819 Sir Robert Peel, a Tory cotton-master, introduced a long-discussed Bill to regulate the working hours of the mill children. Unlike most of his liberal colleagues, Graham expressed some sympathy, though strongly opposed to any interference with adult labour. Within weeks, however, he hotly condemned a petition signed by many clergymen, employers, medical practitioners and operatives of Stockport. The petitioners, to him, were 'no other, for the most part, than idle, discontented, discarded and good-for-nothing workmen, who conceived that they did too much, when in employment, for the wages they received'. This monstrously unfair attack on overworked operatives by a brash young roué was neither forgotten nor forgiven in the Northern textile areas.

The junior Member for Hull did not follow any purely party line in his early parliamentary career. In March he opposed a Bill to amend the electoral laws, particularly condemning proposals to make freeholders prove land-tax assessments, to finance county hustings from the rates and to increase officials' powers; he feared that returning officers 'might make a job at the county expense'. In April he condemned Burrell's motion for an enquiry into the wool trade and for the free export of wool, denying any decline and supporting old restrictions. Equally strongly, he opposed the Country Bank Notes Bill, condemning easily-forged Bank of England notes and praising the country-bank issues. He voted for Peel's Act restoring cash payments, primarily (he later explained) because he was convinced by Ricardo's bullionist arguments. He was fair-minded enough in May to defend Lonsdale's recent purchase of the Barony of Kendal, against unfair attacks by Brougham.

Graham's first major speech was delivered in support of Sir Matthew White Ridley's motion of 18 March to reduce the number of junior Lords of the Admiralty in proportion to the reduction in post-war Naval strength. Sensing an opportunity to combine a popular demand for economy with a sneer against Tory patronage, Graham prepared a bitter harangue presumably designed to please the public but certainly displeasing the House. Wellington thought that Graham and Russell were 'sacrificing their public duty at the shrine of popularity', and Henry Lascelles considered that Graham's career was ruined. Even the Whig leader, George Tierney, referred to 'the manly puppy'.[2] Criticism apparently mattered little to the arrogant young politician, though privately he worried over his failures. In later years he was to change his attitudes both to the Admiralty and to Parliament; in 1832 Le Marchant recorded that Graham, as First Lord,[3]

> speaks in the House as if he was under an awful sense of responsibility, which is singular, as he was remarkably bold and slashing when on the Opposition side. No man was ever more changed by the move.

Socially, Graham's career made progress. He was courting a

much-admired beauty and had an entrée to the sparkling Whig society of the capital. But the events of the summer of 1819 roused his anger. On 16 August the Lancashire Yeomanry slashed their way through a Radical crowd waiting to hear Henry Hunt at St. Peter's Fields in Manchester. This 'Peterloo Massacre' provoked Whig condemnation, Radical protests and the Government's repressive Six Acts. Graham joined in the general alarm, reporting the arming of Northern workers and the fears of an outbreak of violence at Carlisle; he demanded Government support. In general, his attitude pleased neither party, though he secured Castlereagh's acceptance of an amendment to the Bill 'to prevent seditious meetings and assemblies of more than fifty people'; the original measure would have restricted the rights of non-resident parliamentary candidates. Peterloo had other consequences, however. Earl Fitzwilliam, the leader of West Riding Whiggery, was dismissed from his Lord Lieutenancy for condemning the 'crime'. In protest, Graham resigned his commission in Lord Grantham's aristocratic Yeomanry in October. His parliamentary career, dogged by unsuccessful speaking attempts, appeared to be a failure.

On 29 January 1820 the demented King died and was succeeded by his paunchy son, as George IV. Custom and law still demanded a dissolution of Parliament and a new General Election soon after the Monarch's death. This convention posed several problems for Graham. With a majority of four votes he could scarcely regard Hull as safely loyal; furthermore, the seat was expensive, and Graham still owed the money borrowed for the 1818 contest. Rather belatedly, the Carlisle Whigs offered their nominations to Graham and William James of Barrock Lodge. But Carlisle still presented difficulties. It would be costly to fight the powerful Lowther interest; and Graham remained reluctant to embarrass his father by contesting the local borough under the Carlisle Whigs' blue colours. Before the dissolution on 28 February he supported Russell's unsuccessful proposal to postpone the issue of writs for four notoriously corrupt boroughs.

Graham's predicament became increasingly complicated. In the Westminster election he supported the Radical John Cam

Hobhouse,[4] who was elected with Sir Francis Burdett, against the
orthodox Whig George Lamb — a brother of his colleague in
Sicily. This action would scarcely commend him to the closely-knit
aristocratic families which dominated his party. Worse still, he
had promised support to Curwen in Cumberland, and feared that
Morpeth and the Howards might be offended. However, personal
political worries were solved by the offer of Whig support in a
distant seat.

The borough of St. Ives in Cornwall was at this time, as its
historian rather grandly explained, at the height of its prosperity:
'its mines were all working, its fisheries remunerative and its
agriculture in full swing' — and it had become 'the metropolis of
West Cornwall'. It was vastly different from Hull, but Graham
soon forgot his expressed horror of 'insignificant boroughs' and
commenced his canvass. Since 1558 St. Ives had returned two
Members, often the choices of the Whig Stephens family of
Tregenna Castle or of the Dukes of Bolton — or of the Tory Praed
family. In 1820 there were about 340 electors. Graham had high
hopes: he knew the Tory, Lyndon Evelyn, a Herefordshire squire,
and the local manipulators of the constituency promised success.
The optimism was well founded; although a previous Member, Sir
Walter Stirling of Faskine, added to the expense by fighting
again, Graham was returned at the head of the poll. With 205
votes he was 45 ahead of his fellow-M.P., Evelyn; Stirling had 146
supporters and a Mr. Meade 98. But the triumph excited both
some excitement and, as soon became obvious, considerable
enmity.[5]

The victory was followed on 7 April by the birth of the Grahams'
first child, Frederick Ulric, at their London house, 36 Montagu
Square. 'My wife and my boy, both of whom are dearest to my
heart, [are] out of all danger and safe and happy by my side',
Graham told Sir James seventeen days later,

> and I venture to look forward with the purest pleasure to seeing
> you again take the same delight in the company of your little
> Grandchildren which you used to evince towards me in my tenderest
> years. I am anxious to return into Cumberland, and the time will
> appear long until I put the little boy in your arms, and I anticipate

with the most perfect joy the happiness and peace of my residence
so near you: it will add a charm to the remainder of your life to
watch the growth of the young plant on which our common hopes
depend, and everything about Netherby has to me a double
Interest when I look on the face of my Child and think that he will
reap the benefit of all that you and I can effect for the Improvement
of our happy home ...

The equally proud mother also wrote to Sir James, thanking him
for his kindness.

At Westminster Graham maintained his campaign for economy,
generally opposing the Government's proposed increases in the
Royal Family's Civil List. In May he supported Joseph Hume's
motion for details of Court expenditure since 1815, Brougham
and Russell's proposals to postpone the settlement of the Civil
List until the annual estimates were presented and Brougham's
plan to reduce the number of Scottish Barons of the Exchequer.
His periodic friend Brougham, as the Queen's Attorney-General,
was engaged in defending the popular Caroline from the new
King's charges and divorce proceedings. The issue divided the
nation: most Whigs (apart from Earl Grey and Lord Holland's
'set') and the London mob supported the Queen, while most
Tories — with varying degrees of enthusiasm (Liverpool and his
Lord Chancellor, Eldon, disagreed over how far the issue should
be pressed) — were against her. Graham joined the majority
Whigs on this unpleasant issue, which only closed with the
Queen's death in August 1821. There were many opposing appeals
in the case: gallantry to a nymphomaniac Brunswick Princess or
loyalty to a grossly lecherous Monarch; delight in metropolitan
'popular' support or desire to follow the smart set of Brighton;
Whiggish cosmopolitanism, rationalism, liberalism and 'tolerance'
— backed by a desire for revenge on 'Prinny' — or Tory determination to maintain the *status quo*, to support even a former
Whig King, to keep the Great Families from establishing a classic
oligarchy of power and, in several cases, to support Evangelical
denunciations of sin or insubordination.[6]

Graham supported the views of his friend Curwen on the
protection of agriculture; the squire of Workington was moving

from the 1815 Corn Law's principle of high duties on foreign imports to the policy of a small permanent charge. Politicians of both parties were regularly concerned about the real and alleged burdens on the land, and Brougham and Curwen often raised the subject. Furthermore, Brougham was emerging as a prominent Whig leader. J. L. Mallet was convinced, in June, that he was 'seriously engaged in the formation of his little party' — which would include Curwen, Graham and John George Lambton and would follow 'some broad principle of Parliamentary reform, disregarding the opinion of the aristocracy and placing [its] lever on a strong popular feeling'. But Brougham's work on the Queen's behalf was soon to absorb his time. In June and July Graham joined such Whigs as Althorp, Hume, William Lamb, Russell, Tierney and Lords Duncannon, Folkestone and Milton in opposing the Aliens Bill; and he supported Hume's probing questions on thefts by revenue collectors. As a loyal Whig, he also supported the Queen against the Government. But Graham's parliamentary career was both undistinguished and brief. By 1821 he was neither 'flattered in the belief that he had achieved any great success in Parliament, nor very hopeful as to the agricultural interests with which his fortunes were cast . . .'[7] He was still in debt for political expenses and was deeply concerned over the financial state of the family property. When he heard, early in 1821, that some St. Ives electors had got up a petition against Evelyn and himself, Graham must have felt that his career was ruined.

Captain John Tregesthero Short — locally known as 'a Rebel' for refusing to sign a petition against Hunt — was an interested observer at St. Ives. On 27 March he recorded that 'according to their evidence the jury found indictments against the two elected members [for bribery], the evidences returned from Launceston having sworn against Messrs. Evelyn and Graham'. Evelyn fought against the allegations, but Graham, fearing the expense of further proceedings, sadly decided to leave Parliament. He accepted the Chiltern Hundreds, and a new writ was ordered for St. Ives on 16 May. He might have retained his seat. Short noted on 22 June that

The evidences for Mr. Halse arrived from London, and before their departure the two Members, Evelyn and Graham, were declared by a Committee of the House of Commons duly elected, and gross and infamous perjury was pronounced against an Irishman named G.P.D.

The Captain wrote the final chapter on 14 February 1822, when 'the news arrived that G.P.D., the Irish false swearer against Messrs. Evelyn and Graham and Halse, was sentenced on Monday last to seven years' transportation'. Graham's seat was taken by Sir Christopher Hawkins.[8] His high political hopes had foundered.

IV

In 1821 Graham started to manage the neglected Netherby estate, and henceforth much of his time was devoted to agricultural and financial matters. But his interest in political life continued. He made up for the wasted years at university by wide reading, especially in political economy. Smith, Hume and Ricardo's economic writings were balanced, however, by Graham's literary favourites, Dryden, Pope and Shakespeare. And, perhaps because of his doubts about his own oratorical abilities, he constantly read the speeches of Edmund Burke. It was suggested by McCullagh Torrens that the saddened politician at Croft Head felt a particular affinity with Burke's mixture of optimism and depression, ambition and melancholy. Consciously or unconsciously, Graham prepared for a further political career.

His sojourn in Cumberland allowed Graham to take part in county affairs and to meet members of various classes. The independent 'statesmen' of the district were a remarkable race of yeoman farmers, owning their own land and often carrying their hardy and vigorous personal philosophies into their political activities. By this time Graham's old friend William Blamire was becoming the leader of this important group. A progressive farmer himself, Blamire was also a staunch Whig and became High Sheriff in 1828. Later he was a Cumbrian M.P. and a notable official for agricultural affairs, serving as a Tithe Commissioner from 1836, Copyhold Commissioner from 1841 and an Enclosure Commissioner from 1845. His tireless zeal led to some of the most far-reaching reforms affecting English land.[9]

John Rooke of Akehead came from a 'lower' order, an old family of lesser yeomen. His father owned a hundred-acre farm and was surveyor of roads and bridges around Wigton and Aspatria. Such men did not send their sons to university and Rooke was briefly educated at village schools before becoming a farmer. But this virtually self-taught yeoman became a man of some influence in Cumberland. Following Curwen's example, he drained his little property by modern methods, thus attracting Graham's attention and starting a lifelong friendship. Rooke was a Tory, though of an individualist variety. He learned the elements of current economic theories and gradually became an opponent of the Corn Laws. Since 1814 he had contributed to the *Farmers' Journal*, and in 1819 he published a pamphlet of *Remarks on the Nature and Operation of Money*. There followed an *Essay on the National Debt* in 1822, a large *Inquiry into the Principles of National Wealth* in 1824, a pamphlet (which was to cause Graham some trouble) on *Free Trade in Corn* in 1828, a book on *Free and Safe Government* in 1835 and a semi-theological volume on *Geology as a Science* in 1838. Such an output was obviously a great achievement for a working farmer. This eccentric Tory churchman and philanthropist was among the pioneer advocates of Free Trade, though his most prominent public office was the presidency of the Wigton Mechanics' Institute. Graham was his regular correspondent.

Rooke was helped by two other friends of Graham, Blamire and the Rev. Richard Matthews, a man of similar background but less energetic habits. The son of the squire of Wigton Hall, Matthews was born in 1771, nine years before Rooke and nineteen years before Blamire. He was educated at St. Bees and St. Catherine's College, Cambridge, and was ordained as a priest of the Church of England. On succeeding his father in 1798 he retired to Wigton, where he lived a studious life in the family manor house, nursed a delicate constitution (which kept him alive to the age of 75) and was tended by an unmarried sister. The allegedly delicate

clergyman was an active J.P., botanist, meteorologist, archaeologist and politician, and he advised many of his neighbours and
friends on Whig policies.[10]

On 5 April 1821 Graham entered Cumbrian politics with a
speech at a county meeting at Wigton. He had steadily supported
the 'Blues' since 1816, but had been restrained by and suspected
on account of his father's 'Yellow' Tory sympathies. However, he
still hoped for the county nomination — which probably influenced his desertion of Morpeth in 1820 in favour of the ageing
Curwen. Now, with Matthews as his introducer and counsel, he
roused a crowd of over 10,000 people with a 'radical' speech. 'The
agricultural interest,' he told the rural throng, 'the stay and
strength of the country, its prop in war and its pride in peace, was
brought to absolute, almost irremediable ruin.' Such sentiments
uttered against any Government rarely failed to stir county
constituencies. When followed by denunciations of taxes, rates and
the waste of public money they were almost irresistible. Graham
illustrated the last theme with his favourite reference. 'We are
blessed,' he declared, 'with Lords of the Admiralty at enormous
salaries — Lords who have something to do and Lords who have
nothing to do — active and passive Lords — dead corpses
chained to living bodies.' Even the wily Brougham, who followed
him, could not gain more applause.

Henceforth, Graham worked hard to convince the 'Blues' of his
worth. The most obvious, but very difficult, field of operations lay
in the county administration; and here, during worried years of
estate work and financial stringency, Graham achieved some
fame. Cumbrian local government in the 1820s was nepotic and
inefficient. The town corporations had long ago fallen under the
influence of the Lowthers. At Carlisle the parliamentary electors
had formerly been limited to members of the city guilds, freemen's
sons and men who had served apprenticeships under freemen. But
in 1784 the Tory Corporation had ended these ancient rules by
creating 1,195 new voters, all Lowther supporters. When such
creations of 'mushroom voters' were opposed in the Commons, the
more normal methods of bribery were employed. Party energies
were first released when Sir James Lowther fought Henry

Aglionby for the mayoralty in 1765 and, on winning, started to change the old régime. Cockermouth was more entirely under Lowther control; although not lord of the manor, Lonsdale owned most of the burgage tenements.[11] Throughout the county, in the days before the late-century reforms of rural administration, local government was even less 'responsible' than in the boroughs.

The county magistrates, normally recruited from the greater and lesser gentry on the nomination of the Lord Lieutenant (almost inevitably Lonsdale) transacted their business of trials and appeals in leisurely fashion in the two old boroughs. After this toil, they adjourned to The Bush at Carlisle or The Globe at Cockermouth for refreshments; and then, fortified by walnuts and wine or brandy punch, they proceeded to consider the county's quarterly accounts, in private. Their activities were no more dishonest than those of some of their more democratic successors; but nineteenth-century reformers bitterly attacked the real and alleged misdeeds of their non-elected local rulers. Occasional scandals fed the growing resentment against a system which allowed the secret expenditure of public money. The costly new Eden Bridge, from the price of which the architect and the Clerk of the Peace both obtained 'cuts', sparked off a major controversy and encouraged reformers to action.

Graham naturally opposed the erring Clerk, William Hodgson — a solicitor who also acted as Town Clerk (and ultimately Mayor) of Carlisle and clerk to the magistrates. He launched his major attack in 1828, when he opposed any new county works until current debts had been paid and also attacked the clerks' salaries. Supported by Lawson and Howard, Graham also campaigned in 1829 against local Poor Law administration. Paupers had long known Cumberland as a lenient county; horrified liberals reported that Irish and Scottish migrants begged food and travel costs and that vagrants habitually travelled between Bristol and Penrith. 'The expenses incurred for "removing vagrants through and out of the county of Cumberland" amounted in the year 1820 to the almost incredible sum of £865. 2s. 7d.!', noted a local writer, with awe. 'What a blessed county was Cumberland in those days for over-reaching lawyers of

James Graham as a child. Portrait by Raeburn

pious show, make-believe overseers and proletarian vagabonds!'
Graham led the side most popular with the ratepayers, opposing
the lax, generous Poor Law system, the inefficient supervision of
county officials from coroners to bridge-builders, the mismanagement of local prisons and the general expenses of the county.[12]
While undoubtedly partisan, his criticisms were largely true.

By taking the lead in liberal demands for cheap local government Graham established his position in Cumberland. No doubt
he felt sincere anger over maladministration in county affairs; but
Graham was not actuated by pure altruism. Curwen was growing
old, and Graham had rising hopes of a county seat. Already
well-established in London society, he now fostered his local
connections. In particular, he became well known in his native
county as a determined agricultural improver — a role of
importance in Cumberland.

E

3

The Agricultural Reformer

Major agricultural improvement requires a reasonable measure of
political stability and some certainty of ownership, conditions
which came late to the Borders. From time beyond record the
Grahams had lived there. They themselves claimed descent from

> the renowned Graeme, who, *anno* 404, commanded King Fergus
> the Second's army and was governor of Scotland in the minority of
> his grand-child, Eugene II. In the year 420 this gallant person made
> a breach in the mighty wall which the Emperor Severus had
> erected between the rivers Forth and Clyde, which has ever since
> borne the name of Graeme's Dyke. From the time of this eminent
> man, the Graemes are to be found in the records of Scotland,
> enjoying the very highest influence . . .

A modern observer may be content with John Burke's comment
that 'it is certain, however, that no family of North Britain can
boast of greater antiquity'.[1] And this long genealogy had
considerable influence on James Graham.

I

Several Grahams played prominent roles in the bloody history of
later medieval Scotland. Sir David of Kincardine established the
family at Montrose by exchanging his Cardross estate for Royal
property with King Robert I. His son, Sir David, a notable war
leader, gave his own son Patrick as a hostage for King David II's
ransom after the battle of Durham in 1346. From Sir Patrick's
first marriage descended the Earls, Marquesses and Dukes of
Montrose and Viscount Dundee, men destined for important
places in Scottish Royalist history. His second wife was Egidia
Stewart, a niece of King Robert II; and his son, Sir Robert,

married Eupheme Stewart, daughter of David, Earl of Strathearn and Caithness, and inherited the first title. When the Graham Strathearn was killed by Sir John Drummond in 1413, the earldom passed to his son Malise, who changed it with the King for the earldom of Menteith. Malise married Anne Vere, daughter of the Earl of Oxford.

Menteith's second son, Sir John Graham of Kilbride — 'John with the Bright Sword' — was the ancestor of the Grahams of the Borders. Shocked by the ingratitude of the Scottish Crown, he gave his allegiance to the English and settled among the bleak and oft-ravaged 'debatable lands' of Dumfries and Cumberland. From this desolate area Graham and his clan carved out their kingdom around the site of a Roman camp over the valley of the Esk near Netherby, by acts of terrorism which yet included a gallant protection of the poor. Their descendants inherited their marauding habits, martial prowess and control of parts of the long-disputed areas of northern Cumberland. They were one of several families of rough lairds who constantly menaced the inhabitants of both sides of the Border. 'Among the names figuring largely on the list of lawless borderers — the Armstrongs, Elliotts, Fosters, Rootledges, &c.', wrote the local historian, 'that of Grame is by far the most conspicuous of all.' But while Sandford described the Grahams as being 'all stark moss troopers and arrant thieves, both to England and Scotland outlawed', local tradition was

> a shade more lenient towards the family, and averred that there were two sorts of Grames — 'the Gallants' and 'the Cart-tail' lot (the broader Saxon phrase is omitted); the first named were lucky in their forays and showed gallantry in escaping the penalties of the law; the latter were known as having been whipped at the tail of a cart, or handed out of it in the same direction under the gallows-tree.

This division of the clan was long maintained. 'Long Will' Graham, for instance, was banished from Scotland in 1516 on account of his banditry; and 'Pear Tree Jock' saved his arrested brother by kidnapping the Sheriff's son.

Lord Dacre's attempts to put down the family on behalf of

Henry VIII failed, and an Anglo–Scottish division of the area in 1552 had little effect. But the Grahams' generations of brigandage drew to a close late in Elizabeth I's reign. In 1593 Lord Scroope, the Lord Warden of the West Marches, summoned the leaders of the Grahams, Armstrongs, Fosters, Bells, Nixons, Hethertons, Taylors and Rootledges, 'with other very insolent members appertaining to them'. To promote 'the early subduing of the bad and most vagrant sort of the great surnames of the Border', he ordered the clan heads to give sureties for their future behaviour; the first to be called were two Grahams, 'Will of the Rosetrees' and 'Rob of the Fauld'. But despite an Act of 1600 and many promises, the families did not greatly change their habits. Legal enactments could not easily repress the Grahams and their kind. In December 1603 James I regretted his 'lack of means to provide presently for [their] transportation elsewhere, to the intent that their lands might be inhabited by others of good and honest convictions'. However, the Royal means increased and in 1606 Cumberland and Westmorland were taxed for the eviction of the clans. Between August 1606 and September 1607 some 400 Grahams, under the heads of the Nuke and Netherby lines, were transported in three shiploads from Workington to Ireland and the Netherlands. In 1614 a proclamation was issued for the arrest of illegally-returning clansmen, and 'Belted Will' Howard of Naworth Castle, the Warden of Eskdale, maintained a stern rule. The 'debatable lands', which the Grahams had denied to either kingdom, were granted to Francis, Earl of Cumberland, who paid a fee-farm rent of £150 for 2,895 acres of meadow and arable, 2,635 of pasture and 2,870 of marsh and moss.

When the families were exiled (or hanged at Carlisle) Fergus Graham of Plumpe was allowed to remain. This respectable member of the family married Sybil Bell of God's Brigg, by whom he had four sons, who enhanced the family's status. Richard, the second son, served at Court as a Gentleman of the Horse to James I, Master of the Horse to the great Duke of Buckingham and a member of Prince Charles's retinue in Spain in 1622. He was first knighted and then, on 20 March 1629, created a baronet. Through him, the family established its fortune and future in Cumberland.

On 21 May 1628 he bought Netherby Hall, the barony of Liddell
and the manors of Arthuret and Rodillington from Lord
Cumberland, later adding further properties and paying an annual
rent of £200 (later reduced) to the Crown. The penitent Grahams
thus returned to the scene of their former raids, battles and
kidnappings: their estate lay in the traditional Graham area,
bounded by the rivers Sark and Esk, the Scottish dyke and the
Solway sands.

Sir Richard remained a loyal courtier, providing a celebrated
jester (Archie Armstrong of Arthuret) and serving the Royalist
cause in the Civil War. He was severely wounded at the battle of
Edgehill in 1642 and stayed with Charles I until 1648. His sons
continued this loyalty after the baronet's death in 1653. The
elder son, Sir George, was cautious during Republican times, but
his brother Richard was an active Cavalier and was rewarded
with a baronetcy by Charles II in 1662 and established a line of
baronets at Norton Conyers. Sir George was followed in 1657 by
his eldest son, Sir Richard, 3rd baronet, of Esk. This product of
Westminster and Christ Church maintained the family's attachment to the Monarchy. He served with distinction in the Commons
as Member for Cockermouth and Cumberland and, from 1681,
also sat in the Scottish Parliament as Viscount Preston of
Haddington. From 1682 to 1685 he was Ambassador in Paris,
returning home as a Commissioner of Excise, Chancellor to the
Queen Dowager and a parliamentary manager for James II and
becoming Secretary of State shortly before the King's flight in
1688. A loyal Tory Anglican, Preston would not recognise William
III and was briefly imprisoned in 1689. But James granted him the
English barony of Esk in January 1689 and Preston was again
arrested, for accepting the title, in November. These affairs were
minor inconveniences, but Preston lost his valuable post of Master
of the Wardrobe in a costly legal case with Lord Montague.

Preston — or Esk — remained a Jacobite, though opposed to
James's Roman Catholicism. After a conference with leading
supporters, he set off to visit the 'Pretender' in 1691, but was
dramatically arrested and charged with high treason. He cleverly
defended himself, and his wife (a daughter of the 1st Lord

Carlisle) pleaded with the Queen; but he was sentenced. Eventually, William granted a pardon; and many among both Whigs and Jacobites believed that Preston had turned informer. In fact, the Grahams remained loyalists, and Preston was again imprisoned, while his brother Fergus fled abroad. Political reasons gained his release, and he spent his last years at Nunnington in Yorkshire translating Boethius, until his death in December 1695. The Preston line soon ended; Richard's son, Edward, died in 1709, and his son Charles, the 3rd Viscount, died without issue thirty years later. The noble title was now extinct, but the baronetcy and estates passed to other members of the family.

The first Preston's brother, Dr. William Graham, had lived a quieter life, as Dean of Carlisle and Wells and Clerk of the Closet and chaplain to Queen Anne. On his death in 1712 he was succeeded by two clergyman-sons, Charles (Rector of Southchurch and father of the Reverends William (6th baronet of Esk) and Thomas) and Robert. These Whiggish clerics did not, however, obtain the Jacobite inheritance. The last Preston left his estates to his aunts Catherine and Mary, the first peer's daughters. When the younger sister died unmarried, the whole property fell to the elder, the wife of William, 4th Lord Widdrington of Blankney. Widdrington was an active Jacobite who was attainted for his part in 'the Fifteen' — and pleaded guilty. However, he lost only his own property and died peacefully in 1743, fourteen years before his wife, who retained Netherby.

While the Esk baronetcy and estate passed to the Rev. William and his sons Charles and Robert in succession, the substantial Preston property was devised by Lady Widdrington to Dean Graham's second son, the Rev. Dr. Robert Graham, Rector of Arthuret and Kirkandrews. This Whiggish parson, who thus inherited the neglected Netherby estate, was another memorable personality in the saga of the Grahams. He married Frances, daughter of Sir Reginald Graham of Norton Conyers; the family often complicated their genealogical tree by marrying distant relations. Dr. Graham founded a new line of Netherby Grahams.[2] And he played an important part in restoring the family's impaired fortunes.

II

Dr. Robert Graham was one of the pioneers of agricultural reform in Cumberland. In several parts of England landowners were carrying out or encouraging those changes in crop rotation, stock-breeding, 'scientific' farming and estate management which many historians were to see as an Agricultural Revolution. But the new crops and methods introduced in East Anglia and other favoured areas only slowly attracted Northern proprietors. Graham was among the first Cumbrian squires to support the cause of 'improvement'. He gave up his living at Kirkandrews to devote himself to the estate and borrowed large sums to finance a wholesale reform. In 1785 a contributor to the *Gentleman's Magazine* commented on Graham's achievement, continuing a series of papers on 'the delightful improvements' of some Northern estates with the statement that Netherby 'far outstripped them all'. On Graham's succession, the writer declared,

> the rent-roll was said to be near £2000 per annum; and how it could produce that I can hardly conceive, for of all the lands I had then been over those appeared the most unpromising and the least capable of improvement. But let us see what a good understanding, common sense, attentive observation and the love of his family and country will do.
>
> In 16 years after his residence at Netherby, the nett produce of this estate was £10,000 per annum, and before his death, I have been informed, was advanced to £13,000 per annum; and if his son, Sir James Graham, the present possessor, treads in the steps of his father, it will, in the course of a very few years, amount to £20,000 per annum, clear of all deductions.

The observer went on to analyse the causes of this phenomenon:

> how has this immense increase of fortune been obtained? Not by rack-renting his tenants, for that would have reduced his 2 to £1,000 per annum! Not by mines, for I never heard that he had any in his estate; nor by raising their rents; no, nor by fines, for that would have disenabled them to labour for the advantage of their landlord and have operated like the taxes laid on the Americans.

It was simply thus: by draining, manuring and planting. His method was to drain and manure 1000 acres fit for tillage, grass or meadow land, then build villages consisting of eight or ten houses, with the necessary out-buildings, allotting to each so many acres, and then letting them to the most industrious among his married neighbours, frequently rent-free, for one or two years or until they were able to pay rent.

At the same time he was thus improving and peopling his lands, he was reviving or building towns, erecting churches, building inns and furnishing the industrious with the means of accommodating the traveller, the gentleman and the nobleman with carriages and post-horses. In short, this worthy member of society so improved this part of the country, from a cold moist clay, heath and peat land, that it is now the garden of that part of the country and wears the appearance of the most improved soil about the metropolis.

This was praise indeed from a sophisticated Southerner.

Graham himself was the active leader of the activities on the estate. His work met occasional set-backs, notably on 16 November 1771, when a 'black and nauseous inundation' of Solway Moss advanced upon Nether township and eventually, driven by heavy rains, drove 28 families from 500 carefully-improved acres. The slime was drained by one A. J. Wilson, under the orders of the worthy Doctor, who recompensed the homeless tenants; by a system of dams and canals 'the extraneous matter was carried away and the plain restored to its former fertile state, as if no such astonishing event had happened'. Graham's work was, indeed, eminently successful from all eighteenth-century viewpoints:

He had raised a princely estate for his family, added so many thousand acres to the national stock and at the same time been a singular blessing to his tenants and to all around him, as well as to many gentlemen in that Country, who trod in his steps . . .

Nor did he neglect 'the comforts and elegancies of life, having built himself a very handsome house, with every convenience in and about it, fit for a gentleman of fortune, with doors of hospitality to it'. He laid out his grounds in consultation with his friend Philip Howard of Corby Castle; and as his new mansion was being built at Netherby he lived at Lord Carlisle's castle of

Naworth, where his second son, James, was born in April 1761. The journalistic eulogy closed with an appeal to other landowners to 'go and do likewise', for[3]

> How greatly to their credit, advantage and satisfaction would the rest of the nobility and gentry in this island tread in the steps of the worthy Dr. Graham, instead of employing their time and fortunes in corrupting the electors of a county, town or paltry borough to make *dependant* members of Parliament, to the destruction of that constitution they are bound by every tie of conscience, duty and interest to preserve and defend.

Graham's work was long remembered in Cumberland. He had 'raised the Netherby estate nearly from a state of nature to that of a rich, fertile and beautiful demesne'. He had built free schools, corn mills and a harbour at Sarkfoot, raised Longtown from a virtual slum to 'a neat market town' and provided decent housing throughout the estate. And he played an active part in local Whig politics, thus breaking with family tradition. By helping Portland against the Lowthers at the 1768 election he brought his family's political 'influence' into a position of some importance. The Doctor died on 2 February 1782, leaving several children. As the eldest son, Charles, died twelve days later and had fathered only a daughter, the estate passed to James, a 22-year-old product of Magdalen College, Oxford, who was created a baronet on 28 December.

III

As lord of the old barony of Liddell, Sir James inherited a sizeable property. Although consisting only of the parishes of Arthuret and Kirkandrews, the barony was 20 miles long and 5 miles wide, stretching through northern Cumberland. Arthuret, recently enclosed, contained much good land, several stone quarries and an 'abundance of hares and partridges'. The hamlet itself was a tiny place, including the church and rectory — often occupied by younger Grahams. The parish also contained the townships of Brackenhill, Lineside, Longtown and Netherby, with a total population of 2,418 in 1801 and 2,953 in 1821. The 'small neat modern-built market town' of Longtown, which was 'much admired for its beautiful and healthy situation', had a market, two fairs and annual races. Many of its inhabitants were hand-loom weavers for Carlisle masters. The parish contained no other 'assemblage of houses worthy of the name of village, the buildings being all scattered over the townships in convenient situations on the different farms. . . . It was the peculiar custom of this part of the country to give the appellation of *town* to even a single dwelling.' Graham owned almost the whole parish.

Kirkandrews parish was similar in composition, with the townships of Kirkandrews Middle, Nether and Moat and Nichol Forest, containing 1,762 people in 1801 and 2,237 in 1821. The annual values of the two parishes in 1829 were £10,737 and £10,717. But the Grahams also had land in Bewcastle parish where the manor had been presented by Charles I to Richard Graham. The decayed 'town' retained an ancient bad reputation, and its inhabitants were still attacked as 'horse dealers'; the trade was one in which 'some of [them] indulged freely, and perhaps with as much honour as the generality of those in the same occupation had credit for'. In addition to owning the land and houses of such hamlets, Sir James had the patronage of the churches, game rights in the woods and moors and control over the lime and stone quarries of the area.

Evangelical connections did not deter the young baronet from fully enjoying the estate's large rents and splendid facilities. He did not inherit his father's abilities, or his capacity for constant hard work, but benefited from his labours by being able to increase rents in 1784, and to grant fifteen-year leases. On the other hand, he did inherit his father's substantial debts, though the real burden became relatively less onerous in years of rising income. It seems likely that too little was re-invested in the estate. But when Graham sought to follow the Doctor's interests, the results were almost disastrous. Patriotism and profit both encouraged further enclosure and utilisation of land, especially during the war years from 1793, and Sir James liberally limed his fields to improve their yield. Gradually much of the land was ruined:[4]

The wet clays were *mortarized*, and the light soils worked and disintegrated till their texture was destroyed, and both were rendered almost sterile, until drained and re-cultivated with manure and no lime.

An ill-informed squire, untrained in estate management, encouraged the emergence of an idle tenantry, and Netherby started to slip back to its old ways.

From his youth, Sir James's son was closely concerned with his future inheritance. At 17 he was advising his father about a Chancery case over land claimed by Sir Robert Graham of Esk; and in 1812 Starkey told Sir James that young Graham 'dearly loved the inhabitants of Netherby: there all his warmest passions centred'. While abroad, Graham regularly wrote to his father of 'dear old Netherby' and estate affairs; he never forgot 'the charms and beauties of that dear place'. Even in Palermo he worried over the debts on the property. On reaching his majority he signed his consent to the breaking of the entail and urged Sir James to take full advantage of his new freedom:

> Use this power as you and our friends may think best; and if all other resources fail, I even consent — sooner than you should any more labour under difficulties — to the sale of such a portion as may be deemed expedient.

After the war he took an increasing interest in the affairs of the estate, though apparently without yet realising the full extent of his father's mounting debts and mismanagement. In 1821, with his political career seemingly in ruins, Graham was for the first time able to examine the state of the property fully.

Much depended, in a large agricultural estate, on the honesty, skill, vigilance and energy of the steward. Rascally agents who extorted from the tenants and cheated their employers were not merely the creation of later novelists. The great reformation of what amounted to the largest early managerial class had just begun; and certainly it had not reached Netherby. Sir James's manager, Ellis, followed his master's lethargic rules. Audits and even simple accounts of the substantial income were considered unnecessary; Ellis ruled, declared his successors, 'almost without control'. Later agents were scarcely unprejudiced recorders, but their observations were accepted by young Graham. They asserted that the farmers and labourers deposited money with Ellis, 'by whom a running account was kept of these deposits as against rent'. The baronet drew on Ellis as necessary, ignoring balances. And the banker-steward charged or allowed interest on the accounts, with the result that 'while he became virtually master of all around him, neither laird nor tenants could tell, or wished perhaps to inquire, exactly how they stood with regard to each other'. Graham consequently found not only a difficult financial situation, caused by debt and neglect and likely to worsen with the provision of incomes for his brothers and sisters, but also an almost complete absence of estate accounts. Netherby's finances depended on Ellis's memory — which, apparently, was not very good.

If there had remained a reasonable income, after paying debt charges and family expenses, the normal recurring investment needs of the estate could have been met; and the rents from an efficient property might gradually have paid off the debt capital. But, unfortunately, honest book-keeping was not the only reform needed. In a wet county and in an area long renowned for its bog and marsh (and traditionally reputed to have risen from the Solway), little attention had been paid to drainage since Dr. Graham's time. The farms, buildings, roads and hedges which had once earned praise were now decrepit and unrepaired. Scores of small tenants, generally holding traditional farms of 40 to 100 acres, abused their land and, through the vagaries of Ellis's financial system, often contrived to avoid rent payments. The estate was 'in a most ruinous condition', claimed the later agents. 'The good land had been exhausted by repeated corn crops. . . . The estate was over-burdened by an excessive population; a great portion of it was unenclosed . . . three-fourths of the land was completely saturated with water. . . .' Stock and crops, buildings and woods had degenerated; non-rotational cropping, over-liming, under-fertilisation and neglect of drainage had spoiled the land. And the poor, ignorant small farmers could not be rescued by their landlord; the estate was burdened with war-time debts and peace-time rent arrears. Even Ellis diagnosed many of the troubles, in 1819; but he could do little to cure them.

Sir James eventually and reluctantly was persuaded by his wife to entrust the management of his decaying property to his son, thus giving himself even more leisure and Graham the first of several experiences of trying to retrieve a very difficult situation. After a thorough examination, Graham inaugurated major reforms. His methods and enquiries displeased Ellis, who was 'allowed to leave'. The rent accounts were so muddled, with some 300 tenants in arrears, that £6,000 of debts were cancelled. But such generosity, the tenants were warned, would not be repeated. With 26,000 acres (21,000 of them in Arthuret and Kirkandrews), including 19,000 arable acres and containing only 6,000 acres of good land, Graham faced a major managerial task; and, financially embarrassed as he was, he could not afford to wallow in sentiment, though his reforms were carried through with remarkable leniency.[5]

The first task was to replace Ellis with a really efficient agent; and Graham chose wisely in appointing a Scot, John Yule, who was a fervent supporter of the historic squirearchy and had prepared for his work (as he once wrote) 'from his cradle'. For a maximum salary of £500 he served Netherby extremely well and became prominent among the developing race of honest, scientific, hard-working managers of English agriculture, in addition to running Graham's local political campaigns. One of his most difficult early duties was to advise on and carry out Graham's schemes to reduce the number of uneconomic small farms on the estate; between 1823 and 1851 such tenancies were cut from 300 to 140. Similar work earned opprobrium for his great contemporary, James Loch, head agent to the Marquess of Stafford (who became Duke of Sutherland in 1833); this remarkable man, who organised an extraordinary industrial and agricultural empire, was to be remembered mainly as the arranger of the 'Highland Clearances'. No doubt, many of Graham's tenants liked their move into modern times no more than the Duke's even more backward retainers. But Graham and Yule carried out their reforms gradually; and no one has written a sentimental account of the changes on the Border.

Perhaps the principal reason for the comparative slowness of the 'consolidation' of the Netherby estate was financial trouble. The loss of £6,000 'which could not have been enforced without resort to great severity' was serious. Yet Netherby's beauties were maintained. The 'elegant seat' was 'a handsome villa situated upon an eminence in a beautiful park, with neat gardens, walks and pleasure grounds, commanded a fine view of the Esk river and its adjacent fertile plains . . . [and] was elegantly furnished and contained an excellent library' — along with Dr. Graham's museum of Roman antiquities. It was later claimed, with some justice, that

> Few sights in England can be more charming than Netherby, placed on a natural knoll that slopes gradually downwards to the richly-verdured park, studded with noble beeches and other forest trees, traversed by the Esk . . .

But the decaying realities behind such splendid façades compelled the family to reduce expenditure on the great house; and Graham, like many of his kind, closed the mansion for long periods. A side effect of this economy was a local reputation for parsimony. But more important was the problem of raising capital for the modernisation of the estate.

Nineteenth-century landowners enjoyed a new source of low-interest loans. The insurance companies offered splendid facilities, which many squires hastened to use. In 1815 Sir James had borrowed £30,000 and in 1818 £25,000 from the largest such body, the Equitable Assurance Society; and in 1825 Graham borrowed a further £45,000. While charging only $3\frac{1}{2}$ per cent interest, the Society naturally demanded substantial securities.[6] But its loans allowed Graham both to consolidate debts and to embark on a desperate — and sometimes despairing — attempt to save the estate by extensive modernisation.

IV

The gross rental of Netherby in 1818 was £17,946. During the following twenty-seven years Graham spent about £93,000 on the property, including over £6,000 on planting, nearly £1,000 on lime, over £36,000 on buildings, over £28,000 on 'improvements', over £12,000 on tiles and nearly £8,000 on flood defences. By strictly economic criteria, the investment did not pay, as Graham sadly and regularly noted, although the gross income reached £21,638 in 1845. £7,650 instantly disappeared on debt charges, and after deducting estate and family payments the squire was left with about £7,000. The debt in 1823 amounted to about £120,000, and although interest payments were reduced by changing creditors, further essential borrowing increased the Grahams' troubles. But, between periods of anxious depression, Graham pressed ahead with his reforms. As the family's future as landed gentry depended on his success, he closely watched every move. His own expenses were now severely cut. 'I shall be anxious about the Sale of my Horses and Stock,' he told Yule in October 1822: 'anything which is out of condition it will not be prudent to sell'.

Graham's capital was largely spent on rebuilding the estate's property. The decaying houses of clay and thatch were cleared. Fences, roads and bridges were renovated. And the gradually growing farms were taken over by a new race of improving tenants. As the number of farms declined, previous small farmers (whose backward methods 'had shown the landlord . . . that the granting of a lease was destructive to both parties concerned in it, as well as the land occupied') left the area, became paid workers or emigrated, often with financial assistance; and the farms were rationally divided. Graham encouraged his farmers by giving cheap loans and prizes at the farmers' society's competitions. Large new afforestation schemes were followed by the construction of a timber mill, in 1837; eight years later the 2,300 acres of woods included 1,300 planted since 1818. And the new schemes eventually helped to change the 'dissolute' habits of the inhabitants, who had maintained their traditional customs of smuggling and farming lethargy. The new, carefully-selected tenants had to follow detailed rotational and maintenance plans.

Most of the classic features of the Agricultural Revolution were followed by Graham and Yule. While small tenants were

rarely granted leases, larger farms were held for 13 or 14 years.
Early enquiries revealed that no grain was being produced and
the stock consisted mainly of inferior pigs and bullocks. Graham
himself 'had less faith in tillage than in stock-farming, for the soil
and climate of Cumberland'; and even Ellis, during his twenty-
year rule, had considerably improved the home farm's pigs,
horses and shorthorns by importing a fine boar, stallion and bull.
Now Galloway cattle — hardy, beef-producing animals, which had
already found favour among several English breeders — were
introduced on the estate. Graham had a fine herd, and gave calves
and stirks as prizes to his tenants. He founded the Longtown
Agricultural Society largely to encourage the showing of improved
stock, and he freely allowed his bulls to service the better herds.[7]
By a mixture of encouragement and compulsion, Graham slowly
turned the estate into an efficient producer of animals, cereals,
wood and vegetables.

Undoubtedly the biggest problem, in an area considerably
affected by water, moss and sedge, was drainage. While visiting
his uncle, William Phillips Inge (husband of Lady Euphemia
Stewart) at Thorpe Constantine in Staffordshire, Graham saw the
advantages of tile drainage schemes. Border drains had relied on
an inefficient mixture of stone, wood and turf, but Graham
introduced the new Midlands methods. A Tamworth expert was
brought to Netherby, to prospect for local clay, and an estate
tile yard was started (probably by T. G. Patrick, later a leading
Cumbrian tile-burner). For his own land Graham hired Robert
and James Lucock (who also became prominent local pioneers) as
drainage organisers. Tenants who followed the squire's example
were rewarded — though the form of the prize, a monetary award
for the farmer using most tiles, attracted some men's customary
deceit. At first tiles were given to tenants without charge, and
gradually a major improvement was effected on both the old farms
and the new enclosures. Graham drained the poorer lands
generally 'without charging the tenants any interest on the
outlay, and in no case was more than 3s. 6d. per acre added for the
cost of drainage. Where land had been thoroughly run out, he
would sometimes take it for a time into his own hands, that he

William Huskisson

might superintend more closely the process for its restoration.'
In 24 years from 1822 about 4,800 acres on tenants' farms were
tile-drained. Graham himself became something of an expert on
the adaptation of general drainage techniques to local conditions;[8]
and he firmly believed that agriculture must be treated in the
same way as industrial concerns.

The reformation of Netherby greatly impressed Robert Brown,
who surveyed the property in 1821 and returned nineteen years
later. He told Yule that Graham had 'raised an imperishable
monument to his honour . . . a monument that he will contemplate
with pleasure all his life, and his memory will be revered during
ages when he is gone'. But present and future prospects often
seemed less glorious to Graham. His father died on 13 April 1824,
and he inherited the baronetcy and complete control of the
heavily burdened estate, which now had to pay both debt interest
and considerable bequests. For years to come, the rents from the
growing property scarcely rose; only after 1842 did the tenants
reluctantly agree to increases, despite the large investment which
had benefited them. Brown might write in 1840 of the changes as
'a work of magic rather than of art' — for 'where you saw a
wilderness you now see everywhere the country like a continued
garden'. But Graham faced years of doubt and worry: in real
terms, his debt charges had risen considerably. As his family grew
and his expenses multiplied, the morose baronet often wondered
whether the maintenance of landed property was worth while.
Other men appeared to make larger incomes with more ease and
less risk.

Even when the Hall was closed, Graham carefully controlled
the estate from London. The lax, easy-going tenants often
dismayed him. 'I am very much annoyed by the perverse conduct
of James Birrell', he told Yule in March 1825,

> and I cannot imagine what his plan is or what his hopes can be. You
> must watch his cropping and proceedings narrowly; and I am very
> much disposed to insist on his signing his lease or to break with him
> at once and to give him notice to quit. . . . Such conduct on the part
> of tenants is disgusting to landlords and calculated to make them
> harsh, ungenerous and unrelenting. I am beginning to be disgusted

F

with Landed property, burthened so that I cannot reside upon it and every day bringing some fresh annoyance or some unexpected demand.

As to Mr. Ian Thupin, he need not write me letters; generally, I wish only to communicate with the tenants thro' you, for both my conversations and my writing are misinterpreted and misrepresented by them, and I will henceforth have no direct personal communication with any of them. All the letters, therefore, which they may write to me will be answered by you. I shall not lower Mr. Ian Thupin's rent a farthing; and most glad shall I be to get rid of such a tenant — I cannot wish to have a worse, and if a sacrifice in rent is to be made I shall hope to find a better.

Thus Graham laid down his principles of managerial delegation. But he continued to take an interest in detailed problems, large and small. 'I decidedly object to the shooting of rooks,' he wrote in April:

My father tried the experiment, and the damage done to the plover and the disturbance of the game, just at the time of the pheasant sitting, was intolerable. The nests may be destroyed by boys sent up the trees; but Wood must not have the management even of this, since under his pretext of killing rooks all the blackguards of Longtown come into the woods. The rooks, after all, do more good, by destroying grub and worm than harm . . .

In these difficult times, it was suggested to Graham that the new rail-roads might be useful to him. Certainly, several landowners greatly relieved financial embarrassments by railway investments, land sales, promotions, directorships and improved facilities. Graham did not share some squires' antagonism to the new locomotive monster in the countryside. But he told Yule in May 1825 that although 'the Newcastle and Carlisle was of great importance to the country, he found it would not pay the subscribers, and alas! he had no ready money and could hardly keep his head above water'. It was difficult to visualise the effects of the proposed line, but Yule and his employers were fascinated by the possibilities. Yule sent Graham 'a memorandum with regard to the Newcastle Rail Road', which, wrote Graham, appears to contain some useful suggestions and to be founded on probable grounds. I shall carry the substance of it before Keith Douglas and Mr. Irving, and consult with them in what manner we should communicate with the Newcastle directors. But the Manchester and Liverpool Rail Road has been thrown out: a strong feeling exists among the Landed Interest against the principle, and considerable doubts have been thrown by the evidence before the Manchester and Liverpool Committee on the expediency of the locomotive engine and the estimated expense of rail roads generally. I hear also that the Newcastle and Carlisle will be opposed by Lord Carlisle and most of the Northumberland proprietors, thro' whose land it is meant to pass. I think their ignorance will oppose, for it is the interest of any proprietor to raise up his estate by every possible means, especially at the expense of others; but if it be opposed stoutly, however ignorantly, it will fail, and I am not sanguine as to the progress of the measure.

Graham was to some extent in advance of his fellow-landowners, in his appreciation of squirearchical self-interest. But in time the Border proprietors were converted; the Howards of Naworth, Corby and Greystoke all provided railway directors, even for the Newcastle and Carlisle line.

Graham told Yule in June to prepare detailed analyses of the costs of Solway sea-carriage to Annan, as compared with the expense of possible railway extensions to Maryport and Workington. 'Tho' a Rail Road would certainly be beneficial to my property', he wrote, 'yet I do not think the advantage would be very great to me.' And he went on to tell Yule that 'he must keep down the rate of wages as much and as long as he could'. Every economy, every possible gain and every productive investment mattered in the fight to save Netherby.

Yet Graham retained growing doubts about the wisdom of continuing his struggle. He was tempted to sell the estate and to use the capital thus gained to buy a partnership in the London banking house of Pole, Thornton, Downe and Company. Negotiations to this end had already begun, when James Bailey, the Bristol banker, advised him 'to hold fast by Netherby and keep clear of banking'. Graham followed this advice, and soon afterwards realised his narrow escape, when Peter Pole's firm collapsed. Nevertheless, late in 1826 Yule was ordered to assess 'the real state of matters'. In November the agent reported that

> If you choose to sell your whole property in the County your fortune in real cash, paying off *every incumbrance*, might be about £448,000, which at 4 per cent would give you a clear income of £17,920 yearly.

He advised Graham that other schemes might 'pay off almost all your debt and incumbrances by sales', while leaving Graham

> the very heart of your estate, all your political power, the presentations to the livings, the village of Longtown and lands adjoining and also the manorial rights of Arthuret, Kirkandrews, Nichol Forest and Solport

— and an income of £13,775 or £13,361, depending upon which plan of sale he adopted. Yule's plan to deal with total debts and obligations of £194,500 involved selling up to £182,000-worth of land, reducing the £20,500 rent-roll to £14,400 or £15,228 and paying either £625 or £1,867 annually on the remaining debt. After his detailed report, he added:

> I have done my utmost to improve this great estate, and, plebeian tho' I am, I cannot bear to see it go out of the possession of an old and honourable family, who have always been beloved by their retainers, into the hands of a hardhearted grinding speculator, without lifting up my humble voice against such a measure ...

However proud he might be of his genealogy, Graham was now impervious to such sentiments. His next letter announced that he could not give a final answer, in his current financial dilemma. He would pay off his brothers and establish a sinking fund for his debts. But, he told Yule in November,

> I shall expect on your part the most rigid management, an exaction from the tenants of all the outlay to which they are bound by their leases and the saving of every shilling which you can fairly keep in my pocket; and I cannot think that the diminished scale of my money transactions can much longer require the assistance to you of a clerk ... remember always that you and I are fighting for our joint credit, that if I am turned out of the estate by my own outlay

upon it, both I who committed and you who advised will be defamed, however strong may have been our reason.

Here was a blunt exposition of the partnership between landowner and steward which dominated most nineteenth-century estates.

Graham gradually followed parts of Yule's schemes. Late in 1826 he was borrowing further sums and preparing to sell the Bewcastle and Nichol Forest estates, though the Equitable's securities held up the sales. In December he told Yule that he had borrowed £10,000 for six months at 5 per cent, and[9]

I proposed to borrow £30,000 on mortgage which I intend to appropriate as follows:

New Bond	£10,000
Mortgage on House in Grosvenor Place	8,000
Purchase of a Government Annuity for Mrs. Sheldon	7,000
Trustees of my sister Catherine	2,500
Miss Callander	1,600

Early also in the Spring I intend to sell all my out-lying property, to pay off all the mortgage debt upon it and likewise to pay £5,000 to my brother William, £3,000 to my brother George and £2,000 to Miss Johanna.

The Mortgage debt will then stand on the estate £100,000 to the Equitable at 4 per cent, £30,000 to the Mortgager at $4\frac{1}{2}$%. One jointure instead of two; my brothers paid off, excepting the annuity to my brother Charles; and the estate will run against the lives of my mother and my sisters, who are annuitants.

This is my last effort to save my estate; I can never borrow again, having experienced the utmost difficulty in clearing a security for this £30,000 by the most complicated arrangements with the Equitable, and if I rush into fresh difficulties the estate itself must go. Our management therefore must be cautious in the extreme; and with care and exertion I hope we may struggle on.

This was not the last occasion on which Graham doubted the wisdom of remaining a large squire. But during the 1830s he gradually contrived to transfer his debts to the low-charging Equitable, which by 1838 had invested £200,000 in Netherby.

And other considerations, despite his great financial difficulties, induced Graham to retain his property.

V

J. C. Curwen, the Cumbrian Whig champion, undoubtedly exercised considerable influence over Graham. In addition to being second only to Lonsdale in the county's coal production, he was an important agricultural improver. From 1805 his Working- ton Agricultural Society organised shows which attracted such great names as the Duke of Bedford, Coke of Holkham and 'Agricultural Sir John' Sinclair. As Curwen's 'favourite pupil', Graham regularly attended these gatherings — and he made his first speech at one show. Here he met his friends from the agricultural classes, ranging from the great Howards to such yeomen as Blamire and Rooke. The attractions of appearing among such neighbours and such aristocratic celebrities as a great landed proprietor must have been considerable.

Furthermore, landownership carried political influence, and Graham had not lost his hopes of representing a local con- stituency. Curwen was now aged 70, and in 1826 Graham bluntly asked him whether he intended to continue to sit for the county. 'Speculations for my own benefit', he told Yule in April, 'on the death of one of the dearest of my friends are by no means amicable; yet such is the business of life that provision must be made for contingencies like this. . . .' Yule was ordered quietly to make preparations and if possible to gain the Duke of Hamilton's support. 'Under all the circumstances,' wrote Graham,

> tho' most anxious for a seat in the House of Commons, I really believe it is my interest to wait and not spend any money in the purchase of a seat on an uncertain treasury, when I have so good a prospect in more quarters than one. But life is moving fast away, and idleness is odium to me . . .

Although retaining the county seat (and also rejecting Brougham's requests), Curwen urged the Carlisle Whigs to 'lose no time in calling a meeting . . . to propose asking [Graham] to stand' and hoped that the proposal 'would meet with general concurrence'. Graham gladly accepted, told Yule to send a gift of £25 for the relief of the 'manufacturing poor' of the city and welcomed his agent's advice. 'It must be made to appear rather a favour which I confer on them', he wrote in May,

> than an honour which means me representing Carlisle. It will be a troublesome place to win, but I think that I shall strengthen my position in the county. I want a seat in Parliament, and even one in my own immediate neighbourhood is after all most honourable.

In preparation for the re-opening of Netherby, he ordered the hiring of two laundry-maids, a kitchen-maid, dairymaid and housemaid and the opening of the furniture.

If, however, Graham saw his property as a means of political advancement, he had also developed a keen interest in agricultural problems, both technical and economic. His own reading and the conversation of the amateur economist Rooke led Graham, particularly during the 1825 depression, to consider the Corn Laws and their effects. His conclusions were published in a pamphlet of 114 pages on *Corn and Currency*, in 1826. He argued that the best interests of the landowners would be served by liberal economics rather than by protection. High duties on foreign corn had failed to help British agriculture and should be cut to a level where they simply balanced the landowners' taxes and rates, for

> High prices, by increasing rents, benefit the landlords, but they confer no advantage on the labourer; they are an injury to the productive and a tax on the unproductive classes of the community.

Furthermore, high prices necessitated high wages, which reduced profits:

> The landlord's best customer is the manufacturer; but his prosperity depends entirely on high profits, which it is the avowed tendency of high prices to reduce. If corn be dearer in England than elsewhere, wages must be higher; and if wages be higher, profits must be lower; thus our foreign competitors obtain the greatest possible advantage: and if the system become permanent,

manufacturing employment, except for the home market, must cease in this country.

Such 'classical' themes were to become famous. And Graham connected the land's troubles with the Bank of England's currency policies: the deflation caused by the return to the 'gold standard' in 1819 had harmed the landed proprietor and benefited his creditors. In liberal fashion, he advocated a moderate Corn Law, a reform of monopolies, reductions in both taxes and Government expenditure and taxation of annuitants. Throughout his paper, Graham assailed the 'unproductive' creditor and urged the nobility and gentry to act together:[10]

> They will be opposed by the moneyed interest as by one man; they will be opposed by the present Ministers, few of whom are connected with land or with the aristocracy — some of whom, by far the most able, having risen by their talents from an humble origin, are disposed, very naturally, to envy the existence of any power in this country which genius cannot win and which birth alone bestows.

Liberal economics were thus buttressed by Whiggish 'caste' attitudes.

The paper aroused considerable interest. While Government apologists defended the Bank, utilitarians condemned land-owners' attempts to 'rob' their creditors. And many agricultura-lists could not accept Graham's arguments — and probably few of them could understand the pages on currency (a subject, wrote Graham, 'foreign to the tastes of the country gentlemen'). But Carlisle electors expressed interest in his views on Protection, and in May he told Yule:

> As to the Corn Laws, I cannot dissimulate my opinions: the existing system it is impossible to uphold. There must be free importation *with an ample protective duty*; the amount of that duty must be the result of a most careful and difficult enquiry, and I will give no pledge whatever relative to my vote on the subject of the duty. But it does so happen that entire publicity will be given to my real opinions, since I have a work now in the press, which will be published in a few days . . .

Although not all Whigs could approve of the pamphlet, the Marquess of Lansdowne 'read it with great pleasure' in July.

The noisiest comments came from the highly individualistic Radical journalist William Cobbett, editor of the popular *Political Register*. Cobbett started to attack the 'young fellow' in September. The landowners, he asserted, 'were the cause of all the taxes and all the debts; and now let them *take the consequences*!' Graham wanted 'to commit all sorts of acts of injustice', claimed Cobbett, to preserve 'the base reptiles who are called country gentlemen'. By late September, when he had apparently read the paper, the former sergeant-major's wrath had reached fever-point. Graham was a 'conceited and impudent plagiarist, or *literary thief* ... the "Magnus Apollo" ...', author of a 'contemptible' publication wherein he had stolen Cobbett's views on Peel's Bank Act and suggested 'sponging the fundholders and *leaving Messieurs the Parsons untouched*!' Cobbett continued to pour out sarcastic attacks on the 'stupid, empty-headed, insolent pamphleteer', the 'son of "John with the bright sword" ', 'this barefaced plagiarist . . . '.[11]

Prejudiced and unfair though many such criticisms were, Cobbett certainly hit on one side of Graham's character. The Radical propagandist's regular references to Graham's ancestors — the Menteiths and 'the seventh Earl of Galloway, K.T. (taking care, for God's sake, not to omit the K.T.)' — were fair comments on Graham's strong and sometimes snobbish sense of family tradition. Perhaps, among many conflicting ideas, it was this feeling which led Graham to maintain his position as the third greatest Cumbrian landowner.

Netherby still faced many difficulties, but draining, farm consolidation, the selection of good tenants and the enclosure of neighbouring wastes continued gradually. Only in 1842 did Graham dare to raise his rents, and even then he had difficulty in persuading Protectionist farmers to accept the new valuations. Yule found the larger tenants 'a set of cunning fellows and very ill to manage', although he sympathised with their fears. Only about a third of the new gross rent of some £26,000 went to Graham, and in March 1845 he again thought of selling most of the estate. The sale should produce at least £700,000, which would allow him to pay off his debts, provide for his younger children and invest enough to produce £15,048 annually; after deducting family charges, he would still receive £13,868. The prospect was tempting; but Graham never sold his inheritance.

Graham's first major personal achievement was his work as an agricultural reformer, and his reforms were often admired by contemporaries. Although hopes of discovering coal under the estate never materialised, Graham sold land to three railways and in April 1847 rejoiced in telling Yule:

> I consider myself on velvet . . . immense benefits will be conferred
> on my estate. It will do more to restore prosperity to my concerns
> than any other transaction of my life.

He continued to encourage tenants to adopt and improve dairy farming, stock breeding and tillage. And from 1849 he tried to copy the flax cultivation which he saw on Lord Dufferin's County Down estates; this venture was one of his few failures.

In 1873 the 'New Domesday' survey reported that Graham's son had 25,270 acres, with a gross estimated rental of £26,696, in Cumberland. Sir Frederick also had 33 acres in Dumfries and 105 in the West Riding, paying £40 and £85 respectively. In the 1860s he spent about £2,000 annually on drainage alone; from 1879 to 1894, during dark years for agriculture, this expenditure fell to an average of £946, with £1,153 on buildings, and rents were reduced by a fifth. Between 1822 and 1894 some £240,000 had been invested in the estate. When Assistant Commissioner Wilson Fox reported on Cumberland's agriculture in 1895, Netherby's 107 farms covered 30,000 acres. It was, he declared, 'now one of the finest properties in the North', and he noted that it had been saved by Graham.[12] The family were able to remain great landowners because of Graham's example of progressive and efficient management.

4

The Political Reformer

Despite his financial worries, in May 1826 Graham gladly accepted the invitation of the Carlisle Whigs to contest the borough. The ancient city's elections were notoriously riotous and strongly fought. In 1786, 1787, 1790 and 1796 there had been petitions against the results, but in 1802, 1806, 1807 and 1812 the parties had agreed to divide the representation. The truce ended in 1816, when Sir Philip Musgrave belatedly (and unsuccessfully) contested the Whig seat at a by-election, and in 1818 and 1820 the Whigs consequently stood for both seats, though only holding one. There followed a slight change of votes; while Curwen led Lonsdale's nominee, Sir James Graham of Kirkstall and Edmund Castle, by 25 votes in 1818, two years later Graham became senior Member, with 246 votes to Curwen's 239 and the other Whig William James's 149. When Curwen chose to sit for the county, James was returned at a bitter by-election, defeating Musgrave by 468 votes to 382. This contest was very expensive: James claimed that it had cost him £13,000, while Musgrave was supposed to have spent £23,000. Tories complained of Whig intimidation, and Whigs alleged that Tory magistrates had attempted to influence the electors by calling in armed troops. Five years later, on Graham's death, Musgrave was elected to the Tory seat, and thus the balance was maintained.

As a local landowner, Graham of Netherby knew Carlisle politics well. The contest was likely to be difficult, against the entrenched influence of Lonsdale and the Corporation and the growing independent Tory strength of Musgrave. It would also be expensive. And it would probably be violent: the mobs had maintained tradition by rioting against Graham of Kirkstall in 1818 and against Musgrave in 1820.

For the 1826 election the Tories nominated Musgrave of Edenhall against the Netherby Graham. The two baronets might have held their parties' seats without too much expense, had not another Whig group nominated the reluctant James on the hustings. A bitter contest developed and the handloom weavers, already descending the long and wretched road to the extinction of their craft, hotly opposed the Tory. Musgrave, who had represented Petersfield for five years before his election for Carlisle, was a city alderman and a magistrate in three counties. Now he was blamed for what the voteless Carlisle proletariat considered to be the results of the Corn Law and other legislation. Graham's proposals for abolishing slavery and religious disabilities and reducing both Government expenditure and the corn duties were more popular.

While canvassing the Caldewgate in June Musgrave was stoned by a crowd and fled to a weaver's house. City councillors who intervened were thrown into a mill dam, and further rescue attempts by the Mayor and his two constables were driven off with some violence. The magistrates then swore in 300 special constables and called out the Castle garrison of troops from the 55th Foot. When the soldiers were stoned some panic-stricken recruits fired into the mob, killing two people. It was unfortunate for the authorities that the dead were a woman and a girl. Yet small bodies of infantrymen defending unpopular justices from murderous crowds had little choice, in the last resort, but to fire. The provocative crowd nevertheless gave Graham a hero's welcome in the evening; and he delivered a careful speech at the Grapes Inn.

At the nomination on the 9th Graham spoke up for a modified Corn Law, franchise reform and reduction in Government expenditure and patronage. As the voting began there were angry protests over the presence of dragoons in Botcherby Lane. Hodgson, the Mayor, denied any knowledge of this precaution, and the crowd became angry, especially when William Brougham reported that Captain Wheeler, the commanding officer, claimed to be acting on Hodgson's orders. Peace was restored only when the troops left the city. But although Graham successfully pacified the crowd, it is doubtful whether his liberalism greatly influenced the electors. Carlisle now apparently accepted a divided representation, and on the first day of the poll Graham and Musgrave led, with 119 and 92 votes to James's 71. Finally, the two baronets were elected, by 264 and 239 votes to James's 140. Graham professed to see the result as a warning to Lonsdale: 'the noble spirit of independence was rising from [its] dormant state . . . and the Lord-Lieutenant of the county [should] take care, or the lesson which had been taught him in Carlisle would be taught him elsewhere'.

Yet the danger to Lowther Castle did not appear very serious. Lowther relations held one Cumbrian and two Westmorland seats, and Lowther nominees retained a seat at Appleby and two at Cockermouth. And elsewhere the 'No Popery' cry had rallied support to the Government. 'We think [Graham] a good-looking gentleman', commented the Tory *Carlisle Patriot*, '— clever, but too irritable . . . a rash and inconsiderate politician.'[1] This sour view contained some truth about the 34-year-old senior Member for Carlisle.

I

Parliamentary life was leisurely for Graham. He presented a Whig petition condemning Hodgson's call for troops. And he opposed a Glasgow call for organised emigration, preferring public grants to the virtually starving handloom weavers. But the Session was soon over.

His friendship with Rooke was certainly one factor in Graham's developing philosophy. He agreed with Rooke on 'the deadly effects' of Peel's recommended resumption of cash payments in 1819 and forecast a struggle between the aristocracy and 'the moneyed interest'. He was also 'disposed to believe' in Rooke's view that free trade and commercial expansion 'would ultimately enhance the value of all property . . . and of land'; but in January 1827 he was 'not bold enough' to follow Rooke's proposal for free trade in corn, without financial and currency reform. The ultimate result might be 'a general rise of price, accompanied by increased comfort and civilisation to all the people of the habitable globe', but the immediate effect would be a price fall disastrous to encumbered landowners. 'Give me a sufficient circulating medium in our own country', he told Rooke, 'and I am for free trade in every article with every country of the world; but with Mr. Peel's bill on the statute book I dare try no experiment which may lower for one half-year the income of the proprietor of the soil.'

Early in 1827 politics was dominated by the news of Liverpool's paralysis. Old Cabinet divisions now came more into the open, and the King hesitated to summon the able liberal Tory George Canning to form a Ministry. But as Liverpool's health declined and the Right reluctantly considered itself unable to provide a Ministry, the King's choice was narrowed. Speculation mounted in the clubs during what Graham regarded as 'the most exciting interval that could be imagined'. Meanwhile, the Opposition continued to harry the Government — over such issues as the Duke and Duchess of Clarence's grants, the Carlisle riots and Lord Eldon's delays in Chancery cases. Graham was angry also over the Ministers' reluctance to discuss their Corn Law policy. 'This concealment is an evil omen, and to my mind savours of a juggle,' he told Rooke in February:

> A great measure of a wise government should be founded on general principles which will bear the severest scrutiny and the test of publicity and of criticism . . . This check of public opinion on all our measures is, I feel, most salutary; and more severe and sound judgment prevails on all those subjects *without* the walls of Parliament than can very easily be found *within* it.

He did not always follow these high-sounding principles.

Like the Tories, the Whigs were divided by the crisis. Lord Holland's group, including the Duke of Devonshire, Lansdowne and Carlisle, was willing to co-operate with Canning, as was Brougham, intent 'to lock the door for ever on Eldon and Co.'. But others strongly opposed any coalition, even for the sake of Roman Catholic emancipation and liberal foreign policies. Althorp thought that 'Canning courts us merely for our votes and . . . will fall back upon the Tories and leave us only the shame of having been his dupes'. And Grey (described by James Abercromby as being 'as usual violent, ill-tempered and influenced wholly by personal feelings') frankly 'regarded the son of an actress as incapacitated *de facto*' for leadership of a Government. But by early April, despite personal inclinations and professed religious qualms, the King had to accept Canning.

A major political realignment followed. Wellington, Eldon, Bathurst, Westmorland, Melville, Peel, Henry Goulburn and Sir Henry Hardinge left office, and, faced by this exodus of the Right, Canning turned to the Whigs, negotiating terms with Lansdowne and Brougham. Such Whigs as Devonshire, Lansdowne, Carlisle and Tierney remained willing to collaborate, but in late April hopes faltered when Sir John Copley became Lord Chancellor and the King allegedly insisted on an anti-Emancipationist as Lord Lieutenant of Ireland to balance William Lamb, the Chief Secretary. Although reluctant to break with Althorp, Graham supported Lansdowne's coalition manœuvres: 'such proofs of kindness and confidence have been my consolation,' wrote the weary Marquess. At this desperate stage Brougham harangued an assembly in Brooks's club, finally persuading a majority to support Canning. Lansdowne, Carlisle, Tierney and Devonshire entered the Ministry, along with the Canningite Viscount Palmerston; and lesser posts were filled by Lamb, Sir James Mackintosh, Edward Stanley, Abercromby and Thomas Spring Rice.

Many old friendships were thus broken, and — as Canning generally opposed Parliamentary reform and had to maintain an 'open' attitude to Emancipation — many election pledges were forgotten. Whigs to whom Opposition had become almost natural lamented what Sir Robert Adair told Sir Robert Wilson was 'the death of the Whig Party'; Wilson, a friend of Brougham, insisted that 'it had died of exhaustion and revived as a giant refreshed'. The truth was that the old political alignments were breaking up. The Tory Right mourned the passing of the old world so long guarded by Eldon, but 'Church and State', the hallowed war-time cry, had become antique nonsense to new generations in both parties. Most politicians faced some sacrifice; but Sir Francis

Burdett told the Whigs that consistency was the least of political virtues, and most politicians accepted his dictum. Certainly Graham followed the majority decision, sitting on the Ministerial side when the Commons reassembled on 1 May. And when the Tory Right attacked the Government even Althorp changed sides, preferring 'an administration actuated by liberal and enlightened principles [to] one of Toryism in its most objectionable form'.

However, Whig ideals had been considerably changed and Grey's bitter refusal to compromise was admired by many country Whigs. Through the early summer Canning was harassed by Eldonite Tories, while his Whig supporters were assailed by their old leader's group. Graham closely observed the Prime Minister's agony during this extraordinary period. 'The recent struggle of parties', he told Rooke on 29 June,

> has been highly injurious to the public interests, and never was a session less productive of solid advantage to the community. I am not pleased with the present posture of affairs, and I fear that for some time the Government will be disorganised and public attention dedicated to the character and conduct of men, without much reference to measures.

He was increasingly convinced that the 1819 measures 'lay at the foundation of all our difficulties', but 'the Legislature was not yet ripe' for discussion of it. Furthermore, the long uncertainties were scarcely ended by Canning's death on 8 August.

In September Viscount Goderich formed a Cabinet, giving posts to Carlisle, Lansdowne and Tierney but appointing the Tory J. C. Herries as Chancellor of the Exchequer. Goderich was a member of the family which had given the first Sir James Graham his Ripon seat. But Graham was more in sympathy with the Canningite William Huskisson, formerly President of the Board of Trade and Treasurer of the Navy and now Secretary for War and Colonies. Herries and Huskisson were old opponents, and 'Goody Goderich' had little chance of forming a successful Government. As the political manœuvres began again, Graham told Rooke, in November, that he was convinced by his case, though 'not quite prepared to admit foreign corn without the imposition of a moderate duty, as a mere fiscal regulation' and though 'disposed to ascribe even more fatal effects than you do to the permanent operations of Mr. Peel's bill and of a gold standard constantly increasing in value, while our national burthens are proportionately augmented'. Goderich was a weak Minister, harassed by King and Cabinet. Eventually, Herries's condemnation of Huskisson's insistence on Althorp as chairman of the Finance Committee provoked the Government's resignation, before meeting Parliament, in January 1828.[2]

Wellington, a man with slight party feelings but a strong sense of the need to maintain government, now formed a Ministry. The Whigs were reunited as they returned to their accustomed places in Opposition, while several Canningites retained office. But the strains between Ministers continued, and the great general was unable to maintain unity. Russell's plan to repeal the Test and Corporation Acts, the hoary symbols of State opposition to Dissent, was reluctantly accepted. But the more serious problem of Roman Catholic emancipation still loomed ominously over the political scene. And the Cabinet itself was divided over the disfranchisement of East Retford and Penryn; Huskisson's group wished to transfer the seats to new large towns, while the 'High Tories' preferred to pass them to neighbouring districts. When, in May, the Lords rejected a compromise plan, Huskisson resigned, with Earl Dudley, Palmerston and Grant. A more sternly Tory Ministry emerged after these desertions.

II

Meanwhile, there had been a change in Carlisle politics. Musgrave had died in 1827, and a riotous by-election resulted in the return of the Tory General James Law Lushington, with 276 votes to Lawson's 261. And Curwen, the old county Member, was now declining; his sale of his famous shorthorns at a loss seemed to indicate a withdrawal from public life. Graham closely watched for any sign of a political resignation. Curwen already regarded Graham as his successor, though doubting his Whig loyalties, and,

G

as if to disperse this doubt, Graham played an active part in the 1828 Session.

In March Graham supported Hume's attack on the sale of commissions by half-pay officers and the resultant loss to the nation: the system was 'a source of profligate expenditure and of corrupt influence'. But his major speech was delivered on 3 June, against Goulburn's proposal to limit the English circulation of Scottish £1 notes. He admitted that, 'misled by Mr. Ricardo . . . he had unhappily voted for the Bill of 1819' and insisted that Scottish notes 'did not displace the gold currency of England to any extent' and were extremely important in Border districts: 'seven-eighths of the rent of his own estate had been paid in the paper currency of Scotland'. Laws which prohibited notes under £5 in one country and insisted on them in another were ridiculous: 'why not try to amend what was faulty, instead of meddling with what worked well?' After a long speech, Graham proposed that a Select Committee should examine the currency laws; he was defeated by 154 votes to 45.

Such speeches on complicated topics, illustrated by long quotations from Locke and Hume, were scarcely calculated to make Graham popular out of Parliament. But at Westminster he was making some mark by hard work: he joined the committees on criminal commitments, anatomy schools, the removal of Irish paupers, relief of able-bodied paupers and parliamentary printing expenses. And he kept in close touch with party colleagues. In late June he told Althorp that the Government planned to follow the Finance Committee's recommendations on salary reductions but to reject any cut in political offices. The news did not surprise Althorp. 'I am pledged to decided opposition,' he wrote on 2 July:

> . . . My main object being to see the Catholic question carried, I am inclined to sacrifice everything to this. But if there does not appear a prospect of this being done, it appears to me that we must declare open war upon the government, and there cannot be a more hostile measure or one more likely to be effective than blowing up the Finance Committee upon grounds which they are now about to give us.

Late in the Session Graham acted as the counsellor of holidaying colleagues. On 12 July, for instance, he told Edward Stanley that Labouchere was to present a petition on Canada's tangled affairs. 'On the whole, I think the occasion worthy of your appearance', he wrote, '. . . John Russell is out of town, and it is still uncertain whether his motion will be brought on: but the opinion generally is that he will not withdraw it. God send us, if he perseveres, a good deliverance.'

Stanley, grandson of the 12th Earl of Derby, though seven years younger than Graham, already appeared to be a potential leader to him. 'John Russell has withdrawn his notice, and the Session may be considered at an end,' Graham told Stanley on 15 July:

> It is better that it should thus terminate, for the responsibility is awful which now rests on the government . . . I hope you will take the field in force; and I think you will find a strong and respectable body willing to act under you. Much, of course, must depend upon the events which may occur before Parliament reassembles; but the aspect of affairs is so clouded by difficulties that the chances are some capital blunders may be committed, and then will arrive the golden opportunity of forming a party in the H. of Commons on some broad and intelligible principle, without any reference to leaders in the H. of Lords and without any direct compact with Brougham, whose assistance must, of course, be desired, but whose interference as *against* our leader must be resolutely resisted.
>
> You are the person on whom I rest my hopes: you contain all the great requisites: you may reunite a scattered force which it is the interest of the country to see consolidated; and by concerted and judicious management I really am disposed to believe the road to power is open.

Graham had serious hopes of creating an alliance of Canningites and moderate Whigs. But political events moved too quickly for the original plan to have much chance of success.

If Graham was often a carefully calculating politician, he was also a generous and loyal supporter of his friends. With Earl Spencer, he had acted as surety for the 2nd Lord Lyttelton. 'I shall never forget the great obligation you laid upon me and my family, how freely and in how gentlemanlike a spirit of honourable friendship you came to my help,' wrote Spencer's son-in-law, the 3rd Baron, when his brother died in November. Yet Graham continued to watch for political opportunities. Curwen died on 10 December, and Graham acted instantly to gain the Whig nomination for the county seat. The principal difficulty, it seemed, was the resentment which Lord Carlisle (the former Morpeth) might feel over his preference for Curwen in 1820. On 11 December Graham told Carlisle of his intention 'to abandon my seat for Carlisle and to declare myself a candidate for the county'. He recalled 'family connection, past intimacies, long habits of good neighbourhood and general coincidence in political opinions', admitted that Carlisle might think he had 'acted unkindly' and chose 'to throw myself on your generosity and to trust to my general character as it may now stand in your Lordship's estimation'. The Earl was more generous than Graham imagined or had the right to expect, and gave the vital support of the Howards. The Curwen influence was also behind Graham, who carefully announced that he would 'satisfy the Catholics without injuring the Church' and take care not to 'swamp the influence of property' when reforming Parliament.

Lonsdale observed the 1802 compromise, by which the county representation was shared. 'This will find you in the bustle not I hope of a contested election but of a canvass,' Althorp wrote on 17 December:

... I am of course very doubtful as to the course which the Duke of Wellington intends to pursue, but I am very much inclined to think that he will propose something in favour of the Catholics — not enough probably, but something. With respect to ourselves, I think our course is clear, agreeing except in one point as to what it ought to be with Brougham. All our members ought to be present on the first day, and in case the Government do not declare their intention to bring forward something in favour of the Catholics we must get up a debate to last at least two days, and for this purpose put up all the Irishmen we can to describe the state of their country, and we must if possible keep this debate to the Catholic question and the Catholic question only. If, on the other hand, the

Government say they do intend to do something, we must wait to see what it is and be careful not to commit ourselves in any hostilities. The difference of opinion between me and Brougham is that he thinks we ought to have all our foxes in the field; I think we need not bring up the foxhunters . . . I think it wrong to bring up those who are only useful in a division. I told Brougham that he had no experience of the annoyance of being brought up for nothing at that time of year but I had . . .

Althorp denied his own ability to lead the party:

No man ever underrates himself . . . I believe with you that a great many of our party fancy that I should be a good leader (so they did about Lord Lansdowne), but I know I should not. I should not have been leader two months before I had fallen into the greatest possible contempt. At present I am overrated, then I should be underrated . . . I am not equal to the post of the leader of a party.

The election was uncontested, and so on 16 January 1829 Graham joined Lonsdale's brother, Sir John Lowther, as M.P. for Cumberland, the position which he had long coveted. 'The triumph is not mine,' he told Rooke:

the freeholders of our native county have evinced their energy and spirit, tempered by a discreet moderation . . . it was a proud day, not to me only, but to those free-born statesmen whose character I value more as I understand it better.

The *Carlisle Patriot* strangely claimed him as 'a good sound Tory' — which the rival *Journal* hastened to deny.[3]

III

Despite his popular election and comparatively 'progressive' opinions, Graham had not yet achieved any success in the House as a whole. A dandified appearance and over-rehearsed delivery weakened the effect of his long and carefully-planned speeches. Fortunately, Graham himself realised his failure. 'I have tried it every way,' he told Sir Francis Baring of his speech-making: 'extempore, from notes and committing all to memory, and I can't do it. I don't know why it is, but I'm afraid I shall never

succeed.' He even apologised to the Commons: 'he never rose in
the House without embarrassment,' he admitted in 1830. But he
was courageous enough to continue his attempts.

Early in 1829 the Roman Catholic problem came to a head. In
the previous June, on Grant's resignation, a popular Irish squire,
William Vesey Fitzgerald, had become President of the Board of
Trade and Treasurer of the Navy. But when he sought re-election
in County Clare he was defeated by the 'Emancipationist' Daniel
O'Connell. The victor, recorded the horrified Tory Mrs. Arbuthnot, 'talks very big and very treasonably . . . [and] is doing all he
can to blow up a rebellion in Ireland. He sent 120 priests into
Clare to organise the voters and force them, by threats of
excommunication, to vote in opposition to their landlords.' She
thought 'the Government are very much to blame', through
weakness. But it was obvious that O'Connell could repeat his
success — and that only a small swing of parliamentary opinion
would reverse the narrow majority of 1827 against 'Emancipation'.
By late July Wellington was chatting about plans for Roman
Catholic relief with Mrs. Arbuthnot; and gradually a detailed
plan was prepared, not without very great difficulty. 'Every one
was up with the news of the day — that Wellington had decided
to let the Catholics into Parliament,' Creevey told Miss Ord on 3
February 1829. There were still many troublesome problems. The
'pro-Catholic' Viceroy, the Marquess of Anglesey, had been
recalled and replaced by the Duke of Northumberland. Peel felt
it necessary to vacate his seat for Oxford University, where he
was succeeded by the more rigid Anglican, Sir Robert Inglis. But
the policy change was clear. Creevey thought that Wellington
envied Anglesey's Irish popularity and 'so had sacrificed the man,
while adopting his opinions' and that 'the Whigs were as sore as
be damned at Wellington distinguishing himself'.[4] By April
'Emancipation' was carried.

The Duke had, in fact, 'dished' his opponents. 'Our Whigs,
who hate the Beau [Wellington] and Peel and Grey with all their
hearts', Creevey noted on 2 March, '. . . are today more chopfallen
than ever.' Two days later Graham attacked Inglis and 'the High
Church doctors of the University' for opposing the Bill, at the

same time praising Peel's 'manly avowal of his change of opinion'. But if the Tories were divided between stern Eldonites, Lord Blandford's ring of parliamentary reformers, 'middle way' Peelites, Wellington's bloc and the individualistic Canningites, the Whigs were also seriously split. Old loyalties, already weakened — especially since Liverpool's resignation — were now of little consequence: party, it appeared, was again subordinate to personality. Graham had to content himself with hard work on committees dealing with such mundane matters as the militia, Scottish entail law and vestry constitutions.

At Easter Graham returned to Netherby, to perform the varied duties incumbent on a county M.P. and magistrate. 'You see how true all our predictions have proved,' he told Rooke on 10 April: the suppression of £1 notes and the maintenance of the Corn Laws had 'again brought this unhappy country to the verge of ruin', and Graham had 'never thought so ill of the real state of the country as at this moment'. Twelve days later he was the chairman of the great cattle show at Carlisle. 'Born and nursed in the county, I have always taken pleasure in the cultivation of the land,' he then declared. 'It was here in this county that I spent the happiest portion of my life.' And he continued his campaign to reform local administration. With other Whig gentry, he supported the *Carlisle Journal*, the owner of which was imprisoned for libelling the Lowthers. In January 1828 the editor secured permission to attend the Quarter Sessions and started to publicise the hitherto secret transactions of the county's rulers. Graham himself pursued his aim of cheap government in Cumberland as well as at Westminster. With liberal zeal and backed by Lawson, he assailed, publicised and prevented many types of 'extravagance'. Ratepayers naturally welcomed the reduced expenditure; but local social services suffered equally with overpaid Lowther nominees. Not all of Graham's schemes were successful, however, and he soon regretted his support of the *Journal*, when other backers left him to face its debts. In September 1830 he complained to Brougham that[5]

The paper has now fallen into the hands of a violent, illiterate editor; and you cannot wonder at his ignorance and blunders when

I tell you that he was a working weaver a very short time ago; and falsehood also is natural to him, since he is an avowed disciple of Cobbett, the father of lies ... civil convulsion is his object and a new division of property the end in view ...

Graham's seemingly reformist speeches during years of Tory rule had encouraged a real Radicalism which was to horrify him.

Despite such troubles, Graham had certainly consolidated his position in Cumberland. Equally, despite his parliamentary failures, he had continued to improve his standing in the Whig hierarchy and established cordial relations with Huskisson. Althorp's group had gone further, forming close contacts with Sir George Murray (the Secretary for War and Colonies) and Sir Henry Hardinge (the Secretary at War). But the situation was further complicated by Grey's support for the Ministry — which led to the Earl of Rosslyn becoming Lord Privy Seal and Grey's son-in-law, John George Lambton, becoming Lord Durham. In June 1829 Hardinge told Wellington's friend Mrs. Arbuthnot that the Government should give posts to 'respectable' Tories and Whigs, suggesting an under-secretaryship for Graham ('an unexceptionable man, clever and respectable', to Mrs. Arbuthnot). Shortly afterwards Lord Ellenborough told Charles Arbuthnot that Graham might replace Lord Ashley at the Board of Control and 'could manage the business in the House of Commons which Ld. A. was quite unequal to'.[6] Graham neverthe-less maintained his campaign against Government expenditure. From February 1830 he again developed the theme in Parliament. On the 12th he delivered a major two-hour speech, although he had only recently recovered from an illness. He claimed that economic distress was general, attacked currency depreciation and stressed the difficulties of landowners: if they 'were called on to submit to another reduction of 25 per cent, he would say boldly to nine-tenths of the landed interest — at once sell your estates'. And he described the wretched conditions of Cumbrian weavers earning 4s. 2d. weekly, condemned the 'gold standard' and listed some recent official salary increases. Althorp himself could not follow Graham's policy, but Peel, when replying for the Govern-ment, praised his 'eloquent and impressive sentiments'. As the

Ministry decided to reduce expenditure by about £1,000,000, Graham withdrew his motion.

Through the spring Graham kept up his 'retrenchment' campaign. On 12 March he advocated the abolition of the old sinecure of Treasurer of the Navy, but was defeated by Peel. Graham next turned on the job of Lieutenant-General of Ordnance, sparking off an argument with military Tories. And early in May he asked for returns of the public incomes of all Privy Councillors and lists of their services. He rejected Goulburn's offer of a complete list of all placemen and pensioners with talk of 'flights of voracious birds of prey' — a phrase which became popular in the country while arousing conflicting emotions in Parliament. On the 14th he delivered an important speech, insisting that 'the representatives of the people, the guardians of the public purse, were entitled as of right to call for statements of what sums of public money had been received by any particular individual or number of individuals or class of individuals . . .' He carefully listed the incomes of the 169 non-Royal Privy Councillors: 113 of them were receiving £650,164, including £86,103 for sinecures, £442,000 for active service and £121,650 in pensions. Thirty pluralists had £221,130; 29 diplomats received £126,176; and 47 peers and 22 M.P.s shared £378,840 and £90,849 respectively. Graham again attacked civil servants' increased salaries and finally demanded 'a measure of substantive retrenchment, economy and reform'. Although the motion was defeated by 235 votes to 147 it caused a considerable stir, and Graham's speech was of major importance to his career. 'Whatever Sir James Graham undertakes he does extremely well,' noted Mallet next day. 'Nothing could match the spirit, the talent, the propriety of his speech . . . His success was immense and the cheers unbounded . . . What with his industry and talents, his fine manner and person, his aristocratical bearing and connections and his factious independence, Sir James Graham may go a great way.' Palmerston, Grant and Stanley had voted for him, with Althorp as a teller; Brougham expressed 'great pleasure' at his '*perfect success*'; and Jeremy Bentham, always delighted by attacks on governmental inefficiency, sent Graham a copy of his

Official Attitude Maximised and Expense Minimised.[7]

Another event had also strengthened Graham's position. While Grey still half expected a Cabinet seat, the ineffectual George Tierney had remained the Whigs' nominal leader in the Commons until his death in January, leaving the active work to Brougham — a choice unpopular to the great aristocrats. In March, allegedly angered by G. R. Dawson's description of the Opposition as 'only a loose bundle of sticks', E. B. Portman, Francis Lawley and E. W. Wynne-Pendarves (Members for Dorset, Warwickshire and Cornwall) urged Althorp to take the leadership. Althorp was now less reluctant, but insisted that he must consult Russell, Graham and Brougham, and that Portman's group must secure the support of at least 45 Members. At a subsequent meeting in the Albany, Althorp became leader of a new Whig section. He told Grey and Brougham that he would support retrenchment but would not help either group of discontented Tories or try to bring down the Government. But Graham informed Huskisson of the scheme and hoped to work with the Canningites. From the start, he was in the inner circle of Althorp's party, which had about 60 members by May. And he continued to act as the spokesman on 'economy'. In June he strongly attacked the cost of diplomatic missions in South America, losing two divisions by only 19 and 23 votes. Mrs. Arbuthnot bitterly resented the Althorp group's attacks and its professed friendship. 'Lord Rosslyn the other day suggested to me taking Sir James Graham and Lord John Russell', she noted on 6 July, 'and when I said they were pledged upon currency and Parliamentary Reform, he said, "Oh God! that's nothing. They'd throw all that overboard. No principles of that sort would make any difficulty"!! It makes me sick.'[8]

Such speculations had little importance. On 26 June the King's death led to the dissolution of Parliament. As the politicians started to negotiate for constituencies, the Whigs' testing-time was approaching.

IV

In the summer of 1830 Graham had two roles to play: to strengthen his hold on Cumberland and, as a Whig leader, to help in national manœuvres. Palmerston solicited advice and gave his views in detail: '. . . it does not appear that Government will gain much by the Dissolution', he wrote on 28 July,

> at least not enough to enable them to carry the heavy weights which press down the Treasury Benches in the two Houses. There seems to be no likelihood of their securing any reinforcements from other parties, and their own ranks do not furnish the means of much new development . . . The King declared three days ago, after dinner, that he should keep the Duke as his Minister as long as he lived, and desired the foreign Ministers present to report this to their Courts. Of course there can be no doubt that resolutions so announced are unchangeable.
>
> Charles 10 seems now to have at last passed the Rubicon; how long will it be before he also passes the alps?

The news of a French revolution arrived as the election proceeded. 'It does not seem to me that the Government are realising the expectations of gain which they entertained from the new elections,' Palmerston wrote on 4 August:

> This French Revolution has come upon its instigators and authors like a thunderbolt, and I suspect that our Duke is as much surprised by it as Polignac or Metternich can be . . . The contrast between the conduct of the French now and in the time of Louis 16 is truly striking. Then the resistance which patriotism rendered legitimate against tyranny seemed only to be the pretence for arriving at the most horrible Excesses; now no violence seems to have been committed beyond what was absolutely necessary for the security of the Constitution. Is not this the most triumphant demonstration of the advantages arising from free discussion, from the liberty of the Press, from the diffusion of knowledge and from familiarising even the lowest classes with the daily examination of political questions? . . .

Graham's seat was safe: no opposition appeared against him or Lowther. But when Blamire arranged a great dinner in his honour at Dalston on 5 August Graham's request that the affair should be open to all parties led the *Carlisle Journal* to issue a reprimand:

A man can only belong to one party, that which means right or that which means wrong. Let Sir James and his friends make their election between the two; but don't let them hope that they can so trim their sails as to please both.

These were trying times for convinced partisans; but some 800 freeholders attended the dinner and Graham took the opportunity to deny rumours of his 'trimming'. Excited by his support and by the news from France, he deserted his prepared speech and delivered a strong address. 'Blue I am, Blue I have always been and Blue I trust I shall always continue to be,' he declared. The Tories were a 'Court party' aiming at 'the advancement of kingly power', while the Whigs, the 'Country party', fought to 'uphold popular rights, defend popular feelings and forward the happiness of the people'. Graham denounced the *Journal*'s libels and promised that he would 'urge and support with all his power a further reduction of taxation [and] moderate but effective reform in the representation'. The Government must learn from France, 'where the mad career of an infatuated and bigoted tyrant had been arrested by the all-subduing voice of freedom'.

Two days later, at a Whitehaven dinner, Graham talked of Charles X as 'that reckless tyrant, that heartless monarch, that insane man' and warmly welcomed the revolution, hoping for a liberal monarchy. Lawson excitedly went much further, proposing a toast: 'May the heads of Dom Miguel, King Ferdinand and Charles Capet be severed from their bodies and rolled in the dust — and the more speedily the better.' Such heady sentiments delighted Whig diners in Lonsdale's capital but struck a discordant note at Brooks's Club. Graham was returned next day, however, having reached a new height of popularity in his native county.[9] Above all, he had secured the confidence of the freeholders. 'I hope and think that this tower of strength is now on my side, and I hope I shall never either abandon it or be driven from it,' he told Rooke on the 28th. 'Clouds and thick darkness hang over the future. Great events, I am persuaded, are about to happen; sturdy principles and firm resolution will be required to shape a course in the midst of the gathering storm.'

Wellington lost several supporters at the election, and the

return of Brougham for Yorkshire and Hume for Middlesex demonstrated a new force in public opinion. But the Ministry remained in office and the political scene remained fluid. Graham acted as a Whig contact with the ailing Huskisson, whose support could have been vital.[10] 'I have suffered a good deal . . .', he told Graham on the 26th, 'but . . . I shall be able to keep my engagement to be at Liverpool for the opening of the Railway on the 15th of September.' He revealed his views:

> The great Captain, you know, is to be there with all his tail. Of course one object is to throw me into the background at this ceremony; another is, by extending his visit to Manchester and other places, to cater a little applause and bid for a little popularity before the meeting of the new Parliament. The Times (I do not mean the Newspaper only) favour this expedient. The harvest is abundant, the price of provisions falling and the manufactures (silk, cotton, woollen) are all in full employment. He will therefore meet with nothing but good humour, and with his usual luck will endeavour to make the most of it, though it will require no small degree of self confidence and a presence to claim for himself any share in having contributed to this satisfactory state of things.

Huskisson 'looked at the political horizon, both at home and abroad . . . entirely through the same medium as' Graham:

> I agree with you that the present Ministry ought not to stand the shock of the next session and that it is the interest of all public Men (I might say the interest of the public as well as of Party) that they should come to an understanding not to listen to any separate overture for reinforcing it, unless upon the preliminary admission of an entire reconstruction, so as to exclude no one and to admit to a fair participation of influence and power in the deliberations and management of the State persons more competent than those who have now the charge of some of the most important Departments. I do not expect, I own, that the D. of W. will consent to negotiate upon such a principle, but I am sanguine . . . that he will not find in the country any man of real weight inclined to treat with him upon any other. When I say this, I mean men of real weight in public opinion (and without that support no Ministry can long go on) and not of weight from mere station and borough interest. The conduct of some of the latter is to me inexplicable upon any

principle but that of the lowest trimming and shabbiness. When I see the Nominees of one or two (themselves claiming to be opposed to the Minister) so nicely selected that one half will go one way and the other half in the opposite direction, I am at a loss for any more favourable solution of their conduct. Seeing these things, I am by no means confident that it will be easy to beat down the Ministry at the first onset — however well combined and vigorous it may be — in the new Pt. Indeed I do not see that they are likely to fall, even should the attack be successful, because the principle of the Duke appears to be not to stick to his own measures but to be always ready to take up those of his opponents, if he is driven from his own, but, on the other hand, to stick to office, so long as the King will stick by him. The question therefore will be what impression the weakness of his Government is likely to make on the mind of the King. At this moment I believe him to be in a fool's paradise after all these matters, his mind wholly sanguine and with looking after his immense inheritance in palaces, furniture, personalty, etc. — and in courting, by means not always very exalted or wise, a vulgar and undignified popularity.

Huskisson urged Graham to join him at the opening of the Liverpool and Manchester Railway, when they could 'talk over these matters more at length in the Opposition long coach, as it ran along the railway'.[11]

Whatever hopes existed for a Whig-'Huskissonite' alliance were dashed on 15 September, when a fashionable party attended the railway's opening. 'I must go and shake hands with the Duke on this day at any rate,' Huskisson exclaimed; he and Wellington had, in fact, already exchanged civilities in the country. After talking to the Duke and Mrs. Arbuthnot, Huskisson (perhaps still weak from his illness) moved too slowly to his coach and was run over by the *Rocket*. He died within hours. Contemporaries recorded both the horror of the scene and its political implications. 'The Canning faction has lost its corner stone and the Duke's Government one of its most formidable opponents,' mused Creevey. 'Huskisson, too, once out of the way, Palmerston, Melbourne, the Grants, &c., may make it up with the Beau.' Charles Greville thought that the event 'cannot fail to have an important effect upon political events; it puts an end to his party as a party, but it leaves the survivors at liberty to join either the Opposition or the Government . . . As to the Duke of Wellington, a fatality attends him, and it is perilous to cross his path.' Brougham saw 'the consequence' rather differently — and thought the Company 'nearly accessory' to the disaster. The Canningite 'party', he told Graham,

is now worth but little to anybody — though Pam and Grant are clever and good men — but it is not any longer a party for the Beau to reckon upon as a port under his lee — into which he may go when driven, *on paying high dues*. The remnant joining him would not give him a month's respite — Hn. himself could hardly have given him a session's. But he *may* make an offer now, and I hope and trust for their own sakes nothing will induce them to accept. Our policy now should, as it strikes me, be to join openly, for the arg[umen]t ag[ains]t it is unhappily now gone — i.e. the fear of driving off the ultras.

If this doctrine is sound, it should be acted on. Personally, one is very indifferent how it is, but I think their late refusal of the large offer to Mel[bourn]e gives them large claims.

I hear from town that Cumb[erlan]d is more furious than ever against the D. of W., and that Wn. talks of 'making the good Queen Reg[en]t'! This seems incredible, but he is so damned rash and foolish, I wonder at nothing. Sir George Warrender regretted the 'deplorable event' and 'ardently wished' that he might see Grant, Palmerston and yourself with your mutual friends acting together in the House of Commons; and in that case, whether in office or not, you would in fact direct the march of affairs and the Ministers be as harmless as they are incapable. I am quite convinced that in the present temper and feeling of the country, the junction of any individuals with the present men, who have been opposing them during the last Session, can only destroy the character and station of such persons, without giving any real strength or very prolonged existence to the administration — a total change can alone enable such a Government to be formed as can serve the Crown and country with advantage and preserve the character of public men already too generally and too justly suspected by the people.

As a former Ministerial supporter, Warrender explained that

'after the men with whom you know I have sat and voted of late years, I feel for you the greatest respect among all those who have taken a prominent part in Parliament . . .'. The grieving widow told Graham that Huskisson had shown her his last letter 'with the renewed expression of his high opinion of your character and endowments' and that her husband had considered that it 'perfectly expressed his own sentiments'.[12]

Both large parties regretted Huskisson's death, as the Government stumbled towards its end. It appeared possible that Wellington might yield again and introduce a Reform measure and that the Canningites, with Graham and Stanley, might support him. But Brougham, with some support from Graham and Stanley, was already planning a Reform Bill; and Graham had frankly demanded at Dalston a reduction of election expenses, more county polling stations, votes for copyhold and customary tenants, the redistribution of 'rotten' borough seats and an urban franchise qualification of a £10 or £20 rate. Although the Government made belated attempts to gain Canningite support, Graham and the Whigs were able to offer alternative inducements; Wellington's reluctantly-made proposals were rejected by Melbourne and later by Palmerston.

Reform and rural agitations developed in the autumn, as the Duke's long popularity waned. Reports from the country revealed a worsening situation. Hugh Percy, the Bishop of Carlisle, told Graham that one 'Johnson from Preston has been through the neighbourhood and classed the manufacturers, threatening those, few in number, who refused'; each 'class' of ten, according to the Bishop's agent, was to be armed — 'several smiths were of the number and were manufacturing pikes'— and 'Johnson named Hunt as the head of the proceedings'. It was as easy to be over-alarmed by exaggerated accounts of some repetition of the Radical organisations of the 1790s as it was for later writers to deny possibilities of violence; and it was tempting for Opposition politicians to use the real or alleged threat. Wellington's 'days of power are numbered', Graham told Rooke, in new style,

unless he be prepared to satisfy the reasonable expectations of the middle class, which is the life and marrow of the State; and this he cannot effect without the concession of great reforms and a new adjustment of the entire scheme of our taxation and commerce. The crisis is awful, and I hope the peace of the country will be preserved . . .

But when Parliament met in November Wellington showed his hostility to any constitutional change. On the 2nd he bluntly told Grey (only recently realising that it was not only the late King who had kept him out of office) that the Constitution's 'excellence' precluded any reform. This startling avowal led to almost nation-wide hostility to the Government and an alarming spate of rumours of an impending revolution. And many politicians knew that Peel, cold, calculating and clever as he appeared, was opposed to the Duke on several points.

The Whigs faced the temptation to strike at once. Brougham's Bill was ready, and he gave notice that he would propose it. But Brougham did not personally appeal to many Whigs; varying degrees of conservatism divided them, and it seemed important to attract Palmerston's group. Althorp, Stanley, Brougham and Thomas Denman 'all agreed that it would be highly expedient if [Graham] could . . . see any of the Palmerston folks, and ascertain how far they were prepared to go, the heads being — Great towns, Expenses of poll, etc., Non-resident voters in boros., Scotch Cos. and boros., *General* rights of . . . householders, Disfranchisement of rotten boroughs and small towns, such as Barnstaple and Cornish nuisances, to the extent of one member to make room for great towns'. Graham replied that he 'could have no difficulty in lending his feeble but cordial assistance' and agreed to 'ascertain the sentiments of Lord Palmerston'. But he urged Brougham to 'conciliate general support in Parliament by as large concessions' as possible. Their 'common object', he reminded Brougham, was 'to reform to the extent necessary for preserving our institutions, not to change for the purpose of subverting'. Graham developed this conservative theme in a further 'lecture' to the headstrong lawyer:[13]

In this matter general concurrence can only be obtained by mutual modifications of opinions . . . and I rejoice that the question is in

H

your hands, because the public will be satisfied with less from you
than from any other member . . .

Much discussion, negotiation and arrangement will be required,
not only before we can bring Palmerston's friends into line in favour
of Reform, but before you can meet the views and wishes of our
own friends in *both* Houses of Parliament.

Would it not, therefore, be better if, instead of a formal motion,
you in your speech tomorrow notified your intention to bring this
vast subject forward in all its details without pledging yourself to
the precise Time, since it may be convenient to postpone it till after
Christmas and yet if you now fix the day an adjournment may be
prejudicial.

Let the subject rest in your hands, the Giant's hands, and let the
Public know that you have grasped it: but do not bring it to
discussion prematurely, and give us time to digest, to conciliate and
to arrange.

Brougham apparently accepted this advice, telling the House
that his purpose was 'not revolution, but restoration'. And
Graham joined Althorp's group in drafting Brougham's motion
that a committee of the whole House should consider 'the state
of the Representation of the People in Parliament, with a view
to remedy such defects as may appear to exist therein'. But
Brougham was not destined to make the proposal.

There were, however, last-minute possibilities that Wellington's
administration might be saved, despite its general shortage of
ability and the increasing coolness between Peel and the Duke.
On Arbuthnot's insistence, Wellington made approaches to
Palmerston, but failed to gain support because the Duke refused
either a large Cabinet reconstruction or an admission of Whigs. On
1 November E. J. Littleton, the Member for Staffordshire,
suggested to Arbuthnot that Palmerston, Graham, Stanley and
Charles and Robert Grant could be won over if the Government
would accept a moderate reform scheme for the gradual enfran-
chisement of the large towns. Littleton was over-optimistic;
Palmerston and the Grants had already 'quite determined to vote
for' Brougham's motion.[14] Graham undoubtedly favoured
considerable reform, but by maintaining contacts with both the
Whig and Canningite camps he was able to earn both 'radical'

and 'conservative' applause. Perhaps, despite previous avowals, his real time of decision came with Wellington's 'fatal declaration' against any reform. If the Duke had not adopted seemingly 'ultra' phraseology a new Conservative party might have been born — and it would probably have included Graham.

On 8 November the King's cancellation of a visit to the City caused great alarm and a fall in consols. The Cabinet, alarmed by growing violence in several parts of the country, resolved not to risk the chance of major trouble in the capital. Whig, Radical and ultra-Tory alike mocked the Ministers with unfairness and, in some cases, dishonesty. The Duke's 'violent and uncalled-for declaration against Reform', Greville thought on the 8th, had 'without doubt sealed his fate'. Wellington's ill-considered speech had caused the panic, Graham declared: 'his Grace was at direct issue with the people of England . . . not merely the lower orders, but the middle classes of society, in conformity with whose sentiments the Government must be conducted, or it could not stand'. All waited for the Reform division on the 16th; petitions in favour of Brougham's Bill came in daily. And the crumbling Government continued to make mistakes: Graham angrily condemned its gift of the valuable rectory of Stanhope to Henry Phillpotts, the new Tory Bishop of Exeter. But on the evening of the 15th Sir Henry Parnell surprisingly defeated the Government on the Civil List by 233 votes to 204. Next day — at least partly in order to evade the Reform debate — the Ministers resigned.

The King asked Grey to form a Ministry, and the egoistic, surly Earl at once forgot his previous denials of interest in office. 'Dear Sir James,' he wrote on the evening of the 16th, 'I have been commanded by the King to form a new administration. In this arduous and difficult undertaking, I look anxiously to your assistance. Can you call here tomorrow at one?' Graham excitedly drafted his reply (taking care to change 'very faithfully yours' to 'very sincerely yours'). 'I fear my humble assistance can avail little in the arduous task imposed on you', he wrote,

> but when I gave my confidence to your Lordship, I gave it without reserve : and any arrangement will be supported by me which at this critical juncture may seem to be conducive to the public good.

On the 17th Graham called on Grey in Berkeley Square and was offered the post of First Lord of the Admiralty, with a seat in the Cabinet — a triumph indeed for one who might so recently have joined the late Government. Graham thus entered the aristocratic Whig Ministry, with Lansdowne, Althorp, Holland and Carlisle, the Canningites Melbourne, Grant, Palmerston and Goderich, the radical Durham, the Tory Duke of Richmond and the newly-ennobled Lord Chancellor Brougham.

By Saturday the 20th Graham was hard at work at the Admiralty, with Sir Henry Hotham, Vice-Admiral of the Red. Already there were offices to fill; and an address must be prepared for a by-election in Cumberland. Graham expressed gratitude to Grey for his 'great kindness . . . and for [his] confidence . . . : it should be the endeavour of his life to repay it and to prove himself not altogether unworthy'. On the 22nd Greville had 'a great day and very amusing', watching the new Ministers receiving their seals of office from the King. Not everyone shared Graham's pleasure in his appointment: Brougham thought it 'prematurely high' and Greville considered Graham 'too inconsiderable'. Sydney Smith was also surprised: 'The appointment is excellent', he told Lady Grey, 'but I should have thought there must have been so many great people who would have been clamorous.'[15] In December the cartoonist 'H.B.' probably summed up Graham's own attitude, in his print 'Drawing for Twelfth Cake, a Hint to Cabinet Makers', wherein he portrayed Graham remarking 'Who ever thought of seeing me First Lord of the Admiralty ?' It was a fair question.

5

The Reform Minister

On assuming office Graham faced considerable hostility. Greville, who had briefly known him at Oxford, thought his appointment 'the most monstrous of all', bitterly recalling that

> thinking he could do better [Graham] cut me, as he had done others before ... I take vanity and self-sufficiency to be the prominent features of his character ... I think he will fail.

By March 1831 Mrs. Arbuthnot was maliciously recording Brougham's belief that Grey was 'in his dotage', Althorp 'a blockhead' and Graham 'a puppy'. And Graham's attacks on public expenditure (even Greville thought that 'in that line [he] was now the best speaker in the House') had obviously earned him enemies among sinecurists of all kinds. Against such opponents, as against attacks in the *Carlisle Patriot*, Graham 'put his trust in the honesty of his intentions and in the sound judgment and good sense' of his constituents. This 'trust' was aided by his popularity among some young politicians. 'There were a few political men whom he wanted to know — very few', Monckton Milnes told his father in May, '— the Grants, Palmerston, Sir J. Graham and Spring Rice ...'[1]

Graham's principles were now to be tested. He was in charge of a great department, which he and other advocates of 'economy' had often attacked. And he was soon recruited, with Durham, Russell and Lord Duncannon, to the committee charged with planning the Government's Reform scheme. The latter was patently the more immediately important task; after long years in the wilderness and amidst a crisis partly caused by themselves, the Whigs must now prepare a realistic policy.

I

The Whigs had never been united over Reform, and it was important that the planning group should represent a cross-section of party opinion. Although Grey allegedly entrusted the task to Durham and Russell in an aristocratically casual way on the steps of the Lords, the composition of the celebrated committee was not purely fortuitous. Even in a closely-related, ultra-aristocratic Ministry different viewpoints must be represented. The rash, wealthy Lambton was the most radical Minister, and suffrage reformers like Francis Place could rejoice that he was to preside over the committee. Russell, also born in 1792, not only bore a great Whig name but had also proposed sundry parliamentary reforms, including motions in February and May to enfranchise three 'new' towns and to transfer sixty small borough seats. Duncannon, eleven years older, was related to the 'heart' of the Whig Establishment, as eldest son of the 3rd Earl of Bessborough, Althorp's cousin, Fitzwilliam's nephew and Melbourne's brother-in-law — and was an experienced party whip. Graham was presumably added to this noble trio because of his advocacy of middle-class legislation. Grey excluded the troublesome, unpredictable Lord Chancellor Brougham, whose external popularity did not endear him to the Cabinet and who was soon complaining to Althorp that his advice 'had been rejected by all his colleagues, without the least consideration'. But Graham was delighted by his own invitation: 'no honour which Lord Grey could have conferred on me', he told Durham, 'would have gratified me more . . .'[2]

Although Graham had the most onerous ministerial responsibilities of the four men, he played an active part in the committee's secret deliberations. But following his Government appointment he first had to seek re-election. 'Lord Grey has urged me at this eventful crisis to accept office with him,' he told Aglionby on 20 November. '. . . With such colleagues, and reform, peace and retrenchment the avowed principles of the Government, it was difficult to refuse, and I hope you will not object to my acceptance.' He was returned without opposition, and his political promotion was signalised in December by admission to the exclusive Grillon's Club.

Through the Government's early weeks the committee met at Durham's house in Cleveland Row. The Whigs could never accept the radical schemes of provincial demagogues; indeed, only Wellington's affirmation had forced their largely unwilling hands. Yet the insistent clamour outdoors must be pacified and could not be repressed by Melbourne's methods with rioting agricultural labourers. The remedy, it seemed, lay with conservative reform. Any change should be broad and general, but reform should follow Whiggish principle. Property must have fuller representation; and the measure should be final. The glorious constitution might require some amendment, but its bases should not be weakened. Reform, in fact, should preserve and defend State and Society. Yet within such general beliefs there were varied immediate policies. 'Democrats' demanded the abolition of old and minute boroughs and the granting of household suffrage and the Ballot, but Brougham favoured both a redistribution of seats and the retention of some small boroughs (whose patrons had sometimes aided young men of small means). Althorp hoped for a generous scheme and Russell was resolved on a liberal policy.

Russell's policy statement aimed to enfranchise 'the greatest number of independent men'. He would take 150 seats from 100 boroughs, enfranchise 18 boroughs, give additional Members to London and 20 counties and extend the county franchise to copyholders and 21-year leaseholders. His colleagues raised the number of new two-Member boroughs to 'about thirty' and advocated a general £10 rate qualification for borough electors. Boroughs with under 2,000 inhabitants would lose both Members and those with under 4,000 one Member, while 'new' towns with over 10,000 would gain seats. Typically, Graham proposed the administrative provision for the registration of electors. Russell had avoided the Radical demands for shorter Parliaments and the Ballot, and there was some controversy over the rival merits of a £20 or £10 franchise. A compromise on five-year Parliaments was agreed, but the Ballot was more troublesome. Durham, inevitably, favoured it. Althorp had been a supporter but in December 'supposed' (to Russell) 'for the present he must give [it] up'. Duncannon, Graham and Russell have all been named as the single opponent on the committee. Eventually, a recommendation of the Ballot was balanced by a suggested £20 urban franchise.

Grey was kept informed and on 14 January 1831 received Durham's final report. With the exception of the Ballot, he was prepared to accept the recommendations; and in Cabinet the Ballot was dropped, the urban qualification was reduced to £10 and the nomination boroughs were scheduled for abolition. 'The measure on the whole was well received,' Graham told Durham on the 25th, 'Brougham alone dissentient and disposed to carp by raising little points when he could find no real objections, and very much inclined to defend the Nomination Boroughs.' When Creevey dined with Lady Grey six days later he found that the Earl 'was gone to Brighton . . . to lay his plan of reform before the King' and told Miss Ord that 'Grey says the King's conduct was perfect'. Durham reported to Graham on 1 February: 'I have just received an express from Lord Grey. *All is as right as we could wish.* The King approves entirely of the general view and effect of our Reform, and was particularly pleased with the Report. This is really too good.' Next day Grey praised William's 'noble conduct'. 'I congratulate you very sincerely on your complete success with the King,' Graham replied. 'His wise and generous conduct has saved his throne and averted civil war; and for one I am disposed to serve him more zealously . . .'[3]

In the weeks before Russell was due to introduce the Bill there was much back-stage activity among Ministers. In December Graham was urging Edward Ellice to rouse Whig Members against Warburton's motion on the Duchy of Lancaster and discussing the Corn Laws, finance and Ireland with Creevey's old friend Charles Western. The King and his generally Tory-minded Court were thought to be personally unsympathetic to Reform. But Whig opposition to Radical attempts to interfere with his Lancaster rights somewhat mollified the King; and his Tory secretary, Sir Herbert Taylor, was a capable and honest man. William had accepted the measure, but as appeared later, without fully comprehending its scope, and insisted that he would not tolerate either universal suffrage or the Ballot. And there were suspicions that some courtiers were indiscreet in their political conversations. In January Graham reported to Grey on a recent gathering at the Speaker's house,[4]

> when Croker and a party of the late Ministers were present. It is not important to state to you their angry abuse and their empty threats; but in boasting of the advantages which they still possessed, Croker declared that the Army and its Patronage were never more entirely under the control of the D. of Wellington ... [and] that they knew from [Somerset] all our Movements ... They alluded to their friends in other departments ...
>
> Of the King they spoke more confidently of the influence which they hoped to gain than of any influence which they now possess; but Sir A. Barnard and Sir William Freemantle were the channels of communication, which they schemed to have always open to them.

Such Tory claims may have been idle boasts. But further trouble was to come.

At the start of the 1831 Session the Government resolved to make an exception to its policy of economy by passing a generous Civil List (on which, said Greville, 'some economical novelty' had been expected). Charles Grant, however, opposed the Queen's outfit allowance, even threatening to resign. Palmerston, 'sincerely grieved', told Graham that the affair 'might be, I will say it, *Disastrous*':

> It is a common jargon for Ministers to pretend that their official existence is necessarily linked with the welfare of their Country, but in the present state of things this is true with respect to us. I am *very* sorry for the sake of Grant ... But in this Matter, or at least in the issue to which he has put it, he is in my opinion quite and entirely wrong ... I still hope the King may give way, but I have no hesitation in saying that with the great objects we have before us and the great interests which are at stake, we ought to face even the loss of the Grants, great and immense as that would be in the H. of Cms., rather than retire from our Party at the present Moment.

The crisis was ended when the King and Queen gave way, though the Court remained suspicious of parliamentary invasions of Royal prerogatives and privileges.

Ireland caused constant concern. Graham, Durham, Duncannon and Melbourne discussed its state in December, when Graham told the Premier that he felt a 'strong desire' that 'while force was of necessity used to repress insurrection in Ireland, every endeavour should all the same be used to redress real grievances and to prepare remedial measures . . .'. Graham shared his colleagues' strong dislike of O'Connell. He sent to Stanley, the Irish Secretary, 'a sharp intelligent Fellow of the name Dombraine', a coast guard inspector who knew Ireland well. 'He is a Servant of the Crown removable at pleasure; thus perhaps you may be able to make use of him to advantage,' wrote Graham. Dombraine wished to expose 'a little hut of jobs' in the Fishery Board, but, Graham told his friend,

> I fear you have greater Fish to fry; and the big One of all I wish were brought to your net. Be cautious, do not haul up too soon, and you will have him.

O'Connell was now campaigning for the repeal of the Union and, in January, Anglesey arrested him for advocating a run on the banks. Stalling tactics postponed any trial, and in the end O'Connell escaped indictment. He was 'devilishly frightened and trying to bluster', Stanley told Graham in January, '— which won't do'.[5]

Further difficulties mounted. Althorp's Budget was a failure, and the Ministers thought of resigning. *The Times* took to attacking all the leaders but Brougham. And the Government's parliamentary showing was poor. Though 'strong in the House of Lords (which is a secondary consideration)', observed Greville, it was 'weak in the House of Commons to a degree which is contemptible and ridiculous . . . Palmerston does nothing, Grant does worse, Graham does no good, Althorp a *great* deal of harm; Stanley alone has distinguished himself . . .' Graham's attempts to help Althorp had been failures. A series of indiscreet statements in a speech on Ireland led Graham to the humiliation of apologising to O'Gorman Mahon. Even the drafting of the Reform Bill moved very slowly. 'In ten days from the present Time this great question, on which the fate of the government and of the Country depends, must be fully opened in the H. of Commons, and our credit as an Administration will be at stake', Graham complained to Grey, in February,

> yet I doubt whether the Draft of any of the three Bills is complete, and we have not yet agreed on the modifications of the Principles which are requisite. It appears to me that these Bills should be discussed in the Cabinet Clause by Clause, in the presence of Ld. John Russell, Ld. Duncannon, the Lord Advocate and the Attorney General, and no time and labour can be ill bestowed which may give the most perfect form and arrangement to the most important measure ever undertaken by a Government. Without some such preparations I anticipate disaster; and we have already suffered much from the imperfect discussing of great Questions in the Cabinet before they have been brought forward in the H. of Commons.

He might have found added justification in a later note from Stanley telling him of Palmerston's complaints that supposedly pro-Government journals had created the impression that 'we are identifying ourselves with the Radicals and breaking down all our established institutions'.

On 1 March Russell moved for leave to introduce his Bill, in a crowded House. Shocked Members heard the Schedule A list of sixty boroughs destined to lose both seats and the Schedule B list of forty-seven towns losing single seats. As Peel did not immediately divide the House, a long debate ensued, thus giving the Government time to rally support. Russell asked Graham to

> call Ld. Grey's earnest attention to the present state of things. It is probable the house will force us into maintaining the numbers of the house. It is essential that if we should be so forced we should not give members to all the manufacturing parishes in the North. Respectable towns and 3 each to large divisions of counties would be the best bodies to receive the surplus of our schedules . . . I hope the Cabinet will agree to a clause that a person accepting office shall not hereafter vacate.

Graham spoke on the sixth night, answering Peel's charge of irresponsibility in proposing such a measure at a time of unrest and his expression of regret at the non-representation of the 'lower classes'. The Bill was necessary, declared Graham, and 'they had not thought it consistent with their duty to bring forward half-measures'; nor was there 'any good cause for delay', for 'the withholding of just claims only led to claims such as at first no man dreamed of making'. He quoted Fox's view that 'the best system of representation was one which secured to a country the largest number of independent voters, and the worst was one which embraced the largest number who, from being in dependent circumstances, were incapable of deliberation and must act as they were commanded'. Such principles justified the exclusion of the poorer classes. And Graham could not understand

> how Monarchy could be endangered by making it rest on the affections of a loyal people ... The Government of the country would be put upon a more solid foundation, for he knew none so safe as the extension of the suffrage to the most intelligent and industrious classes of the community.

After the long debate the First Reading was allowed without a division.[6]

Although after the initial shock many Members had been 'converted' to the Bill, opponents remained numerous. An indication of hostile strength was given on 18 March, when the Government's proposed timber duties were rejected by 46 votes. The Cabinet then considered the danger of defeat on Reform. A dissolution appeared the best course; but the King was angry when Graham mentioned the possibility of such an exercise of prerogative. Yet even now not all Whigs were prepared to stand by the whole Bill. In a private (and, as usual, undated) letter, Brougham wrote

> Above everything, let me warn you, if you would not throw out both the Bill and the Ministry, not on *this* occasion to dream of staking our existence on it. I only ask any one to consider what possible chance we have of getting our Bill carried, if we hold out this inducement to all our enemies and even to our friends who hate our Bill, namely: You have only to oppose the Bill and you *must* throw out both it and us. The case is a clear one. We are to fight it bitterly and give it every chance of success, and if the House are

corrupt and selfish enough to throw it out, *we are to go on*, and
dissolve when we can. It is time enough to go out if *that* dissolution
fails.

Most of the Cabinet favoured an early dissolution, which the
King (fearing riots) opposed. But on the 22nd the Second Reading
was carried by 302 votes to 301, at 4 in the morning. 'The dreadful
race', Graham told Durham, was 'won by an accident at last'; the
reform of the House had been decided by the tardy conversion of
either John Calcraft or Sir Andrew Agnew.

Anti-Reformers relied on the Lords and hoped that the King's
opposition would not be weakened by public celebrations over the
Second Reading. But Peel, speaking on the Irish Reform Bill,
complained that Parliament was about to fall under 'popular'
control. Brougham professed to be 'astounded' by 'this *radical*
speech', which was 'advertising for a rebellion'. The Tories
remained divided, however, and Peel was hamstrung by Wellington's declaration. Nevertheless, if late Ministerialists and strict
'ultras' could not unite, they could act together against the Bill.
On 18 April Russell announced changes, adding 31 new M.P.s by
creating and reprieving several seats. But next day General
Gascoyne had a majority of 8 in Committee for his motion against
reducing English and Welsh Members. Regarding this vote as
important, the Government formally advised a dissolution, and on
the 21st the King reluctantly agreed and even consented to
prorogue Parliament next day in person, to prevent hostile
motions by Tory peers. Amidst Whig and Radical rejoicing and
Tories' angry premonitions, Parliament was dissolved, 'for the
purpose', said the King, 'of ascertaining the sense of my
people . . .' Everyone knew the certain result of a new election.
'I give you joy,' Anglesey wrote from Dublin. 'All is right. We
have a King and we *have* a Government. Nothing short of His
Majesty's vigour and honesty could have saved him.'[7]

II

For long a supporter of dissolution, Graham had carefully
maintained contact with Cumbrian Whig leaders. Local men now

felt that two Blue candidates should fight the Lowthers, but Graham could not agree. The county's 'state of feeling . . . was not encouraging,' he told William Browne of Tallantire, and he was 'quite clear that neither directly nor indirectly could he interfere with the choice of a second Blue candidate'. If former supporters must 'try an experiment of this kind' they must be responsible for the result, which very likely might be the return of two Yellow Members.' Graham would fight alone, without expense or canvassing, standing on 'his character and his services . . .' County tradition and political expediency both supported this view. But another factor apparently influenced Graham. The second nominee was Blamire, who was far from being considered socially suitable for a county seat. 'Oh, Mr. Blamire is a good fellow, who farms a small estate of his own, and beyond that I know of no further pursuit he has except horse-dealing,' Graham allegedly told Parliamentary friends: 'but don't be alarmed; he is not going to ride over me'. Yet Blamire had been his ardent friend. 'There was no one who possessed more entirely his confidence, or to whom he was under greater obligations,' Graham had declared at Dalston in 1828. Now he tried to dissuade Carlisle supporters from nominating two candidates, finally demanding, 'Am I to carry Blamire on my back?' John Graham of Carlisle instantly retorted, 'Take care, Sir James, that Blamire hasn't to carry thee on his back!'

Even admirers were somewhat shocked by Graham's apparent hostility to an old friend. Few shared his apprehensions over the Lowthers' influence; and few realised his financial difficulties. But Graham did not come out well in any account; his snobbery and ingratitude seemed both unforgivable and unforgettable. Perhaps his explanation to the Rev. E. Stanley allows a more generous interpretation. He understood the Whigs' optimism, though their policy 'must put his seat in jeopardy and expose him to expense and inconvenience'. He would not 'be justified in complacency', but feared the risk of Lonsdale taking both seats; consequently, 'he had resolved not to coalesce with any other Candidate, but to stand alone . . .'. If Blamire were adopted, wrote Graham,[8]

I need not assure you of my respect for his character and of my friendship and long attachment to him; but he has always told me that he would not hold a seat in Parliament ... Moreover, ... the joint Expense must be borne by a contribution from me and by a subscription. I well know how fallacious these subscriptions are; and for one, I would never owe my seat to assistance afforded me in the shape of money ... But you say, and say truly, that the run will be made at me, and if so, and the Lowthers split on Blamire, I shall still have to pay and he will have the return ... The loss of my seat for Cumberland will be the surrender of the highest object of my ambition, but if I am to be turned out it must be done after an open trial of strength.

But the local Whigs — correct in their interpretation of county feeling, but scarcely aware of the embarrassments of a pessimistic Minister — insisted on their scheme, and Graham reluctantly joined forces with Blamire.

The Cumbrian election of 1831 aroused excitement throughout the five wards of the county so recently 'discovered' by the romantics. Against Lonsdale, exercising his influence through his money, his nominated officials and his tough Whitehaven colliers, were ranged most of the aristocracy and gentry and many of the 'statesmen'. Graham issued an address on 25 April, urging the electors not to 'baffle the exertions of the Friends of Freedom', and he delivered a series of speeches against the Lowthers. Canvasses indicated a large majority for Reform, but rumours spread that Lowtherites would use their second votes for Blamire. A Ministerial defeat might be serious, and Blamire generously assured Lady Graham that he would retire rather than unseat her husband. Blamire also arranged with the Whig committee that Graham should head each day's poll. 'Your good news gave me the greatest pleasure,' Grey told Graham on 2 May. 'We have excellent accounts from all quarters ...'

On the 5th Graham and Blamire led a mounted procession into Cockermouth and addressed the freeholders in the festive little town, challenging Lowther to explain his attitude to Reform. 'I have just come from the Hustings, where a Poll has been demanded by Ld. Lowther, after a show of Hands which was very

decidely against him,' Graham excitedly told Grey. '. . . I fear that
we shall be put to great Expense, but I hope and think my Seat is
safe: the contest, however, is likely to be a protracted one and I
shall be detained here much longer than I could wish . . .' By the
evening Graham had 218 votes, Blamire 215 and Lowther 71.
Next day the Whigs toured Lonsdale's kingdom around Whitehaven. 'We sported with a double-barrelled gun and at every rise
we brought down a brace,' Graham boasted on his return. That
night, with 542 votes, to Blamire's 532 and Lowther's 236, he
could afford to joke about Lowther as 'a great gallant among the
ladies' and 'a libertine in his way' who courted both Cumberland
and Westmorland.

On Saturday the 7th, despite desperate Tory efforts, Graham
and Blamire headed the poll, with 942 and 917 votes to Lowther's
453. 'I wish you joy, with all my heart, of your victory in
Cumberland,' wrote Grey:

> It is one of the most important that we have gained. Our success
> has really been most extraordinary. The only failures of any
> consequence [were] Cambridge and Barking . . .
>
> All our other concerns are, upon the whole, going on well. But
> there are, as you are well aware, points of considerable difficulty
> and uneasiness, which we have not much power of improving.
>
> The King does not go to the City. He really is not in a condition,
> with the gout still flying about him, to expose himself to the fatigue
> of such a ceremony. But the disappointment is very great and not
> unmixed with suspicion . . .
>
> The truth is, the King is not in good spirits: full of uneasiness
> about what is going on and dreading the result, as likely to make
> the House of Commons more unmanageable than ever. His kindness
> and confidence do not, however, appear to be at all diminished . . .

On the 8th a messenger rode to Lawson's place at Brayton, to
confirm Lowther's retirement, and next day Graham and Blamire
were declared elected. 'England is gone perfectly mad,' thought
Mrs. Arbuthnot, amazed that Blamire, 'a seller of fat cattle at
Liverpool, [with] hardly a qualification', should be preferred to
Lowther, heir to £50,000 a year in the county, locally active and
'an excellent man of business'.[9]

Parliamentary Reform was uppermost in the minds of both electors and Members. The next Parliament 'would be the most important that ever met since the Revolution,' declared Graham; and the Lords' power would not be 'shaken', for

> surely the Russells, the Cavendishes, the Howards and the other great names who have given [the Bill] their support are as good judges as the Noble Lord [Lonsdale] of what is necessary for their true dignity.

He saw his own victory as a Reform triumph: aristocratic 'sacrifices' were 'dust in his eyes when compared with the sacrifices of the yeomanry of Cumberland'. The men who had walked 30 or 40 miles, refusing any hospitality, were 'proofs which convinced him that the spirit of Reform pervaded all classes and that it was utterly impossible any longer to resist its force'.

There were some loose ends to be tied in the North. Graham's retorts to the personal attacks of *John Bull* caused heated exchanges with the alleged instigator, Lowther. His own comments on Sir James Scarlett were soon to provoke further arguments. Local Press contacts had long been embarrassing, and Graham gladly sold his inherited shares in the Tory *Carlisle Patriot* and helped to promote the Whig *Whitehaven Herald*. But now he had more serious business in London.

III

The Reform candidates' victories had made Grey's position safe; his followers had solicited and obtained a mandate in a novel way. No longer need the Cabinet worry over the King's requests for modifications. Now, apart from Palmerston (recently defeated at Cambridge University), Ministers were resolved to stand by 'the whole Bill'. The Commons debates, though certain to be acrimonious, could end only in success. But the Lords still presented a serious danger. The danger of a clash between the two Houses had often worried the King, and Graham became increasingly anxious. On 20 May he told his uncle, Galloway, that the King and Government were concerned over the election of the sixteen Scottish representative peers; strife between the Houses 'would be *a fearful Event*, and nevertheless the Anti-Reformers appear disposed to play this desperate game' and consequently 'a vote of a single Scotch peer is at this juncture a matter of importance'. Graham arranged for the ailing Galloway to take the oath at home and to sign a blank proxy, maintaining that 'the King is cordially with us and is anxious with respect to this Election of the 16'. But Galloway had 'long been politically extinct and was determined to remain so'; while favouring the Bill, he 'viewed it only as the least of two evils'. At the election on 14 June Lords Lauderdale and Melville almost justified their boasts; that twelve of the victors had sat in the 1826 Parliament inevitably embarrassed Grey.

Graham did not relax. 'In the Commons our Game is safe; in the Lords everything is threatened', he told Stanley,

> and I dread a collision between the two Houses and an insane struggle against public opinion so pronounced as not to be gainsaid. I hope better from the wisdom of their Lordships, for reason does not operate on headstrong passion but something perhaps may be expected from their fears. The next three weeks will be a sort of lull between the breakers; and the occasion must be improved and every exertion made to win a Majority: as it stands now, the aspect of the Lords is most menacing. We shall want on the 1st day Ld. Anglesey, Ld. Plunket and every Peer whom Ireland can produce, and if you have not enough, by heavens we must make *some*.

As Graham worked on the minor details of the Bill, collecting statistics of £10 householders in the industrial towns, his mind played on the major political issue — the possible creation of further Whig peerages.[10] The King's bestowal of a Garter on the Premier was of some political importance. It 'annoyed [the Tories] almost more than anything else', Lord Howick told Charles Grey, 'as it put an end to their lies about the King . . .' Graham told Stanley that Grey's 'Blue Ribbon' had 'exasperated the Ultras beyond all measure' and given a 'warning to the timid and convinced them of the stoutness of the King'. He now found it impossible to recall Anglesey, but still hoped for Plunket's attendance: 'the battle would rage on the first day'. Old Creevey and his friends meanwhile joked about Grey 'wearing his Garter upon pantaloons or trowsers'.

Amidst political and administrative work, Graham faced a personal problem of 'honour'. Sir Robert Wilson discussed with him Press reports of his comments on Scarlett, to whom he reported privately. To Wilson's 'astonishment and regret', *The Times* obtained and published the correspondence, and Scarlett angrily demanded apologies. While Wilson tried to patch up the affair, Graham maintained that he had been misreported. 'I am glad you had not to fight him,' wrote Richmond, 'it would be inglorious to be shot by a Special Pleading Lawyer, who knows little of the Laws of Honour.' Richmond asserted that the King was 'perfectly satisfied' and that Grey agreed that 'it would not do to call [Scarlett] out'. Greville was less tolerant: 'Formerly, when a man made use of offensive expressions and was called to account, he thought it right to go out and stand a shot before he ate his words, but nowadays that piece of chivalry is dispensed with, and politicians make nothing of being scurrilous one day and humble the next.'[11]

Ireland also — inevitably — presented problems. 'Your account from Ireland of the Distress is grievous', Graham told Stanley on 31 May, 'and some relief must be administered. Provisions sold at Cost and Employment in public Works yielding Wages are the only Remedies, alas! very inadequate in sad cases of this kind. As to the insurrectionary spirit of Careless Rapine in Clare, it must be met by strong measures, and a new Edition of the Insurrection Act or Martial Law alone will quench it.' Graham had long been prepared to send Naval forces to Ireland. But in June he arranged for the carriage of Naval food supplies, though telling Grey that Melbourne and Duncannon agreed that the flour, peas, biscuit and salt meat at Deptford were 'moie expensive Provisions than it was necessary for him to supply' and that the same money might relieve many moie people 'with the supply of that food which from habit they liked the best'. In any case, Parliament must certainly repay £10,000 to the Navy. Stanley had reported that 'large masses' of people in Mayo and Galway were at 'the verge of famine', and the

Treasury made money available to the Irish Government. As further relief was necessary, Graham sent Commissioner Hill of the Naval victualling department to organise the scheme. 'I need not observe', he told Stanley,

> how contrary to all sound Principles this Measure must be admitted to be; but no Government can allow its People to starve according to the most approved Rules of Political Economy: only be it observed that the necessity of such extraordinary aid proves the urgency of taking into consideration some Scheme for the future Relief of the Poor by local Assessment . . .

The anxious Stanley gladly received Hill at Phoenix Park. But trouble developed with some Irish landowners. Government would not 'contribute one Shilling of Public Money except in aid of private Charity and in conjunction with the exertions of the [local] Proprietors . . .', Graham insisted. In August 'as usual the Irish affairs pressed . . . most grievously'. But Hill worked well: 'by his intrepid firmness and stirling honesty', Graham told Grey, 'Captain Hill resisted a lavish expenditure and at the cost to the public of no more than £15,000, effected all the objects of his mission . . .'. Yet Hill 'had been so much abused by the Irish Landlords, whose hands he kept with difficulty out of the public purse' that Graham proposed that he should be knighted.[12]

In June Graham told Rooke that 'he almost envied the agricultural pursuits which occupied his time instead of Politics. The present moment was full of difficulty; and temper and caution were necessary.' Burdened with worries over foreign affairs, Ireland, the Navy and Reform, Graham could at least welcome further proofs of the King's honesty. 'I do not think he is much frightened, but Ministers must not be too violent in Parliament, and the less their friends are the better,' wrote Richmond on the 2nd, adding next day that 'K. is Gallant, Honest and straightforward'. And Graham still spared time for his friends. Lord Blandford, having reputedly lost £26,000 at Doncaster races, turned to him for help: 'What to do I know not. Sometimes I think of quitting Parliament and going abroad.' He insisted that the Marlborough Trust had 'been plucked by [the administrators] as well as any Pigeon ever was'. Graham anxiously commented on Lord Spencer's declining health, supported Goodenough's claims to preferment and wrote testimonials for Wilson; and Bentinck wrote to say 'how gratified he had been with the late changes, that had brought forward the men of the principles which he most approved'. Graham did not neglect his family amidst so many other interests. He enquired about a preparatory school 'where attention would be paid to [Frederick's] morals and where he would be trained in making Latin verses . . .' He exerted himself to secure the Carlisle postmastership for his brother Fergus. And in August he suggested to Lawson that

> As you possess the ancient and large Property connected with an honourable title, and as you have a son to whom you may transmit the Title with the Estates, it might not be disagreeable to you to have the old Brayton Baronetage restored . . .

Lawson promptly and 'very gladly' accepted — 'feeling as he did that it would be a kind of restoration of the title to the estate'; and Graham immediately wrote to Grey of Lawson's 'large Estate . . . of a clear 10,000 £ a year'. By such means were the Coronation honours of the Reform Government decided.

Reform, however, remained the great and dominant theme of politics. From 24 June the Bill was again debated by the Commons. Although far from meeting the ultra-Radical opinions previously propounded, it now appeared to satisfy the demands of most active reformist groups — perhaps simply because the Tories opposed it. Government supporters might talk in radical fashion, but the Ministry acted conservatively and finally accepted Lord Chandos's famous amendment granting the vote to £50 tenants-at-will in the counties, thus adding to landowners' political powers. Grey told Lord Somers in September that he was convinced that 'the more the Bill is considered the less it will be found to prejudice the real interest of the aristocracy'. Graham had insisted to him that additions to the traditional 40*s.* freehold qualification would not convert counties into 'close boroughs' and explained his own views, when writing on the proposed increase of county seats:

Large property will certainly give great influence; but if you deprive the Aristocracy of the power of nominating to Seats in Parliament, and if by conferring the Franchise on Large Towns you increase the democratic influence at the same moment, the Equilibrium cannot be preserved, unless in the Counties you give to Landed Property a preponderating sway. In the subdivisions great Estates will carry the Return, and this is the compensation for the loss of direct nomination; but in the Counties at large, with the Constituency extended as we propose, the influence of the great Estate will hardly be perceptible, and the democratic Principle will prevail. No more important Change can be made in our original Measure; none which will more justly excite the alarm of the Aristocracy. If the £10 Qualification in Cities and Boroughs be sound, this countervailing arrangement of the subdivision of Counties cannot be reversed without seriously affecting the whole measure. I am quite certain that any such alterations of the Bill would estrange many of its supporters.

When a Cabinet committee discussed memorials against the amalgamation of Selkirk and Peebles into a single constituency, Graham and Richmond opposed the majority by favouring separate representation. Tradition and rented value were their criteria, and Graham was not dissuaded by fears that the Tory Duke of Buccleuch might extend his powers: 'If the D. of Buccleuch has in Selkirkshire so large an Estate', he told Grey, 'I cannot think it unreasonable that he should exercise a commanding influence in the return of the County Members.'[13]

On 8 July the Second Reading passed with a majority of 136. But the Tories prolonged the discussions in Committee and there were hints of strong opposition in the Lords. 'We have had hard fighting in the Commons, and I was not in bed this morning till eight o'clock,' Graham wrote to Anglesey on the 13th. 'We shall win the day; perhaps, however, by making Peers.' Yet Graham was not always treated as seriously as he wished: the sick Grey was greatly cheered by Creevey's imitations of 'the genteel comedy man'. Grey himself seemed 'as stout as a lion' to Creevey: if the Lords defeated the Bill he would prorogue Parliament and create 'a new batch of peers'. Even Holland thought that a rejection would raise the question 'Will you have revolution or . . . a larger House of

Lords?' The Committee's report was accepted on 15 September and the Commons Third Reading was passed by a majority of 109. On the 22nd Creevey reported that 'Johnny has taken up his child in his arms, followed by a rare tribe of godfathers . . .' Now all depended on the attitude of the House of Lords.

Subsequent events are well documented. On 8 October the peers opposed the Bill by a majority of 41, despite a great flow of (sometimes threatening) advice from mass meetings and after five days of splendid debate. Within days violent mobs condemned the aristocracy in many large towns and attacked the property (and sometimes the persons) of Tory peers. While Radical crowds demanded the abolition of the Upper House, Ministers faced a perplexing problem. On 3 September Grey had told Graham that he had read Brougham's 'long paper on the subject of a large creation of Peers, ably argued . . . but not carrying complete conviction to my mind'. Greville hoped that the defeat would prove 'the necessity of a compromise; for no Minister can make sixty Peers . . .' The Commons expressed their continued support of the Bill and the Government, but the King frankly told the Cabinet a large creation was impossible: 'no Government could propose and no Sovereign could consent to [it], without losing sight of what was due to the honour of the Aristocracy and the dignity of the Throne'. The Ministers reluctantly accepted the King's view, while insisting on their right to promote another Bill.

Graham, while careful to avoid giving offence to the King (who had strongly objected to Russell's description of the Lords' vote as 'the whisper of a faction') did not change his views. In September he told James Abercromby (the Chief Baron of Scotland) that the country was quiet only because it believed the Lords 'would not be mad enough' to oppose the Bill; if they acted unwisely, they would be 'awakened from their day-dream by a voice of thunder, which would shake their House to its foundations'. He agreed with Anglesey that 'all was lost if the Bill were defeated', but feared that the Lords would 'rush on their own destruction'. And he told Western to rely on 'the stoutness of those in power'. But Graham and Durham were concerned by Ministerial timidity and the possibility of compromising over the Bill. The King,

Durham insisted to Graham on 19 October, was a staunch Tory, 'but public opinion controls him. This is now in your favour; mutilate the Bill, and you lose it.' And individual Ministers had great power, for Cabinet unanimity was essential. On 23 November Althorp told Grey that Graham was prepared to resign if the King's consent to new creations were not given, because he thought a second defeat in the Lords would have 'most disastrous consequences'. Durham and Brougham expressed similar sentiments to the harassed Prime Minister.

Although Graham was persuaded to accept the policy of the majority of Ministers, he insisted on presenting a detailed confidential memorandum to Grey on 25 November. He still believed that safety lay only in 'an early understanding with the King on the subject of Creation of Peers'; concession on the Bill was unthinkable and fear of the consequences would scarcely move 'a noble and high-spirited Assembly of English gentlemen'. The Government's strength rested on popular support and Royal backing, and if the King 'be not prepared to trust us . . . we cannot save him'. Rather than face a second defeat, Graham 'would run the risk even of a large creation of Peers' and believed that 'the known possession of the power [was] the surest means of averting the necessity of using it'. And he reserved the right of proposing an appeal to the King at a later date.

Government negotiations with Tory 'Waverers' broke down, and the problem of what action might be taken if the Lords repeated their vote remained undecided. Parliament met on 6 December, and six days later Russell introduced a third Bill containing some modifications which the King and Ministers hoped might influence the 'Waverers'. On the 14th the Commons carried the Second Reading by 324 votes to 162. But Christmas was an anxious time. Graham could feel that he had been right throughout the discussions. 'The accounts which I have of the House of Lords are very unfavourable,' he had warned Grey on 27 September, predicting the opposition of Harrowby and the Bishops. 'I hope you may be right about your majority in the Lords,' he wrote later. 'I am not sanguine, and anticipating the worst I look anxiously forward to the measures which . . . it may be wise and necessary to adopt.' When Althorp wrote on 29 December that 'We have a Cabinet about the Peers on Monday, when I expect our decision will be for the creation', Graham must have felt that his vindication was at hand. Althorp added, however, 'How many will go out upon this I do not know, but I think some will.'

Support for the plan to obtain the King's preliminary assurances was certainly growing. Holland found it 'strange' to 'prefer the danger of having no House of Lords to a temporary enlargement of it' (by 'calling-up' elder sons). Even Grey now sympathised with Brougham's plan; but he knew that Lansdowne, Palmerston, Melbourne and Richmond were hostile and feared the 'quite fatal' effects of any resignations and the King's opposition. Stanley (himself an opponent) told Graham of the proceedings at the Cabinet of 2 January 1832. Durham wanted 'forty or fifty Peers' and Brougham 'a good batch', but it was ultimately decided that Grey should ask for two creations and up to eight 'call-ups' and warn the King that 'a considerable number' might be necessary later. Grey expected to be in a minority of twenty, or at best to be defeated in Committee, and the King realised his difficulties. But an exercise of prerogative to overturn the vote of the Lords was a serious matter: the angry Duke of Newcastle even considered it 'a criminal breach' and virtual treason. Consequently, the King — who behaved with great constitutional propriety in a difficult situation and offended many Tories by so acting — demanded a written statement of the Cabinet's request and accepted their proposal of 13 January under the condition that a maximum of three creations should be supplemented by calling-up heirs and giving United Kingdom titles to selected Scots and Irish peers.

With excitement rising again throughout the country, Parliament reassembled on 19 January and the Committee stage of the Bill opened next day. Lords Harrowby and Wharncliffe carefully approached their fellow-moderates among Tory peers, with some hopes of 'converting' them; but the Government faced several difficult problems in the Commons, and Wellington and Peel remained firm opponents of the Bill. The 'Waverers' could not be trusted, and the King gave periodic hints that he preferred a Reform compromise to any creations. Furthermore, some Whigs started to demand that Grey should proceed with the creations, to guarantee success in the Lords. On 9 March Graham told Grey that 'it is clear that the House of Lords now stands before the public pledged by a large majority to resist even the first principle of Reform'. He maintained that the necessity of 'the large creation of Peers' was accepted by 'the great body of the nation', that it was vital to act quickly, that if the 'Waverers' allowed the Second Reading they would insist on amendments subsequently and that by that stage the Government would have lost the confidence of both the King and the electorate. The Cabinet 'contained within it the only men who had a chance of governing the country on the principles of freedom and at the same time of stemming [the] flood of democracy . . .' Furthermore, if Wellington's supporters left the Committee they could still defeat the Bill at the Third Reading and form their own Ministry: 'my fears, therefore, are almost equally great', wrote Graham, 'whether we succeed or fail in the second reading, unless Peers be now made'. In any case, he was 'persuaded that a large infusion of popular spirit and feeling was wanted in the House of Lords', so that 'Liberal' government might continue and a 'counterpoise be established' to the 'weight of Tory influence' created by Pitt and his successors. Althorp now agreed, wondering whether to resign (or even to commit suicide) and finally asking Grey on the 10th, 'Would you create Peers . . . rather than that I should resign?' But Grey held that a majority was very probable on the Second Reading, and possible in Committee; and he had 'extreme repugnance' to 'a measure of extreme violence' which was 'very uncertain of success', as old supporters and 'converts' might desert the Ministry, while the Lords might be ruined. He could not agree to 'a large creation of peers', but admitted that Althorp's resignation would lead to a fall of the Government. On the 11th the Cabinet accepted the Premier's policy of relying on the threat rather than the fact of creations; on the previous day Grey had gained some assurance of the success of Greville, Harrowby and Wharncliffe.

The Commons carried the Third Reading on 22 March and the

Bill went up to the Lords four days later. Now Grey faced the test of his theories. 'If the Bill is lost by Grey not using his power to make new Peers', Creevey had told Miss Ord on 27 February, '. . . even his *life* will not be safe; to such a pitch is the reforming part of the press now goading the publick on this subject.' The Premier knew the risk only too well, but bravely persevered. On 27 March the Cabinet could only decide that if defeated they would prorogue Parliament and create peers. But the King hinted that his support was at least weakening, and Grey had to insist that the basic essentials of the Bill must not be compromised, as Harrowby and Wharncliffe demanded. Detailed negotiations followed. The King was shocked by the suggestion that 50 or 60 creations might be necessary and maintained his previous policies. The Ministers had thought of possible 'peer-ables' — Graham rejecting a revival of the Preston title in his favour — and King and Cabinet politely disagreed over the all-important issue, while angry Tories talked of 'packing' the Upper House.

The Lords debate opened on 9 April and continued for four days. At length, after further great oratory and a final all-night sitting, the Bill was passed by 184 votes to 175. Provincial and Metropolitan rallies hailed the news with delight and Ministers relaxed over Easter with a mixture of optimism and concern about Royal attitudes: Grey himself was worried over the King's rumoured change of heart. The Lords went into Committee on 7 May and discussed Lord Lyndhurst's secretly-planned move to postpone the disfranchising clauses, which was carried by 151 votes to 116. This defeat on procedure warned the Cabinet of trouble to come, and next day they resolved to resign unless the King promised to create a majority. On the 9th the King replied that he could not create the desired minimum of 50 peers, and the Ministers resigned, not entirely without relief.

There followed the dangerous 'Days of May', when disappointed and often ill-informed Reformers lashed Grey, the King, the Queen, the Royal Family and the numerous Fitzclarences. Threats to refuse taxes were widespread and a network of agitations developed under Francis Place and Thomas Attwood, backed by more menacing revolutionaries. Distrusting Lord Ellenborough's promised compromise, the Commons still favoured the Ministers. But the King (perhaps after considering a Ministry under Brougham and Richmond) perforce turned to the Tories, through Lyndhurst. Wellington and Peel both adhered to their belief that the Bill was bad, but both knew that most of it would be passed. The Duke felt that duty demanded that he should serve the King, while the politically-minded Peel saw the virtues of party consistency. Harrowby, Peel, Alexander Baring and the Speaker (Charles Manners Sutton) having in various ways refused, Wellington was prepared to become Prime Minister. Place then invented his celebrated slogan 'To stop the Duke, go for Gold'. It could have little meaning for the proletarian Radicals whom Place despised, but might have great effect if adopted by bourgeois reformers. But the Whigs noisily assembled at Brooks's Club on the 13th, were harangued by the angry Stanley and Lord Ebrington and finally followed Althorp's advice to accept Tory Reform. Next day Palmerston expressed delight to Graham: the decision was 'infinitely wise . . . [and] perfectly honest', and 'the idea of standing over the new Ministry with the rod of adjournment in one hand and the physic-boat full of Reform in the other and compelling them to swallow the dose properly was excellent'.

A bitter Commons debate on the 14th, when Whig and ultra-Tory alike denounced in violent terms the plan for a Wellingtonian Ministry to carry Reform, led the Duke to abandon the post which he had never officially accepted. The King then wrote to Grey (which, thought the suspicious Creevey, 'was not civil, as he ought to have sent for him') and the Cabinet insisted on the Bill and on a pledge to create the necessary peers. The King hedged on the request; and his illegitimate son Lord Munster kept the Tories informed of Court musings, while William tried to gain Tory peers' support for Reform. There were last-minute hitches; the Duke's men would promise support to His Majesty but not to Reform. Amid rising melodrama created by Radical threats, the Cabinet on the 18th demanded 'full and indisputable security' for the Bill. Through the afternoon London anxiously awaited the King's reply. Every possibility had now been examined, and

William had no real choice. In the late afternoon Lords and Commons learned that Government had a guarantee that the necessary peers would be created (provided that, as the King explained later, 'no permanent increase to the peerage' was involved). Sir Herbert Taylor played an unexpected role by informing Opposition peers that the King would now allow any number of creations. With Wellington retired from the scene, the Lords' opposition withered away; many peers left the House rather than help to swamp it with new creations. The Third Reading passed by 106 votes to 22 on 4 June, with little changing of the Bill, and the Royal Assent was given three days later. As Grey confessed to Graham, 'Taylor had done excellent service'. And Graham might feel some pride in the fact that the Bill which he had helped to draft had been carried by the means which he had advocated.[14]

IV

Throughout the period of struggle over Reform Graham was also working hard at the Admiralty. In November 1830 he both inherited problems from his predecessor (Viscount Melville) and faced completely new administrative and diplomatic situations. An advocate of retrenchment was naturally expected to reduce Naval costs; and equally naturally, Naval men and those who believed in the maintenance of British sea power were scarcely predisposed to support a man who seemed to follow Hume's militant economy drives and pacific defence policies. Graham's first task must obviously be to secure reductions in Admiralty costs. But a consciousness of British Naval greatness gradually grew, and Graham was to become a great First Lord.

As soon as he was appointed Graham consulted with Sir Henry Hotham, the Tory Vice-Admiral of the Red, and Sir John Pechell; and he started to prepare 'retrenchment' plans. But the Navy had many duties to perform, with the ever-active Palmerston at the Foreign Office. In November the great powers considered the problem of Belgium's revolution against the Dutch Crown and tried to divide the Netherlands, displeasing both nations and also the French. By June 1831 the Belgians had been dissuaded from demanding a French king and had reluctantly modified their territorial demands. But two months later the Dutch condemned the Belgian choice of Leopold of Saxe-Coburg-Gotha (the Powers' recommended candidate) as King and invaded Belgium. A British fleet and a French army were sent to the defence of Belgium against Holland. British distrust of France had become almost traditional, and Palmerston alternately used public opinion in negotiations with the astute French Ambassador, Talleyrand, and flouted it by allying with Louis-Philippe's liberal France against the absolutist supporters of Holland. While French troops held the Dutch in Antwerp, British and French ships blockaded the Dutch ports, until Antwerp surrendered two days before Christmas in 1832.

While Britain thus defended traditional interests in the independence of the Low Countries, her old ally Portugal was undergoing painful experiences. Dom Pedro, the Emperor of Brazil and from 1826 King of Portugal, had passed the latter throne to his child daughter, Donna Maria, to forestall the claims of his absolutist brother, Dom Miguel (whom he also proposed as a husband for his own daughter). Pedro granted a constitution in 1827, and Canning then sent British forces to repel Miguel's attacks. When Britain withdrew, Miguel drove out Maria; and in 1832 Pedro took a Brazilian fleet under Charles Napier to Oporto to oppose his brother, eventually defeating him in 1833. Again, Palmerston balanced suspicion of France with positive dislike of the Eastern absolutists, and in April 1834 Anglo-French influence jointly persuaded the Portuguese Regent to expel Dom Miguel — and the Spanish (less successfully) to exile Don Carlos, brother of King Ferdinand VII and since 1833 claimant of the throne.

The liberal British Ministry generally backed Palmerston's support of 'constitutional' monarchies; Napier's activities were condoned, and British volunteers were allowed to serve against the Carlists. But 'official' power could be exercised only through the Navy, and it was virtually impossible for Graham simultaneously to meet increasing commitments and to prove his sincerity on economy.

While working 'like a dog' on Admiralty business, Graham

carefully observed social courtesies. In December 1830 the plump, pathetic but increasingly presumptuous Duchess of Kent took her 11-year-old daughter Victoria to Portsmouth, to see 'everything calculated to impress on Her mind the Naval greatness of this Country'; and Graham (unlike Melville) obligingly promoted the Princess's attendant midshipman. The First Lord was also a generous host. T. B. Macaulay dined successively with Althorp and Graham in August 1831, and 'both of them gave him exactly the same dinner . . . Turtle, turbot, venison and grouse formed part of both entertainments.' But Graham soon earned Radical praise. On 25 February he told the Commons of previous over-spending 'without a vote or the sanction of Parliament' and of over-manning paid for by cutting expenditure on ships and arms. Opponents were thus attacked for unconstitutional behaviour, but in fact the Government could not reduce its Naval and marine forces at this juncture. In December 1830 Graham had made a show of strength by sending two ships to the Tagus and was concerned over the danger of paying-off two vessels: 'the difference in point of Expense will be very great', he told Grey, 'and in a sudden emergency we could man a Fleet at very short notice'.

For some time, Graham suspected the Navy's leaders, including Sir John Barrow, Permanent Secretary of the Admiralty. Sir Pulteney Malcolm, he complained to Grey, 'only gave information to Ld. Melville'. But by January 1831 he was receiving information from secret agents abroad. An observer in Toulon and George Napier in Paris 'both confirmed the fact of a rising warlike Spirit throughout France'; but, insisted Graham, 'at present we have nothing to fear from it, and as far as the Navy is concerned, we should not be found unprepared'. Warships could be sent to Ireland, and 'the arrangement possessed the double advantage of the salutary moral Effect which it would produce . . . and of cloaking the real cause of our anxiety to retain un-diminished our naval strength . . .' Graham was torn between conflicting views. He was 'ready to bring the whole Question of our Naval force before the Cabinet', he told Grey on 6 January; but next day agents in Europe sent frightening reports:

> . . . affairs daily assume a more angry and hostile appearance. I am most anxious to reduce the Naval Expenditure . . . but if you anticipate the early probability of a Call arising, when it would be necessary to augment our Maritime force, it would be an ill-advised Economy to pay off Ships in high Orders . . .

He assured Grey that he would 'have a Line of Battle Ship at each Port ready to take Troops to Ireland'.[15]

It was obviously difficult to align intended Naval reductions with the Government's foreign policy. On 11 January Graham told Palmerston that

> An earnest desire to reduce the Naval Expenditure without diminishing the real efficiency of the Force has led me to pass in review our Squadrons on Foreign Stations, and carefully to consider the necessity which may justify the maintenance of each on its present scale.

The expensive and unhealthy African station caught his notice: 'the prevention of the Slave Trade was its only employment . . . [but] no Force could ever really be effective while France . . . sustained this Trade of Blood'. Surely, France, with a 'Government founded in the Principles of Liberty and Right, and just emancipated from oppression and wrong, must see the necessity of meeting the unanimous wish of Freemen in every Clime and the impossibility of braving the opinion of the Civilised World'. The real point to this wordy epistle was that if Palmerston could convert the French, 'a single Cruizer, with the aid of Steam' would suffice for African patrols.

The 'Sailor King' took considerable interest in his Navy, and Graham faced some uneasy situations with the last Lord High Admiral. 'I am not versed in the correct means of writing to Kings', he nervously told Grey, 'and I fear [my] style may be informal'; and he asked Grey to look over his letters. The King wished Sir James Cockburn to be Deputy Adjutant-General of Marines, but 'the obstacle was his deprivation in early life of a Commission in the army, to which the Commanders in Chief had repeatedly refused to restore him'. Naturally, the King 'did not much like the close investigation of past Navy Expenditure

without the consent of Parliament' — especially on the Weavel
and Woolwich works which he had authorised. Graham thought
that 'the line to be taken was that tho' [the King had] ordered the
works to be begun he never sanctioned the subsequent concealment from the House of Commons'; the King must be told, 'firmly
but respectfully, the intention of vindicating the large votes of the
present year by an exposition of past abuses and of the serious
misapplication of public money'. And Graham promised to
present details of supply shortages 'as conclusive proof that the
neglect of the Appropriation Act had not been harmless . . .' The
King's old friends, like Sir Byam Martin, the Tory Comptroller
of the Navy, also argued with Graham. But eventually Royal
agreement to the Navy accounts was secured. 'It is clear that the
King listens to Reason and surrenders even prejudices to the
force of Truth,' Graham wrote to Grey. 'It is a rare instance of
good fortune to serve in Government under you with such a
Sovereign on the Throne.' But relations actually often remained
difficult. In June Graham warned Sir Edward Codrington that
'there were those who had constant access to the King [and] were
his Enemies', who would attack him for quoting confidential
documents in his own defence. And in September the King
angrily wrote of dismissing Colonel Robert Torrens of the Royal
Marines, who had talked of abolishing the Lords. Grey hoped
that the Cabinet would 'positively resist the proposal'; Torrens's
language was 'indecent, violent and indefensible' but his dismissal
would be ruinous to the Ministry. Graham later 'had a most
satisfactory interview with the King, [who] appeared entirely and
freely to assent to their view'.[16]

Foreign affairs continued to present serious problems. 'Shall we
take immediate measures for sending out a Line of Battle Ship to
the Mediterranean, with the intention of sending a second in the
course of three weeks,' Graham asked Grey in January,

> or shall we put the War Complement of Men into both of them at
> once, detaining them in our Harbour until the *Scheldt Question* be
> settled? The present state of the Question would afford a fair
> pretext for a partial Navy Armament and might be used to lull the
> watchful jealousy of France . . .

K

He insisted that the number of men ('on which the framing of the Estimate depended') required must be decided urgently. His principles were at stake. There were currently some 21,000 seamen and 9,400 marines employed — 1,000 seamen and 400 marines above the last vote. 'I am rather disposed to ask for 22,000 seamen and 10,000 marines, stating the fact that the number voted has hitherto always fallen short of the number employed,' wrote Graham. He gained his increase of 3,000, but actually employed 29,336 men and boys (a reduction of 1,824 on the previous year's maximum).[17]

By February Graham had achieved only minor economies and actually had to ask for increased supplies, receiving £7,221,797 for fifteen months compared to £5,594,955 in the previous year. The international situation and the late Government were naturally blamed for the rise, and there was considerable controversy over Graham's censures; in particular, Sir George Clerk defended the Victualling Board and Martin spoke up for the Admiralty Board. But while Hume criticised expenditure on Royal yachts, he and his colleagues could only admire Graham's strict accounting and an economy campaign which ended both ancient sinecures and seamen's beer. Gradually Graham fashioned a new administrative machine. Nothing was too hallowed to be questioned; nothing was too trivial for examination. Every penny in the Victualling Board's ramshackle accounts was probed; the size of the Falmouth packet service and the Canadian Great Lakes station was investigated; clerks' hours were lengthened, the meat ration on guardships was reduced and some salaries were cut. Such measures, often backed by curt notes from the First Lord, were naturally more popular with middle-class taxpayers than with Naval men. But Graham endeavoured to distribute appointments fairly, although he opposed Admiral King's plan to stop impressment: 'this Power must never be surrendered', he told Grey, 'tho' it is wise to use it sparingly and, by rendering the King's service acceptable to seamen, to encourage as much as possible voluntary enlistment'. He favoured the restoration of the Earl of Dundonald's commission, gave the maligned Codrington the Mediterranean command and appointed the Tory Cockburn.

As always, Graham fretted over current dangers. 'Pedro is gone to Cherbourg and Maria di Gloria to Brest,' he told Stanley: 'and this little ingredient in the Cauldron of confusion just at the moment when the French threaten to bombard Lisbon and when the Dutch and the Belgians are on the very verge of war, adds to the difficulties which assail us on every side'. But the Dutch blockade was inaugurated; Sir William Parker was stationed off the Tagus to protect British lives and to prevent Spanish forces from supporting Dom Miguel; the West Indies station was augmented during the months before the abolition of slavery in 1833; a squadron was sent to the Dardanelles; ships and marines were periodically sent to Ireland; and Sir John Gore was ordered to India, to support Bentinck's negotiations with China, although Graham insisted that 'trade with China is our only object; conquest there would be as dangerous as defeat'. While ordering such forces, Graham carefully tried to avoid provocative actions. 'A naval demonstration is harmless and produces no European convulsion', he told Grey, in September 1832, but Palmerston's plan to land troops at Ostend 'would be a signal for war'. Grey agreed that war 'must, if possible, be averted' and believed that 'if we could but get rid of this Belgian business, our prospects would be very good'. But Graham thought that 'affairs were critical' in France, Belgium, Portugal, Spain and Ireland and urgently needed 'a manly, united effort'; and by 30 September Grey himself was 'in a state of feverish excitement' over the Belgian crisis. Graham was relieved that the Russian fleet could not act in the winter, though 'the Northern Powers' remained 'most hostile' and the Dutch were adamant for some time. But by March 1833 the excited King was allegedly 'loathing his Ministers, particularly Graham, and dying to go to war'.[18]

The strain of meeting varied overseas commitments caused some embarrassment, and by late December 1832 Graham was employing 3,000 more seamen than allowed by the parliamentary vote. But by August 1833, the outlook was improving. Donna Maria had been accepted at Lisbon, where Parker had brilliantly followed orders to maintain 'strict neutrality'. 'Having settled Belgium', Graham wrote to Grey, 'we shall, I hope, arrange

Portugal, and then we shall be in a position to talk boldly to Russia.' At last, in June 1834, he reported that Grey's 'cause had triumphed' in Portugal and 'congratulated him sincerely on this happy termination of a struggle which had so long endangered the peace of Europe'.[19]

Amid these difficulties, Graham pressed ahead with his Admiralty reforms. The supplies voted in 1832 totalled £5,045,827, falling to £4,803,647 in 1833 and £4,716,894 in 1834; the authorised strength of 27,000 was exceeded by only 328 and 701 in 1832 and 1833. Sir Byam Martin (who, Graham thought in 1831, 'hates both us and our measures' but who was a friend of the King and had electoral influence in Plymouth) had been left at the comptrollership, despite Hume's protests. But Graham 'laid up [Martin's] misdoings in store for the day of account'. Martin was eased out of office, and on 14 February 1832 Graham announced his major administrative reforms. The old semi-independent Admiralty, Navy and Victualling Boards were replaced by five new departments (under the Accountant-General, the Store-keeper-General, the Comptroller of the Victualling, the Physician of the Navy and the Surveyor of the Navy), each controlled by a Lord of the Admiralty. 'There would thus be', claimed Graham,

> a just division of labour, an undivided control and a due responsi-
> bility on the one hand, and, on the other, that unity and simplicity
> which he held to be the very essence and life of public business.

The Admiralty thus took over the duties of the civil adminis trators, generally with success. Detailed annual audits were inaugurated, which provided a model for financial reforms in other Government departments; Lord Welby told C. S. Parker in 1905 that 'from a financial point of view, [Graham] was the first statesman who grasped the method in which alone the financial control over expenditure can be secured . . . [he] may lay claim to being the first statesman to understand and enforce the only real check on public expenditure; and that achievement estab-lishes him with financial students as a great financial authority and a great administrator'. Graham's financial reforms earned the praise of the Radical *Black Book* and the Victorian financial administrator Sir William Anderson alike.[20] His administrative changes, if less unanimously praised, were widely supported by politicians and Naval men. The determination to achieve economy, efficiency, honest use of public money and an end to political and nepotic appointments which Graham had first developed in Cumbrian local government combined with his growing devotion to the Navy's interests to make him a notable First Lord of the Admiralty.

6

The Break with Whiggism

As his 42nd birthday approached in the summer of 1834 even the
morose Graham might feel some pleasure in his situation. He had
confounded his critics by becoming a successful Minister; and if
not personally popular, he was widely admired for his energy and
ability. The Navy was reformed and, although impressment
remained, seamen's conditions had been improved. The Reform
Act was operating safely, and Melbourne at the Home Office
appeared willing and able to repress 'dangerous' Radical agitations. Even European peace seemed secure. Yet Graham was soon
to break with his colleagues and re-examine his political
philosophy.

I

Ireland continued to provide troubles for the Government. 'What
an immense maze of embarrassment we all have around us!'
Anglesey had written to Graham on 30 July 1831. 'You should
legislate for Ireland with the rapidity of lightning . . . the only
way of rendering O'Connell harmless is by anticipating him . . .'
Graham agreed that the Government should act first, 'but', he
wrote, 'we are distracted with the daily cares around us, and I am
sorry to own that "the rapidity of lightning" is not our charac-
teristic'. Anglesey, however, continued to hope for reform for
'frightfully oppressed and degraded Ireland', which, he told Grey,
'suffered injury and insult and oppression and exaction that no
other people upon earth would stand'; his 'only astonishment was
that Ireland was not in open rebellion'. He was particularly
concerned with the tithes of the Church of Ireland (which his
Chief Secretary, Stanley, supported) and the equally complicated

and emotionally-charged problem of land tenures. Early in 1832 he planned a series of reforms, including tithe composition, a State take-over of Anglican revenues, official payment of Anglican (and later, Roman Catholic) priests and the provision of a Poor Law system.

The Government angered the Lord Lieutenant by insisting on its Tithe Recovery Act, and Anglesey was soon sending Graham 'letters which presented a fearful picture of impending civil war'. Consequently, Graham sent a Naval force under Sir Pulteney Malcolm to Ireland in July. Although Anglesey was often dismayed by Ministerial slowness, while Graham and Richmond disapproved of Anglesey's relations with O'Connell, the Government maintained its aim of first enforcing order and then redressing grievances. 'I know not what to hope or think respecting Ireland,' Graham told Anglesey in August. 'There appears no alternative left but to govern by force . . .' If moderation were impossible, 'then we must either resort to Protestant Ascendancy or rule by the mandate of Catholic agitators . . .' But Anglesey had already told Melbourne that 'the bare mention of governing Ireland by means of the Protestants horrified and appalled him'.

Anglesey tried to 'convert' several Ministers. 'If you do not reform the Church to the full extent recommended, you will soon be without one,' he warned Graham in October. '. . . Do let us draw the teeth of these confounded agitators . . . Stanley's views upon Church matters are not sound, and will not be tolerated nowadays.' Not unnaturally, Stanley wished to leave his unpopular office, but Grey asked Graham to dissuade him, as 'nothing could be more fatal to the Government'. Both Graham and Richmond offered to give up their posts for Stanley. However, as Graham explained to Stanley, Grey could not dismiss Anglesey or any other Minister. The O'Connellites would always 'rage' against firm Irish Secretaries, but, he wrote, 'though they hate you, they fear you'. Furthermore, if Stanley had failed to carry his Tithe Bill ('which remedied the real grievances and was a barrier against spoliation') in the Cabinet and had then resigned, he 'would not have resigned alone'. Stanley reluctantly retained his post, to Grey's relief and Graham's delight. He had 'sacrificed

himself for the Government,' wrote Richmond, who hoped that
Stanley might soon be promoted: 'the day would arrive when he
would be Prime Minister, and a very good one he would make'.[1]

Graham had made his views on Ireland only too clear in a
speech on the Army estimates on 18 February 1831: 'though he
considered civil war as the greatest of all possible evils short of
dismembering the empire, he, for one, would fight for Ireland as he
would fight for Kent — *toto certandum est corpore regni* ... and
he was sure the whole people of England, who had never been
conquered, would not allow themselves to be overcome by the
people of Ireland'. He tried to amend this tactlessness by adding
that 'it was not the people of Ireland who threatened, it was only
some demagogues ... who sought for the repeal of the Union'. As
the only Irish Member present, O'Gorman Mahon asked whether
the attack referred to O'Connell and himself and, being dissatisfied with Graham's reply, sent a Major Macnamara to call on
Graham and Althorp. A duel was avoided and the controversy
temporarily settled when Graham told the House that he had
intended to refer to O'Connell and made some apology.

In November 1832, as Stanley's Irish plans were considered
(along with his hopes of becoming Colonial Secretary), Durham
threatened to resign if Stanley were promoted. Although the
troublesome peer withdrew this blackmail, he and his friends
remained hostile to the men who in some ways formed the
Cabinet's 'Right'. Durham 'looked to being the head of a *mouve-
ment* Government', Graham told Stanley, who agreed that he
would 'await a more favourable moment for breaking with us'.
Stanley resolved to call Durham's bluff by calling for 'the decision
of the Cabinet between us', although 'nothing would suit
[Durham] better ... than breaking with us on the Church policy,
if he dare'. It was probably only loyalty to the long-suffering
Prime Minister that restrained several Ministers from condemning his insufferable son-in-law. However, on 26 February
1833 Althorp stumblingly introduced a strong Coercion Bill.
'Poodle' Byng told Greville that Althorp 'made a very bad speech
and a wretched statement ... and the debate looked ill till
Stanley rose and made one of the finest speeches that were ever

heard, pounding O'Connell to dust . . .' To Anglesey's pleasure, a Church reform measure was introduced which provided for the abolition of ten of the twenty-two bishoprics. But after Grey had told Anglesey of his concern over his relations with Stanley in January, the Marquess had offered to resign. In the end, it was the tired, angry Durham who resigned in mid-March, being compensated with an earldom. Goderich took his position as Lord Privy Seal and Stanley moved to the Colonial Secretaryship, with the difficult task of abolishing slavery. Sir John Hobhouse briefly succeeded Stanley, being followed by E. J. Littleton; and Anglesey gave up his task in September. Meanwhile, Stanley had managed to remove the Church Temporalities Bill's provision for using the suppressed sees' revenues for 'secular' purposes.[2]

Marquess Wellesley succeeded Anglesey. Littleton then found 'nothing discouraging' and 'much . . . that was promising' in Ireland and believed that 'a great effort ought to be made to propitiate' O'Connell. But in October Graham opposed Littleton's two plans for Irish tithes. 'If you wished to drive us to our wits' end, that is the approved mode,' he wrote. 'For Heaven's sake send us only one, and let that be the one on which you are all agreed . . .' Acts of 1823 and 1832 had made composition first possible and then compulsory and transferred payment to the landlord; but Roman Catholics still demanded abolition. As arrears totalled £1,200,000 by 1833, new schemes were considered, involving a parliamentary advance of £1,000,000 to tithe-owners and further attempts to collect the sums due.

The Cabinet was deeply divided over such issues. Stanley had been willing to reform the Irish Church by amalgamating dioceses, taxing wealthy benefices, commuting tithes, banning sinecures and abolishing Church cess. But, as a churchman, he strongly denied the right of the State to use Church revenues for other purposes. Russell, on the other hand, considered it expedient to pacify Ireland by applying unpopular Anglican wealth to causes approved of by the Roman Catholic majority. Many conflicting beliefs, principles and emotions were involved in such a controversy. Variations of Stanley's view could be held by such diverse groups as ultra-Protestants intent on maintaining the Ascendancy, the embryonic Anglo-Catholics roused by Keble's Oxford sermon on 'National Apostasy' or simple defenders of corporate and private property rights. And Russell could appeal to the need for liberal treatment of Ireland, a standard of 'fairness' in judging between a rich minority and poor majority and to the utilitarian and Erastian 'spirit of the age'. Edward Ellice put this view to Graham in February. 'The question which will make or mar the Government is the Irish Church', he wrote, 'and I am at a loss to discover what of principle there can be involved in a satisfactory settlement of it, beyond one of degree and expediency.'[3] It was against this background that the 1834 Session opened.

On 13 February O'Connell attacked Sir William Smith, a Baron of the Irish Exchequer Court ('a very able, but fanciful and disaffected' judge who 'would never suffer any but policemen or soldiers to be hanged', Greville had recorded in 1831), hoping to remove him from the bench because of his eccentric court hours and a recent Orange-style address. Ministers naturally opposed the motion, but while Stanley and Graham were absent, O'Connell demanded an enquiry, to which Littleton, Althorp and John Campbell agreed; 'they had gone ding-dong' into O'Connell's 'trap', thought Greville. Stanley angrily supported the Government, but Graham, 'in a maudlin, stupid sort of speech' declared his opposition — and O'Connell, 'quite satisfied with what he had done', dropped his demand. Regretting that Smith was 'to be handed over by the Government to his enemies' for 'an indiscreet charge, levelled against agitators', Graham tendered his resignation to Grey. He believed that O'Connell had achieved another public triumph: as Smith could only be removed after addresses by both Houses, the case might cause a 'dangerous' quarrel with the Lords and would surely anger the judges. Grey, 'distressed to the greatest degree' but accustomed to threatened resignations, dissuaded him, and the Commons soon reversed its vote. But the Ministers' attitude rankled with Graham and Stanley, and moderate conservative Whigs began to wonder whether Althorp, despite his virtues, was a reliable leader. Some, no doubt, were influenced by reports of Earl Spencer's illness; if Althorp succeeded him the Government would probably fall, unless Russell or Stanley could control the Commons.[4]

The climax came on 6 May, when Stanley introduced his Tithe Bill, converting tithes into lower State land taxes. He humorously quoted O'Connell's repeated statements that the Irish opposed not the amount but the ultimate applications of tithes. But Russell openly disagreed with his colleagues. 'If ever there were a just ground of complaint on the part of any people against any grievance', he declared, 'it was the complaint of the people of Ireland against the present appropriation of tithes.' He was prepared to break with the Cabinet to support lay appropriation, to do 'justice to Ireland'. As Russell enjoyed the 'loud and general' cheering, Stanley passed a celebrated note to Graham:

> John Russell has upset the Coach. We cannot go on after his declaration that 'if ever a nation had a right to complain of any grievance, it is the people of the Church of Ireland'.

Brougham 'never was more disgusted or indignant in his whole life than with J.R.'s effusions of mere senseless vanity', and several Ministers unsuccessfully tried to persuade Russell to withdraw. H. G. Ward (according to Palmerston at the instigation of 'Durham and Co.') then tabled a motion for lay appropriation for the 27th. Considerable Ministerial discussion followed. Russell's 'outbreak . . . had excited no sensation at all', Brougham now maintained. 'So it had blown over.' And Palmerston urged Graham and Stanley to postpone any decision on resignation until the forthcoming Government reconstruction.

The Government faced a difficult choice. Ward's proposal might be avoided, but there was little hope of satisfying supporters of Durham, Russell and Stanley. On the 27th Greville thought that 'the Government was on the very brink of dissolution', adding that 'Stanley, *they think*, would have knocked under if Graham had not been very fierce and urged him on to resistance. They attribute all the present bother to Graham, who pleads conscience and religious feelings.' Stanley had visited the King, and some Ministerialists 'suspected that Graham kicked up this dust with ulterior views and . . . aimed at a junction with

Peel — Stanley of course included — and coming into office with a moderate mixed party . . .' The finale arrived that evening, after a levee. After seeing the King, Grey told a group of Ministers that Ellice and Holland thought that immediate resignations would prevent a 'most angry and very unpleasant' debate. Palmerston and Lansdowne protested, but Richmond, Ripon (the former Goderich), Stanley and Graham — all perhaps misunderstanding Grey's sentiments — tendered their resignations to the King.[5]

II

Reactions to the resignations varied widely. According to Greville, the King told Richmond that 'the four . . . who had quitted were the four [Ministers] whom he liked best'. But the Earl of Sefton 'never was so happy in his life' (which seemed a bad sign to Greville) and O'Connell rejoiced at the removal of 'the worst part of the Government'. Brougham thought Stanley 'honest and open' but that Graham had used the Irish Church controversy as an excuse for an already-planned resignation. Greville busied around to obtain 'a tolerably correct understanding', finding that Cabinet differences had long existed on the question and that 'Stanley and Graham were both vehemently opposed to any Parliamentary appropriation of the surplus revenues . . . but not exactly on the same grounds'. While Stanley denied any right of parliamentary interference with property, Graham simply thought it inexpedient: the Union principally rested on the Church and 'any meddling with the Establishment would inevitably lead to its downfall'. Greville thought that Graham 'stood upon religious grounds'. He did not understand either man, being 'lost in astonishment' that they should oppose minor corollaries to the Reform Bill, especially when public opinion, justice and contemporary Irish conditions necessitated them. Stanley later told him of his several attempts to resign, while Graham insisted that the argument 'involved the fate of the Irish Church, and with it the connexion between the two countries'.

Friends were more sympathetic. Stanley's father, Lord Stanley, naturally gave support. 'I congratulate you and your seceding brethren on the relief to yourselves', he wrote, 'though I cannot but regret the occurrences which have rendered such a secession necessary.' But even Stanley wondered 'how on earth was it to end'. Goodenough, now comfortably placed as Dean of Wells, thought that 'the country owed [Graham] the deepest debt of gratitude for the noble stand [he] had made in behalf of the Church'.[6] Old colleagues like Althorp, Lyttelton, Poulett Thomson, Holland, Palmerston and Anglesey (who feared that he might accidentally have hastened Graham's resignation but still maintained that 'really the Irish Church should not be left as it is') expressed regret, while Grey promised always to 'bear testimony to [Graham's] zeal and ability'.

Undoubtedly the principal motive behind Graham's resignation was his determination to protect the Church from spoliation. 'It was [also] a consolation to act in perfect concord with [Stanley], whose example he was proud to imitate and whose principles he entirely espoused,' he told Lord Stanley. The Stanleys' support proved that he had not opposed 'genuine Whig principles, which . . . were not incompatible with the firm maintenance of the Established Protestant religion, that religion of perfect freedom, which the Revolution of 1688 bore triumphant over Popery and regal tyranny'. And he told Bentinck that

> Though anxious to reform the Church, I could not consent to measures which appeared to me calculated to overthrow it; and, believing sincerely that the maintenance of the Protestant Establishment in Ireland is necessary for the preservation of the Union, now so fiercely assailed, I could accept no compromise.

To Francis Aglionby he pointed out that he was a devoted supporter of religious liberty and Church reform; 'but having made these large concessions . . . he was nevertheless a devoted friend to the Protestant religion and to the Established Church'. He could not support 'the voluntary principle' or any weakening of the 'parochial Church Establishment, which in his opinion was the best and purest part of their Church discipline'. Furthermore, 'the growth and boldness of Dissent', the rising demand for the disestablishment of the 'United Church of England and Ireland' and Graham's own knowledge of 'the course in which the Government was about to move' made him glad that he would not share future responsibility.[7] His early tuition under the Evangelical clergymen of Carlisle had left a lasting impression, and Graham could never forget his duty to protect and forward the interests of the Church. Yet, if (contrary to opponents' suspicions) religious views were of primary importance, growing disillusion with the Ministry had conditioned him for the resignation.

III

As Graham handed over the Admiralty to the Earl of Auckland not all his work was finished. When, in August 1833, Silk Buckingham had again raised the question of seamen's impressment, Graham had talked of providing registration and a ballot. The only move yet made was the Merchant Seamen's Registration Bill; the press-gang remained and, indeed, seemed inevitable. This measure and a Bill on tonnages were still before Parliament in June, and Althorp asked Graham, as the man who 'understood [them] better than any one else' to manage their slow progress.

In March Graham had acted as the Cabinet's spokesman in an embarrassing debate on the Corn Laws. On the 6th Hume proposed to replace the sliding scale of 1828 with a 10*s.* fixed duty, as a move towards complete free trade. Though divided, Ministers resolved to oppose the change, but left junior colleagues free to vote at will. Graham defended Huskisson's system, insisting that 'an exorbitant price of corn was at present impossible'; the level of protection was too low to hurt industry but appeared the last defence to farmers. If rents fell the landowners would collapse and there 'would be a complete change in the existing frame of society'. Next day Poulett Thomson, Vice-President of the Board of Trade, replied. 'He had no belief in cheap bread [and] believed that reducing existing duties on imports would not materially reduce the price of corn. What was really to be anticipated from such a change was the steadying of prices.' And he justified his views by quoting from Rooke's pamphlet on Free Trade, first published as written 'by a Cumberland Landowner' and often ascribed to Graham. In fact Graham had taken the manuscript to Ridgway, the publisher, in 1828, but was not responsible for the contents, though he did not deny the charge until Rooke acknowledged the authorship. The debate was 'very dull', but Greville found it 'very pretty to see Graham and Poulett Thomson like to gamecocks got loose from one pen, pecking at and spurring one another'. The motion was defeated by 312 votes to 155.

On 12 May Graham's last task as a Minister was, appropriately enough, concerned with economy and efficiency, when he introduced a Bill to reform the Exchequer Office. Following the recommendations of a commission of which Graham had been a member, the measure abolished old Exchequer sinecures, reduced the staff, ended the tally system and medieval record-keeping and considerably cut costs. The Bill was carried.

Graham's resignation caused a considerable change in his life. He had worked hard at the Admiralty and carefully thanked his staff on leaving them. One of his last actions — in the circumstances, a gracious gesture — was to promote Anglesey's son, Lord Clarence Paget. Naval affairs had even intruded into his private life; Macaulay was once shocked when a duchess had tearfully appealed for a better posting for her son while dining with Graham at Holland House. Now Graham and Stanley had the freedom to think out their position as the emerging leaders of the independent, more conservative Whigs.

On 2 June Ward persisted in demanding appropriation of Irish tithes, though the Government promised a commission. Graham and Stanley heard the debate from the second bench below the gangway. Before Althorp carried the previous question Stanley 'spoke very well' (thought Greville), though with 'considerable acrimony and in a tone which demonstrated the breach between him and his old colleagues to be irreparable'. Graham did not speak, but both former Ministers voted with the Government. 'We are now sure of a violent measure next session, and the more quiet we can keep everything till then the better, provided the Church is on the alert,' Graham wrote to Stanley, who 'even wished matters could rest as they were'. It was important to Stanley that 'Grey should not be driven from the helm'; but he knew 'how little would drive him'.[8] Further trouble was soon to come over the renewal of the Coercion Bill.

Wellesley agreed with Althorp and Russell that coercion could be modified, but Grey insisted on retaining the force of Stanley's measure. On 3 July Graham reported to Stanley that he had met Grey and that 'it was clear that he had carried the Coercion Bill by force against the majority of his Cabinet'. He had also met Peel, to concert opposition to Littleton's new proposals to alienate Irish Church property. But Littleton had virtually promised O'Connell that strict 'coercion' would end, and the Irish leader now protested. The Ministry was bitterly divided, and Grey's tolerance had allowed a complicated series of manœuvres to develop among some Ministers. Littleton appeared to have persuaded his father-in-law, Wellesley, to change his mind over coercion — perhaps with Ellice's help. Althorp knew of Littleton's meetings with O'Connell, but not of his indiscreet pledges. Brougham, it was supposed, might have instigated the trouble. On the 7th, after a harassing day, Althorp told Grey that he could hold out no longer: following Stanley's vicious attack on his former colleagues, O'Connell had routed Littleton. Next morning, the Premier resigned and recommended that the King should summon Melbourne. 'Then there is an end of the Whigs, Graham commented. Littleton, 'a man powerless to serve his party', thought Greville, 'had contrived to destroy it'.

The obituaries were premature. Melbourne succeeded Grey and persuaded Althorp to return to the management of the Commons. 'Almost everything depends upon the course which Althorp takes', thought Greville on 12 July, for there was 'no such feeling as animosity against Althorp'. With such help, Melbourne — 'considered lax in morals, indifferent in religion and very loose and pliant in politics' — patched up a Government which had lost much of its prominent talent. The first task was to deal with Court suggestions of some coalition with Peel, the second to face the Lords' rejection of the Irish Tithe Bill.

If old-style Toryism was already decayed, a new Conservatism was developing under a textile magnate's son, Peel. It was a cautious, empirical faith, seeking for new policies for the Right in an age of extended electorates, institutional reforms and industrial development. Peel 'presumed' that Conservatism's 'chief object' would be 'to resist Radicalism, to prevent those further encroachments of democratic influence which would be attempted (probably successfully attempted) as the natural consequence of the triumph already achieved'. Conservatism would defend Church and Constitution while seeking to remedy abuses; Peel 'was for reforming every institution that really required reform, but he was for doing it gradually, dispassionately and deliberately, in order that the reform might be lasting'. As Peel told his Tamworth tenants and electors in December, 'If the spirit of the Reform Bill implied merely a careful review of institutions, civil and ecclesiastical, undertaken in a friendly temper, combined with the firm maintenance of established rights, the correction of proved abuses and the redress of real grievances', he and his colleagues could 'undertake to act in such a spirit and with such intentions'.

Such a Conservatism obviously had attractions for Stanley and Graham. But while Wellington and Peel considered a coalition with Melbourne impossible, because of party divisions, personal considerations prevented the ex-Ministers from collaborating too closely with Peel's group. On 26 September Graham told Stanley that he had met Melbourne and Palmerston at dinner and that 'Melbourne without saying it, . . . wished to [say] "Let us continue friends. You and those with whom you act differ less from me than many of those with whom I am now associated. I may have to fall back on you; do not be impatient." ' George Dawson had told him that 'Peel was quite ready to enter on government with the view of meeting the just expectations of a Reformed Parliament, removing every abuse and rectifying every imperfection, both in Church and State, to the utmost extent consistent with the maintenance and safety of the institutions themselves'. When Whiggism tired of 'radical' measures Stanley might still achieve power. But he confessed to Graham on 30 September that he 'could not make out' the Government's Irish

L

policy: 'they truckled to and courted O'Connell, and did not appear to have made the smallest progress towards gaining him'. Consequently, Melbourne no doubt 'would be very glad to have other friends to fall back upon in case of need'.

During the fine autumn Graham relaxed in the country. He spent a week with Richmond at Goodwood, he told Stanley on 21 October. Such country house sporting holidays led to many political contacts. Graham went shooting with Althorp; and Brougham, in his roundabout way, asked Richmond to 'sound' him about succeeding Bentinck in India. Graham 'could only entertain such a proposition when made to him by the head of the Government' and believed that Melbourne 'would be sorry so to weaken that band of former friends from whom in his extremity he still looked for support'. After some controversy, Auckland accepted the Governor-Generalship.

Leisurely dreaming and planning soon ended. Graham and Stanley had only ceased to lament the burning down of Parliament when they heard of Earl Spencer's long-expected death on 10 November. Althorp succeeded as 3rd Earl, and Melbourne virtually tendered his resignation. After a jovial dinner at Brighton the King not only ordered the Whigs out but gave Melbourne the task of carrying the summons to Wellington. Brougham ensured that his colleagues first heard of their dismissal from *The Times* of 15 November. 'The town was electrified by the news,' recorded Greville.

Rumours of a Tory plot were disproved by the news that Peel was touring Italy. It transpired that the King had resolved to rid himself of a 'radical' Ministry, largely by refusing to accept 'that young man' Russell as Althorp's successor. As James Hudson, a Gentleman Usher to the Queen, hastened to Rome to find Peel, Graham and Richmond were visiting Lord Lichfield. 'Affairs have taken a sudden, I hope not a dangerous, turn,' Graham confided to Stanley on 18 November. 'It will be melancholy indeed if, after waiting so long, His Majesty should have made his rush at the wrong moment. I think also he has put up the wrong man to ride this second heat. Bob was the lad who had the best chance of winning.' This objection to Wellington was invalid. The Duke temporarily took several offices, but only until Peel returned. Three days later Graham told Stanley that the Duke of Sutherland's party at Trentham Park was hostile to 'a Wellington Government and very decided in favour of you and of an Administration framed on liberal Reform principles, opposed to Destructive'. Richmond pointed out that Stanley could only take the lead if he had a party; and Graham insisted that the group should refuse to help the new Ministry — which 'would lead to Peel's joining us, not us him'.

Old Lord Derby — who allegedly disapproved of his grandson's activities — had died in October, and Stanley had inherited a courtesy viscountcy. He entertained Graham and Richmond at Knowsley in late November, when it was decided to refuse Peel's expected invitation. On the 29th Greville was giving Wellington different news, heard from Lord George Bentinck, who had it from Richmond. Stanley, he reported, 'was not at all desirous to be mixed up in the new concern, but had no objection to take office under Peel', but fear of attacks by old colleagues made him insist on a Government of 'Liberal principles' and the inclusion of his friends. The Duke wisely 'took very little notice of this'. On 2 December Hardinge told Greville that 'Peel would at once make a fair and cordial overture to Stanley', and Greville decided that the Government 'would like ... to take Stanley and Graham and wash their hands of Ripon and Richmond' but that Stanley could obtain posts for all four. However, Stanley was firm. 'It is quite clear that when Peel returns there will be a battery opened upon us,' he predicted to Graham on 5 December. 'But I am the more satisfied the more I reflect on it that we have judged well and wisely in declining a junction.' By supporting Peel without office they could make him carry liberal measures, 'gain the credit with the public and strengthen their own party'.

IV

Peel reached London on 9 December, accepted the Premiership and started to form his Ministry. An ideal Cabinet, Lyndhurst had told Greville, would contain 'four Stanleys, six of their own people and two High Tories'. The Whigs rejoiced at Stanley's refusal of office, but (asserted Greville) 'were sorry that Graham did not join, for they hated him and wanted to be rid of him'. To avoid duplicating Stanley's letter, Graham discussed the invitation with Peel on the 13th and instantly reported to his friend. He told Peel that 'If his measures were good their support out of office would be more effectual, whereas their junction with him would render them powerless and his opponents united and uncompromising.' Wellington's attacks on Grey were put forward as a reason for not joining the Cabinet, but both Stanley and Graham made it clear that they had no objections to Peel.

As the Ministers kissed hands on the 16th Hardinge told Greville that 'the arrangements would in some respects be only temporary and made with a view to the subsequent admission of Stanley and his party'. Ripon's brother, Earl de Grey, did join the Government, as First Lord of the Admiralty, giving the little party one official contact. Certainly the Stanleyites could expect to enjoy considerable prestige. 'One of [Peel's] first acts was to make [an] earnest appeal to [Graham] for his co-operation as a Minister of the Crown', and it might even be possible for Peel himself to join them. Nevertheless, they were resolved to remain independent. By late December Greville noticed that both Stanley and Graham were uttering Whiggish sentiments, favouring 'Conservatively Liberal principles' and opposing any alliance. On the 23rd Graham told Edmund Hornby that the Duke of Hamilton 'and the best part of the Whigs in Scotland' would be 'anxious to join a Third Party occupying the middle ground between the Radicals and the ultra Tories' — though, after Tamworth, 'it was hard to say where an old Tory was to be found'. But the Stanleyites were disappointed with Peel's Cabinet. 'He cuts the ground of support from under our feet,' wrote Stanley on the 29th; and on New Year's Day Graham replied that he also regarded 'the composition of Peel's Government with great distrust', though 'not anxious to scrutinise the materials to which [Peel] had been driven to resort by their refusal to join him'. The 'party' might be weak in numbers, but it was rich in talent. Early in January 1835 Ellenborough suggested to Wellington that Graham might run India. The Duke (recorded Greville) 'though it better not to have anything to do with that party at present' and, when a tentative offer was made through John Barrow, Graham, though flattered, rejected it.

The Cumbrian electors, so recently freed from Lowther domination, were uncertain of Graham's loyalty. There were stories of a King's Messenger bearing Peel's offer of the Home Office or Admiralty to Netherby, missing Graham near Shap and delivering secret messages at Arthuret. Graham attempted to allay local Whigs' suspicions. He still supported 'all reforms which he considered necessary and safe and [would] resist all changes which were urged in a restless spirit of innovation', he told the High Sheriff, Henry Howard. In an address to the electors he insisted that he still favoured peace, economy and reform. Some Blue partisans remained hostile, but the gentry generally accepted his professions. Only family troubles prevented Aglionby from proposing him at the nomination for the General Election in January 1835. Lawson took Aglionby's place, and Lord Carlisle was prepared to support Graham, except over the Irish Church. Graham could only condemn the Ministry's composition, but was convinced that its 'measures would be good' and 'most decidedly opposed [any] Government formed on Radical and destructive principles'. Such sentiments scarcely reassured his more radical supporters.

On 12 January Graham appeared before an audience of over 10,000 people at the nomination in Carlisle market place. Although there was no Tory opposition, the affair was important and Graham arrived with over 400 'tenants and friends, on horseback'. At the Bush Inn he was joined by Blamire and on the hustings was proposed by Lawson and one John Bowman. He delivered a polished speech to the partly-hostile crowd. There was an appeal for sympathy; he had just left his ailing brother, Captain Charles. There was a reminder of past work for Reform, economy and local progress. And there was a denial of the slander that he had received Durham's patronage. 'I never had a patron', he declared, 'because I never was a client', and it was untrue that he had solicited titles from Canning and Wellington or office from

Grey. He supported both Roman Catholic rights and established institutions: 'there was but one fatal subject of difference' with Grey, 'and that subject was the Irish Established Church'. He denied being controlled by Stanley, for they had disagreed over Smith. And he had rejected Peel's offers 'because he believed that coalitions of the kind proposed seldom led to a good end . . . they had invariably ended in doing great injury to the characters of public men, they shook public confidence and public opinion was decidedly opposed to them'. Furthermore, it would not have been proper or honourable to turn against his old friends. The *Morning Chronicle*'s claim that he rejected Peel's overtures through fears for his seat was untrue. He did not, in fact, like the Government, which 'was as bad as he could well imagine, [being] entirely composed of men to whom and to whose measures he had all his life been opposed'. Consequently he would support or oppose its measures on their merits. Above all, Graham remained a reformer in Church and society:[9]

> There ought to be no pluralists . . . [and] the sinecures of the cathedrals were indefensible . . . He was a most strenuous advocate for a settlement of the tithe question . . . [by] a commutation on liberal principles . . . He was prepared to put an end to all exclusive and self-elected bodies . . . He wished to see the advantages of education shared equally between nonconformists and Churchmen [and] every cause for discontent on the marriage question removed [and] that provision should be made for the fabric and service of the Church without having resort to the collection of a parochial rate.

Although the county representation was the 'earliest and highest object of [Graham's] ambition', he would not sacrifice his conservative principles. The Reform Act, he now maintained, 'was like fire — in the hands of the honest artisan a purifying element, but in the torch of the incendiary a consuming flame'. His courage in announcing such views in Carlisle was weakened by his denial of complete concord with Stanley. The fact was that Graham had always looked for a leader to serve, although he was rarely a loyal disciple for long. Nearly eight years ago he had told Lansdowne that he would follow his views:

> From my entrance into Parliament I have considered you the safe
> depositary of those principles to which I honestly adhere and to
> which power in your hands is best calculated to give effect.

Several politicians subsequently received similar professions. And
in 1835 Graham felt it necessary to explain his denial to Stanley.
'It is clear that I am not a popular character on a Cumberland
hustings', Stanley replied, 'and that you have to deal with a much
more Radical constituency than I have.' But Graham and Blamire
were returned unopposed.[10]

The 'Stanleyites' now planned their tactics. J. E. Denison and
Lansdowne hinted at further support, but although Stanley
agreed to attend a 'cabinet' at Goodwood he doubted the wisdom
of Graham's plan for a party meeting: 'our numbers are so small',
he wrote, 'that a formal meeting would only indicate our weakness'.
Stanley was right, and Graham, for once, was over-optimistic; but
George Bentinck rashly estimated supporters at 86 and Hornby
thought 87. And Stanley himself strongly opposed the possibility
of Graham becoming Speaker: 'come what may, your post must
be ἐν προμαχοισι not judge of the lists.'

Peel's first Ministry was far from strong. It was defeated in the
Speaker's hotly-contested election, and a close Whig–Radical–
Irish alliance was created solely to attack it. After the King's
Speech on 25 February Sir Oswald Mosley arranged a meeting of
33 'moderate' Members, who were persuaded by Graham to meet
Stanley. By the evening Greville thought that 'the Stanley party'
numbered 45 or 50; and the next day there were 'about fifty [and]
other adhesions and half-adhesions occurred in the course of the
evening'. But Greville noted the 'party's' inherent weakness:
Stanley 'could only lead them the way they were minded to go,
and the design of his friends was to show themselves Conservatives
without being Tories, to save this Government, not from love of
it but from fear of its opponents and of the alternative'. Perhaps
the group briefly saved the Government, but it soon crumbled.
Yet it enjoyed temporary power, observing 'a suspicious and
suspected neutrality': Greville thought that 'the Government was
at their mercy whenever they joined the Opposition, or, indeed, if
they kept aloof'. Of course, Greville was often wrong, but he did

in many ways represent well-informed society (and often had access to 'confidential' — though not always accurate — sources) and was wisely cynical about the group. Stanley's own leisurely impartiality scarcely encouraged the growth of party discipline and the dwindling group gradually disintegrated.[11] O'Connell soon gave it a title which stuck, quoting Canning's lines in the *Anti-Jacobin*:

> Down thy hill, romantic Ashbourne, glides
> The Derby Dilly carrying six insides.

The 'Derby Dilly' was soon to be attacked.

Graham's hustings speech had aroused considerable opposition. On 26 February Gisborne quoted his attack on the Ministry during the debate on Morpeth's amendment to the Address. When Graham sat silent the Radical dandy Tom Duncombe 'drew' him. In reply Graham frankly admitted his pain at leaving the Whigs, that he trusted Peel more than any other Minister and that his views were unchanged. Whatever his past criticisms, he believed that the Ministers should be given an opportunity of acting on their liberal professions; he strongly opposed 'a factious opposition' and any such motion against even the present Government. He attacked the 'Babel Opposition . . . [of] new and old Whig, of the Moderate and the Ultra, of the Radical and the Repealer', and strenuously denied Opposition slanders about Stanleyite agreement with the Government. But Ministers did not escape 'Dilly' attacks. When Lord Ashley introduced the Naval estimates on 16 March, Graham could not resist pointing out that his former denigrators were now accepting and even extending his own economies.

The uneasy middle course was maintained, but on 17 March Graham introduced amended Bills on merchant sailors' registration and Naval impressment, considerable moves towards emancipating the long-exploited seamen which finally passed in the summer. And Graham could support Peel's ecclesiastical reforms. But the Irish Church again provoked major arguments after 30 March, when Russell proposed a debate on temporalties. Supporting Peel principally because he would 'resist the application of Ecclesiastical Revenues to secular purposes' and

believing that the alienation of corporate funds would render all
property insecure, Graham was hostile. As major principles were
at stake, he could not accept the argument on 'proportionate
rights' in Ireland; 'once admitted ... they must of necessity
extend it to England, and thereby the existence of the Established
Church would be not only endangered but ultimately destroyed'.
Graham personally followed Whig ideals, believing in 'the utmost
liberty of thought and of action in all matters, whether of politics
or of religion, consistent with law, order and constitutional
authority'; but Church property was sacred. His two-hour
speech, burdened with (sometimes unhelpful) quotations, was not a
parliamentary success, but delighted old Lady Graham, Ripon and
W. E. Gladstone. The Irish Church debates were, however, fatal
to the Government. By 3 April, after the first defeat, Greville
thought that 'Stanley and Graham were angry that [Peel] didn't
resign directly'. Two further Opposition victories led Peel to yield
on the 8th.

The 'Dilly' had foundered, and Graham, who had largely
formed it, felt some bitterness. When Greville lengthily discussed
'general politics' with him on the 9th, he considered that Graham
and Stanley 'looked *now* solely to a junction with Peel ...'
Graham hoped that a '*well endoctriné*' King would refuse O'Connell
any office and create no peers. And when told of Tory anger at
Stanley's flippancy, he frankly examined his friend: despite 'great
talents', debating ability, 'high principles [and] unblemished
honour', Stanley 'followed politics [merely] as an amusement'.
Though Stanley would serve under Peel, Graham percipiently
doubted 'whether it would be possible for two such men, so
different in character, to go on well together in the same Cabinet'.
Another leader had proved too weak and already Graham was
again changing his allegiance: again 'Bob was the Lad'.

Whether addressing Carlisle crowds or old friends, Graham still
asserted his own consistency, conservative and Anglican. 'I, ...
adhering to Whig principles', he told Howick on 13 March,
'regard with peculiar jealousy a dominant Catholic Church, and
... am convinced that the Union cannot be maintained if the
Protestant connection be severed and if Popery be established in

[Ireland], as the triumph of agitation over Law.' But the King's reluctant recall of Melbourne appeared to herald another brief Ministry, despite Radical and Irish support. Graham succinctly described his attitudes in a memorandum of 1 May describing his repeated refusal to rule India under either party. Having rejected Peel's offers because of 'imperfect confidence and the evils of premature coalitions', acceptance of 'a lucrative appointment' would be personally ruinous. Acceptance of Melbourne's offer was equally impossible, as Graham opposed the new Government's 'principles ... composition ... support [of "Radicals and Repealers"] ... and the destructive changes which avowedly it contemplated'.

'Dilly' policy, 'the Knowsley Creed', had largely rested on the defence of the Church and support of municipal reform. Melbourne's Government planned a measure on the latter subject in the spring, amid considerable interest and anxiety. But, apart from arguments over London University's charter, there was little to arouse Graham in the Government's early months. Russell introduced the Municipal Corporations Bill in June, dissolving the old Corporations (which had been condemned, not always fairly, by a Commission of 1833), setting up elected councils for English and Welsh boroughs and granting votes to householders paying rates for three years. While many old Corporations were virtually indefensible, the proposal to abolish freemen's rights was strongly opposed. When, on 23 June, Sir William Follett proposed to retain their privileges, Campbell attacked the whole body as corrupt and Peel defended it. Graham agreed with Peel, primarily because the new franchise proposals broke the agreement on which the Reform Bill rested. When Russell scoffed, Graham hotly replied that the Reform Act 'provided a resting-place whereon he might resist steadfastly, manfully and constantly, all further change' and although it would lead to Church and municipal reforms it did not justify franchise changes. Stanley supported Graham and their dwindling group joined Peel's followers in tabling a series of unsuccessful amendments.

If the 'Dilly' were unsuccessful, the Stanleyites must look to

Peel for the Conservatism which they demanded. And of all the
Stanleyites — and despite Peel's inclination to distrust him —
Graham was already the most sympathetic to Peel. Ever busy in
planning and organising, he joined the Conservative agent,
F. R. Bonham, in arranging electoral 'influence'. When Greville
dined at Ripon's on 20 June, he found that Graham 'held nothing
but Tory language'. Ten days later, as Graham crossed the House
after again voting with the Opposition, some Government
supporters challenged him to stay on the other side; and he
angrily took his place on the Conservative benches. Next day's
newspapers made much of the affair, the *Chronicle* urging Cumbrian electors to disown their Member. Stanley had been a teller
and also changed his place, because (he explained) of Ministerial
attacks and (according to Greville) largely through Graham's
influence. A little group of loyalists — Lord George Bentinck,
Gally Knight, Sir Matthew Ridley and Stratford Canning —
followed their leaders. But the centre party was dead. Stanley's
leadership was over. And Graham's search for a personal leader
must continue.

V

From the Opposition benches Graham continued to support
amendments to the Municipal Reform Bill. His own proposal, to
transfer beer licensing from councils to magistrates, was defeated
in the Commons but adopted by the Lords. Based on his own
common-sense appreciation of local politics, it was to have some
importance. And Graham worked hard to save Greville's sinecure
Jamaican Secretaryship (Greville having 'whipped up the old
friendship' for the occasion). When the Irish Tithe Bill came up,
he and Stanley were naturally active again. The Government
proposed to commute tithes for rent charges and to transfer
payments from tenants to owners. Graham opposed the Bill on his
usual grounds, defending the Establishment and the rights of
property. Although the measure passed the Commons, the Lords
rejected secular appropriation and a modified Bill did not
succeed until 1838. In the meantime, Stanley and Graham con-

tinued to condemn O'Connell, whose support of the Whigs was a principal reason for their own defection.

To the melancholy Graham the outlook appeared bleak, as O'Connell's influence with the Government and popularity outdoors seemed to grow. 'Every effort to induce men, from philosophical and humane considerations, to lay aside their party differences and to concur in patriotic measures of pure philanthropy is, I fear, at the present moment quite hopeless', he told Rooke on 27 July,

> For, unhappily, religious differences have become intertwined with political dissensions; and this compound has never failed to produce the bitterest potion which can be administered and the strongest incentive to the worst passions of mankind. I hope our country may struggle on without some fierce convulsions; but my fears are stronger than my hopes.

Increasingly, it appeared that the one hope of saving the Church and established institutions from Radical and O'Connellite desecration lay with the union of all conservatives. J. C. Colquhoun later remembered asking Graham's advice in the summer. 'Whatever may be our present position, it can only end in one way, and that is in a cordial union with Sir R. Peel and the conservative party,' replied Graham — though he hoped for a gradual merger 'so as to be evidently the result, not of personal ambition but of honest agreement . . .' Already the break with Whiggism was widening with each major debate. 'To Peel it is nuts to see Stanley and Graham drawing down unpopularity on themselves and every day widening the breach between them and their old friends,' noted Greville, who, however, expected Stanley to rejoin the Whigs.[12]

The major problem facing the 'Seceders' was, in fact, whether to maintain any semblance of independence. They approved of Peelite Conservatism but still disliked the old-style Tories who formed a sizeable proportion of the party. Their inclinations remained largely Whiggish, but they hated the O'Connellite alliance and any move towards a more radical liberalism. For Graham at least constituency pressures caused some concern.

Stanley, with the power of the house of Derby behind him, could always be virtually sure of a Lancashire seat; but the Cumbrians had already shown resentment against Graham.

For a time, the little group decided that it would have more influence in conserving what it held dear by retaining a nominal independence. But it continued to support the Conservatives in major debates. The Tory-dominated Lords, which Graham had hoped to overcome in 1831, now became the bastion of Conservative principles on such issues as Ireland, the Church and the Corporations. 'It is needless to advert to my secession from the Whigs,' Graham told Granville Somerset on 17 December 1836. 'They retain the name, but . . . have changed their principles. I adhere to my principles and am indifferent to the name.' He continued to maintain that he had upheld true Whiggism against a degenerate (majority) version, for some time: Russell's battalion was out of step, while Stanley's section kept true time.

Ireland continued to be the great divider of the Whigs. Graham would not tolerate even modified versions of Whig–O'Connellite policy. 'A Tithe Bill without the Appropriation clause, introduced *by the present government*, would be a monster of political deformity', he told Hardinge, 'revolting even to the lax morals of the days of political expediency in which we live.' A Bill to reform the close Irish Corporations excited Graham to strong opposition in the spring of 1836; twenty-seven years later McCullagh Torrens thought that his hostility was Graham's 'most signal and lamentable, because the most gratuitous and uncompensated error . . .'. Graham had planned joint action with Stanley and Peel in February and doubted whether 'Ireland [was] fit for municipal institutions identical with those of England'.[13] The Government's theory was 'that it was necessary in legislation to proceed identically with all the three nations which formed the empire', he told the Commons sarcastically. Yet the Scottish 'municipal qualification [was fixed] at £10, and in England at rating and residency for two years and a half with payment of rates, which was generally admitted to be equivalent . . . yet the Bill for Ireland placed the qualification at £5. Where then was the alleged identity?' While O'Connell ostentatiously yawned,

Graham quoted de Tocqueville on the dangers of extending the franchise.

The root of Graham's belief was a conviction that Irish legislation should be considered in the context of Ireland's unique state: to pretend that 'what was good in one case must of necessity be good in another, without reference to circumstances, was . . . pedantry and imposture'. Furthermore, the Government's 'identical' policies were not in fact consistent: the Irish Reform Act differed from the English; even the present Bill gave police powers to the Crown instead of to the Irish Corporations; and Ministers had certainly treated the English and Irish Churches differently. Graham accepted past concessions but would go no further, believing that the new Corporations 'would become schools of treason and rebellion, the last fatal symptom preceding the overthrow of the Church and the dissolution of the legislative Union'. He recalled the recent dissolution of the Orange lodges and refused to 'repel threat by threat'. He wished 'to secure to all classes of the community, without reference to sect or creed, perfect freedom and the full enjoyment of their lives and properties, under equal laws, firmly and impartially administered'; but the Bill was 'an unconditional surrender of important means for securing these ends'. On 10 March the Government succeeded by 307 votes to 243. But Graham persevered in April debates, still defending his own Whiggish consistency and attacking the influence of demagogic O'Connellites. Again the Lords opposed the Ministry; although Richmond proposed a compromise, Lyndhurst rallied a Conservative majority. On 19 May even Graham regretted the impossibility of compromise, blaming Irish agitators' insatiable demands and regular threats. Irish Corporations were to cause further trouble.

Graham also worked as a member of a 'Select Committee on the State of Agriculture', which proposed to investigate the fall in cereal prices. Good harvests had considerably reduced farmers' prices and increased landowners' difficulties. Graham had strong views on the situation, but thought that the remedy did not lie with Free Trade. 'Although I assent to the abstract truth of many of your positions', he told Rooke on 25 January, 'yet I doubt the policy of throwing open the corn trade, when I consider the many and mighty burdens imposed on land in this country and the highly artificial state of society in which we live, with a debt of eight hundred millions, the interest of which is double the annual expenditure of the State.' To him, currency depreciation was still the panacea. But as the Committee could not agree it simply reported the evidence which it had heard. Graham complained about Ministerial inaction, but the depression was still lifting, as he admitted in April, when opposing Lord Chandos's motion to reduce agriculturalists' taxation. The lightening of current burdens appeared dangerous to Graham because it would only lead to new demands and weaken the case for Protection; and constant complaints by the Landed Interest would increase Radical hostility.[14]

As parliamentary life became increasingly frustrating, Graham's personal reputation and relationships developed even more distressingly. As a Minister he had carried an Act on Cabinet salaries and pensions. His successor, Auckland, had demanded £2,000 a year pension before giving up official salaries of £1,600 on accepting the post. On Auckland's resignation and move to India in September 1835 his stipulation became known. A rumour then spread that Graham's Act had provided a similar sum for himself. The story was completely untrue, for the Act excluded men with private incomes. But Graham could only dispose of the matter when Sir Edward Codrington raised it in the Committee on Naval Estimates. That such a slander should be uttered was perhaps a measure of Graham's own unpopularity. He had tried to cultivate good relations with rising politicians; for instance, in November 1833 Macaulay was surprised by his 'warmth of kindness'. But Graham roused little affection among most contemporaries, and strongly resented attacks by old colleagues. His resignation from Brooks's marked a further abandonment of Whiggism. But such breaks were less worrying than the decline of his mother, who died on 20 September. When his interests were at a low ebb, the ever-attentive son was overwhelmingly depressed by his loss.[15]

With a stalemate at Westminster and O'Connell's new General

Association growing in Ireland, 1837 opened gloomily. Graham went shooting at Netherby, refusing to support Peel as Lord Rector of Glasgow University but entertaining him on his return journey. No doubt he heard of growing local opposition. In August the Radical William James had succeeded Blamire without opposition, supported (to Graham's horror) by 'all my old Whig supporters'.[16] The Irish Church (as Greville had noted on 9 July) remained 'in one way or another the insuperable obstacle' to Irish peace and Ministerial stability. A developing financial crisis and the prospect of further long, balanced and ultimately futile debates suggested an even less attractive future.

When the Session began in February Stanley and Graham were again attacked as apostates. Lord Francis Egerton's motion against Irish municipal reform was again debated, and Graham used the opportunity to explain his views yet once more. Graham was no 'ultra' and hoped for a settlement; but the parties were too committed for manœuvre, and on the 25th the Government had a majority of 80. On 11 April, during the Third Reading, Graham even promised 'not [to] oppose the erection of municipal institutions, if they could only satisfy him that they could be granted with safety to the Church'. The Tithe Bill's appropriation clause (soon to be dropped) was a greater stumbling-block. And on 22 May Graham lengthily condemned Radical moves to abolish English Church rates. Party passions and hopes were high, and Graham provoked further exchanges (but eventually a mere legalistic quibble) with an investigation of a writ for a Glasgow election.

Graham's partisan energy inevitably annoyed old friends. Greville mused over Graham and Stanley's previous refusal of Peel because he might not be liberal enough; now, sure of offices in a Conservative Ministry, they would (he thought) bring Peel only 'an addition of bigotry and illiberality'. Peel's coldness would balance oddly with Stanley's 'intemperate and often injudicious vivacity'; but Graham's 'principles would not be found too inflexible'. The Whigs were shocked 'at the contrast between Graham's 'extreme violence' in 1831 and his current views; 'he was in fact the most ultra Liberal of Lord Grey's

Edward Stanley, Fourteenth Earl of Derby

Cabinet, and now he is little better than a Tory'. What a sophisticated diarist thought privately was more bluntly announced elsewhere. Sympathisers had already suggested a retreat from hostile Cumberland to Liverpool or Middlesex. But Graham would not run away: 'on the whole', he told Granville Somerset, 'my game is not desperate — and if it were, I cannot with honour retire unless defeated'. 'A violent attack on me here is inevitable and the result is doubtful', he admitted to Peel, 'but my honour is at stake . . . If I am to be turned out, defeat is more honourable than a surrender, and nothing can befall me which I did not anticipate . . .'[17]

Whatever the dangers ahead, Graham would not desert his supporters. A warning shot was fired in April, when the Rev. Thomas Ramshay and 202 Brampton district electors charged him with breaking his party allegiance and demanded his resignation. Graham retorted that 'he was not their delegate' and that 'they formed only a small portion of the great constituency'. But the Whig Press followed up the attack, and the Whiggish gentry, including even Lawson, left Graham's camp. The King's death on 20 June precipitated the threatened struggle. When Russell arrived at the Commons with the first message from the young Queen Victoria, the Speaker ordered Members to remove their hats. Watchful journalists noticed that Graham alone did not obey. Next day Graham explained that he had observed conventional etiquette by awaiting the mention of *Rex* or *Regina*. The Speaker admitted that he had been wrong. Graham, almost inevitably, was right.[18]

M

7

The Move to Conservatism

On Queen Victoria's accession the political situation somewhat
altered. The Government, long declining, hoped for the sympathy
or at least neutrality of the Crown; and both sides were prepared
to use the young Monarch's personal 'appeal' in election
propaganda. 'The object of the Whigs', wrote Greville, 'was to
remain in office, to put down the Radicals and Radicalism and go
on gradually and safely reforming', though some had 'more
extensive and less moderate views'. Meanwhile, the Tories were
'thirsting for office' and their impatience was restrained 'within
moderate bounds' only by 'the prudent reserve of Peel (in which
Stanley and Graham probably joined)'. An exciting election was
at hand. And Graham knew that his contest in East Cumberland
was virtually hopeless. The *Chronicle* urged electors to 'leave him
to the house of refuge of the Lowthers [for] a penitentiary would
not reclaim such a big offender'. Graham's defeat would give the
Whigs 'extreme satisfaction, for they hate him rancorously', wrote
Greville, who could understand their feelings about 'political
conduct . . . neither creditable nor consistent'. Durham claimed
to have extremist letters from Graham over the Reform Bill; yet
now Graham was a near-Tory, 'a very high Churchman and one
of the least liberal of the Conservative leaders'. If London Whigs
held such views, local men could scarcely be expected to be silent.
At a Carlisle meeting in June 1837, under Henry Howard,
Graham was strongly condemned; and 2,590 of the 4,688 electors
signed a requisition for Major Aglionby and James to contest the
seat.

In addition to the charge of deserting his principles, many
attacks were made on Graham. Yule's unpopular reorganisation
of Netherby was ascribed to a harsh squire. And Graham's

aloofness, even a gloved handshake, provided ammunition. He had made few preparations, but on 28 June issued an address from London claiming consistency and stressing his support of the Church. A second message appeared from Tory Edenhall on 3 July. Graham was not 'conscious of any departure from one principle' and would 'not fly from the threats of coalitions and subscriptions'. He was fighting bravely, but his self-justification was laboured (though largely accurate):

> Mr. Howard . . . has asserted . . . that my cause is identified with the anti-Reform principles of 1831. Allow me to observe that there was then no compact alliance between Lord Grey's Government and Mr. O'Connell; that the reformers of that day sought strictly to limit, not indefinitely to extend, the new portion of democratic influence they added to the constitution; and that the Whigs had not renounced the leading principle of the Revolution of 1688, which is the maintenance of the Reformed Protestant religion in every part of the United Kingdom.

He 'stood on his old ground' as 'an independent country gentleman'. But while doing little good locally the attack on Melbourne's relationship with O'Connell angered London Whigs. 'This was too bad,' Lord Tavistock told Greville: the Government's only 'understanding' with O'Connell was over Irish elections and Graham had been a Minister when only Lansdowne and Richmond had prevented O'Connell's entry into office. 'It was not extraordinary', thought Greville, that the Whigs should consequently hate Graham and the Tories 'rejoice in him'.

Graham had his back to the wall, and his courageous fight was one of the nobler episodes in his career. His attacking address of 6 July asked how Aglionby could support James's Radicalism and cast doubts on the requisition. But the yeomen whom he had so proudly represented had deserted him. The Whig *Journal* published regular attacks, notably a widely-quoted letter by 'John i' the Gate' (one Thomas Wannop) who assailed Graham's 'affected cant' and 'endless appeals to [his] conscience'. And the influential gentry had followed Aglionby, Lawson and the Howards. Some old friends remained loyal, however. 'The contest will be very severe', Graham desperately told Rooke (who, with

Matthews, voted for him), 'and every vote important; and if, on the whole, you think my principles sound and my conduct honest, I hope you will rescue me from this attempt to dismiss me like a worthless servant.' But it was mortifying to have to rely largely on Tory churchmen and the Lowthers, who sent their agent Billy Holmes. In the spring some religious crusader had daubed the Eden bridge with an admonition to 'Flee from the wrath to come'; and before the nomination a Whig partisan added 'Oh Netherby apostate'.[1]

<h1 style="text-align:center">I</h1>

Although there was a considerable swing to Conservatism elsewhere, East Cumberland held aloof. Whig and Radical united to attack Graham on every count, from his 'tergiversation' to his support of the unpopular 1834 Poor Law (though he and Richmond had opposed the establishment of the hated workhouse 'Bastilles').[2] On 3 August, as a great Whig horde entered Carlisle from Harraby Hill, Graham led his depleted cavalcade from Netherby. He reached the Court House with difficulty, amid fights and stone-throwing. The Whig leaders — Howard, John Gill, William Crackanthorpe and Salkeld — were pledged to James and Aglionby, and Graham was nominated by two Tories, Musgrave and Captain Thomas Irwin.

On the hustings Salkeld (himself to be an unsuccessful Conservative candidate in 1852) bitterly accused Graham of 'hypocritical cant', warning him that 'principle and political integrity could not always be abandoned with impunity'. Only appeals by Saul, the Under-Sheriff, and H. A. Aglionby secured a brief peace for Graham. He coolly defended himself (though young Henry Lonsdale, standing nearby, heard very little above the heckling) and attacked James and O'Connell. But the noise eventually prevented him from speaking. Twenty-five years later P. H. Howard thought that 'it was no doubt a mistake not to have persevered rather longer'. But at the time, amidst mounting violence (including the knocking-down of Graham's son), it seemed wise to leave the crowd and start canvassing.

If Lowther support could ensure a substantial Tory turn-out, victory might still be possible; the loss of one brother-in-law, Lawson, might be balanced by the support of another, Musgrave. But county visiting gave little cheer when old friends like Mrs. Stordy of Thrustonfield and Mrs. Twentyman of Hawksdale received him coldly. Holmes valiantly tried to rouse the Lowtherites, but, as he later explained, 'the Yellows could not be brought to forget [Graham's] conduct in 1831, [although Lonsdale], forgetting the past, did everything in his power for him'. The poll took place on 7 and 8 August, when Aglionby received 2,294 votes, James 2,124 and Graham 1,605. His native county had punished its erring Member.

The result was not unexpected. 'I have sustained here all the annoyance of a bitter contest and extensive canvass,' Graham told Peel in July:

all the influence of Greenwich Hospital and of the Government, subscriptions in London and in the country, the malignant hostility of the Press, the united forces of the Cavendishes and the Howards, outraged friends who are the most implacable of enemies, Whigs and Radicals, Dissenters and Unbelievers are banded against me . . .

Nevertheless, the blow — and the size of the majority — pained Graham. He had spent £4,000 on the contest and could not afford such expense again. 'I have been deceived and am defeated,' he announced in an address on the 10th. 'In the senate and in our own county, in office and in my private station, for twenty years I have laboured to advance your popularity; and it cannot be laid to my charge that I have, in any instance, from sloth neglected your business or sacrified your interest to my ambition. No!'[3] He returned to estate work, reading and extensive letter-writing (especially to Peel); but his long service to the county was ended, along with many old friendships.

Graham could not bear to leave political life and soon sought for a new seat. In September he stayed with Peel at Drayton, further extending a growing relationship. The Marquess of Exeter was willing to give him a Stamford seat, but Graham did not wish to enter any controversy over nomination boroughs. He firmly refused to consider contesting east Cumberland again, but on 4 January 1838 he was the Conservatives' guest at a dinner in the Bush Inn. Several hundred Tories and Netherby tenants with some Whig friends attended, under E. W. Hasell. 'Defeat itself was not half so painful as the circumstances attending it,' Graham bitterly told them: 'he did not suppose that he should be hunted almost like a mad dog through the streets ...' He talked of the Whig 'conspiracy' against him and of Melbourne's reliance on O'Connell. Personally, 'he held by the principles he professed in 1828, and he was neither bigot nor renegade, but averse to the downward path of revolution' — while the Howards had followed a Radical. And in a celebrated passage he declared that

> There may have been more wicked governments, there may have been more powerful and dangerous governments, but I defy any one to produce from the annals of our country a more shabby government than the present.

The three-hour speech was instantly successful, and Lord George Bentinck uged Graham to publish it. Graham soon decided to join the Cumberland Conservative Association, and, after thinking of a new 'sound, constitutional, independent newspaper', backed the *Carlisle Patriot*.

Negotiations for a seat continued. Hoping for a major constituency, Graham rejected James Freshfield's offer to vacate Falmouth. But after discussions with Stanley and Peel early in 1838 he obtained a nomination at Pembroke from Lord Cawdor. Here the ancient Owen family of Orielton had long controlled both county and borough seats, often sitting personally. Sir John Owen, M.P. for the county since 1809, now ordered his son, Colonel Hugh Owen, to make way for Graham in the town; sympathetic journalists asserted that local electors had demanded the change. Graham was elected unopposed in February and instantly confessed to Peel, 'I have ... departed from my good intention of allowing no vacancy to be made for me by private arrangement ... [but] my wish to sit beside you in the House of Commons has been stronger perhaps than my strict sense of right.' The arrangement was to be short-lived. In 1839 Sir John's debts led him to flee from his creditors and by 1841 he found it necessary to return to his borough seat.[4] But this was in the future. In March Graham gladly returned to Westminster.

II

The Government apparently had few plans. Peel thought in November that the Royal Address 'abused the privilege of saying nothing'. And Graham himself 'could not understand her Majesty'; surely, she 'must have been struck with the ungenerous baseness of the conduct of her Ministers . . . Yet Melbourne would seem to enjoy her favour in a high degree.'[5] The Queen's close friendship with her Prime Minister was to be of some importance.

Parliament was again noisy, with arguments over the Ballot, Canada and the elections. Graham quickly entered the fray, working increasingly closely with the Conservatives. On 12 March he opposed Hume's attacks on Lord Lichfield (the Postmaster-General) for alleged nepotism, but condemned Ministers' general abuse of patronage. And he arrived in time for the third introduction of the Irish Corporations Bill. Tory hostility to Irish legislation was becoming unpopular, and Wellington, Peel and Graham tried to plan a compromise. Wellington, indeed, went further, rejecting the half-way scheme devised at a series of party gatherings and preferring to swallow the Irish Corporations. Eventually, the Conservative leaders resolved to accept both the Corporation and Tithe Bills, if appropriation were dropped. The Government adopted this scheme, and although old rivalries sometimes flared up during the debates and past speeches were recalled, the compromise measures were ultimately passed.

Attendance at the planning meetings of the increasingly organised Conservative party involved Graham in considerable work, especially in deciding how to avoid contact with the Radicals. But he was also assiduous in parliamentary work. On 24 May he complained of the violent riots at the Roxburgh election. On 21 July he proposed that the new Railway Bill should allow arbitrators to consider companies' capital costs when deciding mail charges. But the session provided few excitements: the Queen's Coronation in June provided more interest than did the debates. 'Stanley and Graham have said little or nothing,' wrote Greville on 23 August, believing that the parties' rough equality prevented 'any great triumph on either side'. Privately, Graham was worried over Russell's apparent conversion to the Ballot. 'My part was taken at the passing of the Reform Act,' he told Tavistock. 'I pledged myself to resist the Ballot, short Parliaments and further extension of the Suffrage.' However hopeless his cause might seem, he was determined to stand by his 'fixed principles'.[6]

In January O'Connell had denounced Graham at Dublin for not fighting O'Gorman Mahon. This challenge to 'honour' quickly roused Graham. 'When Friendship, tried Principles and sound Judgment are necessary, I naturally turn to you,' he told Hardinge, who consulted Wellington, Peel and Stanley. Hardinge dissuaded Graham from writing to O'Connell's chairman (Lord Charlemont) and asked Stanley to urge Spencer to explain the full story. Spencer generously complied, telling Charlemont that Graham had acted 'by his advice and under his directions'. Other friends also denied that Graham had made any 'base and trickling apology' to avoid a duel. 'The atrocity of O'Connell's attempt to affix a stigma upon you', wrote Hardinge, 'is only to be equalled by the heartless hypocrisy with which he pretends that Christian feelings and penitence caused him, after he had killed his antagonist, to register a vow in Heaven never to lift his hand again against the life of a fellow creature.' O'Connell had only become 'more blustering, quarrelsome and foul mouthed'; Peel 'had a year's correspondence and a volume of printed letters with this blackguard fellow in his case . . .' Honour was salved by the publication of Spencer's letters.[7]

Party bitterness did not, however, prevent the maintenance of some old friendships. Graham corresponded regularly with Tavistock, who 'always regretted that [Graham had] quitted the neutral ground he occupied to take up a hostile position with the Tories'. When Russell's wife died, Graham wrote movingly to his former colleague. 'Stanley and Graham are two men for whom I shall always retain cordial feelings of attachment,' Russell then told Tavistock. 'I cannot, when I part from a friend, go to St. James's coffee-house and get a new one. I hanker after my old affections and am very slow with my new ones.' Graham, deeply moved, 'felt over again the real bitterness of the pang which separated him from John Russell'. But, he told Tavistock, 'the permanent occupation of neutral ground was impossible', although he 'still hoped to preserve the remains of friendship'. The Queen herself rejoiced to hear of such friendly relationships. But, as usual, Graham's interest was not wholly sentimental. A recent letter from Tavistock, he told Stanley, 'makes it clear to me that John Russell, or rather Tavistock for him, is anxious to keep open, as the *last* Resort, a friendly and confidential channel of communication with the Conservative party'.[8]

The year ended with a novel experience. In October Colquhoun told Graham that he was likely to be nominated as the students' Rector of Glasgow University. Graham hoped, however, that Wellington would stand. He knew Glasgow and Lanarkshire through his friendship with the Duke of Hamilton, feared that he 'would be opposed with more than ordinary bitterness' and firmly opposed the 'reformism' of Dr. Thomas Chalmers and a majority in the General Assembly, who were now condemning lay patronage in the Scottish Church. 'When I reflect on the certain tendency of the course on which the General Assembly is now entering', he told Stanley,

> and when I foresee that, unless they stop short in this career, they will surrender the key of our strength in Scotland, ruin the Kirk itself and seriously endanger the Church of England, I feel that I am ill fitted to bear a high office in a University closely connected with the existing authorities of the Kirk . . .

He doubted whether Chalmers's group would still support him, but in November, having informed his 'principal friends' of his 'strong opinion on the Patronage question', was 'told that this was no objection and that probably he should be elected'. He then accepted nomination.

Stanley warmly supported Graham's cause: 'at all events', he wrote, 'your election after a frank avowal of your views will be a significant indication to [the General Assembly]'. The once Whiggish university had accepted a 'conservative' dominance with the election of Stanley in 1834 and Peel in 1836.[9] But Graham's opponent was the eccentric, liberal-minded Duke of Sussex, the sixth son of King George III. After a bitter struggle, on 15 November the Principal, Professor MacFarlane, told Graham that he had been elected. John Morier, his campaign organiser, jubilantly told him that he had won by 273 votes to 209.

The result was gratifying, both personally and politically. 'If this can be taken as an index of the feeling of the middle classes in Scotland, it is very consoling,' Graham told Stanley. 'At all events, it is a proof that the rising youth entertains sound and decided principles; and when they prefer a country gentleman to the Queen's favourite uncle, they rescue their countrymen from the charge of time-serving sycophancy and of interested calculation.' But he refused to attend celebration dinners with the Peel Club and the Edinburgh Tories, considering it the best policy to await a clash between the Whigs and Radicals.[10] A university election still seemed politically important, and friends hastened to congratulate Graham. Hamilton invited him to his palace; Goodenough talked of 'the *glorious* result'. To Stratford Canning 'the triumph was not the less satisfactory for being connected with the progress of conservative opinions, not the less brilliant for being achieved at the expense of a Royal competitor'. And Peel welcomed his successor.[11]

There remained the troublesome inauguration. Morier warned Graham against commenting on the Auchterarder case, in which a lay patron's nominee had been rejected by his congregation in 1834 and had therefore appealed to various courts. The legal battle had become a vital struggle in the Kirk and was difficult for an Englishman fully to comprehend. 'It is my decided opinion that in your inauguration speech . . . you should not launch upon this matter at all,' wrote Morier. Graham chose to ignore this advice at the ceremony on 21 December. 'I could not shrink from it', he told Stanley of his invitations, 'and expose myself to the

charge that I sought a hole and corner. I wish the whole affair were
well over; and the day of my return will be far happier than the
day of my departure.' He delivered lengthy and innocuous eulogies
of academic life and warnings on wasted opportunities; and then
he praised the constitutions of the Kirk and Court of Session
(which had upheld the Auchterarder minister's appeal) as
examples of beneficial connections between Church and State.
Near uproar between rival factions led to a hasty ending of the
speech. Yet, Graham told Stanley, 'the Glasgow affair was
successful'. He received the freedom of the city (which had to be
purchased from the churlish Corporation for Peel in 1836) and
was well received by the citizens in the Trades Hall.[12]

Although 'none but Scotch Reporters were present, and it was
clear that they did not yet understand English, when spoken
without the drone of a Bagpipe', friends delighted in reports of
Graham's address. It was a 'brilliant success' to Stanley, 'a most
excellent exposition' to Lord Wharncliffe, 'a masterpiece of
vigorous yet discreet cutting up' to Hardinge, a 'complete success'
to Peel. Baron Alderson of the Exchequer Court was 'highly
pleased' and added:[13]

> I look on all these things as working out a favourite theory of mine
> that Principle not Expediency must ultimately prevail and govern
> the people of this Kingdom. And I trust that your success will give
> confidence to your leader, whose weak point, believe me, is that he
> is too fond of the (immediate) Expedient. That which is *ultimately*
> Expedient is only another word for an adherence to fixed and good
> Principles.
>
>   You see that I call Peel your leader — trusting to the Reports
> of your speech at Glasgow — and in truth he will soon be your only
> leader in the House of Commons, for Lord Stanley is clearly soon
> destined for the House of Lords.

The dreaded Glasgow visit had, in fact, been a considerable
success. In the centre of Scottish Liberalism Graham had defended
the Established Kirk to the University and the 'finality' of the
Reform Act to the city.

Alderson was partly wrong; Derby, though ill, was not dying.
Graham made a similar mistake. He had been asked by Stanley

to invite Lord Douglas to contest North Lancashire, but found Douglas's father very ill. 'I should say that Ld. Derby will survive the Duke of Hamilton', he wrote, 'and I am quite certain that . . . you must look to some other arrangement, since in the present state of the Duke's health, even if he live, Lord Douglas would never think of embarking in a serious contest.' Stanley's uncle, Edmund Hornby, 'is by far the best Candidate that you could produce, and I doubt whether Towneley would dare to fight him on the single vacancy', explained Graham — though Hornby would need financial help and his son, 'young Edmund, I fear, is an impracticable Radical and out of the Question . . .' By such careful help Graham demonstrated his still close alliance with Stanley: 'every thing which affects your happiness is felt warmly by me,' he wrote. But Alderson correctly forecast Peel's growing influence. 'I value more highly than I can express your friendship and good opinion', Graham told Peel, 'and amidst the change and dangers which surround us on every side I rejoice in the conviction that I possess your esteem and in the hope that I shall never forfeit it.'[14]

III

Peel prophesied that 'Corn Laws, Canadian affairs and Lord Durham [who had recently returned from Canada after angrily resigning his Governor-Generalship] will be the most prominent Topics of debate at the Beginning of the Session, unless some fresh atrocities in Ireland or some disaster in India force Ireland or India into immediate Notice'. Graham, as usual, approached the Session in sombre mood. 'The opening of every Session brings with it the general impression that a crisis of unusual importance is at hand', he told Peel,

yet, making an abatement on this score, I cannot help feeling that the present Emergency is very awful. The state of Ireland, the price of provisions, the cry for cheap Bread raised by the Govt., the angry temper of the manufacturing community, the reckless profligacy of the Ministers, the active participation of the Crown itself in the most disastrous Policy, form a combination of adverse circumstances which baffles human foresight and crushes confidence.

In the industrial areas the long refusal of the Government to amend either the 1833 Factory Act or the Poor Law had encouraged older agitations to merge in a wider Radicalism. The varying strands of Chartism demanded more than the six points of political reform postulated by the Charter; the factory operatives and the ever-declining handworkers dreamed of wider social and industrial reforms. From Manchester the Chartists' rivals, the predominantly Liberal cotton-masters, were mounting a campaign against the Corn Laws and against the aristocratic interests which allegedly supported them. Both groups of agitators were prepared to utter violent threats against both Government and established institutions. Graham was not frightened of imaginary dangers.

Graham was now becoming a Peelite Conservative and his views at this time were explained in detail to Peel:

The Canadian and Foreign Difficulties, excepting the State of Parties in France, are to be ascribed in great measure to the wayward conduct of our own Govt. and would vanish, as I hope, under the influence of the steady Counsels and firmer Policy which you and the Duke of Wellington would impart to any administration you might form. But the Domestic difficulties would come to a Head at once, and you would have upon your Heads, before the Administration was well formed, a Catholic Insurrection in Ireland and a movement of the masses in Great Britain. I believe that Property would rally round you: but in our highly artificial state of society one week of suspension of Credit, of cessation of Labour, of interrupted communications and consequent famine, would present such a scene of havoc, of bloodshed and horrors as the civilised world has not yet witnessed: and when I look out of my window and see all my finest and oldest Trees prostrate, their size the growth of a century, their destruction the work of an hour's hurricane, I fear I see the emblem of our Country after a week of civil tumult. I do not say this to dishearten; but it is wise to be forewarned, and this consideration bears directly on the question of active measures to overthrow and displace the Government. When the Storm runs high, it is one thing to take the Helm, when the Steersman runs from it, another to wrest it out of his hands and by force, as it were, to take charge of the vessel . . .

He was concerned at the 'health and age' of the Duke, who could be a 'Tower of strength'. And the Government seemed to be moving to Radical policies:

> Every day throws fresh light on the intention . . . to raise the question of Corn Laws: whether they mean to go out on it or to dissolve is not so clear: the decision on this latter point must be influenced by the division in the Commons. As at present advised, I do not think we can refuse to join issue in defence of the present Corn Law. I believe it to be the best Protection of Agriculture which can be devised, and without Protection the greatest interests in this Country will be involved in ruin and confusion. When Principle is attacked, it is dangerous to talk of concessions in detail. I know not whether the scale of duties may be perfect, but the principle of a vanishing scale is the vital point, and no 'fixed duty' would be to any avail when prices from scarcity become high . . . With these discussions in view, I think it is rather a fortunate circumstance that Lord Chandos has been withdrawn from us in the Commons: while every protection which Agriculture really requires must be defended, every concession which can be made to Trade, in its close rivalry with foreign skill and industry, is justly due. The tax on the import of raw cotton is most impolitic and indefensible, and a substitute for this tax, in which Land should bear its share ought to be provided.

On Opposition tactics Graham was 'in exact accordance' with Peel:[15]

> Without regard to possible consequences in both Houses, we must resist every proposal which in our conscience we consider to be dangerous; we ought to be most careful in originating any motion intended to displace them; we should steadily avoid all concert and private communication with the Radicals; we should touch Brougham like hot iron with pitch on it; but directly or indirectly, let the Motion come from what Quarter it may, we must avoid a single vote which implies the least confidence in the men entrusted by the Queen with the Government. With a Dissolution in view, the grand object is to keep the Conservative party united and in good heart. Any marked fear of undertaking the government, or

any wish evinced to shelter the present Administration, would
therefore be fatal. But on the other hand any eagerness to seize
power would be a most dangerous indiscretion. The course lies
between the two shoals. It is a narrow one, but under your
guidance I am not afraid, if the crew are under command and will
implicitly obey you.

Graham could become a Conservative, though not a Tory. And
his long search for a leader had reached its goal.

IV

Despite high expectations, Graham's career was comparatively
quiet in the early months of 1839. 'The Government', recorded
Greville on New Year's Day, 'is in a wretched state of weakness,
utterly ignorant whether it can scramble through the session . . .
tottering and staggering between one great party and one fierce
faction, and just able to keep on its legs because both are, for
different reasons, willing to wound but afraid to strike.' On the
same day the Earl of Norbury was murdered at Kilbeggan, and
further arguments began over Ireland. 'Protestantism is the only
weapon with which we can encounter Republicanism,' Graham
insisted to Bonham. Lingering hopes of defeating the Ministry
soon evaporated, although Greville thought that 'a pretty correct
analysis' of M.P.s gave 267 'Government people, including the
Irish tail', 66 Radicals, 5 doubtfuls and 315 Conservatives, with
four vacancies. As usual Graham was 'very gloomy', wrote Peel.

Graham remained interested in Ireland. 'It is quite clear', he
told Sergeant Jackson of Dublin,

> that the Roman Catholics have basely cheated all those Protestants
> who trusted them when the grant of equal Civil Rights was
> conceded . . . It is impossible to overstate the moral turpitude of
> this conduct or to adduce more conclusive evidence of the altered
> Spirit and debasing Influence of the Romish Creed; and the warning
> is impressive against the concession of further Power to a Religion
> so dangerous, so deceitful and so encroaching.

He was also angered by attacks on his reform of the Marine
Artillery and the Coast Guard and demanded the relevant

Admiralty papers from Lord Minto.[16] In March he called for the transfer of the Mediterranean Fleet to American waters.

The 'new' controversies now became more important. On 4 February the anti-Corn Law agitators held a London conference, after which their delegates called on various politicians. Graham had no sympathy with their demands: Repeal would ruin British agriculture. A short parliamentary debate on the subject was spoiled for the Repealers by George Wood's talk of national prosperity. C. P. Villiers's annual Free Trade motion was easily defeated on 20 March, after what Greville considered an 'extremely long and dull' debate. Graham lengthily defended Protection — and his own former defence of a fixed duty, which was quoted by Poulett Thomson — recalling that he had supported Huskisson in 1821 and 1828, drawn up the 1833 report, supported the Corn Law in 1834 and opposed Russell's fixed duty plan in 1836. He admitted that his 1826 pamphlet contained 'many errors' and 'held himself no longer bound by any part of that publication [as] he should always endeavour to deal with all questions ... as he thought the necessity of the time and the interests of the country demanded'. But low corn prices involved low wages, unemployment and a general decline in consumption. Thomson,[17]

> in the lofty phraseology of the economists, spoke of labour as a commodity and as though labourers were without feelings, habits or attachments; that they might be dealt with as machines; and that as long as they could find employment they would be content to receive it in any part of the country. Oh! let the House well reflect before they took any steps which directly or indirectly tended to these displacements of labour. Little could they estimate the wretchedness which sprang from change of habit, of house, of manners, of the mode of life itself ... The proposed change ... was the first step towards making England the workshop of the world, dependent for its daily food upon foreign supplies ... were it to succeed, he should say with his friend Lord Ashburton that this was the last country which he should wish to inhabit.

Graham thus gave a standard defence of agricultural Protection. Ireland again affected politics, however. On 21 March the Orange

Sir Robert Peel

leader Lord Roden narrowly secured a Committee on the state of
Ireland since 1835. 'John Russell has just announced to the House
that . . . he himself will take the sense of this House . . .' Graham
told Stanley next day. The Government treated the Lords'
motion as a question of confidence, and Russell (wrote Graham),

> says that Melbourne only holds office while he retains the
> confidence of the Commons . . . The rumour was general that they
> intended to resign, and I had a communication from Young,
> Melbourne's secretary, last night, which led me to believe they
> wished to take this course; but after a long deliberation they have
> adopted this other alternative . . .

Graham wondered whether the debate might not be extended to
cover 'the state of the nation', but Peel would 'come to no
decision whatever until [Stanley] and the Duke of Wellington
returned to London'. Stanley was with his ailing father, but
Graham gave him exciting news:

> Hume has announced that he shall be at Paris . . . and I think it is
> becoming every hour more doubtful whether the Radicals will
> come to the rescue. It will be retributive justice with a vengeance
> if a vote of confidence sought gratuitously by the Ministers should
> end in a declaration of the want of it . . . yet the risk is imminent
> that this will be their fate. Peel, I think, inclines not to evade the
> Irish Question but to repeat in moderate terms our Policy with
> regard to that Country and to add an expression in distinct terms
> of disapprobation of the general conduct of the Government.

The scent of victory drove Graham's usual caution from his mind.

The wily Greville, though considering the Cabinet 'the most
second-rate one this country ever saw', thought it would be
disastrous for Peel to gain office on Irish controversies. 'A pretty
scrape you would have been in if Government had resigned upon
this vote,' he told Graham, who 'shrugged up his shoulders and
said "I own I am better pleased as it is."' Hearing that the overworked, mourning and pessimistic Russell might support a
moderate Ministry under Peel, Greville called on Graham on 9
April, to urge that Conservative attacks should be toned down.
Graham was apparently impressed by the chance of uniting

N

Whigs and Conservatives against 'the movement', though
sceptical of its reality. Stanley welcomed the suggestion, but Peel
was 'excessively annoyed and *put out*' at the loss of an oratorical
triumph, though realising the importance of Graham's report: 'he
must go down to the House of Commons with two speeches,' he
told Stanley. In the debate on the 15th the leading Conservatives
acted moderately and the Radicals, though threatening, helped
to save the Ministry.

The Government survived the Irish vote by 330 to 308, but on
5 May Greville noted that 'the Jamaica Bill is about to produce a
fresh crisis much more difficult to get over than the last . . .'[18]
Graham, with help from Wellington, Arbuthnot, Ellenborough
and Wellesley, had been preparing to attack Auckland's warlike
policy in Afghanistan, but withdrew his motion when the
adventures led to British military defeats. The battle with the
Government took a new turn early in May, when the Conservatism of Russell's *Letter to the Electors of Stroud* shocked many
Radicals. On 6 May Russell proposed, as a compromise settlement of Cabinet differences, to suspend the Jamaican Constitution for five years, ostensibly because of the Assembly's refusal
to accept a Prison Act and actually because of threatening racial
violence. The Government had a majority of only five votes and
promptly resigned. Melbourne advised the Queen to summon
Wellington, who recommended Peel. The breach between the
Whigs and Radicals, which Greville thought essential, was not
yet made. But the Queen, tearful at losing her avuncular Premier,
unwillingly accepted the reluctant Peel on 8 May. In the evening
Peel met his leading colleagues, including Wellington, Lyndhurst,
Stanley and Graham, who were to manage the Foreign Office,
Chancery, Colonies and Home Office respectively. But Tory
rejoicing was premature. Complaining that they wished to treat
her like a girl the Queen determined to 'show them that she was
Queen of England', by refusing to change her Ladies of the
Household. 'I have stood by you, and now you must stand by me,'
she told Russell; and the Whigs resolved to support her. The
bedchamber crisis drove out Peel, and (to the Queen's pleasure)
Melbourne returned to office. Graham was appalled. He shared

Croker's 'apprehensions and sad forebodings', he wrote on the 22nd: 'the Crown in alliance with Democracy baffled every calculation . . .'[19]

The next crisis was over education. Since 1833 small State grants had been made to the Anglican and Nonconformist voluntary societies in England and to Scottish educationalists. Now Russell proposed to establish a central board to control public expenditure and a central training college. Churchmen, Methodists and Tories protested at such Erastianism, and Peel, Stanley, Ashley and the Bishops fought against any weakening of the Church's control over its extensive educational system. Graham could not approve of grants to Dissenters: 'if aid was to be granted to dissenting teachers, how could it be denied to dissenting chapels, and how could endowments be refused to Socinian chapels?' For him, education must rest on religion, and the State's duty was to promote the system of its partner, the Church. Although a Committee of the Privy Council on Education was established, the Opposition succeeded in preventing any further extension of secular control.[20]

Recent disappointments rankled with some Tories. On 31 May Brougham flayed the Government in the Lords, in a 'boiling torrent of rage, disdain and hatred', but Wellington annoyed many of his supporters by ignoring the outburst and assuring Melbourne of support if he maintained his promised moderation. Greville noted that the Duke's statement 'exasperated his own people to the greatest degree', producing 'a sulky article in *The Times* and the usual complaints at White's and the Carlton of the Duke's being in his dotage . . .' But he 'entirely concurred' with Wellington's view that 'a Tory triumph' should not be achieved 'at the expense of the highest Tory principle' by endangering the Monarchy. Graham, however, was furious. Wellington's speech had 'produced a great effect and given rise to doubts and uncertainty among our friends, at a juncture when a Dissolution is impending and when confidence is of primary importance', he told Wellington's associate, Arbuthnot:[21]

It was natural that the Duke should be anxious to disclaim all alliance or tacit understanding with Brougham . . . [but] he

probably went further than he originally intended, and protected
Melbourne to an extent of which at the moment he might hardly
be aware . . . It is asked, then, what are the intentions of the Duke?
Is he prepared to grant to Ministers an amnesty for the past? Does
he wish to avert their overthrow? These are the doubts which fill
the mind of every man who has read the speech.

Graham was convinced that the Opposition should use every
weapon, although he had favoured moderation in January.
Arbuthnot understood his concern. 'I am in despair,' he replied.
'I have not known what to do. I resolved on writing to the Duke
in a way that would not hurt him and still would show him that
great evil would arise from what he has done . . . Intimate as I am
with him, I must ever bear in mind who and what he is.' Russell's
expected acceptance of the Ballot as an open question to maintain
Radical support made the matter more serious in Graham's eyes:
the 'fatal Bill' would be 'the death-warrant of the Monarchy and
of the Landed Interest'. But Arbuthnot would not hurt Wellington by reporting further criticisms. The Duke had been 'deeply
wounded by the censures . . . He had dreaded lest Lord
Melbourne should have to give way and retire before his more
Radical colleagues; and this it was which induced him to speak
as he did'. Arbuthnot was glad when Graham called on
Wellington. 'I really believe, from what you now tell me', he wrote,
'that the language the Duke held gave some support to Melbourne
against some of his more Radical colleagues; and if this be so,
great good may arise from it.'[22]

Wellington, in fact, was probably right; and Graham, now an
eager partisan, was for once too optimistic. 'He is very proud of
his foresight,' Graham told Stanley. 'His secret information on
this occasion has not failed him.' And other affairs were pros-
pering. Russell's education scheme had failed. 'A grave question
of nice discretion now presents itself', wrote Graham,

which is, shall we become the Assailants and address the Crown for
the Revocation of the Order in Council appointing the Committee
of Education? — or shall we be satisfied with our present Triumph
and resist the new principle of Distribution of the £30,000 to be
granted . . . ? . . . Never was a Government so knocked about as

this has been in the last week, and next week we probably shall beat them on the Jamaica and Canada questions . . .

Stanley agreed that 'the Duke is a great Diplomatist. I don't know how the F.O. might have suited him, but he is evidently great in the Home Department.' But Graham remained worried about lay control and inspection of education. 'I think we need move no Amendment,' he told Stanley. 'There is ample ground for resisting this proposal.' On 7 June, however, he found the new version 'hardly less objectionable than the first'.[23] The appeal to the Crown was rejected.

As angry discussions opened in July over Birmingham riots the Opposition appeared to have the Government in its power. But Graham was unwilling to desert principles to overthrow the Ministers, and refused to join the Tory–Radical campaign against the Poor Law. On the other hand, he favoured a mitigation of the severity of the workhouse 'test', particularly for widows and sometimes for able-bodied unemployed men. In his own Longtown Union, he told the Commons on 22 July, it had been vital in 1838 to relieve the hand weavers. Typically, though he knew of faults in any strict 'Benthamite' application of the Act, he resisted the temptation to make party capital out of them.

Before leaving London Graham called on Wellington. 'I never remember our party in better humour or more united,' he then told Arbuthnot. 'The firm and decided measures of hostility [to the Government] adopted by the Duke, tempered with his never-failing prudence, have greatly contributed to produce this happy result.'[24] Graham returned home with rare pleasure.

V

Many problems still confronted Graham. Young W. E. Gladstone, a Tory and High Churchman, had published a volume on *The State in its Relation with the Church* in 1838 and was now deeply concerned about a new Church Discipline Bill. Although disappointed in February that Peel, Graham and Stanley had never mentioned his book, he approached Graham about the Bill, which was 'a fatal wound to the most essential principles of our

Church government, without attaining any single object of utility . . .' He was glad that Graham agreed with his opposition to a measure which 'filled him with sorrow and amazement'.

Owen's troubles caused Graham some alarm. In September Cawdor warned him of the danger to his seat. 'It is probable that I shall be compelled to relinquish my seat', Graham replied, 'but in the present uncertain state of affairs it would be unwise in me prematurely to form a decision, as by making any application elsewhere to create the necessity of a change which may even yet be avoided.' He confidentially gave the details to Somerset and Bonham ('who directed their attentions to Elections generally') — 'and in case of necessity they would be on the outlook for some port under his lee'. But although Owen was 'overthrown', Graham still trusted his own supporters. 'If, however, Sir J. Owen or his son intimated to him a wish that he should not stand again, he should hold himself in honour bound at once to comply . . .'

Cabinet changes in August and September appeared to do nothing to strengthen the Government and were 'received with considerable indifference', Greville observed, 'nobody much caring and the generality of people finding fault with some or all of them'. Lady Holland's statement that the Government had 'nothing to rely upon but the Queen and Paddy' struck him as 'epigrammatic but very correct'. Stanley believed that Russell and Lord Ebrington would be 'the only two of the present Government who would have increased their reputation by holding office'. Graham agreed: Russell alone had 'first-rate abilities, [but] his talents and many virtues were debased by his love of party, which was stronger than his principles'.[25]

The summer's optimism gradually yielded to bitterness in the Tory ranks, and local associations took to blaming the Queen. The Government's majority was 'very small, but I consider it sure', Graham sadly told Stanley in November:[26]

> The Radicals, when it comes to a pinch, to a man will rally round them. O'Connell will stand by them to the last extremity, and the Queen almost identifies their existence with her own. On our side also there are some serious difficulties. The declining health of the Duke, our position in the House of Lords when he is gone, the

hostility of the Queen, but above all the mad impatience and indiscretion of a large mass of the party, are more than enough to counteract all the caution of Peel. In such circumstances, it will be most difficult to keep the party together. Yet in the country it is gaining strength.

By December Graham and his friends were rejoicing at Wellington's recovery — whatever his indiscretions, the old man was still a national hero — and planning tactics over the grant to the Queen's future husband, Prince Albert of Saxe-Coburg.

When Peel solicited his colleagues' views on policy for 1840, Wellington and Stanley favoured moderation, while Graham (noted Peel) was 'more inclined . . . on account of the position of the party, to hostile measures'. Graham certainly believed that the Duke's 'age and growing infirmities' made him too cautious. 'The constant legitimate object of an Opposition was the overthrow of an Administration which they considered bad and hoped to replace by a better'; and perpetual opposition would break any party. 'The possession of power in our popular form of government is the sole object of political warfare', he insisted to Stanley, '. . . Let it once transpire that you are afraid to take the government, and your party is gone.' Despite Wellington's reluctance, Greville found 'boiling impatience in the party, indoors and out';[27] and when Parliament met in January Sir John Yarde-Buller gave notice of a motion of no confidence.

On 29 January the Government's proposal to grant £50,000 a year to Prince Albert came under fire. Hume's suggestion of £21,000 was rejected but the eccentric Tory Colonel Sibthorp's figure of £30,000 was carried by a majority of 104. After participating in this bitter debate, next day Graham spoke on Yarde-Buller's motion, attacking Ministers over their divisions on the Ballot, the suffrage, Protection, appropriation and Ireland; Greville thought it was 'one of his usual speeches'. After four nights the Government won by 308 votes to 287.

Despite this militant start, the Opposition — and the Commons as a whole — was soon divided over the question of privilege raised by the celebrated case of Stockdale v. Hansard. In a series of actions since 1837 the Court of Queen's Bench had rejected

Messrs. Hansard's claim of parliamentary authority as justification for publishing libels on J. J. Stockdale in official papers. But when the sheriffs executed the court's writ they were committed by the Commons for contempt and breach of privilege. R. V. Richards's demand for a writ of Habeas Corpus on 23 January heightened the drama. The Whigs and Peel supported the claim of privilege, while 'the great bulk of the Tories and all the second-rate lawyers' were on the other side. Graham deeply regretted 'the evil which would probably flow from their fatal disunion', he told Arbuthnot, after supporting Peel: 'if honestly we could have taken the opposite course we should have destroyed the Administration'. But in February he felt that Peel was 'most imprudent' in asserting privilege and told Stanley that 'the Ministers evidently feel that they have a wedge by which they will split the Conservative Party'. It was 'curious that Peel, who often was languid in his attack on his adversaries, put forth superior energy and strength when he combated his followers'.[28] Wellington's followers ultimately accepted Peel's line in April, and the privilege question was settled by legislation, after long efforts by Graham to heal the party's divisions. The division had amounted, at least, to an unpleasant augury; but for Graham there was now no possible leader but Peel.

During a debate on Exchequer pensions on 27 February Graham caused an argument by attacking the incompetent policies of Spring Rice (now Lord Monteagle). 'I never saw John Russell so angry,' he told Arbuthnot.[29] On 26 March he supported Stanley's Irish Registration Bill, designed to prevent unqualified voting. The Government lost by 250 votes to 234, but Stanley had a majority of only three in Committee in May and his controversial measure was not enacted. But, apart from peace-making among his colleagues, Graham's major interest was currently in foreign affairs.

Thwarted in his attempts to prevent the Afghan War, Graham was now determined to condemn Palmerston's bellicose attitudes towards China, where 'incidents' had occurred in 1839. Britain's interest, he maintained on 7 April, lay in 'consulting the feelings and respecting the prejudices of a people who had continued to be excellent customers, but whom it was very undesirable we should ever have either as foes or tributaries'. The Government, he thought, had needlessly insulted the Chinese, tacitly sanctioned the opium trade and misdirected the Superintendent at Canton and now faced the possibility of an unnecessary and distant war. Quite apart from party advantage, many old Tories opposed imperialistic ventures on principle, as products of brash manufacturers' minds. But after three nights' debate, the Government won by 271 votes to 261. The narrow majority was encouraging for the Conservatives. But when Lord Stanhope raised the question in the Lords, after hostilities had begun, Wellington stoutly supported the Ministers. Graham's attempts to prevent war seemed to be doomed to be too late. Wellington's speech 'put [him] in a mortifying position', thought Greville on 17 May, 'for (it) was a complete answer . . .' Foreign affairs were not to be Graham's *métier*; but he was apparently most concerned that he might have offended Macaulay, the new Secretary at War.

Divided over Privilege, Ireland and China, the Conservatives faced another party difficulty on the Bill to follow Durham's recommended union of Upper and Lower Canada. Graham 'foresaw very serious difficulty', as Peel supported and Wellington opposed the measure. The Duke feared that union would lead to Canadian independence — as, indeed, it ultimately did. But in the end, after making his own protests, he persuaded the Peers not to reject the proposal in July. As over the Irish municipalities, he sacrificed his predilections to save party unity. 'We serve the noblest leader that ever led any army or a party to victory,' Lord Ellenborough then told Graham. Yet, though Wellington generously gave way in the last resort, Graham was concerned to bridge the gap between the Conservative leaders, who so often differed and so rarely met. He and Stanley always hoped 'to promote the union of the great party which admitted them so generously . . .' They respected their leaders, and, he told Arbuthnot, 'no sane man could contemplate a Conservative Government without the Duke'. Arbuthnot then urged them to consult Wellington regularly. 'I have known upon many occasions that Lord Stanley and you were the persons chiefly consulted by

Peel', he wrote, protectively, 'and upon all occasions I have seen that the Duke had the same feeling.' Arbuthnot spent some time trying to convince Graham that the Opposition leaders were not so far apart as he feared; and Graham kept Peel informed of the correspondence.[30]

VI

As Ministers trembled in the summer at the likelihood of Palmerston involving them in a Middle Eastern war, Graham worked hard to heal Conservative differences. He was eventually convinced that Wellington and Peel, though apparently remote, could and would work closely together. And in January 1841 he formally signified his own complete allegiance by joining the Carlton Club, on the nomination of Somerset and Hardinge. It was 'a proof of cordiality and perfect union', and Stanley followed him.[31]

The 1841 Session opened pleasantly for the Tories with several by-election victories. It seemed that the only major problem was the method of the Government's death, one strong possibility being the Irish registration, on which Stanley and Morpeth promoted rival Bills. Graham was 'ready cheerfully to be guided by [Peel's] opinion' on strategy. When, at Howick's suggestion, Greville approached him on 12 February, he 'soon found there was no possibility' of compromise. Graham 'expressed the greatest alarm and disgust at Morpeth's measure [which would extend the franchise] . . . he would never consent to transfer power from the landed interest to the multitude' and bitterly condemned the priest-politicians. On the 24th he opposed Morpeth in the Commons, and the Government succeeded only by 299 votes to 294, later being defeated and withdrawing the Bill in April.

Conservative strength was mounting again, though not always in forms of which Graham could approve. He was uniquely bitter in attacking his former colleagues; but he liked the spectacle of Tory–Radical alliances, of the sort which resulted in John Walter's return for Nottingham in April, no more than did Russell. He now strongly approved of Wellington's 'vast experience, superior judgment and magic influence' being utilised by any Conservative Cabinet.

The Budget, introduced on 30 April, followed a succession of classic Whig failures. A deficit of some £2,400,000 was to be remedied by increasing colonial (and reducing Baltic) timber duties and cutting foreign sugar duties. The Opposition prepared for the final blow. On 3 May a meeting under Peel resolved that Lord Sandon should oppose the sugar proposals. Graham expected victory, 'with the aid of the Anti-Slavery party . . . the East and West India interest and [tacitly] . . . the Whig landed interest . . .' The Ministers were defeated on the 18th by 317 votes to 281. Undecided as to future policy, they tried to fall back on existing taxes, and Peel replied with a motion of no confidence on the 27th. Meanwhile, on 7 May Russell had revealed the Government's counter-thrust, a small fixed corn duty.

A tense debate began on the 27th, and Graham spoke on the second night. He lashed a crumbling enemy. 'Retained in power by Royal favour, [Ministers] crouched under the prerogative and hoped to protract their miserable existence . . .'; but 'never was a country cursed with a worse, a more reckless or a more dangerous Government'. Early on 5 June the Opposition won by 312 votes to 311. On the 7th Russell announced a dissolution.[32] The Whigs hoped to benefit from Court sympathy and anti-Corn Law feeling, while the Conservatives relied on their new organisation, middle-class reactions to 'Whig mismanagement' and, in several areas, on Radical alliances. After the dissolution on the 23rd, the politicians looked to their constituencies.

8

A Condition of England Minister

The 1841 elections gave Peel a majority of almost eighty. Long years of Conservative planning, organising and hoping had been rewarded at last. Graham had faced the extra labour of finding a new seat. Since 1839 he had considered and rejected such 'proprietary boroughs' as Ripon, Thirsk and Woodstock. Eventually, Robert Williams gave up his seat and influence at Dorchester to Graham, who canvassed the entire electorate in June and was returned unopposed, with the Evangelical Viscount Ashley.[1] And so Graham shared in the victory for which he had toiled in Parliament and party. With Stanley and Ripon he was certain of office, but Richmond could not be persuaded to accept.

While awaiting Parliament's reassembly and the Government's inevitable fall, Peel discussed the difficult financial situation with Goulburn, Stanley and Graham. Wellington had been 'very much struck' by *The Spectator*'s suggestion of tariff reductions and property taxation. Also impressed, Graham nevertheless insisted that 'there was no safety in this tariff operation unless the imposition of the income tax preceded or accompanied *pari passu* the remission of the duties'. Herries, the Tory spokesman on finance, strongly favoured an income tax, but he was now out of Parliament and Goulburn and Stanley were hostile. However, Peel and Graham supported the plan, allied with tariff reform and retrenchment.[2] They were already moving towards the economic liberalism which was to cause increasing Tory resentment.

Early on 28 August the Government was defeated on the Address by 91 votes — an Opposition majority greater than Ripon secured in the Lords. Two days later Peel visited the Queen, and on 3 September the new Ministers were appointed at a Council at Claremount. Lyndhurst, Wharncliffe, Buckingham,

Wellington, Aberdeen, Haddington, Ripon, de Grey, Lincoln, Goulburn, Hardinge, Ellenborough, Granville Somerset, Lowther and Knatchbull were joined by Graham and Stanley, who took the Home Office and Colonial Office respectively. Now came the great challenge. The new Conservatism faced many enemies, and at this testing time it was confronted by several urgent problems.

I

In 1841 various agitations were making a wide range of demands. Textile-workers, with Ashley as their parliamentary leader, still campaigned for a Ten Hours Bill; and as their pioneers, like Richard Oastler, had been Tories, they now looked to Westminster more hopefully. With this cause was linked the anti-Poor Law agitation, to which many Tories were pledged in different degrees. Indeed, if the middle classes looked to Conservative rule for sound finance and administration, many workers hoped for social and industrial reform. Even Chartists had often supported Tory candidates, though many remained hostile to all parties and demanded a new social organisation. Among bourgeois Radicals and others the Anti-Corn Law League revived Free Trade agitations. For their varied purposes the agitators could point to increasing distress in the industrial towns, where ill-paid factory operatives and technologically-obsolete handworkers were suffering under slump conditions. Constant poverty, alternating overwork and unemployment, hunger, ill health and bad conditions at home and at work had provoked sections of the proletariat into dreams of revolt — a possibility enigmatically hinted at by the Chartists' blustering demagogue, Feargus O'Connor, on many platforms.

One of Graham's major tasks as Home Secretary was the maintenance of public peace amid trying conditions. Four years later he was to recall that 'there was hardly a day that he did not find it necessary to have personal communication with the Horse Guards, as well as with the heads of the police'. But although extremely busy he could always spare time for minutiae. In 1839 Graham appears to have been particularly disliked by the Queen. Perhaps for this reason he took particular care to soothe Royal susceptibilities in 1841: in December he relieved the angry Greville of the task of arranging the baby Prince of Wales's coat of arms. The Ministers treated the Queen 'with profound respect and the greatest attention', he explained. 'He made it a rule to address her as he would a sensible *man* . . .' During Parliament's brief autumn meeting he managed to renew the Poor Law for six months — but not before a young Yorkshire Tory, Busfeild Ferrand, had roused party passions by assailing it and the factory masters. The Government postponed the announcement of its proposals, and Parliament was prorogued on 7 October. Ministers then started their long task of preparing answers to the problems posed by contemporary agitations. They were expected to work hard; 'the limitations of a Ten Hours Bill [Peel] never applied to himself'.[3]

Through the winter the Government prepared important fiscal reforms. It was decided that tariff reductions, aimed at promoting increased trade, should be guaranteed by an income tax for at least three years — which would also wipe out the expected deficit. Even on the near-sacred Corn Laws the inner duettists of Peel and Graham were prepared to be empirical. On 12 December Graham told his leader that his own experience proved that it was 'dangerous . . . to dogmatise in matters of this highly speculative character'. The Leaguers, in many ways as violent as the Chartists (and vastly wealthier) regarded the abolition of agricultural Protection as morally, economically, politically, socially and intellectually desirable. The products of Dissenting academies, Manchester societies and cotton markets felt themselves to be the new *élite*; while privileged, effete landowners busied themselves with Gothic dreams, Game Laws and Anglican exclusiveness, they had built the brave new Jerusalem of the cotton manufacture. Peel, descended from their kind, could not deny their achievements, their rights or, ultimately, their arguments. Arrogant Leaguers soon regarded any opponent as wicked, stupid, or both. But strict empiricists could accept such views even less easily than the opposite contentions of the Lord Privy Seal, Buckingham, and his followers from the shires.

Peel's party contained many shades of opinion. Behind the rashly-spending 'Farmer's Friend', Buckingham, were ranged cohorts of neo-Mercantilist squires. Sulkily brooding off-stage was the self-made Benjamin Disraeli, offended at being refused office; Stanley would not have served with 'that scoundrel'. Ashley, earnest and suspicious, was waiting with declining hope for an announcement on factory reform. A delegation of his Yorkshire supporters who called on seven Ministers gave a mixed report. Only Buckingham was completely sympathetic, while Graham 'urged most of the reasons adduced by the free trade party', though denying his acceptance of them. 'The impression produced [by Graham] . . . was less favourable than in [Peel's] case. [He] seemed to them to have drunk too deeply at the fount of Malthusian philosophy.'[4] Peel delayed his decision, and only in February 1842 did Ashley become convinced of Ministerial hostility. Oastler suspected the Government from the start: 'The people were sick of Whiggery [and] would not endure it even under the name of Conservatism.' From his cell in the Fleet debtors' prison, he angrily expressed his disappointment, soon selecting Graham as the principal villain: in him was 'incorporated the very essence of the soul of 'liberal principles' . . . [and] it was . . . clear that [he] must be thrown overboard or that the Conservative vessel would sink'.[5] A considerable body of Tory opinion came to agree with the outspoken 'Factory King'. Peel's distant superiority scarcely mitigated the party's unrest. But his trump card was the lack of any alternative leader.

Reports of extending distress and unrest kept Graham busy. The lax tolerance of Russell and Normanby was quickly changed. Graham expected disorder and was determined to quell it forcibly. In time, he would look for its causes and try to eradicate them by legislation; but for the moment disturbances of public order simply vindicated his old fears, and no lingering Whiggish sentimentality would prevent him from suppressing them. He sympathised with Greville's concern at politically unfair magisterial appointments, though eventually giving standard party explanations. 'Trade was very bad and distress very great', he told Greville on 23 January, but 'the people [were] very enduring and well-behaved'. Even the curious Greville could obtain no indication of Government intentions, apart from platitudes about 'liberal and impartial' rule in Ireland. But Buckingham's resignation in January seemed to presage some move 'in the Anti-Corn Law line'. Certainly the League tried hard to convert the Government.[6]

When Parliament met on 3 February it received little information, though invited to consider recent financial difficulties and to look at the import tariffs. Buckingham's resignation was explained six days later, when Peel proposed to change the sliding-scale charge on corn imports. Whig supporters of a fixed duty, Liberal free traders and Tory Protectionists alike were hostile to Peel's proposals of a more gently-rising tariff with a lower maximum and an improved method of determining average prices. But Greville found some Conservatives accepting the change as simply a temporary halt. The Duke of Buccleuch's acceptance of Buckingham's post, Graham told de Grey, 'blunted the edge of the cut', for the rest of the Cabinet was united. 'We shall succeed with Corn; our great difficulties will be taxation and finance.'[7] Graham was closely involved as the most fervent supporter of liberal trade policies in the Government.

The Corn Bill introduced on 14 February provided for a duty of 1*s.* when prices rose to 73*s.* a quarter, rising to 20*s.* at 51*s.* Leaguers initially regarded it as 'an insult', and Russell advocated a fixed duty of 8*s.* Graham, still favouring some protection of home producers, lengthily defended the proposal, largely because of its administrative virtues. The Government was in a strong position, easily defeating 'fixed duty', 'free trade' and 'full protection' motions. Its policy succeeded 'as well as [Graham] could have hoped'; the Bill's main 'aim was to meet the reasonable expectations of moderate men, without offending or injuring the Landed Interest'. But, Graham confided to de Grey, the financial proposals were crucial. 'If [Peel's] proposed measures be accepted by the country, we are irresistible; if they be rejected, power has departed from us.'[8]

After years of Whig rule the nation's finances were precarious. In 1841 there was a deficit of over £2,300,000 which was likely to rise in the 1842 financial year. Peel's great edifice rested on two bases, which he had previously opposed. His Budget on 11 March proposed to restore the income tax, at 7*d*. in the pound on incomes over £150, except in Ireland. More important to the over-all plan was the massive change in the tariff. Old prohibitions were removed and duties on raw, partly-manufactured and fully-made imports were limited to maxima of 5, 12 and 20 per cent. The loss occasioned by reducing duties on 769 of some 1,200 dutiable articles would, it was hoped, be covered by increased trade and production, thus allowing income taxation to be abolished. Graham played a major role in planning this policy, and, after long anxiety, he considered in mid-March that 'the public had accepted [it] and the position of the Government was secured'. Whigs, Radicals and Tories might voice doubts, but in these early days of the Ministry much was taken on trust, and, as Greville noted, Peel had 'complete mastery over both his friends and his foes'. The Conservatives, '*nolentes aut volentes*, had surrendered at discretion . . .',[9] though some already grumbled that party performance differed from electoral pledge. And public protests against income taxation would be voted down by the Chartists, prophesied Melbourne, while Greville felt that military reverses in Afghanistan could only rally support for a 'strong' Government.

To have revived the income tax, modernised the tariff and liberalised agricultural protection was no mean achievement. Whatever opponents of all parties might declare, the Budget was a masterly affair. The Government's ultimate goal was already realised by Graham. The next move on corn, he told Peel in December, 'must be to an open trade . . . But the next change must be the last; it is not prudent to hurry it: next session is too soon; and as you cannot make a decisive alteration, it is far wiser to make none.'[10] Such views would have dismayed back-bench Tories in 1842.

II

Meanwhile, the slump so variously invoked by Leaguers, Chartists and Protectionists to support their assorted panaceas steadily worsened. Reports from harassed magistrates in industrial towns soon justified Graham's fears of 'a winter of great excitement and

o

considerable tumult'. By the early months of 1842 widespread
unemployment and near-starvation had produced a combustible
situation. Small groups of Radicals could quickly become large
mobs. And current experiences, at the bottom of a cycle,
heightened older grievances about industrial conditions and (for
some) working-class exclusion from political influence. Old and
new creeds merged and mingled in many permutations to offer
their solutions. But Chartist, socialist, working-class Radical
and operative Conservative alike looked for some dramatic
remedy for proletarian distress. And Peel and Graham were not
given to 'dramatic' gestures.

The League's veiled threats angered Ministers. Peel, for
instance, was annoyed by 'specific allegations of extreme privation
[made by] . . . Bowring, Villiers, Cobden, &c.' and even feared an
election in South Lancashire because of League 'attempts . . . to
influence the people'. As the hot summer approached, the
Leaguers' rhetorical violence and working-class militancy both
rose. In the spring, wage reductions led to bitter strikes in the
Midlands. While Chartists threatened to organise strikes for
political ends, Leaguers thought of provoking them for similar
reasons. In early August Lancashire cotton operatives started
their 'Plug Plot', as gangs toured the textile towns closing the
mills by drawing the boiler plugs. When the movement spread to
the West Riding woollen and worsted towns it developed into
something approaching a Northern 'General Strike'.[11] Inevitably
it produced some violence and ended with many arrests.

While the immediate participators in the riots were easily
recognised and punished, many Ministerialists suspected that
ultimate responsibility rested with Liberal capitalists. The
Leaguers had often threatened lockouts; they had inaugurated
or threatened wage cuts; they were alleged to have encouraged the
mobs, or to have hindered resistance, as mill-owners or magistrates.
In mid-August Graham regularly reported on the riots to the
Queen. 'In some of the disturbed counties', he told her, he 'was
by no means satisfied with the activity of the magistrates; and the
millowners had show a want of proper spirit in defending their
property'. He confessed to Lord Powis that he was 'overworked',

and told Galloway that 'he had not been one day absent from [his] office since February'.[12] He was prepared to use any force, including Chelsea Pensioners (whom Wellington considered 'a rabble' without proper officers) and the Yeomanry (loyal, generally Tory and, in this splendid summer, anxious to return to harvesting), against an insurrection; but he 'much preferred the assistance of regular troops', and controlled the military employed in police actions under Arbuthnot's brother, Sir Thomas. He had already asked for additional soldiers, but he would 'be slow to apprehend [Radicals] for words spoken, unless a breach of the peace was imminent . . .'.[13]

Suspicion of League provocation lingered on, and Graham always tried to distinguish between maintaining order and enforcing employers' claims. The Government was not 'prepared to force the workers to resume labour at what they might consider inadequate wages', he told General Arbuthnot. He insisted to Talbot that he was 'by no means prepared to use Military force to compel a reduction of wages or to uphold a grinding system of Truck', for 'to preserve peace, to put down plunder and to prevent the forced cessation of labour by intimidation [were] the sole objects of the Government . . .' To Croker he maintained that the riots amounted to 'a social insurrection of a very formidable character and well organised with forethought and ability' and wished that 'they could get at the authors'. Even when the North began to quieten down, Graham found its state 'by no means satisfactory', explaining that the 'sullen and discontented' workers were returning 'with great reluctance to their employments':

> they have just cause of complaint against their masters; plunder is their object and plunder is their weapon; and a state of social disorder is advancing with fearful rapidity, for which legislation can supply no remedy and against which force is the only safeguard.

Magistrates who had neglected their duties through idleness, fear, 'economical' reliance on the Army or desire to embarrass the Government were censured. The Government could not 'provide troops for every [manufacturing] town and village', Graham told Townley Parker; 'and if men of substance would not furnish means for defending their own property and would risk nothing to guard it from outrage, lawless violence and plunder must necessarily prevail'. Local rates could pay for local policing, and squires and manufacturers could form armed patrols. If local leaders evaded such tasks 'they must bear the consequences', for the Government 'could not be everywhere and do everything'. League mill-owners, Graham thought, 'were at first inclined to smile at the disturbance, but when it reached their own doors were the first to cry aloud for soldiers'.[14]

Home Office efficiency, rapid troop movements and widespread arrests soon promoted a general return to work. Croker meanwhile prepared a vindication of the Ministry. 'The true line ... is to dwell upon the enormous difficulties to which we have succeeded,' Peel advised him in February, and in July he maintained that 'the difficulty would be to prove that they had gone far enough *in concession*, that is, relaxation of prohibitions and protections, not that they had gone too far'.[15] Graham had 'never read a more able or satisfactory article' than Croker's first paper in September. But he still hoped to establish the cause of the riots, telling Peel in August that 'we are on the track of the real authors of the mischief'. Hopes of exposing League machinations rose, but simultaneously, Graham maintained,

> we must not neglect any appliance which can improve the moral feeling and disposition of the people. We must augment the means of Education; we must keep down the price of articles of first necessity; we must endeavour to redress the wrongs of the Labourer; we must mark an honest sympathy with his wants; and while we uphold the authority of law with firmness, we must temper it with mercy.

In November, considering the coal-owners 'insane, if they drove their men to a second strike in the dead of winter', he urged Talbot to 'exert his influence'. As legal proceedings started in the autumn, he told Peel that the Chartists were in 'a strait' and that the Government could now 'make a damning case' against the Leaguers. The indictment was prepared by Croker and was published in December. Although Graham admired 'the grand outline', both he and Peel suggested amendments to the draft, leaving Croker free to show League involvement in the outbreak. But no legal action was possible and the matter rankled in Tory minds, especially after the murder of Peel's secretary, Edward Drummond, on 21 January 1843. 'The more we hunt out these Leaguers the viler vermin we shall find them . . .', Croker then told Graham. 'See in the *Quarterly Review* on the League what the Revd. Mr. Bailey says about *shooting* Sir Robert Peel. He says "*a gentleman*" told him that he would willingly do so if it fell to his lot. Would it not be worthwhile to have this Mr. Bailey taken before a magistrate to say who "*this gentleman*" was — *perhaps it was MacNaughten* [Drummond's killer] — most probably it was nobody and a mere lie of the Rev. Mr. Bailey — but, in any case, it would be satisfactory to *expose this villain* . . .'[16] This attitude was widely held among Tories; but the only sufferers for the recent 'treason' were the arrested Chartists.

III

One result of the 1842 riots was a strengthening of the Government's resolve to lead industry and commerce out of the depression, while Graham determined to hasten social improvements. His time was 'occupied with odious business arising from the mad insurrection of the working classes', he told Brougham in August, 'which will ruin every peaceful occupation and divert thoughts from the contemplation of the means which could not fail to improve their social and moral condition'. But he had no faith in purely legislative reforms: society's malaise was too deep to be cured by Acts. 'I am afraid no legislative remedy can be applied to the undoubted evils which prevail to an extent most dangerous to the public peace,' he told Powis. 'They are inherent in the state of society at which we have arrived, and which is highly artificial. It will be seen that a manufacturing people is not so happy as a rural population, and this is the foretaste of becoming the workshop of the world.' He was moved personally by others' distress, but politically he believed too strongly in liberal economic theory to support State intervention in industry.

Indeed, the removal of controls on commerce was the State's most useful action: 'unless the fall in the price of provisions be counteracted by reduction of wages [as Tory–Chartist Protectionists alleged it would be], the condition of the working classes must be improved'.

Graham's philosophy, however, permitted some positive role to the State. 'I am most desirous that the education of the rising youth should be the peculiar care of the Government,' he wrote to Dr. Kay-Shuttleworth, the secretary of the Committee on Education. 'Its neglect is one of the chief causes of the evil spirit which now actuates large masses of the community' — although an education scheme could not remedy immediate evils, and 'law and civil rights must be upheld by power'. A letter from a Philadelphian operative confirmed his belief that production outstripped consumption in every manufacturing nation and caused 'grievous distress' among workers; but 'legislation could do little in these cases' and 'care only must be taken that articles of prime necessity . . . are not artificially enhanced in price'. Graham thus postulated his constant thesis that strictly 'social' reform required Government action, while 'economic' reform necessitated a Government withdrawal. Peel, touring Scotland with the Queen, agreed on 'the necessity of deeply considering more comprehensive and permanent remedies for disaffection and turbulence than mere measures of forcible repression'.[17]

In the autumn Graham further explored the possibility of a major educational reform. Contemporary conditions compelled education to be religiously-dominated; churchmen had a 'social conscience' long before the State, and mainly voluntary contributions from the Church of England provided the vast majority of elementary schools. Furthermore, many Tories believed that Anglican education provided an antidote to revolutionary ideas. The remedy for 'the perilous materials of present and future pauperism, violence and infidelity', thought Ashley, was the provision of 'opportunities of moral and religious education'. Brougham, with very different attitudes, had also 'entreated and conjured [Graham] to direct his attention to education', recommending 'a general parish plan — permissive if you will'. Although the Ministry would allow the Church 'more sway' than he would like, he believed that 'all real friends of education' except militant sectarians would accept such a scheme, for 'education had now no other chance'. Graham squarely faced the difficulties. 'Religion cannot be separated from the system', he wrote, 'and . . . the state, if it make a choice, must prefer the established creed; and this preference is the signal for an attack on the measure . . .' He respected Brougham's experience, but believed that 'Religion, the keystone of education, was, in this country, the bar to its progress'. Graham knew that Brougham's plan would face 'very great difficulties', as rival religious groups would dominate local rating authorities; indeed, in June 1842 he preferred 'a cautious and gradual extension of the power and the pecuniary means of the Committee of the Privy Council' to 'any plan by the Government'. Nor did he like Peel's suggestion of a Commission on the state of the industrial districts; it would merely show 'the want of education, the need of pastoral care, the insufficiency of Church room', on which religious differences prevented Government action.[18]

Eventually, Graham resolved to deal with the education problem in the industrial districts in a new Factory Bill. The Act of 1833 had limited children under 13 to an eight-hour day in most textile industries and provided for two hours' education in existing schools or specially established classes. The 'factory schools' cheaply run by many masters soon proved unsatisfactory, and in 1841 Ashley's committee on the operation of the Act had recommended a half-time system, allowing children to attend 'schools of a respectable kind' and ending 'the mockery of education now so common'. Graham's own proposals were prepared 'under his direction' by two Factory Inspectors, Leonard Horner ('who had influence with the Dissenters') and Robert Saunders ('who had the confidence of the Bishop of London'). If the Episcopate approved of the Bill, he believed that it would pass.

On 28 February 1843 Ashley appealed in the Commons for 'a moral and religious education' for the working classes, and

Graham promised to try to 'find out some neutral ground on which they could build something approaching to a scheme of national education . . .' The Bill was brought in on 8 March. It prohibited employment in the textile industries under the age of eight and limited children under 13 to $6\frac{1}{2}$ hours' labour, with at least three hours' education in carefully-inspected schools. New schools, financed by pupils' fees, local rates and Exchequer contributions, would be controlled by seven trustees, consisting of the Anglican priest, the churchwardens, two industrialists and two ratepayers nominated by the magistrates. Generally Anglican-dominated religious instruction would be provided, though Nonconformists might contract out.[19]

Ashley 'foresaw great good' from the plan, and Graham was delighted, hoping that 'the reasonable settlement proposed' might remove Ashley's 'honourable scruples' against the Government. But Ashley's and Dr. Blomfield's approval was not enough, and Graham was soon trying to answer clergymen's suspicions. 'It was not an easy task to uphold the just authority of the Church and to respect the honest scruples of dissenters': the Bill was 'a measure of Peace [and] he was afraid that this compound would effervesce with one drop of acid'. Despite Graham's insistence that episcopal sanction 'might justly command the confidence of the Laity, even tho' the Clergy might be disposed to disregard it', many churchmen continued to oppose the measure.[20] Factory reformers disliked a Bill which still ignored their full demands, and a violent campaign was raised by both Methodists and Dissenters (including some Roman Catholics) against what the Congregationalist Edward Baines regarded as 'a declaration of war against all the Dissenters in the Kingdom'. Massive petitions were prepared against the alleged plot to extend Anglican power through public finance — and often against any sort of State interest in education. High Churchmen doubting 'inter-denominationalism', Oastlerites demanding 'Ten Hours' and Dissenters opposing either the Church or any denial of 'voluntaryism' formed a great opposition.

Graham soon realised the extent of hostility. 'The Dissenters will be too much for us,' he told Stanley. 'They will convert my measure of Peace into a Firebrand and a Sword.' But he did not regret his 'honest' proposal. Dissenting opposition must cause the Government to assist and rely on the Church's 'increased exertions'. Every master in the new schools would have been a churchman, he assured Gladstone; but the Dissenters 'would succeed in defeating the measure, at least in the sense which led him to propose it as a scheme of comprehension and concord'. Even Ashley, though refusing to withdraw his 'Ten Hours' motions on adult labour, agreed that the Bill should be amended. In April Graham planned modifications with the Bishops of London and Chester, being 'deeply convinced' that the Bill would 'be conducive to the strength and welfare of the Established Church and to the spread of Christian Truth and saving Knowledge . . .' He had 'never felt greater anxiety for the success of any measure'. But the Methodists, for long the Church's allies, were 'more hostile than [Graham] anticipated, [thus] marking a wide estrangement . . .'; they now went 'the whole length of the bitterest dissent', demanding equality for all but Roman Catholics. Internal tensions were actually responsible for this breach, but Low Churchmen soon discovered their own villain; Graham blamed 'the Pusey tendencies of the Established Church', and Ashley confirmed that Methodists had 'a deep and conscientious fear of Popery', adding that the Anglican clergy had been inactive. On 15 June Graham withdrew the Bill. Ashley continued to blame 'the perilous pranks of Dr. Pusey and his disciples', while Peel considered that Dissent had gained 'but a sorry and lamentable triumph'.[21] Graham's scheme to educate the working classes had been wrecked on the rocks of religious opposition.

IV

The Conservative party remained closely allied with the Church, though generally hostile to the growing Oxford Catholicism which terrified Protestant Dissenters. The Church had already been subjected to reform, with her tithes commuted, episcopal revenues redistributed, cathedral chapters purged, ecclesiastical courts modernised and finances largely controlled by the Ecclesiastical Commissioners. Dissenters might — and often did — complain against Church rates, but Anglicans generally looked to the Government for sympathy. Peel and Graham were devout churchmen, but were not inclined to be dominated by the varied enthusiasms of such men as Gladstone, Inglis or Ashley. 'Judicious measures', Graham told Peel, might extend Christian knowledge and 'Scriptural education' and guard Church property from grasping priests; 'but all this must be done gently, almost silently, and from time to time public aid may be obtained'. The Government opposed Sir John Easthope's Bill against Church rates, but in 1842 passed the Ecclesiastical Corporations Act, allowing the Church to grant long leases and use much of the extra income to raise low stipends. Such minor measures continued to be proposed, partly because any large-scale State support might be disastrous. 'I dread for the sake of the Church and its best interest, stirring up that storm which large demands on the public purse would inevitably excite,' wrote Peel, opposing Inglis's ideas on Church extension: 'you and I know that the Church and religion would suffer, and peace and charity would be sacrificed . . .'[22] Consequently, in 1843 Peel merely legislated for additional endowments, while Graham's attempt to reform the tangled web of ecclesiastical jurisdiction was defeated. In general, the Ministry was content to support Blomfield's internal reforms — and to avoid involvement in Tractarian controversies. The error on 'factory education' was not repeated.

Another established church provided more difficult problems. There had long been differences in the Church of Scotland over the rival rights of lay patrons and congregations (and sometimes presbyteries) in the presentation and acceptance of ministers, and the new Evangelicals became increasingly hostile to patronage. Abolished in 1690, lay power had been restored in 1712 by 'the infidel and Jacobite Bolingbroke', Dr. Thomas Chalmers told Graham in 1840, to punish 'the Church and people of Scotland for their adherence to the House of Hanover'. The Evangelicals gradually defeated the Moderates in the General Assembly, and in 1834 passed the 'Veto Act' providing that 'no pastor should be intruded on any congregation contrary to the will of the people' (as represented by male heads of families). Statutory provision for a patron's presentation of a candidate for parochial and presbyterial decision was thus apparently denied by a Church enactment. The Auchterarder case brought the issue before the Court of Session, which found the 'Act' illegal, as did the Lords in 1839. As other cases followed, the Kirk's disunity widened. While the courts insisted that presbyteries might only test a nominee's morals and orthodoxy, the Evangelicals demanded Church freedom; Chalmers insisted that the Church was 'amenable to no higher power on earth'. The battle was fought bitterly; when the Moderates of Strathbogie followed the Court of Session's order to ordain a vetoed minister, the Assembly deposed seven ministers.

Graham had tried to keep aloof from Scottish affairs. 'A sense of his peculiar position with reference to Scotland and Glasgow' kept him away from Peel's dinner in 1837; his support of Hamilton's reform plans was now an embarrassment. But the Church question gradually grew in importance. The Conservative Chalmers became a friend of Graham in Glasgow and hoped for his support. If the Lords would not allow even a presbyterial veto, he told Graham in June 1839, many of the best clergy would leave the Church, which would become 'a prey for the Radicals and Voluntaries and demi-infidels . . .' He hoped that Graham would promote a Bill to prevent 'an absolute and uncontrolled patronage'.[23] When Gladstone expressed his concern, Graham confessed that he 'had long felt great anxiety' and regretted that Chalmers and Aberdeen had not 'devised some middle term'; it was 'but one step from the veto to voluntaryism'. Wellington also worried over 'the Church question in Scotland'; Arbuthnot wrote that it 'occupied the Duke's mind greatly'. Graham himself firmly opposed the legalisation of the veto. 'It was impossible to over-estimate [the problem's] importance', but 'the controversy had [by December] assumed so angry an aspect that he had little hope of a reasonable adjustment'. And he told Peel that 'the Scotch Church question . . . had assumed an angry aspect of extreme danger'.[24]

Colquhoun and some Scottish Tories sympathised with the reformers; Sir George Sinclair, in particular, hoped for some compromise. But Graham opposed any concession which offended 'the principles which ought to govern an Established Church'. Nor could he trust Chalmers, who had reverted from an acceptance of presbyterial control to a demand for a congregational veto. Peel agreed that it would be 'unworthy' to bid at 'the auction for the short-lived favour of the heated zealots of either party'. And Graham bluntly told Chalmers that the Conservatives could not agree to transfer patronage to 'a variable and irresponsible multitude', while regretting both the conflict between Church and State and the threatened secession. 'Greatly saddened and greatly solemnised', Chalmers then made last efforts to convince his friend. During 1840 a 'non-intrusionist' delegation canvassed Ministers and Opposition leaders with no success, and Aberdeen's compromise proposals were rejected. The struggle between the Moderate League and the Evangelical Covenant was intensified, and Graham revealed his attitude by hurrying to Scotland to oppose Chalmers's election as Professor of Theology at Glasgow. The result of the Conservatives' hostility to theocratic pretensions and to the Duke of Argyll's Bill to legalise the veto was Evangelical opposition to the Tories.[25]

As Home Secretary, Graham was deeply involved in the controversy, since the Government owned patronage rights in about a third of the Scottish parishes.[26] Sir William Rae, the Lord Advocate, told him that Peel had presented the minister desired by the parish but in cases of party differences selected an 'outside' candidate, while the Whigs had allowed parishioners to choose from a Government-selected list. Determined to nominate justly, Graham followed Peel's precedent. He consequently offended some friends; but, as he explained to his adviser, Dr. William Muir, he was 'resolved absolutely to renounce patronage as a source of political influence'. He hoped for ministers leading their parishioners 'to the paths of piety and peace. He did not wish [them] to be politicians, but they must not be Radicals and ... must incline to the side of the law and order.' And 'the admission of popular election', he told Sir Andrew Agnew, still 'appeared to him dangerous and derogatory to the dignity and independence of the sacred calling.' While rejecting the 'ultra' views of such Conservative Presbyterians as John Hope and distrusting Sinclair's suggested solutions, Graham was determined not to neglect the unfairly suspended ministers of Strathbogie.[27]

In 1842 the Assembly issued its 'Claim, Declaration and Protest' against Erastian control. Most delegates subsequently promised to secede if patronage continued, and funds were collected for 'free' churches. In January Graham considered that the Government should reject communications from law-breaking 'non-intrusionists'. By December the impasse between Church and State had become clear and, after consulting Peel, Wellington and Buccleuch, on 4 January 1843 Graham explained Ministerial policy to the Moderator. A parochial veto and abolition of patronage were unacceptable, and the Church already had guarantees through its control of ministers' training and licensing and through presbyterial rights of veto on judicial (but not personal) grounds. But the Veto Act, denying even a trial of patronal nominees, was illegal, for churchmen had 'no exemption from the duty of obedience to statute law'.[28] Fox Maule's motion for further investigation was negatived, but an added complication arose when the civil courts ruled that ministers of *quod sacra* parishes, caring for chapels of ease, were not entitled to act in Church courts. Graham suggested remedial legislation in January and by April hoped to graft a permissive clause to a new version of Aberdeen's Bill. In May he carefully prepared the Queen's letter to the Moderator, promising to secure churchmen's rights of objection and the Church's right to pronounce on such objections. It was too late. On 18 May Chalmers led over four hundred ministers and many elders out of the Church to form the Free Church of Scotland.[29] The Disruption was a sad event for the Kirk, when over a quarter of its most talented ministers chose to renounce the security and social positions given by the Establishment in order to maintain their ideal of the Church.

Politically, the Disruption was distressing to the Government. Few Englishmen understood the Kirk's complicated traditions, and the claims of determined theocrats have always embarrassed legalistic Ministers. The Government was often condemned for not preserving the Church by appeasing the reformers. Yet, finally forced by the 1842 Assembly's declaration that 'Acts of the Parliament [affecting the Church] passed without the consent of the Church and nation . . . were and should be null and void', Ministers could only insist that an Established Church must obey the law. The Free Church was to make a major contribution to Scottish life, while the weakened Establishment became increasingly representative of the middle classes and less concerned with social problems. In later years the old controversies were rendered obsolete. Patronage was abolished in 1874. And in 1900 the Free Church amalgamated with the United Presbyterian Church. A Free Church minority then unsuccessfully opposed the vesting of all property in the new United Free Church before the Court of Session; but in 1904 the Lords decided that the minority, still accepting an Establishment and rejecting voluntaryism, were the true inheritors of both beliefs and property. Because Chalmers had defined the Free Church as anti-voluntaryist its last remnant was able to defend the imperilled rights of a society outside the State. But for the majority Graham had rightly prophesied that 'secession . . . [would become] union with the voluntaries'. Torrens maintained that Graham 'looked back with deep regret' on his policy, but Graham's daughter insisted that, though sympathetic to the Free Churchmen, he never changed his views on the controversy. Free Church rights provided themes for early 20th-century defenders of voluntary societies against the monolithic State. Graham had defended the equally harassed rights of a legal Establishment.[30]

V

Peel's Government played a considerable role in extending social reform, largely because of outside pressures and often by improving rather than inaugurating State interference. In the factory reform field, the 1843 proposals had only been postponed. Northern Tory–Radicals were active through the winter, raising funds for Oastler's release and condemning both Liberals and

Ministers. On 6 February 1844 Graham introduced a new Bill, limiting children in the textile industries to 6½ hours' labour and women to 12 hours and tightening administration and improving factory education (though without the 1843 provisions). But the reformers remained determined to have 'Ten Hours'.

Graham's Bill reached the Committee stage on 15 March, when Ashley moved his amendment to restrict older children to ten hours' work. Ashley had disliked Graham's notions on inter-denominational education in 1843 and 'suspected' his motives. In July 1843 he had recorded that

> Graham . . . has contrived to render himself so thoroughly odious that I cannot find one human being who will speak a word in his behalf. He has done very much to injure the Government, for though he is clever and discharges his business well in the House of Commons, he cannot persuade a single soul, nor produce the least effect by his most emphatic and solemn appeals. He is universally distrusted, and this by everyone, from a prince to a beggar.

These feelings had not been dispelled. On 2 March Ashley heard 'unpleasant rumours' that the Government would oppose him, and two evenings later Graham urged him 'not [to] make an adverse statement'; Graham 'clearly feared a full exposé'. But Ashley collaborated by moving for the Committee on the 5th 'in half a dozen words', and 'Graham thanked him for his silence'. On the 15th Graham announced Ministerial hostility. Ashley believed that he would have won a division, but gloomily expected that 'official whips would produce official votes'. Ministers certainly worked hard to avoid defeat; Stanley even urged Lord Jocelyn to dissuade Ashley.[31]

In fact, Graham acted only reluctantly on the factory issue. Any legislation obviously violated *laissez-faire* principle; and, although young children might be further restricted, twelve hours would be allowed for other operatives. Adults paid on piece-work, as Graham pointed out, naturally 'preferred the establishments where most work was done'. Peel was shaken by the strength of Ashley's Tory support, but 'could not and would not acquiesce'. However, on the 18th Ashley won two divisions. This 'was a virtual adoption of a Ten Hours Bill without qualifications [to which Graham] . . . had an insuperable objection'. Ashley observed that Peel and Graham were 'evidently out of temper' and their speeches 'ingenious in argument, but wretched in principle and feeling, purely commercial'. The Government again tried to rally support and when, on the 22nd, Graham spoke on the clause limiting women workers, he and Peel (thought Ashley) were 'furious in temper'.

By two curious divisions the Commons narrowly rejected both Graham's proposal and Ashley's amendment. And on the 25th Graham rashly condemned Ashley's 'dangerous course' along (in *The Examiner*'s words) 'a Jack Cade system of legislation', thus rousing Ashley's friends to fury. Greville 'never remembered so much excitement . . . nor a more curious political state of things' and noted Ministers' 'chagrin and soreness at being foresaken' by 'nearly half their supporters'. Some blamed 'Graham's unpopularity . . . [and] nothing could be so foolish as [his] taunt . . .' Ashburton told Croker that Peel 'liked to drill his men as our great Duke does his guards', but Members needed 'a little more freedom'; Graham's 'half threat [of resignation] was merely a manœuvre to frighten back some of the stray sheep into the fold . . .' And Ashley, offended by Graham's 'indecent, foolish and stupid' charge, welcomed the Bill's withdrawal and Graham's pledge to reintroduce it.[32]

Graham's new Bill of 29 March allowed children aged between 8 (not 9) and 13 to work $6\frac{1}{2}$ hours and women and young persons 12 hours, strengthened the Factory Inspectors' powers and provided for the fencing of dangerous machinery. Northern reformers now hated Graham, and the Lancashire men even petitioned the Queen for his dismissal. But though assailed on both sides Graham forced his *via media* through Parliament. Tory–Radical rallies condemned what Ferrand called his 'cold-blooded dogged stupidity', but Ashley found it difficult to propose amendments. When, on 10 May, Ashley proposed a 'Ten Hours' clause, the Government made a final threat: Graham on the 10th and Peel on the 13th promised to resign if they were defeated. This was enough to rouse 148 'new' voters for the

Ministry. On the 13th Ashley was 'utterly, singularly, prodigiously defeated by a majority of 138'. He consoled himself by believing that 'the majority was one to save the Government', founded on Sir Thomas Fremantle's threats and Whig inability to form a Cabinet, and forecast 'a high reaction'.

For the time, however, Graham had triumphed. And as passions cooled, it was realised that his interest in administrative efficiency had influenced a major Act. The operation of factory legislation was considerably improved and the insistence on three hours' daily education started the children's 'half-time system'. Furthermore, Greville thought the Act was 'a great triumph to Graham, who deserved it', for 'no man ever rose so much as he had latterly done'; all admitted 'his capacity and administrative powers . . . to be first-rate', and his 'temper and moderation' (instead of 'a bitter and sarcastic tone') had provoked 'a general disposition to do justice to his firmness, ability and honesty on this occasion'.[33] A considerable body of working-class opinion obviously did not share this view.

VI

Many of the industrial reformers had also demanded the repeal or modification of the 1834 Poor Law, which had become increasingly unpopular. Melbourne's Government was able to renew it only for a year in 1839 and 1840, and Graham gained a six-months renewal in September 1841, against Sharman Crawford and Ferrand. The Benthamite cruelty of a system allowing relief only in designedly-bleak 'Bastilles' had been condemned on many Tory and Radical platforms, and *The Times* and many local journals had publicised every real and alleged instance of brutality. Consequently, Graham faced many difficulties in framing new proposals. He had always supported the Act.

Aided by Sir Edmund Head, a Commissioner whom he had appointed, and by many local Guardians, Graham prepared his measure quickly and introduced it on 11 May 1842. He demanded a five-year continuation of the Act, the abolition of the fifteen remaining 'Gilbert Unions' (which still granted 'outdoor relief' under an Act of 1782) and the education of workhouse children.

P

Despite the opposition of 'ultras' on Right and Left, the measure was passed in June, shorn of the last two provisions. Opponents were reduced to making sniping attacks, until in February 1844 Graham introduced a Bill providing for weekly maintenance payments by fathers of illegitimate children, reforming apprenticeship conditions and modernising the administration. The principles of 1834 were thus retained, while their operation was amended. Graham would not bend to the Law's opponents and stoutly supported his officials, even when their reports seemed grossly untrue to local ratepayers. During 1844 Ferrand waged a bitter war on Graham over the former Assistant Commissioner Charles Mott's reports. He accused Graham of procuring false information — and J. W. Hogg of unfairly helping to unseat Walter. When the Commons condemned him in April, Ferrand published a detailed pamphlet which appeared to question Graham's integrity. But by 1845 Graham's interest had moved to the Settlement Laws, which both hampered labour migration and harshly affected the migrant. In February he proposed that entitlement to relief should depend upon either previous orders or the place of birth, that parochial authority on settlement should be transferred to the Unions and that provisions for removal should be liberalised. Widespread opposition led to a postponement and the Poor Removal Bill was finally enacted by Russell's Ministry.[34]

Scotland's Poor Law problems came to a head in 1843. The Scottish system had always rested mainly on voluntary contributions administered by the Kirk Sessions. It was a cheap scheme: even by 1839 fewer than a third of the parishes had levied rates, and the extent of relief was defined in conveniently vague terms. Outdoor relief was given, but the urban rich subscribed too little for a growing pauper population during the extending industrial slump. Paisley especially faced ruin and became the saddest burgh in the tragic story. 'For upwards of a year', Peel told Arbuthnot in October 1842, voluntary charity had supported over 8,000 people on average and sometimes 17,000. He had subscribed twice, 'being satisfied that if nothing were done we might take the choice either of hundreds dying of hunger or of a frightful outbreak and attack upon property', and wondered 'what was to be done with these people at Paisley during next winter'. Chalmers always supported the voluntary system, but his secession undoubtedly increased the demand for national organisation. A Royal Commission was appointed in January 1843 and in 1844 a majority report recommended the establishment of a central Board of Supervision, elected parochial boards and poorhouses and medical provision. The 'independent' Scots, however, retained much of their voluntaryism; the Act of 1845 left a great deal of freedom to local authorities.

Old arguments continued over the English Act. John Fielden, Ferrand, Walter, Oastler and many others continued to produce reports of starved old people, separated families, flogged girls, unsegregated imbeciles, emaciated toilers at tread-mills and the general ill-treatment and under-feeding of 'Bastille'-dwellers. Graham disliked the 'demagogues' who raised such points, whether they were Radicals like the medical journalist Thomas Wakley or individualistic Tories like Ferrand; such men would exaggerate their charges and could usually be answered with the quick cleverness and heavy sarcasm of the 'uncommitted' man flaunting his superiority over 'partisans'. But the scandal of the Andover Union, where starving workhouse inmates allegedly fought over the bones which they were compelled to crush, brought the long campaign to its peak in 1845 and 1846. Graham was forced both to forbid bone-crushing and to accept a contro- versial Select Committee, which eventually condemned both the Union and the Commissioners.[35] Peelite interest in pauperism remained unsentimental: poverty, like other social problems, was seen principally as a problem of administrative regulation. Individuals would certainly perform Christian duties of charity, but it would be wrong to extend State provisions, although their arrangements might be improved.

Such attitudes augured ill for dramatic social reform, but could be applied to useful measures elsewhere. After the 1842 riots Peel and Graham considered employing stipendiary magistrates at Quarter Sessions, along with the 'unpaid, and therefore to a considerable degree irresponsible' local justices. Graham was in favour, while Peel counselled 'great caution' in striking 'a severe blow against the useful influence of the best part of the local and

provincial aristocracy' and wondered how to balance a 'democratic' extension and professional administration with voluntary
service and established custom. Graham showed that assistant
barristers had served usefully in Ireland, but Tory feeling was
generally opposed to a substitution of bureaucratic power for
squirearchic duty and he decided 'not [to] touch the county
magistracy'. Magisterial competence continued to worry him, but
he succeeded only in using experienced lawyers as temporary
justices. Conservative empiricism did not necessarily involve
inaction. Peel suggested an inquiry into industrial relations in the
collieries, believing that there were 'practical grievances —
possibly not to be redressed by law — of which the employed had
just reason to complain' and that 'what law could not effect
exposure might'. He 'strongly suspected' that colliery profits
justified higher wages. Yet, typically, he and Graham were
gracelessly unhelpful to Ashley over his Mines Bill of 1842 and
insisted on modifying it. Equally typically, when the Act was
passed, prohibiting truck, female labour underground and the
employment of boys under 10, Graham and his Inspector, Seymour
Tremenheere, tried to enforce it.[36]

The Government's forte was its administrative ability. But its
general trend towards social and economic liberalism offended
many provincial Tories. 'Am I to be satisfied to have Whig
measures adopted by a Tory Government?' Oastler asked in
February 1842. By May he considered that 'the die is cast — the
mask is thrown away — the Whiggery of Conservatism is now
arrogantly displayed in sight of the deceived and indignant people
of England' — and largely blamed Graham. In November, when
he was transferred to the Queen's Prison, he started to address his
weekly publication to the Home Secretary. 'The higher you rise,
so much the more is your want of principle apparent,' he wrote. 'I
am a Tory of the olden time — you are a Conservative of yester-
day. My employment is to *preserve* the Constitution — yours is to
destroy it.'[37] Oastler was a romantic eccentric, but his views were
widely respected among Northern workers and eventually gained
acceptance among many of the mutely-suspicious squires on the
Tory back benches.

9

The Policy-Maker

Graham earned a special place in Peel's Cabinet, not solely dependent on the extensive powers wielded by the Home Office. His hard, meticulous work commanded (sometimes grudging) respect. Gladstone recorded half a century later that Graham 'knew more of economic and trade matters . . . than the rest of the cabinet of 1841 all put together'.[1] But most important was his closeness to Peel; their official 'intercourse . . . was the most frequent and the most intimate', wrote Peel, and Graham's 'responsibility was equal to [his] own'. In 1848 Graham recalled that 'we seldom failed, even without concert, to take the same view of important questions'. To the new humorous journal *Punch* they seemed 'two persons with only one intellect'.[2] As Peel's *alter ego*, Graham exerted considerable influence on Cabinet decisions; from 1841 he was virtually the Government's second-in-command.

Power and influence, however, did not bring popularity. 'Having arrived at the highest pitch of power by means the most dishonourable', wrote the bitter Oastler, 'you have resolved to use that power so as to disgrace your office as well as yourself.' Politicians never forgot past sarcasm, and Graham's cold personality attracted few close friends. Naturally, his responsibility for public order during disturbed periods did not endear him with the 'disturbers'. Yet he tried to act fairly. He disliked the employment of spies and spent much less than his predecessors on the Secret Service, but he did use his power to order the opening of suspects' mails. In 1842 both Chartists' and Leaguers' letters were examined, and in 1843 the Welsh Rebecca Riots provoked further openings. The practice led, in 1844, to an embarrassing attack on Graham. On 1 March he agreed to Aberdeen's request for the examination of the correspondence of the Italian nationalist Giuseppe Mazzini. The decision became known and Aberdeen was suspected of passing information to the Austrian Government. When Tom Duncombe presented a petition from Mazzini and three other men who suspected that their letters were being examined, on 14 June, Graham refused to comment. Public interest was aroused, the Lords debated the issue and on the 24th Duncombe demanded a Select Committee. Graham faced the problem of all Ministers attacked over security matters; he insisted that he had acted properly and refused further information. Although Duncombe gained much Whig support, his motion was defeated.

Public feeling, stirred by the Whig Press, rose high over the Government's power to examine private correspondence, and on 2 July Duncombe asked for a Select Committee on the General Post Office's secret branch. Now, angered by the hypocrisy of such Whigs as Macaulay, Howick and Russell in attacking him for using a traditional power which their Ministry had freely employed, Graham countered by suggesting an inquiry into the system itself. Committees of Lords and Commons examined the subject in detail and found that no improper use had been made of it. But on 19 February 1845 Duncombe revived the issue by demanding an investigation of the alleged opening of his own letters and attacking the Committees' decisions. 'My Whig friends behaved as ill as they could', wrote Greville, 'and all out of spite to Graham and because they could not resist seizing the opportunity of flinging dirt upon the Government.' Graham again defended himself; the motion was rejected and on 1 April Sheil's proposal to apologise to Mazzini was also opposed. But the aftermath dragged on. Graham accused the Italian of complicity in murder; Duncombe defended Mazzini; and on discovering that he was wrong Graham withdrew. In the end, the Home Office retained its power. It had not been a pleasant task to defend the procedure, and Graham suffered personally. 'I do not recollect ever to have seen any one Minister singled out for attack so venomously as you have been, or on more flimsy pretexts,' wrote Croker. Brougham was 'disgusted at the perpetration of the most gross injustice he could yet recollect anywhere', but told Graham 'you really have come out of the fire unsinged'. Graham himself never forgot the conduct of former friends who relied on 'his honour not to save himself by exposing them . . . From that day [wrote his brother] he never thought so highly as before of human nature.'[3] He had never regarded it very highly.

I

Drummond's murder caused both horror and work, in January 1843. The killer, Daniel MacNaughten, apparently intended his bullets for Peel and soon appeared to be insane. Although the Queen considered 'the proof of . . . madness . . . very slight', expectations grew that a plea of insanity would succeed, and on 3 March the judges accepted it. It seemed strange to the Queen and her Ministers that the perpetrator of an apparently planned murder should escape hanging because of purely judicial decisions, and the Queen (who had herself been attacked) asked Peel whether Parliament could not insist on standard rules. After much work by Graham and other Ministers the MacNaughten Rules were evolved by the judges.

Graham was also concerned with wider penal affairs. In November 1842 he ordered the Prison Inspectors to suggest improvements. As a result, legislation was provided for the continued separation of offenders. And Graham worked hard on schemes to classify convicts, send reformatory boys to the colonies and establish a terrible régime in the new Pentonville prison. In 1843 the 'Graham Dietaries' provided standard sparing lists of convicts' food — though they seemed too generous to some prison governors. Graham agreed with current opinion: imprisonment was a form of social vengeance and its rigours, along with transportation, should be retained; public executions were effective deterrents (though a 'disgraceful' scene at Newgate in 1845 made Graham waver); appeals against court sentences were rarely entertained; prisoners were generally incurable.[4] Again, he offered no major changes, though he improved the existing system by attending to such matters as convicts' food, sanitation, ventilation, heating, discipline and labour and abolishing the

Fleet and Marshalsea prisons. Above all, he insisted on rigorous economy. But he resolutely seconded Ashley's reform of lunacy provisions in 1845, preventing improper detention, extending the asylum system, placing regulation under permanent Commissioners and ordering 'better care and treatment' of inmates.

Public health also entered Graham's sphere. He had offended the energetic Edwin Chadwick by preferring Head as a Poor Law Commissioner but insisting on the rapid production of Chadwick's report on sanitary conditions. The Commissioners refused any responsibility and eventually issued Chadwick's famous *Report on the Sanitary Condition of the Labouring Population* unofficially, in July 1842. Chadwick revealed the horrors of urban life: filth, bad water, bad housing, overcrowding, regular epidemics, ill-managed cemeteries and sparse drainage provided a lethal background to the 'Workshop of the World'. He undoubtedly showed the need for major reform, and in 1843 the Government set up a Royal Commission on the Health of Towns, under Buccleuch, to undertake more detailed investigations. While the Commission was working, Graham parried W. A. Mackinnon's proposals to prohibit burials in urban areas by obtaining another report from Chadwick (who also, unofficially, greatly influenced the Commissioners). Public health interested a growing number of philanthropists and administrators, especially after the founding of the Health of Towns Association in 1844. But legislative progress was slow. 'Such is the absence of civic economy in some of our towns that their condition in respect to cleanliness is almost as bad as that of an encamped horde, or an undisciplined soldiery', wrote Chadwick, '. . . the civic officers have generally contented themselves with the most barbarous expedients, or sit still amidst the pollution, with the resignation of Turkish fatalists, under the supposed destiny of the prevalent ignorance, sloth and filth.' The resistance of local interests and Ministerial reluctance to act on a difficult administrative problem led to delay. The Commissioners finally reported in 1845, when the Government was immersed in other problems; and it was only three years later that Russell's Ministry passed the great Public Health Act. Graham's principal interest lay in reforming, classifying and to some degree controlling medical practitioners. His controversial Medical Reform Bill of 1844 would establish a central council to standardise and register professional qualifications. Heated opposition from many practitioners led to a modified Bill in 1845 and eventually to the withdrawal of the proposal.[5] Despite Graham's hard work and many concessions, the ancient institutions and anti-State suspicions of the profession were too strong.

While working on these varied tasks, Graham remained deeply involved in the problems of public order. After the 1842 riots he discussed with the Attorney-General (Sir Frederick Pollock) the means of securing heavy sentences for the arrested Chartists in a show-trial; the light punishments meted out at the Lancaster assizes of 1843 were no part of the Government's design. But he recognised the need for amelioration of conditions, as well as repression of violence. Amelioration, however, would come through the development of a free economy rather than by 'Jack Cade . . . legislation'. Even starving Paisley was ordered by the Home Office to rely largely on 'Self Help'. For Graham knew that 'eating, drinking, working and dying must ever be the sum of human life among the masses . . .' In 1842 he inevitably opposed the political panacea of Chartism; such 'wild schemes' would subvert 'all our great institutions'. Nor would he support the Ballot, urging the contradictory arguments that the 1832 decision was final and that he was not convinced that secret voting would prevent further change. But he believed that Radical militancy 'mainly arose from the want of adequate sustenance, in consequence of the high price of food and low wages' and recognised Government's role in changing these conditions. In 1843 the Rebecca Riots in Wales, directed against turnpike tolls, Church rates and the Poor Law (but primarily provoked by distress among industrial and agricultural communities alike) again roused Graham's apprehensions. By December he 'grieved' to tell Peel that 'South Wales bids fair to rival Ireland. Poverty and the misconduct of Landlords are at the root of crime and of misconduct in both countries. This is a truth not the less dangerous because it cannot be openly declared.' At the same time he was suspicious of the real motives of Poor Law reformers. 'In many Unions the conscious shame of the Guardians on account of the insufficiency of their workhouse, combined with unwillingness to tax the ratepayers to make good the deficiency, places them in constant opposition to the Law . . .', he told Wharncliffe. 'They therefore shelter themselves under a preference for Outdoor relief, which, as administered by them, would be a recurrence to the old system . . .' The Act's virtue was that 'it had saved to the Ratepayers, with a growing population, two millions annually . . .'[6]

Cool, unemotional calculations, openly based on the tenets of political economy, inevitably made Graham unpopular with Evangelical humanitarians like Ashley, the romantics of the 'Young England' group of Tories and working-class campaigners against *laissez-faire*. But Graham had never cared about popularity. 'We suffer much from the hostility of the Press', he told Peel, 'but we are not its slaves, and I had rather have it for my enemy than that it should be my master.' Careful, largely administrative, reforms continued to be planned, however. With Gladstone, Graham organised one of the series of abortive investigations into the ever-worsening position of the framework-knitters and handloom-weavers.[7] In 1843 he secured a Registration of Voters Act to improve the operation and prevent the abuse of the Reform Act. He provided for the registration and control of Friendly Societies between 1842 and 1846 and was largely responsible, with Lyndhurst, for reforming bankruptcy law in 1842 and legal payments systems in 1845. And the Government was responsible for important legislation on companies, railways and banks, and regularly continued the liberalisation of trade.

II

Though in Britain good harvests and expanding commerce seemed to be proving the antidote for political and social unrest, as Graham and Peel had expected, Ireland, inevitably, remained discontented. O'Connell's association with the Melbourne Government had not been so close as many Tories suspected; but it was certain that his connection with a Ministry under 'Orange Peel' would be less friendly. He expected a reversal of the moderately liberal policies of the Whigs and a restoration of coercion. He was already prepared, as head of the Loyal National Repeal Association of 1840; but the campaign was not yet widely supported, and in November Graham recommended that 'no notice should be taken of these Repeal subscriptions'. The Home Secretary was heavily involved in Irish affairs and was intent on 'an impartial and liberal policy' and 'a steady and marked discountenancing of the Repeal party'. The Irish administration, however, was not very well chosen. De Grey, the Orange-inclined Viceroy, Peel feared, was 'a little apt to keep the [Chief] Secretary [the Catholic sympathiser Lord Eliot] too much in the background'; and de Grey himself found the Lord Chancellor, Sir Edward Sugden, 'a man, though an excellent lawyer, whose judgment in matters of policy and public expediency I do not attach weight to'.[8] The Viceroy and the Under-Secretary, Edward Lucas, soon disagreed with Eliot over the continuation of the national schools set up by Stanley in 1831; and the law officers started legal proceedings without consulting the politicians. The task of composing the differences between the officers at Dublin Castle largely fell to Graham, adding another burden to his already busy life.

Stanley himself considered, in November, that 'the scheme for *united* education had in great measure failed' and suggested State aid for voluntary schemes. Eliot complained that Irish Church promotions were being given only to clerical opponents of National Education, and Graham and Peel disapproved of such a policy. After many complaints about the disunity of the Irish Government, on 8 November 1842 the Cabinet resolved on 'adherence to the present plan [of education], with correction of abuses which may have arisen', and Graham believed the decision was 'politic and right' as a proof of the Government's impartiality. The Government hoped that the policy would prevent religious strife. But more serious divergences arose over an appeal by the Roman Catholic hierarchy for an increased State grant to the seminary at Maynooth. 'If it were not for Protestant feeling, the last thing which I would refuse to the Catholics should be money,' Graham told Stanley; but to prevent controversy an increase was refused. Throughout the discussions Peel and Graham constantly feared that the personal disagreements at Dublin might lead to the collapse of the Irish Government.[9]

Important though religious and educational problems were, they were still overshadowed by the troubled state of Irish land law. The Government was not disposed to interfere, because, Graham told Eliot, legislation would shake 'the rights of property'. Ministerial inaction and extensive distress during the summer of 1842 provoked a rapid growth of O'Connell's Association, with its promise of land reform and social justice. By May de Grey was alarmed by the 'astounding' growth, and Graham was 'uneasy' in April. Ministers were undecided on how to act. Certainly they stood by the Union and resolved to take no notice of journalistic attacks, but Wellington favoured the banning of the Association, the mobilisation of troops and the arming of the Ulster yeomanry. It seemed possible to the apprehensive Graham that the situation might escalate into 'a religious war'. And in this tense position the Government made errors; Lucas resigned; Sugden bungled the legal issues; and Graham unwisely told the Commons on 17 June during a debate on the Arms Bill that 'conciliation had been carried to its utmost limit in Ireland'. But Peel and Graham were soon agreed that while the Irish Church must be defended, Roman Catholics must be emancipated fully, especially by receiving a fair share of patronage. De Grey, as Graham expected, did not approve: to him, 'conciliation was a chimera', and he insisted on retaining the Conservative Lucas while regularly complaining of Sugden and Eliot. Yet the peak of the crisis passed. O'Connell withdrew or modified his more violent threats; and Graham moderated his outburst and tried to persuade de Grey to follow the Government's policy.

Faced by the great Repeal Association, with many allies among Whig and Radical politicians, and by Irish landowners and ultra Tories demanding strong action, the Ministers were in a difficult strategic position. By September Graham had 'begun to despair of the Irish Executive: it did not only sleep; it was dead'. With Wellington, he regretted the neglect of prosecutions and often feared 'a religious struggle directed by the R. Catholic hierarchy and priesthood . . . which would lead to bloodshed and convulse the empire'. Yet even he saw signs that 'the heat of the repeal fever had somewhat abated'.[10]

Graham believed privately that Irish evils arose from 'the bankrupt condition of the landlords and the severance of the religion of the people from all connection with the State'; but typically he held that the Government 'could not heal this gangrene, but might probe it [by a Commission on land tenure] and propose to administer decisive remedies'. At the same time, he hoped to press sedition charges against O'Connell. When the Repealers wrote of 'repeal cavalry' in placards for a rally at Clontarf on 8 October, the Government struck by banning the meeting and arresting the leaders, while Graham 'was pouring troops into Ireland from every quarter'. There followed long anxiety over the result of a trial. But this, Graham told Eliot, was 'the moment for tempering firmness with reasonable concession'. He 'never had so much work' as within the first fortnight of October and told Peel that he 'sometimes almost despaired'. Nevertheless, some progress was being made; a few Catholics received posts; Lord Devon agreed to head a Land Commission; discreet appeals to Rome were planned. But Graham gloomily expected that O'Connell would escape imprisonment.[11]

'It was clear' to Peel in October 'that mere force, however necessary the application of it, would do nothing as a permanent remedy for the social evils' of Ireland. Yet the Devon Commission necessarily took many months over its deliberations, while the trial of O'Connell and seven of his associates was wretchedly bungled. However, with O'Connell detained, his threatening bluff called over Clontarf and his authority already disputed by the 'Young Ireland' group, the Government had a chance to act. In February 1844 Peel suggested to the Cabinet that Maynooth's grant should be increased (with the hope of improving both the educational standards and the political loyalty of its graduates) and that mortmain law should be relaxed to permit voluntary endowment of religious groups and ministers. And while the Commons debated Russell's motion for a Committee of the whole House on 'the state of Ireland', Peel bluntly told his colleagues that he feared impotence in the administration of Irish law; efforts must be made to win over moderate Roman Catholics, by extending education, equalising the franchise and examining land law — while maintaining both the Union and the Church Establishment. Gladstone's religious scruples postponed an announcement on Maynooth, but Stanley agreed with Peel that 'the education of the Catholics was the point to look to' and called for the establishment of three new 'colleges' for further education of both clergy and laity of various denominations.[12] In the end, it was decided that the Maynooth grant should be increased and distinct institutions provided for lay education; Graham and Gladstone supported the establishment of a new, interdenominational university, as it seemed 'inexpedient to open' Trinity College Dublin. Apart from extending education, trying to persuade the reluctant de Grey to appoint Roman Catholic officials, hoping for an improvement in the priesthood and ordering an enquiry on the land (though believing, with Graham, that 'the remedies were beyond the reach of legislative power'), Peel's Government had few plans for Ireland. The 'potato economy' remained.

Graham was meanwhile involved in planning O'Connell's trial, which the lawyers at Dublin Castle mishandled throughout. 'A trial of O'Connell in Ireland seemed [to Greville] a desperate measure' from the start, 'and it was not easy to see how a conviction was to be procured from an Irish jury'. The Irish Government tried to solve the problem by (perhaps negligently) omitting qualified men from the special jury list and then carefully objecting to all the balloted Catholics. Graham was furiously angry. 'How strange it is', he told de Grey, 'that nothing can be done in Ireland without a blunder, when Irishmen alone are employed.' He could not accept that the mistake was 'accidental' and was determined to punish those responsible for such 'gross and palpable' negligence. But he remained convinced that a legal victory was vital: otherwise, 'the days of civil Government were numbered . . . unless the sword might be able to save what the law had ceased to protect'. 'The unhappy trial', Greville thought on 14 January, 'had been one continual course of blunders and mismanagement from first to last', and he condemned the 'stupid, narrow-minded, shortsighted, professional eagerness to ensure a conviction', expecting no 'satisfactory and reasonable solution' of Irish problems. But the Dublin jury found O'Connell guilty on eleven counts, and 'nothing could exceed the satisfaction of the Government'. Greville thought that 'the agitation which has been suspended will not be renewed. The notion of O'Connell's infallibility which had got hold of the people has been des-troyed . . .' And the decision arrived in time to help Graham and the Ministry in a long Commons debate. Disraeli and his aristo-cratic 'Young Englanders' had already opposed Government Irish policy in 1843 (with the result that Graham curtly rejected Disraeli's application for a post for his brother), but now voted with the Ministers, though Disraeli affirmed that 'the Irish question' consisted of 'a starving population, an absentee aristocracy and an alien Church, and in addition the weakest executive in the world'.[13] 'Young England' was still intent on proving that it would follow what it regarded Strafford's policy to have been. But Whiggish support for moderate 'O'Connellism' was worrying. And O'Connell, his bragging claims disproved but his political importance confirmed, decided to appeal against his sentence, gathered liberal support and exploited the effect of his (actually luxurious) confinement.

The Irish Government remained uneasy. In May Eliot, now widely regarded as incompetent, even suggested the abolition of his own post; but Peel would rather abolish the pageantry of the Lord Lieutenancy itself, and Eliot refused a Cabinet post. Lucas again offered his resignation and in July Lord Heytesbury succeeded de Grey, with orders to wean from 'Repeal' the moderate Roman Catholics, 'by the steady manifestation of a desire to act with impartiality and to do that which was just'. Progress was slowed, however, by concern over the new Federalist ideas now gaining ground in Ireland. Federalism, thought Graham, might be 'the middle term on which for the moment opposite parties would agree'; the Whigs would accept 'some scheme of national representation' and O'Connell would secure many of his aims. Peel was active in opposition: 'if Ireland must have Federalism so must Scotland. Why not Wales? Why not Wessex? — and the kingdoms of the Heptarchy?'[14] The ideal initially attracted O'Connell; it would give Ireland some form of internal self-government and some say in Imperial affairs, and it might attract many moderate liberal-minded men (despite Russell's opposition), while repelling the 'Young Ireland' nationalist activists. However, O'Connell soon dropped it to maintain the unity of his own agitation.

Graham continued to watch the progress of O'Connell's appeal. Peel insisted that the case should be decided by the Law Lords and not by a political vote of the peers, and in April Graham was consoled by the law officers' belief that they '*ought* to succeed'. By September the outlook was gloomier. The majority of the English judges agreed with the Irish verdict in general, but Lyndhurst reported that Denman, one of the five Law Lords, might oppose him. This would 'indeed be a serious disaster', Graham burst out, bitterly resenting the political considerations leading Denman to join the Whigs Cottenham and Campbell. His 'whole Irish policy', he told Peel, was 'likely to be subverted and turned into confusion'. Primarily on technical grounds, Denman opposed Lyndhurst and Brougham and thus reversed the judgement. The decision 'came on the world [and Greville] like a clap of thunder', although the released O'Connell was considerably weakened in his political hold and the Government, though shaken, continued to work on other matters. There was great difficulty in persuading suspicious Roman Catholics to accept and support the Charitable Donations Act, and a recurrence of trouble over Wellington's plans for garrisoning Ireland — which Graham considered 'rash, cruel and utterly indefensible'. But to Graham, the failure of the case against O'Connell seemed tragic. The Lords' decision had 'inflicted a deep, perhaps an incurable, wound in a very tender part', he told Croker: 'the administration of justice according to law [would be] more difficult than ever . . . no Irish juries would ever again convict in a political case, and it would be hard to find judges bold enough to do their duty when the House of Lords betrayed its trust . . .'[15] Ministerial duties and worries weighed heavily on the increasingly tired Graham. He was 'on duty about fourteen hours every day in the House of Commons', he told Lord Anson in July 1845, and 'the labour . . . was rapidly becoming too great for human endurance', when added to the burden of administrative responsibilities. When Ministerial weakness in the Lords and Stanley's determination (from preference and feared ill-health) to 'stay no longer in the House of Commons' led to his elevation, Graham confessed to Greville 'what a weight it cast on himself and Peel, and what a loss [Stanley] was to them there'.[16]

III

Peel's policy for Ireland continued to be conciliatory, and Heytesbury was more inclined to follow it than de Grey had been. Roman Catholic members of the 'Board of Bequests' for the first time provided an 'official' body with whom the Government might discuss religious questions, especially on education — which, Graham forecast, would soon lead to debates over Maynooth. It was now accepted that it would be impossible to train laymen and priests together and that State control could not substantially be extended. The 'Maynooth arrangement was the most difficult but the most important part of the whole settlement', giving the Government a last chance of influencing Catholic opinion and the future priesthood, and for this reason Graham was interested in gaining further Papal support against O'Connell and Archbishop MacHale of Tuam. In January 1845 Peel and Graham morosely pondered over a mysteriously-phrased letter from Gladstone, apparently threatening to resign from the Board of Trade if they proceeded with the proposal to increase financial aid to Maynooth threefold and incorporate the College trustees, which conflicted with his published views on the relationship between Church and State.[17] Peel, knowing that the Bill would provoke a political storm and greatly respecting Gladstone, urged him to remain; but Gladstone insisted on resigning, though he subsequently voted with the Government. About the same time Eliot left Ireland on

Q

succeeding as Earl of St. Germans, and was followed by Fremantle, whose own sisters were Roman Catholics.

The Maynooth Bill introduced on 3 April provided £30,000 for college buildings and an annual grant of £26,360 and allowed annual official visitations. Protestant Britain rose to arms immediately, and Dissenting and Evangelical protests soon flowed to Parliament. Passions flared high, cutting across normal alliances: Young England and Anti-Corn Law League alike were divided, and the simmering arguments between Conservatives broke into the open. 'The truth is that the Government is Peel,' gleefully commented Greville, 'that Peel is a reformer and more of a Whig than a Tory, and that the mass of his followers are prejudiced, ignorant, obstinate and selfish.' Disraeli lashed the Ministry, especially Peel, in a celebrated speech, while Graham 'grinned a sort of compelled smile'. George Smythe and Sir George Grey (both, ultimately, supporting the Bill) recalled Graham's words on the limits of concession, whereupon Graham 'avowed his regret' for the expression, affirmed that 'his actions towards Ireland had been better than his words' and strenuously supported the proposal to improve Maynooth's wretched facilities, thus earning O'Connell's admiration.[18] Despite provincial protests, the important division was carried by a majority of 147. But the split in what Disraeli sneeringly called 'the great Conservative confederation, which was destined to destroy so many things' was immensely widened, with consequences soon apparent. 'Peel's speech', noted Greville, 'was considered as clearly indicative of a consciousness that his party was broken up and the termination of his tenure of office approaching'; Wharncliffe 'did not think they should be in office a month hence'. A change would not be unwelcome to Graham at least. He knew that 'our country gentlemen were out of humour' and might destroy the Government, he told Croker, in March:

> We have laboured hard, and not in vain, to restore the prosperity of the country and to give increased security to the aristocracy, by improving the condition and diminishing the discontent of the great masses of the people. We have effected this object without inflicting any real injury on the landed proprietors; yet we are

scouted as traitors . . . The country gentlemen cannot be more ready to give us the death-blow than we are prepared to receive it. If they will rush on to their own destruction, they must have their way. We have endeavoured to save them, and they regard us as enemies for so doing . . . the time will come when this party will bitterly deplore the fall of Sir Robert Peel and when in vain they will wish that they had not overthrown a Government which its enemies could not vanquish but which its supporters abandoned and undermined.

And Peel, convinced of his rectitude and the support of all parliamentary 'youth, talent and real influence,' was 'indifferent' to the storm, 'being resolved on carrying the Bill and being very careless as to the consequences' to himself. 'The Bill will pass', Graham told Heytesbury, 'but our party is destroyed.'[19]

The Conservative leaders now knew the extent of back-bench Tory hostility, engendered over the years by Ministerial 'liberalism'. They were brave enough — and tired enough — to persist in their policy, whatever the consequences. As Lord Devon's report on Irish land problems was published, containing few important recommendations (apart from the suggestion of compensating tenants for permanent improvements) but much evidence on social conditions, the Government pressed ahead with their educational reforms. As usual, political, 'diplomatic' and organisational measures appealed to Ministers. Graham secured an Act for the establishment of three Irish colleges, meeting only slight ultra-Tory hostility to 'Godless education' at Westminster but provoking wide opposition in Ireland. He encouraged Stanley to introduce a Compensation to Tenants Bill (which soon foundered) and told Heytesbury that a County Franchise Bill must be prepared to extend English privileges to Ireland.[20] But Peel considered that 'there was sheer cowardice in dealing with the disturbers of the public peace'. He rejoiced when 'tranquility' was restored at Fermanagh 'by courage and enforce- ment of the ordinary law', but was disturbed to hear of Orange arming. 'How disgusting and horrid is this mutual hatred among fellow-countrymen on account of differences in the Christian faith!' Graham wrote to Heytesbury. He was angry at the

aristocratic Orange leaders' support for violence: 'Our dangers
from without are threatening enough [and] we might be spared
this internal discord,' he told Peel. After all the work, Ireland
remained an apparently unsolvable problem. 'Affairs are rapidly
verging to a crisis,' Graham wrote in late September. He 'saw no
cure for the evils which rendered impartial government . . . almost
impossible'; Protestant opposition would prevent any further
concessions to Roman Catholics. Graham was sadly 'aware that,
notwithstanding honest intentions and constant efforts, the
government of [Ireland] did not prosper under his care'. Peel
agreed: his views on Ireland 'had long been very gloomy', for 'it
was in a state which seemed to preclude honest and impartial
government'; but Graham had 'done whatever could be done to
apply a remedy . . .'[21] Now a new factor was not only to worsen
Ireland's woes but also to have dramatic effects on politics in
general.

In the summer the Cabinet was worried about the harvest. The
gout-ridden Stanley reported potato blight in some areas, and
Graham regretted that 'Ministers were driven to study the
barometer with so much anxiety'. But it seemed likely that while
much of England would have a low wheat crop, Irish crops would
be satisfactory. Later there was concern over the potato crop, but
by late September Graham had received 'more satisfactory
reports' and hoped that 'the failure, though extensive, was by no
means general'. Despite 'the recent terrible rains', on 8 October
Graham was 'sanguine in his belief that the potato crop, tho'
damaged, was not so much below the average as some of the
exaggerated reports from Ireland had led them to apprehend'.
Five days later the blow fell. As the Irish peasants started to dig
up their potatoes they discovered a widespread blight, and
Heytesbury sent an alarming report to Graham and Peel. Their
reactions were similar. 'The removal of impediments to import is
the only effectual remedy,' insisted Peel. Graham hoped that the
reports might be exaggerated, like so many others from Ireland,
but agreed that Heytesbury 'did not readily give credit to false
alarms'. American maize might be provided, 'if the people would
eat it', but free trade seemed to be the real answer and Graham

suggested a remission of duties by Order in Council in November. In a matter 'so momentous and so lasting in its consequence', however, Peel preferred careful planning. He agreed with Graham that, once suspended, the Corn Law could never be re-enacted. Now the Ministers faced a gathering pressure, which Graham prophesied would be 'the most formidable movement in modern times'.[22]

IV

Thoughts of ultimate Free Trade had long lingered in Peel's and Graham's minds. 'I agree with you that we must advance in our present course of relaxation,' Peel wrote in July 1842; in February 1843 Graham had admitted to the Commons that 'free trade principles . . . were the principles of common sense'. Successive Budgets had implemented these ideas. In 1843, faced by a substantial deficit, Goulburn reduced only the duty on Canadian wheat, and in 1844, despite a larger surplus, merely cut the controversial sugar duties. But in 1845, as national prosperity rapidly mounted, 430 of the remaining 813 dutiable articles were freed, other duties lowered, all export taxes abolished, payments on raw cotton and glass ended and timber and sugar preferences modified. This massive change in the Protectionist nature of the economy had been accompanied by 'improving' legislation on the Bank of England in 1844 and the Scottish banks in 1845, designed to stabilise the currency, on business companies and railways in 1844 and on bankruptcy law and county courts in 1842 and 1846. The State finances and the administrative arrangements of the world's workshop had thus been considerably modernised. Doubting country squires had generally followed Peel thus far, though with some reluctance and with occasional temporary revolts. Periodic threats by party whips and the lack of any obvious successor to Peel had maintained discipline among most Tories. But the abolition of the last great symbol of Protection, the Corn Law, regarded with almost mystical devotion in the shires, would inevitably provoke a major outburst. Croker had warned Peel even in 1843 that while 'the country will stand by [the

1842 modifications] . . . if it sees reason to suspect your Government of wavering, mind, I tell you, we are all lost'.[23]

The Government's difficulties soon became apparent to the leading Ministers. Peel called a Cabinet meeting on 31 October, to discuss the need for immediate relief in Ireland and to decide on the Corn Laws; he recommended a suspension. After two days' discussion the Ministers were seriously divided, and at a further meeting on 6 November only Aberdeen, Graham and Sidney Herbert supported Peel's plan to reduce duties by Order, recall Parliament and prepare a new Bill on the Corn Laws. Greville heard that 'Aberdeen was the strongest of any against the Corn Laws [and] the Duke the most determined to support them' (which Peel, unwilling to reveal the extent of dissension to the Queen, ascribed to Wellington's deafness). Perhaps the most hostile to the plan was Stanley, who 'found it difficult to express . . . the regret with which he saw how widely he differed with Graham and [Peel]' and believed that the party would be broken.[24] Graham alone was permitted to read Stanley's argument and 'returned the paper with a heavy heart' to Peel who sent it back to Stanley 'with the deepest regret'. Graham feared the loss of another old friend; Spencer had died in September. While trying to 'convert' other Ministers he concentrated on Stanley, believing, as he told Herbert, that the next Cabinet decision 'would be conclusive for good or for evil'. But on 29 November he found Stanley still 'opposed to the opening of the ports' and insistent that the choice was between Protection and Free Trade; and Stanley told Peel that 'the best thing, for our own credit and for the country, would be that we should agree to differ'. Furthermore, the League's activity was mounting and the Whigs could not resist making a bid against the Ministry. On 22 November Russell wrote from Edinburgh telling his London constituents of his conversion from a small fixed duty to free entry. To the Queen's annoyance, the Cabinet remained divided at meetings on 24 and 26 November and 2, 3 and 4 December, although finally only Stanley and Buccleuch stood out. But Peel knew that the assent of others 'was a reluctant one' and on 6 December tendered his resignation to the Queen, as Herbert had recommended on the 4th.

The public already had some inkling of the Cabinet's deliberations, as Aberdeen had told Delane of *The Times* of an apparent
agreement on 3 December; for some time Herbert was blamed for
this leak. Greville found that 'the whole town had been electrified'
by the exclusive news, despite denials by the Protectionist
Standard; but even he did not know of the resignation until the
11th, when Russell arrived at Osborne. Russell was uncertain
about the possibility of forming a Whig Government with
Conservative majorites in both Houses. Graham assured him that
Peel would offer no 'captious objections' to his Corn Law settlement, but on the 13th the Whigs were still doubtful and Peel
naturally refused to give them close pledges of support. Graham
told Fremantle on the 18th that Russell was 'still undecided', but
that evening Russell agreed to form a Government. Next day
Russell was again 'not certain', because of Grey's objection to
Palmerston taking the Foreign Office; and on the 20th he told
Graham that he could not accept office. Peel returned to his post,
with his Ministers, apart from Stanley, who insisted on resigning.
The Colonial Office was offered to Gladstone, and Peel was
worried that Stanley might dissuade him from accepting. Almost
inevitably, it was Graham who had to 'prevent [Stanley] doing
mischief' (although 'his spell was broken [and] his influence was
gone') and who helped to persuade Buccleuch to accept the
Presidency of the Council. He was amazed at Russell's weakness
and not entirely pleased at resuming his anxious labours.[25]

V

Just before Christmas Graham took up again the many burdens
of the Home Office. In the summer and autumn he had had many
varied tasks. For instance, in August he and Greville had to
provide hasty orders for the continuation of Guernsey liquor
duties. Suspicions of French intentions led him to interest himself
in Herbert's plans for the strengthening of the militia and
defences. But above all, he was closely concerned with the
organisation of Irish relief services. Perhaps unfortunately, the
head of the operation was Sir Charles Trevelyan, who had angered

Peel and Graham in 1843 by publishing a confidential discussion. The Irish Relief Commission was set up in November, but Graham believed that 'the extreme pressure from want would not take place until . . . April or May'. The 1838 Poor Law provided relief only inside workhouses, and the Commission's duty was to give additional help, primarily by providing supplies of maize and Army stores to local committees; and measures to provide employment in public works were quickly prepared. By the end of the year, 'the Irish potato case was beginning to develop itself in its awful magnitude', wrote Graham: '. . . we have a nation to carry, as it were, in our arms . . .' Ireland continued to take much of his time, as he planned an Assassination Bill, complained of apathetic landlords, prevented Treasury officials from interfering with Heytesbury's schemes and urged the Irish Government to meet the emergency with 'great exertions and prompt decision'.[26] If, in the end, his work for Ireland was unsuccessful, the failure was not due to lack of energy, but rather to intractable, long-term causes.

As the Irish tragedy of starvation and disease unfolded, Britain awaited Peel's plan for the Corn Law. Parliament met on 19 January 1846 to hear the Queen announce Peel's proposals to complete his reform of the tariff. Within days, Peel revealed his determination to balance the gradual repeal of the Corn Laws with the abolition of tariffs on many manufactured goods and a lightening of local rates. Long debates followed, principally on the Corn Bill, against which the majority of Tory Members quickly formed a Protectionist party under Stanley in the Lords and the hitherto indolent Lord George Bentinck in the Commons. The Third Reading passed only on 15 May. Meanwhile, Peel and Graham had also pressed ahead with their Custom Bill, passed the Poor Removal Bill to lighten unfair burdens on landowners and led their group, with the Liberals, against John Fielden's Ten Hours Bill, which, largely supported by Protectionists and Whigs, was only narrowly defeated. Lord St. Germans had taken the 'Preservation of Life Bill', strengthening Irish Government powers, through the Lords, and on 30 March Graham gloomily introduced it in the Commons. Ireland 'has ruined many

Administrations and has been the stumbling-block which has caused the downfall of the greatest men', he had told Croker (who, like most Protectionists, denied that Ireland's woes would be solved by Free Trade). 'It has not lost its malignant influence, and it will do its accustomed work again.' Yet the new measure of coercion was both necessary and comparatively moderate. The Bill's principal stages were debated after the Corn Bill, and the danger lay primarily in Protectionist desire for revenge.

Both Bentinck and Russell were originally committed to the measure, but both ultimately decided in early June to oppose the Ministry. This 'rendered the defeat of that measure certain', and Graham favoured resignation. He worked hard to defend both the Bill and the Free Trade measures, but early on 26 June the Second Reading was defeated by 292 votes to 219. Thus the Protectionists punished their former leaders' 'treason'. Next day Peel tendered his resignation to the Queen. On 5 July Peel, Aberdeen and Graham 'parted [from the Queen] with great emotion, and had tears in their eyes when they thanked [her] for her confidence and support'. Many old friendships had been broken; Bentinck raged against Peelite 'deception' in the Commons; Stanley was no longer at home when Graham called; Croker had 'sympathised in his personal struggles and prayed for his political defeat' and subsequently castigated him for inconsistency. Amid all the bitterness, however, Peel recorded his 'grateful acknowledgment [of Graham's] zealous support and able assistance'; through their years in office they had shared 'unreserved confidence'. Brougham, hoping now to lead the Peelite peers, reported a rumour that his 'old and valued friend Graham' was to enter the Lords. The story was untrue, and Peel would 'strongly dissuade him from [such action], for his own sake, under present circumstances, even if he wished it, which [Peel] was sure he did not'. Brougham, as Graham noted, wished 'to organise an immediate Opposition'; and Russell offered Cabinet posts to the Peelites Dalhousie, Lincoln and Herbert, who refused. As Peel and Graham, tired and ill, retired to Drayton and Netherby, there were some consolations in their own friendship and loyalty. They had 'concluded with honour a successful career as well as a desperate conflict', and Graham's 'cordial support and entire and unreserved confidence had been [Peel's] chief stay'. Graham reciprocated such sentiments, stressing his 'fixed intention to act in strict union' with Peel: 'I hope that till the close of our lives we shall never be divided'. Furthermore, the messages from the industrial areas gave further pleasure to the two weary politicians. 'The heartfelt tribute of grateful thanks from poor and suffering millions', thought Graham, 'is some compensation for the malignant hatred and abuse of pampered landowners.' And he was delighted that Blamire gave 'entire approbation' to his views. He gave his old friend 'full credit for his foresight and disinterested boldness and honesty in the early avowal and steady maintenance of these opinions'.[27]

10

The Peelite

On his retirement from office in June 1846 Graham sought no
honour or position, preferring to rest at Netherby. The years of
work had taken their toll on his health. He had been 'an admirable
coadjutor of Peel's, for the business of the House of Commons',
thought Charles Villiers: 'See how these two men do their business
and understand it!' Colquhoun maintained that Peel and Graham
had 'mutual defects', but that Graham had one 'superiority' in
'his power of forecasting the future'. In August Hobhouse,
Shaw-Lefevre and Labouchere made a 'comparative estimate of
the powers of endurance' of leading politicians and placed Graham,
Peel and Russell 'very far above all competition'; Labouchère,
indeed, believed that Graham's office 'gave him more labour than
both put together'. Now Graham had no official position and
little chance of a seat in the next Parliament. When in November
the Prince Consort persuaded him and Lincoln to serve on a new
council for the Duchy of Lancaster, there was 'a great uproar'
among men suspecting a coalition with Russell. Graham explained
his feelings while dining with Gladstone. He agreed with Peel's
desire to 'abjure party and stand aloof for ever and never resume
office . . . He was weary of labour at thirteen or fourteen hours a
day, and of the intolerable abuse to which he was obliged to
submit; but his habits were formed in the House of Commons
and for it, and he was desirous to continue there as an independent
gentleman, taking part from time to time in public business as he
might find occasion and giving his leisure to his family and to
books.' He had been hurt by the 'virulence' of opponents and
deeply resented the Protectionists who had ousted Peel: 'with
those gentlemen he could never unite', although he understood
their feelings.[1]

Gladstone did not believe it possible for prominent politicians thus to cut themselves off from public affairs. But Peel and Graham were not disposed to form a party from the 112 Conservatives who had supported the Corn Bill. They continued to look back with pride on their achievement and watched developments from the wings. Ireland's distress 'could not be met by measures within the strict rules of economical science', Graham maintained, wondering 'whether John Russell would be found equal to this occasion'. By November Irish affairs were 'very alarming' and Graham doubted the value of expensive but unproductive public works and pondered whether the three-year abolition of the Corn Laws should not be hastened. Peel would not accept 'total and immediate, instead of deferred repeal', but shared many of Graham's fears about the worsening situation in Ireland.[2] Such interests in current problems — and in the controversial reduction of sugar duties — did not lessen Peel's pleasure in enjoying what he called to the King of the Belgians 'the coolness and impartiality of a spectator'. As a sign of similar intentions, Graham resigned from the Carlton Club. His principal desire was to support Peel, but he did not favour the efforts of Dalhousie, Lincoln and Edward Cardwell to organise a party. However, the logic of events and a mutual regard for their leader gradually led to the emergence of a 'Peelite' group during 1847. The Liberal Conservatives tended to support the Whig Ministry on Ireland, although (as Graham told Joseph Sandars) 'yellow meal, in the end, would do more for Ireland than O'Connell, Repeal and all the claptrap of a "Liberal Government" '. In February Graham supported the temporary continuation of his public works schemes but urged that workers should soon return to the land; in March he favoured a land drainage Bill but opposed the principle of large loans to a few large proprietors — and he reluctantly accepted the provision of outdoor relief under the Irish Poor Law and a £600,000 grant for Irish aid. On the other hand, he offended Russell in April by welcoming a new English educational grant but attacking Roman Catholic exclusion from its benefits. And he opposed the Government's Bill to advance £620,000 for Irish railway construction, Fielden's Ten

Hours Bill (which several Whig Ministers now supported) and the abolition of transportation. On the English Poor Law he remained firm, voting for Grey's Bill to set up the Poor Law Board.[3] By the summer of 1847 Graham was again working hard.

I

In February Greville found Graham 'not very well satisfied with the Government, though wishing to keep them in rather than let in the Protectionists', whose connections with the Ministers annoyed him. When they next met in mid-June Greville had heard from Bedford that Russell intended to offer Graham the Governor-Generalship of India, on the recommendation of the Company chairman, Sir James Hogg, and with Wellington's approval. But Graham would refuse for a fourth time, as he would not take a post from Russell, who, he unfairly maintained, 'was evidently animated by very implacable sentiments towards him'. Greville insisted that Russell had no such bitterness, but Graham remained 'very low and very much vexed' and refused to discuss the matter again. Russell meanwhile told Ellice that, 'after reflection and communication' with Lansdowne and Wellington, he knew that Graham was 'the best man for the government of India' and sent an official invitation. Graham asked permission to consult Peel, who advised him against acceptance. But even at this stage Russell hoped that Graham might accept, and promised to keep the post open. The fact was that Graham might not have a seat after the July elections.

Dorchester was no longer available, and when Lord Londonderry offered a Durham seat, in February, Graham preferred to 'reserve to himself perfect freedom of future action, unfettered by any obligation' to the Marquess. He soon hoped that the Cumbrian Whigs might again nominate him; but Aglionby wrote to say that Charles Howard and William Marshall (a manufacturer's son) had been selected, and although Graham pledged his support to Howard, Morpeth sent him a cool refusal of help. Greville recorded that 'Graham took this very ill, and was evidently hurt at the way in which he was thus excluded . . .' But

Graham was 'always in the garret or in the cellar', and the flattering offer of India cheered him. However, parliamentary life still attracted him, and his regular searches for a seat caused some embarrassment; in 1852 Palmerston dreaded the possibility of 'having to go abegging like Graham from one place to another'. Eventually, Earl de Grey, who had inherited the Aislabie family's great Studley Royal estate and the political control of Ripon from that formidable Tory patron Miss Elizabeth Lawrence in 1845, offered Graham his father's old seat (which he had considered in 1841). Graham insisted on freedom to 'adhere to [his] independent course', but, backed by the Robinsons' influence, he was inevitably elected.[4]

Graham retained friendly relations with some Whigs. Clarendon, the Irish Lord Lieutenant, was grateful for an offer of advice; Cornewall Lewis appreciated his honest consistency on the Poor Law; Langdale congratulated him on his 'manly and generous course' towards Roman Catholics. In October he suggested that the Government would be strengthened by appointing Cobden to a Ministerial position in charge of the Poor Law. When the new Session opened he was appointed to the Select Committee on Commercial Distress. But Peelite attitudes to the Government remained variable. In December Graham told Greville that 'Peel thought this an excellent Parliament', but in February 1848 he 'expressed a doubt if the Ministers were up to their work . . . [and] said Peel was "more sullen than he had seen him" ' and had the same doubts, but nevertheless was 'more than ever resolved never to take office'. Graham was convinced that the new commercial policy required a new colonial policy: 'we ought to limit instead of extend our colonial empire', make Canada independent, and withdraw wasteful garrisons from the Empire. But the 'Peelite' position was difficult; Peel's own aims were in doubt, and the brilliant coterie which followed him was dwindling in the face of a lack of party policy and a consequent bleak future. Gladstone thought that the group was halved in 1847.[5]

In January 1848 Peel heard rumours that Bentinck was to be deposed from the Protectionist leadership and hoped that Inglis would lead 'a real old Tory, Church of England, Protectionist and Protestant party'. In fact, to Greville's amusement, the nominal leadership passed to Lord Granby in February. Meanwhile, Goulburn had been invited and told Peel of his hopes for eventual Conservative unity. But Peel had long doubted Goulburn's estimate of the 'difficulty of cordially reuniting the Conservative party', believing that 'the elements of disunion' existed 'in a formidable degree long before ... October 1845'. Now Graham admitted that he 'had no faith whatever in the possibility of reuniting under any circumstances the party which [Peel] led in 1841'. The only factor which had bound 'the different shades of opinion' together had been a general support for Peel, which was now lacking; and 'fresh combinations' rather than 'the revival of past agreements' provided the only hope of an eventual restoration of a Conservative party. But in February, when Graham 'thought the appearance of the House very alarming', the Ministers were 'in a state of continual uneasiness about Peel and Graham and the Peelites', because of the activities of Lincoln and the *Morning Chronicle*.[6]

The year of Continental revolutions saw Chartist violence in Britain and outrages among the starving Irish, facing the third successive failure of the potato crop. Both Graham and Peel wrote sympathetically to Count Jarnac, offering to help the exiled French Royal Family, whom Graham had met in Sicily. But Graham found Palmerston's 'rashness and insolence ... almost incredible'; whatever governments existed in Europe, 'he would not only deprive us of every friend but would convert every Power into an insulted and implacable enemy'. At Westminster he supported Russell's further grant to Ireland and his compromise proposals on sugar duties. But Conservative opinion in the country demanded something better than a choice between brilliant Whig-supporting Peelites and virtually leaderless Protectionists, whose divisions allowed Whiggism to retain power. Greville, who was 'in continual communication with Graham', primarily over 'Charles Wood's income tax agony' — on which Wood followed Graham's advice to meet his needs from reserves rather than increased taxation — found him 'by way of being very friendly to the Government but ... not sorry to see their mismanagement and unpopularity'. Graham still insisted that Peel would not return to office: he hated the Protectionists and the Whigs disliked Aberdeen and Graham, without whom Peel would not act. Greville himself hoped that Peel would take over a Whig-dominated Ministry from the ailing Russell.[7] But Peel and Graham were so determined in their hostility to Disraeli and Stanley's Protectionists that they gave no hopes to such ambitious men as Gladstone, Cardwell and Lincoln, who were still held by personal ties to Peel. Inevitably, Graham was 'greatly alarmed at the aspect of affairs both at home and abroad'; European revolutions and Chartist and Irish menaces roused all his apprehensions, and in April he had earnest conversations with the Speaker and Sir George Grey about precautions against the planned Chartist march to Parliament, and with Greville about the dangers of allowing the Irish Arms Bill to expire. 'The distress among the working classes is severe and of long continuance', he told Cornewall Lewis, and foreign examples had encouraged the progress of 'republican doctrines'; 'whether to yield anything, or how much, is the nicest question of practical statesmanship ...'

The great Chartist demonstration failed, and in May Wood asked Greville to sound Graham about West Indian affairs. Graham was opposed to any alteration of the 1846 settlement. 'He and Peel did not want to turn the Government out, nor embarrass them ... but he severely criticised [Palmerston's] conduct and was evidently very glad at his getting into such a scrape [over Spanish policies].' Greville was convinced that Graham

has a great contempt for the Government, thinks nobody has done well but Sir George Grey and Clarendon, but is biding his time and acting on the policy ... of making a junction with the Whigs possible hereafter. He is very much provoked with Lincoln and Gladstone, who he said were 'impatient' and acting in a spirit of most injudicious half hostility and annoyance to the Government ... His object is to have as many doors open to himself and Peel as is possible by-and-by, and he looks to govern upon such popular principles, and at the same time safe ones, as may enable them to

raise a standard that will have attraction for all moderate, sensible
and liberal people.

But Graham continued to support the Ministers, although by
June he thought that 'the Government seemed to be paralysed
and to have lost their understandings', after a succession of
tactical blunders. A Protectionist Government, he considered,
would lead to revolution, but on 23 June he fully expected Russell
to fall and Stanley to form a Ministry composed of Protectionists
and most of the Peelite leaders. Greville soon heard that the more
militant Peelites actually hoped to force Peel to form a moderate
Cabinet, but Graham still insisted that this was impossible.
Busier than ever, Greville acted as a courier between Russell and
Graham, now convinced by Graham's growing insistence that
Stanley should be made to attempt to form a Government that he
and Peel hoped to return to power. He gathered also that 'he and
Peel (who were man and wife politically) were provoked with their
followers and resented their conduct'. Graham meanwhile served
conscientiously on seven committees.[8]

Despite their suspect manœuvres and personal divisions, the
Peelites retained a position of importance in the oddly-balanced
Commons. In September Londonderry 'sounded [Graham] to
ascertain if he would consent to the reorganisation of the
Conservative party . . . and undertake a prominent part in leading
it'. Graham immediately refused; his differences with 'the High
Tory and Protectionist party' were 'irreconcilable', he could never
work with Bentinck and Disraeli and he was freely committed to
Peel. As he wrote, he heard of Bentinck's death, which provoked
'sad reflections'. Several other old acquaintances were dying:
Richard Matthews and Dr. Fletcher in 1846, followed by O'Connell in 1847 and Melbourne, Buller and Carlisle in 1848. In
January 1849 Russell consulted Lansdowne and the Cabinet and
offered Auckland's post at the Admiralty to Graham. To have received invitations from both major political parties within a few
months was a measure of Graham's current importance.

Catching the night train from Carlisle, Graham reached London
on the 12th. He closely questioned Russell on his plans, expressed
no 'wish that any more of the Peel party, of whom he considered

R

himself independent, should be asked to join' and decided to consult Peel. He missed Peel, but returned to Russell's house, where (recorded Lady John) he refused the post on 'the grounds that the Ministry were not prepared to go as far as he should think right in the Cobden line of retrenchment'. Greville thought that Russell was 'not pleased ... and would not make him another proposal if he could help it'; Graham was probably afraid and, as the Protectionists' 'favourite aversion', would have roused opposition. To Peel Graham explained that he disliked the Government's lack of retrenchment, Palmerston's power and the failing Irish policy. Nor would he accept the proffered peerage. Many old friends regretted his decision, but Graham was convinced. He 'had no personal objection' to Russell and indeed 'would have more confidence in his Government if his controlling power were more predominant ... it was not his supreme authority but the absence of it that [Graham] regarded with jealousy'. Greville soon discovered variations in accounts of the interview; Graham had put 'his objections and refusal in a much stronger way [to Peel] than he appeared to have put them to Lord John'. Greville maintained that[9]

> All this comes from his timidity, and I have no doubt the want of a really clear conscience. He pines for office, he dreads to take it; he knows he is an object of suspicion and dislike to people of all parties; he is embarrassed with his own position; he is clear-sighted enough to perceive all its entanglements and difficulties. All sorts of absurd stories are current about his demands and what the negotiation went off upon.

Eventually Greville was 'satisfied that [Graham had] both acted fairly and judged wisely'. Russell, it transpired, had given Graham information not to be repeated even to Aberdeen and Peel. 'I have played some pranks before high heaven in my time,' Graham told Greville. 'I quitted the Whigs once, and it would not do to quit them again; and unless I could subscribe to all their past conduct and policy, as well as feel quite satisfied for the future, it was better not to join.' Palmerston was 'the great obstacle'. One result was a further Tory approach. Londonderry was again selected for the task. He was an old friend of Graham, having been his host (and Disraeli's) at a 'most magnificent banquet' after the Queen's Coronation and later at Wynard Park. 'The enmity between Peel and the great body of the Conservative party is irreconcilable,' Graham replied: Granby's followers still hoped to restore the corn duties, and the debates on the Navigation Laws would prove their 'unabated and fierce animosity' to the Peelites. Graham regretted Peel's aloofness, but could not join an alliance without him; he was nearer to the Ministry than to the Protectionists. The fact was, as Peel wrote, that 'the position of parties — or rather of the relics of ancient parties — was now more complicated and embarrassing than ever'. The Government rested on its own weakness and 'the disunion of all opponents except the Radical party'.[10]

II

The Peelites remained unhappy about the Whigs' unwillingness to balance coercion with concession in Ireland. But they were themselves divided; Lincoln had been 'more surprised than he could say' that Graham should even consider Russell's proposal, and Graham discussed Ireland with both Stanley and Greville (who passed his views to the Cabinet). They remained linked only by their common loyalty to the enigmatic Peel and their hostility to any reversal of his Free Trade legislation. Although shaken by Russell's mismanagement of debates on colonial administration and by Palmerston's connivance at the export of arms to Sicilian insurgents, Graham firmly supported the abolition of the Navigation Laws and the idea of charging tax-exempted Ireland a rate in aid to maintain its own paupers. As the pioneer promoter of the latter plan, Graham was 'prodigiously alarmed' at the violent opposition in comparatively prosperous Ulster and Leinster and even urged Russell to drop the proposal; but a low rate was eventually levied on the wealthier districts. He saw the repeal of the Navigation Acts as a vital step in the liberal march: 'protection or no protection was the point at issue and . . . the battlefield . . . between reaction and progress'. He still favoured 'progress tempered by prudence and discretion'. But with 'no party, no organisation, no Whipper-in', the Peelites felt free, and for a time Gladstone thought of insisting on a reciprocal measure, which had some attraction to Stanley; after all, Gladstone's 'conduct was not placed in [Peel's] hands to govern'.[11] Peel's influential aid allowed the Government to pass its measure in both Houses.

For the rest of the Session Graham worried over the maladministration of Irish relief, joined the general hostility to Palmerston's bellicose foreign manœuvres, supported Russell's decision to transport rather than hang Smith O'Brien and three other Irish revolutionaries and opposed the Lords' right to alter the financial provisions of the Irish Poor Law. It was an unexciting period for one accustomed to great office. But, as Aberdeen told Greville in September, 'Peel thought of nothing but the progress and development of his Free Trade measures [and as] the present Government alone could and would carry them out . . . he strenuously supported them, being perfectly conscious that he had no party and consequently no power'. As Greville observed, 'this was . . . a disagreeable prospect for those of [Peel's] adherents who followed his fortunes to the last, and were now left high and dry'. Graham followed Peel, joining him in advising the Government on Irish policy — though not without recalling the Whigs' very different behaviour when in Opposition. But in the autumn both were concerned at the dangers to Free Trade from the Protectionist revival and Whiggish weakness. In June 1850 Graham told Greville that Peel 'thought of nothing but securing a fair trial for Free Trade and keeping the Protectionists out'.[12]

Peel believed that the Government's main strength would be 'the declared resolution of the Protectionists to restore Protection as a principle'; if the struggle were clear-cut the Ministry could win, although the Whigs were still burdened by previous pledges of a fixed duty. He prophesied 'a furious struggle' if the Protectionists seriously proposed to restore duties, and promised to do 'whatever he could do to defeat the project'. Graham's information on the Whigs' 'secret desire' for a 5s. corn duty disturbed Peel, but he 'totally disbelieved' the rumour that Russell would

reverse his statements of 1845 and face a 'fearful struggle'.
Graham discussed the question with his informant, Ellice,
discovering that Palmerston had never withdrawn his hostility to
the repeal of the Corn Laws and that the Government was
impressed by widespread public hostility to Free Trade. Peel was
inclined to dismiss such talk, quoting such men as Arbuthnot and
Bedford, but Graham retained 'a strong suspicion' that some
Ministers had 'a secret wish to revert to a fixed duty' — though
insisting that he had no doubts about Free Trade and 'even as a
proprietor of bad land, did not despair'. And when Peel quoted
Wood's confirmation that the Cabinet had not discussed the
question, Graham wrote of the possibility of Stanley and Disraeli
engineering a combination with the Radicals and Irish to bring
down the Government and commence 'the fearful struggle' which
would ruin the constitution. He would stay loyal to Peel and
believed that the continuance of the Government was 'the great
object'. Nevertheless, he wished that Russell would not 'excite
delusive expectations' by promising electoral reform. In the
summer Graham had told Russell that he must act on such
pledges and that he would support him. Greville inevitably heard
of the conversation and thought that 'Graham (after his wont)
was afraid of not being beforehand with public opinion or clamour,
and . . . was ready to advocate some Radical, or at any rate
Liberal measure'. But in December Graham was shocked by the
extent of Russell's commitment. He believed that there was a
tenable position 'between Tory prejudice and mountain movement'; but Russell 'had occupied it feebly', causing Graham
'serious alarm'.[13]

In February 1850 Disraeli made another effort to combine the
still large Protectionist party with the Peelites. 'For himself,' he
told Londonderry, 'he had long seen Protection was out of the
question, and he was looking to practical measures.' He recognised
his own deficiencies (being landless, Jewish and suspected) and
believed that Graham 'was the only man to be at the head of the
House of Commons'; under Graham and Stanley 'the country
would have a very strong Government'. Disraeli later told
Gladstone that 'for some time [he was] not without hope' of

Graham's acceptance. But Graham retorted that the Protectionists' changed views 'were entertained in secret', that he 'entirely approved' of Peel's policy and that power obtained dishonourably was worthless. He already knew of the Protectionist quandary; every interest except agriculture was enjoying an upward turn and even for agriculture (insisted Cornewall Lewis) the old Tories made only 'some vague proposal about local burdens and income tax'. Disraeli's view that 'Protection was not only dead but damned' and must now be superseded by remission of landowners' taxation was expounded in Protectionist speeches in support of Sir John Trollope's amendment to Villiers's motion on the Address. Trollope was easily defeated by 119 votes, but on 19 February Disraeli demanded a Committee on Poor Law reform in order to aid the agriculturalists, thus opening a major debate. Ministers and Liberals naturally stood by Free Trade, which Peel drearily and Graham militantly defended; Graham attacked his fellow-landowners for wishing to 'take a large portion of the burdens now resting upon property and place it upon labour and industry'. Gladstone caused 'a considerable sensation' by answering him. The Peelites were divided, and Disraeli was defeated only by 273 votes to 253. As a result, although Peel remained convinced that Protectionism was impossible, Graham pointed out that Stanley 'would now be able to offer the Queen a list which would not be an insult'.[14] Even Peel had only narrowly saved the Government.

It appeared that Peel's influence was crumbling, and the House noted that Graham had held his ground when he and Peel rose together: 'it was probably the first time Peel ever . . . had to give way'. But Peel and Graham still agreed on the fundamental need to protect the great Free Trade experiment against any modification which Disraeli's cunning might produce. Weak though Russell's Government was, they remained determined to maintain it in office. Nevertheless, both continued to deplore Palmerston's uncontrolled reign at the Foreign Office and the regular troubles which it provoked. When the *Globe* rejoiced at Palmerston's 'immunity from all attacks or adverse comments in Parliament' in March, Graham prophesied 'increased audacity . . . [and] some signal disaster'. But he pointed out that

> the present Government is so identified with Palmerston that his
> overthrow would be the fate of the Administration . . . It is a choice
> of dangers and of evils, and I am disposed to think that Palmerston
> and his foreign policy are less to be dreaded than Stanley and a new
> Corn Law . . .

Aberdeen and Peel were both concerned, but Graham welcomed
Peel's agreement: 'old high Tory habits and predilections might
to others render easy and agreeable reunions and combinations of
party which to him were distasteful and undesirable'. In his last
letter to Graham, Peel expressed pleasure at their 'unison' and
recalled their 'cordial agreement . . . and reciprocal esteem and
confidence' in the past. Aberdeen maintained that it was possible
to support the Ministry and simultaneously to condemn the
peccadilloes of its Foreign Secretary. Graham, however, believed
that if Peel attacked Palmerston, even privately, subsequent
debates might force him either to form a Government or to 'a
perpetual sacrifice of principle to expediency'.[15] The risks seemed
too great, and so most Peelites remained silent.

Other Peelites were less loyal to Peel. In March Graham told
Greville that 'Gladstone, Goulburn and Aberdeen would all join
Stanley' in a moderate Tory Government. On the 21st Disraeli
thought that 'the fusion . . . ripens rapidly . . . but our mysterious
friend Graham continues to baffle all conjecture'. He had heard
that

> Peel said to Aberdeen that even he could not make out what
> Graham was after. Some say that, if the Whigs can get their Irish
> Reform Bill well thro' this year, they mean to try their hand next
> session at an English measure, that Graham has an understanding
> with them on this subject, and is to lead the new revolution. A
> pleasant prospect!

Palmerston was the principal reason for the disgust with Whiggism
expressed by Aberdeen's group. He had been Foreign Secretary
in 1830–4, 1835–41 and since 1846. Active, brilliant, liberal and
(in all senses) romantic, he had regularly supported the cause of

moderate constitutionalism in Europe. He disliked the old autocracies, distrusted the French Orleanists, sympathised with emergent nationalism (while opposing some of its excesses) and maintained for Britain a role of high-minded and high-handed interference, combining equally open claims to arbitrate on others' disputes and to defend every British interest. In upholding these principles he was undeterred by the hostility of both Court and Cabinet. By 1850 he had long offended Royal etiquette and sympathies, Liberal pacificism, Tory traditionalism and the standard tenets of his Whig colleagues — and, in Aberdeen's view, had broken Britain's vital friendships; secret diplomacy had yielded to flamboyant eccentricity. A long series of scrapes was climaxed by great consternation over Admiral Parker's forcible extraction of Greek compensation for losses allegedly incurred by a shady (but reputedly British) Portuguese Jew, Don Pacifico. Opponents of Palmerston, of Whigs and of 'gunboat diplomacy' could now unite, as both Russia and France (as well as Cobdenite pacificism) had been offended. On 18 June, in concert with Aberdeen, Stanley carried a censure motion in the Lords. Palmerston would not resign, and on the 24th Russell put up the Radical J. A. Roebuck to defend his foreign policy. The Commons debate was vital to the Ministry, but Peel at last felt bound to oppose Palmerstonian intervention abroad. Having supported such actions in the early 1830s, Graham trod warily but also opposed recent policies towards Spain, Switzerland, France, Austria and Italy. The Peelites consequently broke with the Government, but Palmerston brilliantly defended himself, declaring that British subjects everywhere should know that 'the watchful eye and the strong arm of England would protect [them] against injustice and wrong' as Rome once aided every man who could say '*Civis Romanus sum*'. The Government had a majority of 46 votes.

Peel's last speech was a defence of diplomacy as an instrument of peace, but even he was unable to turn the tide which Palmerston had splendidly drawn to himself. Graham had expected a Government defeat, but had acted from principle. Such actions, Londonderry thought, would 'add to his reputation and give him the applause of his own conscience — though not the road to power'. Soon after the debate, however, the situation again changed dramatically. On the 29th Peel was thrown by his horse on Constitution Hill and was carried home seriously injured. After three days of pain Peel visibly declined and on the evening of 2 July his medical adviser, Sir Benjamin Brodie, summoned Graham to his friend's bedside. At 11.10, with Graham and Hardinge in gloomy attendance, Peel died. Graham told the news to the crowd in the street and to the Queen (who invited him to tell her 'details of the last moments of the dear friend'), acted as a pallbearer and endeavoured to console Lady Peel and her family.[16] In death as never in life Peel discovered an immense popularity, extending from the Court to the thousands who subscribed for municipal statues. And the politicians soon discussed the tragedy's effect on the political scene.

III

For some time Graham had been in touch with Russell, discussing current strategy, administrative reform, foreign affairs, patronage and the Lord Chancellorship. Now, with Peel gone and Palmerston vindicated, a Russell Government seemed the only alternative to Protectionism. But Palmerston's strength had increased, and the Ministry remained divided and reliant on the Peelites. Peel's death, Russell told Graham, 'would necessarily place him in a position more important and responsible'. Party leadership did not attract Graham, however: 'he was quite unfit to influence the opinions and regulate the conduct of other men'. Yet while the group had no official leader its obvious spokesmen were Graham and Aberdeen. Deeply moved by Peel's death, Graham would 'endeavour firmly to do his duty, but his heart was estranged from it and . . . he now stood alone'. It was kind of old Cumbrian friends to take him to the county agricultural dinner in September, when Carlisle proposed his health.[17] Pleasures were few at this time.

Despite professed disinclination, a lifetime's habits drove Graham to resume an active political role in the autumn. He suggested the compromise by which Baron Lionel de Rothschild took oaths on the Old Testament on entering the Commons, supported Hume's proposal to reduce the number of half-pay Naval officers and opposed the planned compensation of depositors in a bank which had failed. But the most dramatic controversy began in September, when Pope Pius IX promulgated a brief establishing a Roman Catholic hierarchy in England with twelve territorial dioceses. Wiseman, the Archbishop of Westminster, set forth his claims in a pastoral letter in October. It was an unfortunate time for such assertions. English opinion had already been disturbed by the spread of Pusey's Tractarianism inside the Established Church and, recently, by the long legal proceedings over the Bishop of Exeter's refusal to institute G. C. Gorham because of his heretical views on baptism. Russell was not initially alarmed by Rome's pretensions, but public hostility mounted rapidly and on 4 November he sent a famous letter to the Bishop of Durham, denouncing both Rome's impertinence and the Puseyite 'danger within the gates'. He had joined the majority side against 'Papal Aggression'; on the 10th Greville noted that 'the "No Popery" hubbub ... was now running its course furiously over the length and breadth of the land'. But there were moderate men who were shocked by both Papal arrogance and Russell's bitter reaction. Greville, for instance, was disgusted by the emotional intolerance of 'Protestant bigots'. Graham's views 'were precisely like [Greville's] own ... He was not only very sensible but very bold on the subject, and quite prepared to confront public opinion in defence of the principles of religious liberty.'

Graham explained his attitude to Howard of Greystoke. As 'a sincere Protestant', he resented 'the haughty tone' of the Pope and Wiseman, but he would not 'join in the No-Popery cry' or in any way limit Roman Catholic rights. In supporting Emancipation he had realised the possibility of an eventual territorial episcopate; as a Minister he had recognised the Irish Bishops and their right of communication with Rome; in opposition he had supported Russell's Bill of 1848 for diplomatic representation at the Papal Court. He did not regret these decisions and would stand by them, while reserving his right to declare them publicly only in the Commons. Other leading Peelites reached the same conclusion, sometimes under the influence of their own High Church views. Graham told Herbert that Russell's 'letter was hasty, intemperate and ill-advised', but as usual refused to give a lead.[18]

As the religious argument proceeded, the political scene was still dominated by the almost equal balance between a weak Government and an almost leaderless Opposition. Consequently, former Peelite Ministers retained considerable power and influence. In December Greville 'hinted to [Graham] that his joining the Government would not be disagreeable', and Graham 'owned that Palmerston would no longer be an insuperable objection' but refused to support 'any measures savouring of religious persecution, or even restriction'. Although Gladstone and Aberdeen were more friendly to the Protectionists, Disraeli was again inclined to negotiate with Graham. 'Personal regard and his high sense of [Graham's] abilities', he told Londonderry, would make him welcome a union, though some settlement of agricultural complaints remained necessary. He would not meet Graham and rejected the superiority of 'a mere reputation for administrative talent' over the support of great interests. But Graham's seeming sympathy led Disraeli to hope that he might enter a Ministry under the less optimistic Stanley; Graham was, in effect, offered Disraeli's post. It was important to settle the matter quickly, and in January 1851 Disraeli told Londonderry that all difficulties could be solved, if Graham would agree to some compensation for agriculture. Londonderry was not the best of negotiators, however, and Graham resented the assumption that he would 'resume his political connection with Lord Stanley' through an intermediary. Protection remained 'an insuperable barrier', and Graham aspired neither to usurp Disraeli's place nor to occupy Peel's; the effects of 1846 had not yet subsided and he would maintain his independence until the pattern was clear.[19] Disraeli then made some approach to Palmerston, while Graham steadily cultivated Whig friendships.

On 7 February Russell introduced his Ecclesiastical Titles Bill, forbidding the assumption of territorial titles by Roman Catholic priests. It was one of the most popular and least observed measures ever passed by Parliament, which accorded it gigantic majorities. Against the widespread hysteria a small group of Radicals and Peelites fought a brave but losing battle. Bright characteristically turned his attack on the 'sham' against the Established Church. Cobden had considered the 'Cockney no-Popery cry' as 'a disgusting display' and observed on 19 February that one result was that 'the Irish Catholic members were determined to do everything to turn out Lord John'. Graham, Aberdeen, Gladstone and their friends earned a reputation among Orangemen as 'Puseyites', by opposing a measure which Graham condemned as both intolerant and inexpedient. Already the Bill had hastened Tractarian submissions to Rome, and (to the dismay of Gladstone) the converts had included Archdeacon Manning.[20]

The 'Grahamites' acted on principle against Russell on the religious issue, but remained prepared to protect him from Tory attacks. On 11 February the Commons started to debate Disraeli's motion for agricultural relief. Graham delivered a sentimental speech about his 'sacred duty' to protect Peel's measures; but on the 13th, despite dwindling Peelite support, the Government succeeded only by 281 votes to 267. Charles Wood's weak Budget pleased neither Radicals nor Protectionists by maintaining income taxation and proposing a house tax instead of the charge on windows. Meanwhile, Russell had reported to the Queen on 'a long conversation' with Graham. He had already proved on the 16th 'the importance of obtaining support like Sir J. Graham's', by suggesting him for Hobhouse's post at the Board of Control. Next day he offered Graham the Home Office, which Sir George Grey would vacate. Graham then told Russell of Londonderry's manœuvres and declared 'that he did wish to support the Government, but that he thought he could be of more use if he did not join . . . and was able to give them an independent support'. The Queen clearly recorded Graham's statements

that he had not attempted to lead Sir Robert Peel's followers; that many who had followed Sir Robert would *not* follow *him*; that he thought the Government in great danger; that the Protectionists,

Radicals and Irish Members would try to take an opportunity to
overset them; that should the Government be turned out, he would
find no difficulty in joining them; or should they go on, that by-and-
by it might be easier to do so; but that at this moment he should
be injuring himself without doing the Government any real service;
besides which, there were so many measures decided on which he
was ignorant of and should have to support.

Graham expressed dissatisfaction with 'the Papal Aggression Bill'
and some aspects of foreign policy. 'In short', wrote the Queen,
'Lord John said it was evident that Sir James thought the
Government in great danger, and "did not wish to embark in a
boat which was going to sink". Still, he was friendly, and repeated
that it would be very easy when in opposition to unite, and then to
come in together.'[21]

For a brief period, Graham, as the most prominent Peelite, was
at a peak of importance, sought after by both parties. The Whigs
urgently needed numbers; the Protectionists desperately required
potential Ministers. The 'Papal Aggression' legislation ostensibly
restrained Graham from a Whig alliance, while Protection — even
when flamboyantly disguised in Disraelian prose — prevented a
union with Peel's traducers. Behind such obvious political
reasonings lay Graham's innate caution. 'He was by nature both
timid and irresolute,' Le Marchant recalled: '. . . to decide when
he incurred serious responsibility drove him to seek the counsel of
someone to whom he looked up . . .' But Peel was dead and the
coldly calculating Machiavellian strategist was flustered when
confronted by historic decisions. Long experience of careful
balancing of interests and meticulous office work were no training
for resolving unique problems. The perpetual second-in-command
postponed action and gradually wasted his opportunity. 'As a
public man, he is considered finished,' Disraeli told Lady
Londonderry in late March. 'A month ago he was the proximate
Premier.'[22] Events had moved too quickly for a man prone to
indecision.

On 20 February Locke King moved his annual motion to extend
the suffrage. Reassured by Russell's talk of future action, he was
prepared to withdraw, but the Radicals forced a division on which

the Government was beaten by 100 votes to 52. 'The Tories purposely stayed away,' Russell complained to the Queen, though Stanley pointed out that his supporters provided 25 of the Government's votes. Even such a defeat seemed final to Russell, and the Queen, though finding it 'very vexatious', agreed that he should resign when 'he was so ill supported'. The Government resigned on the 22nd, when 'the town was electrified with the news'. On being summoned to the Palace, Stanley told the Queen that it would be difficult to form a Ministry unless Aberdeen and Graham would join him, advised her to try a Whig–Peelite coalition and begged her to call him only as a '*dernier ressort*'. Many negotiations followed. Graham was summoned on the 23rd and told Prince Albert of his fears of 'universal commotion' against Protectionist rule, his belief that Aberdeen would not support Stanley, his disagreement with other Peelites over religion and his opposition to many of Russell's policies. Furthermore, he mentioned 'his own utter weakness, calling himself the weakest man in England, who had lost his only friend in Sir R. Peel and had for the last fifteen years not exercised an independent judgment, but rested entirely on his friend'. A long discussion with the Queen, the Prince, Russell and Aberdeen was fruitless. Graham 'raised nothing but difficulties, though professing the greatest readiness to be of use', noted the Prince, who never forgot the incident. Finally the Queen declared that '*one* of the three gentlemen *must* form a Government'.

A further meeting with the Queen made no progress, as Aberdeen and Graham were studying Russell's proposals to maintain Free Trade, revise the Budget, greatly modify the Ecclesiastical Titles Bill, extend the suffrage and reform the electoral law. Graham, as so often, was 'in very low spirits and full of disquiet and apprehensions' and confided his 'most gloomy' anticipations to Greville. The Queen and the clubs now waited for his and Aberdeen's decision. Russell told the Queen that Graham 'might have any office he liked', and the Prince noted that 'the Radicals were very much pleased' at his possible return. The picture became increasingly complicated: Disraeli denied that Stanley had refused office; Russell would not serve under either

Peelite; and Aberdeen and Graham rejected a Whig coalition. The Peelites thought any version of the religious Bill wrong and dangerous and could not agree to vaguely planned suffrage legislation, while Graham personally wanted 'a more rigid economy and a reduction of the public expenditure'. They consequently refused to join Russell, insisted on their own inability to form a Cabinet and (perhaps maliciously) counselled the summoning of Stanley. As Gladstone would not join him, Stanley was unable to form an impressive Ministry, and on 4 March Russell reluctantly resumed office. Old friends viewed Graham's part in the proceedings very differently: Greville thought him 'too stiff' over 'the Papal Bill'; Ellenborough offered support; Newcastle opposed any Stanleyite union; Carlisle hoped for a Whig coalition; and de Grey withdrew his patronage at Ripon.[23] Although Graham's hope of a brief Protectionist Ministry did not materialise, his ultimate aim of proving that only a Whig Government could stand had succeeded.

IV

The Ecclesiastical Titles Bill, even in its greatly modified form, was the stumbling-block to any rapid Peelite conversion — though Greville was probably correct in believing that Graham 'was not sorry to have this excuse for keeping aloof, for if he could have got over this, there still remained behind the great difficulty of Palmerston'. Graham still hoped for a Stanley Ministry, which would provoke a Whig–Peelite alliance in Opposition. In the meantime, however, he continued to oppose the religious Bill and angered some Whigs by opposing them on some other measures. Although hoping ultimately for a Liberal coalition, he knew that only Russell was really friendly and so did not trouble over possible offence to more hostile Ministers. Through March Graham regularly talked in this vein to Greville, knowing that his views would be reported to the Cabinet. Greville tried to persuade him to moderate his speeches to avoid angering the Whigs, while Spencer Walpole made further hints about a union with Stanley, and Russell decided that Graham's recent speeches against the Ministry made another negotiation impossible for a time. 'The truth is', wrote Greville, 'they [the Whigs], most of them, dislike and fear him. They dread his propensity to truckle to the Radicals and to popular clamour, above all as to economy . . .' Palmerston, who had (rather surprisingly) wanted Graham in 1850, now thought his policies too dangerous. By the 27th Greville thought that he understood Graham's position:

> He thinks he can rally round himself a body of supporters, of men who will look up to him as a leader, and, by so doing, when there is a break-up, he may play the part of a political potentate, and, in the event of the construction of a Liberal Government, that he may have a large share of influence and make his own terms. He knows or suspects that the Whigs want nothing of him, but that he should singly join them to help them out of their difficulties, thereby giving up altogether any claim he might have to be a political leader, and all distinctive character as such. This intention of theirs he both resents and abhors, and though he is really anxious to be on good terms with John Russell, with whom he wishes hereafter to act, he can neither conceal his desire nor abstain from his efforts to upset his Government. He is the strangest mixture of timidity and rashness I ever saw. He is generally afraid of everything, and sees many unnecessary and imaginary dangers; nevertheless, he is prepared to hazard almost anything to bring about that consummation on which his thoughts and his heart are fixed, but which can only be worked out by the downfall of this, and the experiment of a Stanley Government.

Meanwhile, Disraeli, angered by the timidity of his own colleagues, maintained his campaign against the Government, mocking Graham and Government alike, over Roman Catholic titles, and on 11 April gaining 250 votes to the Government's 263 for his motion on agricultural distress. Gladstone, Herbert and Newcastle (the former Lincoln) were again thinking of an ultimate fusion with the Stanleyites.

In May politicians (apart from those like Colonel Sibthorp, who regarded the whole venture as a Free Trade stunt) were as excited as the populace by the wonders of the Crystal Palace. A Government defeat by 244 votes to 230 on Hume's motion to limit

W. E. Gladstone

income taxation to one year provided little excitement: 'the world seemed to have thought of nothing but the Exhibition, and all politics had appeared flat, stale and unprofitable'. The apathy aided the Ministers and a few successful divisions carried them safely through the summer. The Protectionists were increasingly divided over Disraeli's attempts to draw them away from their old dogmas, and Disraeli himself became gloomy and despairing. He sounded Thomas Baring about the party leadership, and in August Lord Malmesbury told Derby (the former Stanley) that he was again thinking of Graham.[24] In August Bedford told Greville that Russell 'had a great disposition to invite Graham to join the Cabinet'. Greville opposed the move, but accepted Russell's invitation to negotiate with Graham. However, on 12 September Russell sent Cornewall Lewis to Netherby with messages from himself and the Prince, offering Graham the Board of Control, Frederick Peel the Colonial Under-Secretaryship and Cardwell (ultimately) the War Office. Russell was anxious to secure Graham's 'abilities and experience', but in offering a comparatively minor office (although it would rise in importance during the renewal of the East India Company's charter in 1852), neither he nor Lewis could expect an acceptance. Graham was offended by the offer to himself and refused to be 'shut up in the Board of Control'. Thanking Russell for his 'friendly disposition', he raised difficulties over the Reform Bill (which he thought irresistible but strange from former defenders of 'finality') and ecclesiastical titles. Consequently, although the opportunity of leading the nation had passed, Graham retained much of his old position. 'I never did or could believe', Londonderry had written in February,

> that Lord John and you, with his Letter in no way un-redeem'd or with Clarendon either could arrive at a Common Understanding . . .
> I still hope the Time may not be far distant when Bye Gones may be Bye Gones and that I may still see you and my friend Aberdeen where I wish in my heart you were enrolled, in the great Conservative Party . . .

And Russell still wanted Graham to strengthen the Whigs. On the whole, *Punch* was right in commenting that[25]

S

> The Baronet of Netherby,
> Cold heart and ready tongue,
>
> Beheld himself, with wonder,
> Towards Whig embraces flung.

V

Graham lived quietly at Netherby in the autumn of 1851. He presided at the county agricultural dinner and, for almost the last time, enjoyed fishing and shooting on the estate. He also morosely watched political affairs. Hardinge sought his advice, as 'no fair-weather friend', on his reports on the nation's defencelessness against France. He corresponded on legal reform with Bouverie and on parliamentary reform with several men. 'He is full of gloomy apprehensions', noted Greville on 24 November, 'and seems in a state of contradiction with himself, desperately afraid lest John Russell should go too far, and equally afraid he should not go far enough. With all his ability he is a most strange and inconsistent politician. It is impossible to know what he will do, and I suspect he does not know himself.' Graham hoped one day that the Court would prevent too much reform, and next day talked of wide disfranchisement of small boroughs. 'In short, his fears assumed the most different shapes, and it was pretty clear that whatever the Government proposed he would find fault with their plan.' He disliked the Ballot, but 'in revolutionary movements it was not wise to lag behind', he told Lewis: 'a large measure of disfranchisement would be inevitable . . . [and] a war of classes and interests would commence' over the redistribution of seats. He retained his dislike of Palmerston, who deeply angered the Queen by expressing support for Kossuth's Hungarian nationalist movement in October and November. On 2 December 'the wonderful Electric Telegraph' brought the news of Louis-Napoleon's *coup d'état* in Paris, which alarmed Graham into considering the need for greatly increased military expenditure, while Palmerston rashly welcomed it. But Graham also had time to read Disraeli's new *Life of Lord George Bentinck* and complain of its portrayal of Peel. On the 22nd came the dramatic news of

Palmerston's dismissal. '*Palmerston is out*! — actually, really and irretrievably out,' wrote Greville. 'I nearly dropped off my chair . . .' at the news.[26] It was now obvious that the Government could not survive much longer.

Graham did not share the admiration of clubland for Louis-Napoleon's adventure. 'If the French nation submit to this outrage without a struggle', he told Greville,

> Political experience, learning, eloquence, law, liberty are at a discount, and brute force and military despotism are in the ascendant.

Aberdeen agreed: 'the President had left his uncle far behind, not only in the perfection of his duplicity, but in lawlessness and violence'. Greville kept Graham informed of the news, including Palmerston's dismissal, Clarendon's refusal of office and Granville's acceptance. 'The long postponement of this wise and necessary decision has been unfortunate,' Graham wrote to Aberdeen on Christmas Day; but he still expected it to produce a major change in the parties, prophesying that Palmerston would be 'bent on revenge'. He 'was not so much surprised at his dismissal as at the patience which had endured so long,' he told Lewis. On 7 January 1852 he hurried to London, heard of Russell's intention to approach himself, Cardwell and Herbert through Newcastle and had a four-hour conversation with Greville. Graham thought that Peelite support could not save the Government:

> It will not do to try and patch up the old garment. This Government must be broken up completely, there must be a *tabula rasa*, and then an attempt made to construct another on a wider and more comprehensive plan. John Russell ought to go to the Queen and tell her he cannot go on, and then she ought to send for Aberdeen and Russell together, and desire them to set about the formation of a Government.

Graham still suspected the new Reform Bill, but wished for an early settlement of the Government. On the 8th he told his wife that Russell would 'meet Parliament, but without much hope of long surviving . . .' Next day Lewis 'brought him something like a message from Lord John' to discuss Reform; but Graham was unwilling to help (though Newcastle sympathised with the Government). He realised that an alliance would still be difficult; Greville recorded that

> The Whigs generally hate the Peelites, and Graham especially. The Peelites hate the Whigs. Mutual dislike exists between Graham on one side, and Newcastle, Gladstone and Sidney Herbert on the other. The three latter are High Churchmen, of a deep colour, which makes it difficult to mix them up with any other party, so that the Peelite leaders are extremely divided, and the party is so scattered that it can hardly be called a party.

Consequently, Graham, unwilling to take responsibility for previously planned measures, refused Russell's proposal for co-operation. The Queen herself had doubted the value of such overtures.[27] Neither she nor Graham liked the Puseyism of 'the Clumber party'.

The Queen opened Parliament on 3 February, when Russell and Palmerston explained recent events. 'Sir James Graham says the next fortnight will clear up matters very much,' Russell reported to the Queen next day. Graham was almost right. On the 16th Russell talked of a Militia Bill, and four days later Palmerston 'had his tit-for-tat with John Russell' by defeating the Government's local militia plan with a motion for a national force. Before the Bill was even introduced, Palmerston secured its condemnation by 135 votes to 126. Russell took the vote as fatal and again resigned, complaining to the Queen that the Protectionists and some Peelites had supported Palmerston, while Graham and Cardwell were absent. Derby then formed what the Queen (and probably most other observers) regarded as 'a very sorry Cabinet'; Palmerston refused to join, and St. Leonards, Lonsdale, Salisbury, Disraeli, Walpole, Malmesbury, Northumberland, Sir John Pakington, Hardwicke, Henley, Herries and Lord John Manners gave little confidence. The party remained divided over Protection and a decision was postponed until a General Election had been held. Peelite support allowed Derby a brief reign, however, and the Government succeeded in passing a considerable amount of legislation. Graham took little part in the debates, because of gout.[28]

The Government's weakness in the Commons made an early election necessary, and Parliament was prorogued on 1 July. It had seemed likely that at the age of 60 Graham would be without a seat in the new Parliament. De Grey had refused his support at Ripon because of 'the uncompromising tenor of his opinion upon the Papal question'; and when, for the same reason, Edmund Roche offered his seat for County Cork Graham gratefully refused. In March Graham still had no arrangement and told Gladstone that he would not imperil Cardwell by contesting Liverpool. He had already refused to 'embark in a contest for Carlisle', as proposed by some old friends. But on 15 March a petition was got up to invite Graham and Joseph Ferguson to contest Carlisle as Liberals. On the 24th a large crowd escorted Graham from the railway station to the Coffee House Hotel, where he announced that 'the wanderer had returned: ... he came home at last, after perambulating England', and proceeded to survey his public career. Many old scores were forgotten and forgiven, although Graham's promise to support further Reform led to Gladstone, Newcastle and Goulburn breaking their party connection with him. Graham and Gladstone parted as friends, although Peelite suspicions of Graham had been exaggerated; he regarded 'the issue [as] Free Trade or Protection' and supported only a moderate measure of Reform. On 7 July Graham was returned at the head of the poll, with 525 votes to Ferguson's 512 and the Tory W. N. Hodgson's 419.[29]

At his victory dinner Graham mocked Protection as 'outdoor relief to distressed landlords' and reaffirmed his support for restrained Reform. The Peelites had lost several seats, and in early August Greville found Graham 'exceedingly dejected' over Derby's gains and the state of affairs in general. Graham had now committed himself to Russell's views. Roebuck had proposed a more flattering alternative, writing that he 'looked [to Graham] to be the leader of the Liberal party in the coming Parliament [for] Lord John would never again unite them ...' and urging him to have the courage to 'be the Great Commoner'. Graham replied that Roebuck had over-estimated their power in Parliament, that he had no ambition and that he would act with Russell in the Opposition to Derby. Equally frankly, Graham told Russell of the objections to him becoming Prime Minister again.[30] There were many reports that only Graham could lead a miscellaneous alliance against Derby. But he was determined not to take the lead, although he would obviously be one of the major figures in any new arrangement. Gloomy as ever, he set about the manœuvres necessary to create his own ideal political grouping.

11

The Elder Statesman

The General Election of 1852 proved that the basic problem of mid-century politics — the personal and often emotional groupings which prevented the restoration of two-party domination — remained unchanged. Though the historic parties had never been tightly organised, since 1846 their place had been taken by more fluid alliances in which personalities were all-important. The result was weak Governments resting on transient 'arrangements'; party disintegration involved compromising on party legislation. In January the Radical Sir William Molesworth, though expecting a Tory alliance with Palmerston, had correctly forecast to John Delane of *The Times* that a Derby Government would face the electorate and 'make use of [its] decision to give up the cry of Protection'. He thought 'a strong Government' was vital and that 'a strong Tory Government (supposing Protection abandoned) would be a less evil than a weak pseudo-Liberal Government'; and he despaired of a strong Liberal Government,

> for [which] . . . there must be a combination of Whigs, Peelites and Radicals, but where was the leader to bring about such a combination? Lord John would never agree to it, Graham had not courage for it, Cobden had not had [enough] administrative experience . . . Palmerston alone had courage and ability for anything, but the Peelites wouldn't have anything to do with him . . .

The elections gave the Tories about 310 seats, the Whigs and Liberals perhaps 270 and the Peelites and Irish Roman Catholics between 30 and 40 each.[1] Consequently, despite their widening divisions, the Peelites retained their importance.

I

Graham had undoubtedly proved his unwillingness to lead a party; Prince Albert, among others, had been dismayed by his hostility to the Court's plan to fuse the Whigs and Peelites. But he still kept considerable influence. The young Duke of Argyll fairly portrayed him at this time as

> a tall, handsome man, a little bald but looking otherwise hardly past the prime of life. He was a coalition in himself . . . Although a man of large and powerful frame, he had rather a weak voice . . . no animation in his delivery, no action with his arms . . . But he spoke with a weight and gravity which made his speaking highly effective. I have heard Lord Aberdeen refer to it as 'Graham's sledge-hammer'.

Graham had continued to patronise younger politicians, like Milnes (now an ardent Palmerstonian), who invited him to his first 'public' dinner after his marriage, and Macaulay, of whose literary success 'he was sincerely glad'.[2] To the Court's pleasure, he regularly communicated with Russell; the Queen and the Prince 'rejoiced' to hear that he had 'told [Russell] nothing stood now in the way of their acting together' and urged Russell to form a strong alliance. But in July Graham pointed out some of the difficulties: 'not only a new Administration must be formed, but a definite policy must be provided and announced'. Finance, franchise and education policies were 'probably the groundwork on which this policy must be based', while 'Religion and Ballot were the stumbling-blocks'. He insisted that 'new combinations [of] heterogeneous materials' were essential, as Tory minority rule meant that 'our representative form of government [would be] at an end'.

While Conservatives were divided over Derby's traditionalism and Disraeli's revisionism and Peelites between Gladstone's conservatism and Graham's liberalism, the Whigs were at least as bitterly separated. Russell and Palmerston had personal followings; anti-Reformers looked to Lansdowne; some hated Russell's leadership, while others rebelled against the entire concept of oligarchic domination by the great families. Naturally welcoming Graham's sympathy, Russell thought it essential to 'ascertain whether Gladstone and Sidney Herbert would act with the Whigs and . . . the Radicals'. Graham could not solve such an enigma, though hoping that Protectionist hostility had engendered a reluctance to support Derby. His fellow-Peelites, however, would probably prefer a peer to Russell as a potential Prime Minister. But Russell, while willing to support another Premier, would never lead the Commons for a peer again; 'the Radicals, the Irish Brigade and some of the Whigs would prefer anyone else to him, so that his personal degradation would be a sacrifice to no purpose'. He approached Aberdeen and, like Graham, disagreed with Lewis's notion that the Ballot would prevent corruption (though Graham characteristically thought that 'the demand for [it might] be irresistible'). In early August Bedford, Clarendon, Graham, Lansdowne, Russell and Grey were in constant touch. 'The result . . .', thought Greville, revealed 'a deplorable state of disunion and disorganisation in the Liberal party and the prospect of enormous and apparently irreconcilable difficulties when they came together'. While Russell, Graham and Aberdeen were friendly, 'the question of headship would itself be very difficult to arrange'.[3]

Graham had 'advanced' views on future policy. 'With proper care', he told Lord Dunfermline, the 1832 Act 'might have been sufficient for our day', but after Russell's pledges 'any effort to resist change would be an absurdity'. He now favoured the disfranchisement of tiny boroughs, but also believed that 'station acquired by superior intelligence and industry', the 'Universities both new and old' and perhaps 'the Inns of Courts and other chartered and scientific bodies and East India proprietors and holders of bank stock' should be represented. The Queen had suggested curiously similar 'fancy franchises' to Derby in March. Moderate Radicals might accept such compromises, but Graham feared that 'the Whig grandees would be dissentient, the Conservative Liberals alarmed and the middle classes, now in possession of supreme power, not openly but at heart unwilling to share it'. The alternative was a prolonged Derbyite reign, with disastrous results; and Graham would always defend 'what he considered reasonable and right'. If Derby were succeeded by an 'anti-Reform Administration', however, there would be 'a legitimate division into two parties', for politics flowed 'between the extremes of oligarchy and democracy, but democracy was the flood and would prevail'. Although suspecting that Lansdowne and Palmerston were plotting to rally Whigs and Peelites against 'a disfranchising Reform Bill', Graham told Bedford that Peelite support was unlikely. His long-term plan might now succeed: a Liberal coalition might yet emerge, with arrogant Whiggism restrained by Peelite moderation, though careful manœuvring was still necessary.

In June Graham was glad 'to say or to do anything which was agreeable' to Russell. He had warned Lord John of the opposition to his leadership and had promoted his relations with Aberdeen. As he told Ellice, 'Aberdeen and the Peelites were at heart much more liberal' than most Whigs and Palmerstonians, and 'for his part . . . no effort should be omitted to promote concord.' By mid-August, though reluctant to disfranchise the small boroughs, Russell was willing to serve under Aberdeen. But Gladstone was torn by rival emotions: 'his opinions went one way, his lingering sympathies the other'. In March he had listed no fewer than four types of Peelites and he was conservative enough to be shocked by Graham's Carlisle speech. 'So nice was the equipoise of [Gladstone's] balanced opinions', Graham told Aberdeen in September, 'that he wished to be . . . "on the Liberal side" of the Conservative party rather than on the Conservative side of the Liberal party.' Herbert, who generally followed Gladstone, had been 'surprised' by Graham's liberalism, but commented that[4]

> it is impossible to speculate on his course. With all his ability and experience and his love of straining his sight into the future, he has none of what the French call *esprit de conduite*. He had a great game before him and has thrown his cards away — though I doubt whether he is conscious of it.

Graham's cultivation of younger politicians had scarcely succeeded. 'He had always felt that his age and position were different [from other Peelites]', he explained to Gladstone in March, 'for the habits and connections of his early political life, though broken, gave to him a bias which to them was not congenial . . .' He was 'a strange mixture', wrote Herbert, 'with great ability and experience and considerable foresight as to what was to occur, but none as to how he was to behave'. Peelite disagreements had even been demonstrated in Commons placings: Graham sat with Russell, while the Gladstonians were sandwiched between Cobdenites and Irishmen. Before the dissolution Peelites and Whigs had defeated Government proposals to redistribute four seats, but by late August Graham expected both Palmerston and Gladstone to join Derby. He hoped that the 'redistribution' of the three dozen Peelites would resurrect the great parties and supported Russellite Reform (though Russell, as Greville noted, 'was in this fix' between Whigs and Radicals).[5] Above all, Graham worked for a liberal Conservative Ministry under his friend Aberdeen, the 68-year-old peer who had been Foreign Secretary in 1828–30, 1834–5 and 1841–6.

Although Aberdeen worked hard to bring Whigs and Peelites together, Graham was the real broker of the alliance. As the nation mourned Wellington's death in September, Graham and Russell grew closer: 'We commenced public life together', wrote Graham, 'and I feel that I am drawing to my journey's end.' However, Aberdeen was not altogether pleased at this develop-ment. He did not share Graham's belief that the Gladstonians were lost to Derby, and, while hoping for an ultimate alliance with the Whigs for what he taught Russell to call 'conservative Progress', was unwilling to desert the Peelites and 'could not altogether renounce his Conservative character'. Graham, he wrote, 'might fall back upon Whiggism, in which he was bred, but [Aberdeen] was bred at the feet of Gamaliel and must always regard Mr. Pitt as the first of statesmen'. Naturally offended, Graham retorted that he certainly preferred Russell to Derby, but that Aberdeen's 'tone . . . [had been] more confiding and conciliatory than his' and that Aberdeen and Cardwell were his only Peelite contacts. For once, Aberdeen was more subtly sophisticated than Graham, explaining that he wished to reunite

Graham and the Peelites and to work with Russell — 'but it must be as a Liberal Conservative, and not as a Whig'. Thus reprimanded, Graham recalled their long friendship (to be savoured 'in the evening of life') and insisted that his 'allegiance' to Russell was 'strictly limited to conjoint opposition to the present Government'. He had offered no more; he had shown Russell that he was not a competitor, 'but he had not promised to be his vassal . . .'⁶

Graham's grand design faced other hazards, as well as the Peelite leader's suspicions. In late October Russell told Lansdowne that 'personally he had no objection to serve under him, quite the reverse', and Herbert reported talk of a union between Lansdowne and Palmerston. In such tense circumstances, Graham stayed away from Russell's political dinner on 10 November, though pledging support against Derby. He had shown some courage in making a clear choice between parties; his speech of 15 March, Disraeli told the Queen, was 'elaborate, malignant, mischievous'. But other Peelites' lingering Conservatism made their attitudes doubtful; Disraeli's onslaughts on Peel were never forgiven, yet the expected renunciation of Protection would remove a barrier to reunion. Lewis thought that Palmerston, Gladstone, Newcastle and Herbert would support Derby, while the Irish group 'intended that [Graham] should be their leader'. Aberdeen disagreed, but Graham told Russell that Palmerston 'was anxious to carry Gladstone and Herbert with him to either camp', while 'Joe Hume and Cobden on the one hand and the Irish Brigade on the other rendered the confusion . . . ludicrously complete'; indeed, 'the ball would open with a country dance in which no-one had secured a partner'.⁷

II

The Derby Government's weakest point was Protection, now losing its attraction in a period of rising affluence but very differently described by Ministerialists on the hustings. Consequently, an Opposition motion on the virtues of Free Trade would have the twin virtues of embarrassing the Government and

uniting its enemies. In August Russell reported Gladstone's view
that 'if they were not invited in the Address to deliver an opinion
on the recent commercial policy, they ought to have an amendment for that purpose'. But there were complications: veteran
ex-Leaguers were pressing for such a motion, but the Irish might
abstain unless it were proposed by Graham. The plan did not
appeal to Graham: the Government should not be assailed
prematurely and a carefully-planned Free Trade motion should be
left to Villiers. Opposition strategy was planned with great
difficulty. But in November Russell rejoiced in his own freedom,
the safety of Free Trade (now 'suckled by the very wolf which
opened its jaws to devour it') and the 'clear majority against the
old Tory notions of government and against the new Radical
notions . . .'

Graham's position was now clear. He could never collaborate
with Derby, but would support Russell in opposition. Nevertheless, he 'reserved to himself the utmost freedom of independent
judgment' on 'future contingencies'. While Aberdeen could boast
of his willingness to 'advance more rapidly than probably was
ever contemplated by Peel himself', Graham more fully applied
Peel's philosophy and techniques. Peel himself would scarcely
have approved of later Peelite divisions, though he might have
relished Newcastle's haughty proposal to merge Whigs and
Peelites as equals in a new Liberal party. Despite much discussion,
however, there was no unity. 'We appear to me to meet this
Session, so far as combination is concerned, exactly as we parted
in July last,' Herbert told Aberdeen in October.[8]

Parliament met on 11 November, but 'the real struggle was
postponed by common consent' for two weeks. At a Manchester
rally on the 2nd Cobden had demanded a full denunciation of
Protection, but the Peelites (though dissatisfied with the
generalised approval of Free Trade in the Queen's Speech) did not
wish to humiliate Derby. Graham discussed the problem with
Russell and with Aberdeen, Newcastle, Herbert, Gladstone and
Sir John Young. He prepared a motion supporting 'the policy of
unrestricted competition, firmly maintained and prudently
extended', which Derby would accept. Such moderation did not

appeal to the Manchester Radicals or to Villiers, who produced a rival amendment containing the 'three odious epithets' — 'wise, just and beneficial' — to describe the measure of 1846. When Villiers's proposal was countered by a motion tabled by Disraeli, Graham and the Peelites preferred to follow Villiers. But after the debate began on the 23rd Palmerston came to the Government's rescue by proposing a motion based on Graham's draft. The Peelites were thus bound to oppose Villiers's proposal, which was defeated by 336 votes to 256 on the 26th, and to support Palmerston's amendment, which was carried by 468 to 53.[9] In this strange manner Protection was at last buried.

The Ministers' respite did not last for long. Constantly pressed by the Court to increase military expenditure, Disraeli had to alter his long-awaited Budget 'on the very eve of battle'. On 3 December he presented his proposals to lower agricultural taxation and extend the income and house taxes. A splendid speech ensured an initially good reception, but Disraeli's supporters were no match in the long debates for Gladstone, Graham, Cobden, Goulburn or even Wood. Early on 17 December the Government was defeated by 305 votes to 286.[10] Whigs, Peelites, Radicals and Irishmen had acted together against the Ministers, who promptly resigned; but they were united in little else. Now began a complex series of manœuvres, in which conflicting principles, personalities, loyalties and hatreds were complicated by naked greed for office.

Graham watched events with concern, recording his views in one of his rare journals. On 18 December the Queen summoned Lansdowne and Aberdeen to Osborne. Aged 72, gouty and (as Herbert had forecast) unwilling to lead a Government, the Marquess excused himself, despite Palmerston's entreaties. He expected 'a joint commission' to Aberdeen and Russell, which Graham 'strongly urged' Aberdeen to reject. That evening, over dinner with Herbert, Newcastle, Gladstone, Goulburn and Cardwell, Graham insisted that the new Government must agree on Reform and income taxation before taking office. Next day Aberdeen accepted the Queen's Commission, telling her that 'it was of the utmost importance that only one person should be charged with the task ... and that the new Government should not be a revival of the old Whig Cabinet with an addition of some Peelites, but should be a liberal Conservative Government in the sense of that of Sir Robert Peel'. Russell might have the Foreign Office and Commons Leadership, and Herbert or Graham could balance Derby in the Lords. 'Sir James', thought Aberdeen, 'might gain in moving from the House of Commons, as he [had] lately fettered himself with inconvenient Radical pledges.'

When Russell visited him on the 19th Graham would not discuss Aberdeen's plans, but defended Gladstone's recent appeals to the more liberal Derbyites. A discussion with Newcastle convinced him that Aberdeen's Peelites would 'go as far in the liberal sense as Lord John desired', and would act with Russell but not under him: 'the question now was, would Lord John act under and with Lord Aberdeen?' Next day Russell retracted what Aberdeen had thought was an acceptance of the Foreign Office, and Herbert reported Palmerston's threats to join the Tories. Russell's later offer to join the Cabinet without office (and therefore without fighting a by-election) was unacceptable to Aberdeen and Graham. 'Lord Aberdeen by my advice will make the acceptance of some office by Lord John and the vacating of his seat a *sine qua non*', Graham noted on the 21st, as Aberdeen offered the Foreign Office to Clarendon, some post to Palmerston and 'the choice of the Home Office or the Chancellorship of the Exchequer' to Graham. 'I do not like the look of this drama,' wrote Graham. 'The infusion of aristocracy and of old Toryism will be too strong.' At Aberdeen's house next day Russell proposed to lead the Commons and resign his seat; the appeals of the Court and friends to him and his strong-willed wife over the Foreign Office had failed.

Aberdeen reported on his progress to the Queen at Windsor on the 22nd. 'For the Colonial Office', the Prince then recorded,

Lord Aberdeen wavered between Sir J. Graham and Mr. Gladstone; either could be this, or Chancellor of the Exchequer. Lord John wished Sir James as Chancellor ... We argued the greater capabilities of Sir James for the Administration of the Colonies and Mr. Gladstone for the Finances.

On the 23rd the scene changed again, when Russell accepted the
Foreign Office and Palmerston agreed to join the Ministry. 'There
is no room for Disraeli and Lord Derby', Graham commented, but
'otherwise we had better all kiss and be friends'. It seemed that
the Cabinet would consist of seven Peelites, five Whigs and
perhaps one Radical, and its management would require great
skill — though Graham 'had great faith in the strong cohesion of
office'. He was finally to return to the Admiralty, despite the
Queen's belief that he 'would be very unpopular in the Navy' after
past retrenchments which had later proved 'injurious to the
Service'. The other Cabinet Ministers were to be the Dukes of
Argyll and Newcastle, Earl Granville, the Earl of Clarendon,
Lords Cranworth, Canning and Palmerston, and Russell, Baring,
Wood, Gladstone, Herbert and Cardwell. But Aberdeen's troubles
had not ended. On the 24th Russell demanded three further Whig
seats and was reluctantly bought off when Lansdowne and
Granville displaced Cardwell and Canning. The Radical Sir
William Molesworth replaced Baring, who (with Grey) had been
rejected by Aberdeen, while Clarendon's place was taken by
Russell.

'The Cabinet is now definitely constituted,' Graham wrote on
Christmas Eve. 'How it will work Heaven knows, but the
experiment will now be tried . . . It is indeed a tessellated pave-
ment.' On Christmas Day Aberdeen presented his final list to the
Queen, whom he told that 'he was inclined to let Lord John have
his own way pretty much with regard to minor offices, considering
that he brought 250 followers and he (Lord Aberdeen) only 50'.
Russell was already complaining of *The Times*'s attacks and that
'the Whig share of the spoil was insufficient'. He had been
shocked by Peelite greed: Aberdeen had originally hoped for a
Cabinet of eight Peelites, six Whigs and Palmerston, and the final
arrangement consisted of six Peelites, five Whigs, Palmerston and
Molesworth. Such schemes scandalised even nepotic Whigs, and
Russell had protested at such different treatment of 270 Whigs
and Radicals and 30 Peelites. Whatever variations were made in
the party totals, the distribution of offices certainly favoured the
Peelite clique. 'It is melancholy to see how little fitness for office is

Sidney Herbert

regarded on all sides', Graham noted, 'and how much the public
employments are treated as booty to be divided among the
successful combatants.' What Whigs claimed by prescriptive right
and majority support, the Peelites took with a cool assumption
of their own intellectual superiority.

When Graham 'discussed these matters' with Aberdeen and
Russell he believed that 'if we three were left alone, we could
easily adjust every difficulty'; but 'interested parties' postponed
a settlement. On Boxing Day Russell, Newcastle, Herbert, the
Whig Whip, W. G. Hayter, and Graham 'finally settled the list
of subordinate members of the Government and of the Household
[but] the same wrangle continued for places, and the same
unabated jealousy of Whigs against Peelites'. The Whigs were
kept out of most Irish offices and on the 27th 'returned to the
charge and claimed in a most menacing manner a larger share of
the minor offices'. Wood and Hayter had a bitter discussion with
Graham, and when the trio went to Russell 'the whole arrangement was on the point of being broken off', until Graham called
the Whigs' bluff by threatening to reveal the affair to the
Commons. Next day 'the contest . . . was renewed with equal
pertinacity but with less effect', and Aberdeen was able to submit
his list to the Queen. Graham, who had done much to ensure this
outcome, 'had never passed a week so unpleasantly':

> It was a battle for places from hostile camps, and the Whigs dis-
> regarded fitness for the public service altogether. They fought for
> their men as partisans, and all other considerations, as well as
> consequences, were disregarded. Lord Aberdeen's patience and
> justice are exemplary. He is firm and yet conciliatory and has
> ended by making an arrangement which is on the whole impartial
> and quite as satisfactory as circumstances would admit. Disraeli's
> observation is true that 'the cake is too small for us'.

In fact, however, the Peelites had humbled the Whig Establishment, excluding both men of ability and men of influence from
place. 'A very tiny party', Brougham fairly commented, 'had
entirely swallowed up the great Whig party'. Graham returned to
his first Ministerial post and on the 29th was appointed to a

T

committee on the income tax — 'a pleasant little addition to the labours of the Admiralty'. Next day he left for Netherby.[11]

III

After explaining his attitude to Reform and the need for defence against the Empire re-established by the Bonapartist *coup* in France, Graham was re-elected unopposed at Carlisle on 1 January 1853. 'I have now known this constituency for thirty years', he told Lewis, 'and I see in the new generation the most marked improvement . . . They have confirmed my belief that there is a class between the £10 householders and the old scum of freemen which may be safely trusted with the franchise.' His condemnation of Napoleon III as 'a despot who had trampled on the liberties of forty millions of men' earned Disraeli's rebuke on 18 February. But after Russell's resignation from the Foreign Office in February, Graham joined his successor (Clarendon), Palmerston, Aberdeen and Russell in the Cabinet committee on foreign affairs. Amid the work of preparing the Naval estimates (introduced on the 18th and providing for considerable increases), Graham was thus engaged on several other tasks. He never entirely trusted some of his colleagues (although 'on the whole they were gentlemen'), and Argyll was later 'much amused . . . by Graham saying solemnly that he could not conceive how any Cabinet could stand that was weighted with two Dukes'. Greville had observed in December that, while 'the late Cabinet had two paramount chiefs and all the rest nonentities, and [a] nominal head [who] was also a real and predominant head', Aberdeen's Cabinet included 'five or six first-rate men of equal or nearly equal pretensions, none of them likely to acknowledge the superiority or defer to the opinions of any other . . .' Yet the Government got on well enough, although it had 'no *power* in the House of Commons and lived on the goodwill or forbearance of the several factions of which it was composed'.[12]

In December, when Aberdeen pressed Palmerston to take the Admiralty, he had 'considered it in existing circumstances the most important office . . .' Certainly, amid the current concern over defence, the First Lord must be active. Security was tightened, recruitment raised to 45,000 men (the highest number since 1815), dockyard accounting reformed and the pilot service extended. Graham concerned himself with improving steamships and armaments; Admiralty inspections were increased, a new reserve coastal defence force was established and a great Naval review was held off Spithead. But the attack on France was forgotten as the international scene changed. In 1849 British and French Naval power had been prepared to support the Ottoman refusal to hand over exiled revolutionaries to the vengeful Austrians and Russians, and now a similar alliance seemed possible. One of the periodic disagreements between Orthodox and Roman Catholic monks over their rights in the Holy Places in Bethlehem and Jerusalem brought Russia and France, posing as rival champions, into conflict over the long-decaying Turkish Empire.

Not unnaturally believing that Aberdeen's Ministry (with Palmerston wasting at the Home Office) would be pacific, Tsar Nicholas I sent Prince Menschikov to Constantinople in February, to press Russian claims. He first made friendly overtures to Britain, talking of 'an early dissolution of the Turkish Empire'; but Aberdeen considered that there was nothing 'very new' in the proposal. The Sultan yielded by replacing his Foreign Minister and granting Orthodox (and Roman Catholic) claims; but, supported by British diplomats, he rejected Tsarist patronage of his Christian subjects. The new Russophobe British Ambassador, Lord Stratford de Redcliffe, undoubtedly backed the Porte's defiance from April. Meanwhile, Russian troops threatened the Danubian provinces of Moldavia and Wallachia, and on 8 March French and British diplomats asked for Naval help. A French fleet was sent to the Aegean, but Admiral Dundas refused to leave Malta without Cabinet orders. Late on the 19th Graham awakened Clarendon with the news, and next day Aberdeen, Clarendon, Palmerston, Russell and Graham approved of Dundas's caution. Despite French anger, the affair seemed to have quietened down by early April, when even Graham thought the Government's prospects 'pretty good' and that Ministers were 'going on in great harmony'.[13]

'The Eastern Question' was temporarily thrust into the background when the Government, after several irritating minor defeats, produced its Budget on 18 April. Gladstone extended income taxation to Ireland and (against Graham's protests) to lower income groups, further reduced tariffs and applied Legacy Duty to real property. After first converting his colleagues, he established a great personal reputation.[14] In May a Select Committee condemned the rule of the Derbyites Northumberland and Stafford at the Admiralty, and when Greville met Graham in a train he found him 'in excellent spirits about [the Government's] political state and prospects, all owing to Gladstone', and gloating over Disraeli's wrecking of the Conservatives. Graham minimised the pre-Budget controversies, and did not know of the Queen's displeasure at his postponement of the Bill ending the East India Company's semi-monopoly.[15] From a pacific Peelite viewpoint, the future seemed bright. The Conservatives were thought to be crumbling, after resorting to Radical alliances, and the oddly-matched Cabinet was growing in stature under Aberdeen's uninspired leadership. But neither sacred Romanov nor brash Bonaparte was content with the uneasy balance in the Middle East, and behind the distress at the 'Sick Man's' iniquities towards his Christian subjects lay Holy Russia's urge to reach the Mediterranean.

Inevitably anti-Russian, Palmerston urged Graham in late May to send the Mediterranean fleet within call of Stratford. Despite 'great alarm' and 'vast public indignation . . . against the Emperor of Russia' (whose demand for immediate Turkish acceptance of his terms had been rejected), Graham, Aberdeen and Clarendon hoped to avoid any provocation. Graham certainly did not wish Stratford to have too many 'discretionary powers' and wanted to know more about Menschikov's ultimatum before acting. He reminded Palmerston that

> It is always easy to involve this country in war; but the reaction of the public mind is speedy and violent when the evils of war have become inevitable. To prevent the Russians reaching Constantinople is a British object of primary importance, which would justify many risks and great sacrifices. Nothing but the imminent

danger of so great a disaster would be regarded as a sufficient plea
for a sudden rupture with Russia.

He was frankly pacific, though no pacifist; he moved rationally
between the appeasers and the militants. As First Lord and an
experienced politician, he felt a strong sense of responsibility for
his Service, so often attacked in the past by the club-room
advocates of its employment. And he distrusted Stratford. 'He is
a Bashaw — too long accustomed to rule alone,' he told Clarendon. 'Such temper and such manners are not the pledges or
emblems of peace . . .'[16]

The militants now supporting Palmerston were successful. On
2 June Graham ordered Dundas to sail near the Dardanelles and
accept Stratford's call; and on 2 July Prince Gortschakov
invaded Moldavia and Wallachia. Palmerston was inclined to
treat the seizure as a *casus belli*, but the Cabinet remained
divided, and his scheme to send a fleet through the Straits was
rejected. Stratford insisted on his peaceful intentions, but
maintained that the failure of negotiations must lead either to
'surrender to Russia' or to a major war. Graham replied that
though the Navy was far-stretched, Dundas's fleet was 'the most
powerful . . . for thirty years'. He hoped that the Ambassador
would 'wield this power with discretion and in the spirit of peace',
for 'it would be a miserable end if Europe were convulsed in these
latter days by a Holy War'. When the Powers conferred at Vienna,
Graham considered Stratford's tone 'harsh and ominous' and
urged Clarendon to replace him, as 'he was quite capable of
advising the Turk to be refractory'. To Sir Hamilton Seymour at
St. Petersburg he wrote that 'he was unwilling to abandon the
hope that our amicable relations with Russia would not be
brought to an untimely end', but received a stern reply that 'the
Russians were great rogues', their Emperor was 'worthy of being
at the head of such a people' and 'they sadly wanted a lesson'.
Seymour even regretted that 'the lesson' was not taught before
the Russians improved their Baltic fleet and fortifications, which
Graham was already having surveyed. Intelligence reports did not
support Seymour: in late September Clarendon wrote that 'we
must not in future underrate the naval power of Russia'.

Long negotiations gave reasons for alternating hope and despair during the summer. Russia might accept a compromise, but the Turks (encouraged, it was suspected, by Stratford) became increasingly recalcitrant. Russia had little popularity in Britain, and the warlike attitudes of Palmerston and Russell had more public appeal than the peaceful aims of most Ministers. Graham certainly had no belligerent aims: military ventures would ruin economical government and he saw little reason for Britain to maintain decrepit Ottoman rule. Nevertheless, he had prepared the Navy and secured Sir Edmund Lyons as Dundas's second-in-command. On 3 September he told Clarendon

> I hope you will not allow Europe to be involved in war because [Stratford] thinks he can write better than anybody else, and because he is resolved to embroil matters at home and abroad, in the hope of obtaining a triumph for his own morbid vanity and implacable antipathies.

Greville again 'fell in with Graham in the train' that day and found him 'very hot against Stratford, to whom he attributed all the difficulties'; he was 'inclined to think not only that he had acted treacherously towards his employers but that proofs of his treachery might be obtained'. Graham still opposed the popular cry for the Navy to enter the Dardanelles, 'though he acknowledged that he could not retreat while the Russians remained where they were'. Clarendon observed that Graham was 'very violent against Stratford', but considered that it would be impossible to make a case against him, except in private.[17]

In late September elements of the British and French navies entered the Dardanelles as a precautionary measure. And on 3 October the Divan threatened war unless the Russians left the principalities: 'the beastly Turks', Clarendon told his wife, 'have actually declared war'. When the Cabinet met on the 7th Graham and Molesworth, who (thought Gladstone) 'would both have been strongly for peace', were absent. The worsening situation affected different leaders differently: Clarendon toiled desperately at the Foreign Office; Aberdeen talked interminably; Russell began to demand the Premiership. Russophobe hysteria, aroused by the independent Tory David Urquhart and proletarian Radicals whose East European friends had often fallen before Tsarist bullets, was perhaps as important as the 'war party' in the Cabinet in determining British attitudes. But the Peelites prevented Ministerial changes, although in sending the fleet to Constantinople Aberdeen acted less from conviction than to maintain the cohesion of the Cabinet. This compromise disturbed the Court, and on the 10th the Prince 'had a long interview' with Graham at Balmoral, when Graham agreed that the Queen should have been consulted before the Cabinet acted. He carried the Royal protest to London, telling Aberdeen that if Russell seceded he would rather enter the Lords than serve under Gladstone.[18] Despite all warnings, however, the 'fanatical Turks' (as the Queen called them) were convinced that their incompetent forces would receive Anglo–French support. Their provocations led on 30 November to the Russians smashing the Turkish fleet off Sinope.

IV

As the nation drifted into war, Russell's new Reform plan was considered by Granville, Graham, Wood, Newcastle and Palmerston. Graham warmly supported Reform. 'I am quite satisfied that an extension of the Suffrage may be granted with safety', he told Dunfermline in January, 'and cannot much longer be withheld without danger, after the promises which have been made.' He expected any opposition to come from 'the Aristocratic Whigs, and perhaps from Palmerston'. Greville gloomily expected a £5 franchise to be accepted — by some from principle and by 'Graham from timidity'. Graham actually helped to plan Russell's 'good and safe' measure, and hoped (with most of his colleagues) that Palmerston would also accept moderate Reform. But Palmerston threatened to resign in protest by November. For once he was joined by Graham and Russell in opposing a £10 county franchise; but few Ministers were keen Reformers. On 16 December, long angered by Aberdeen's moderation abroad, Palmerston resigned, ostensibly over Reform: he 'did not choose to be dragged through the dirt by John Russell'. By Christmas, however, a frightened Cabinet ('cowardice was the word', Aberdeen told Russell) was agreeing to Palmerston's requests to return; if Lansdowne had followed his friend and the Palmerstonians had joined a Tory and Radical war alliance, the Government must have fallen. Although Graham had been 'most *tankankerous* and ill-disposed' in November, had joined Russell in refusing to weaken the Reform Bill and was thought by Granville to be 'the man most against' Palmerston, he agreed to the reconciliation, to maintain the Whig–Peelite coalition.[19]

Graham continued to support Russell's plans and cautiously welcomed Gladstone's proposal to implement the recommendations of Sir Stafford Northcote and Sir Charles Trevelyan and open entry to the Civil Service, by substituting examinations for patronage: it 'would be regarded as the greatest boon conferred on the nation since bread was freed from taxation', but required careful examination. Political affairs, however, were again dominated by the Turkish situation. After Sinope even Graham considered war inevitable, and in late December British and French ships were ordered into the Black Sea. 'If they were driven to go to war', Graham told Greville, 'he was for waging it with the utmost vigour and inflicting as much injury as they could on Russia . . .' War-fever was still rising, and even the Court (and especially the Prince) were widely and wildly attacked for apparent reluctance to fight Russia. Graham discussed the possibility of destroying the Russian flotilla at Sevastopol and prepared a fleet under Sir Charles Napier to restrain the ice-blocked Russian navy in the Baltic, indiscreetly hoping for a 'short . . . sharp' war. The Queen recognised his services in April by awarding him the Civil Grand Cross of the Order of the Bath.

Through the summer Graham was in constant touch with Napier about the blockade and hoped-for defeat of the Russians in the Gulf of Finland. The Russian ships did not venture out, and Napier did not choose to risk his force in attacks on strong harbours. By the winter of 1854 the Press was attacking his inactivity, and he was engaged in arguments with the Admiralty. Meanwhile, the Black Sea venture was also progressing too slowly for a nation expecting heroic triumphs. War officially began on 27 March, and Graham immediately hoped for the destruction of Sevastopol: 'all other enterprises were secondary,' he told Lyons in July. But Lord Raglan's army only landed at Eupatoria (35 miles north of Sevastopol) in mid-September and then moved slowly northwards, trailed by the fleet. On the 20th the troops drove Menschikov and Gortschakov from Alma, after a muddled, heroic battle, and thereafter gradually moved round the Russian fort. But on the 22nd the Russians sank vessels across the harbour mouth. Graham, the Admiralty and the Cabinet regretted Dundas's caution in not attacking the arsenal fully while the harbour remained open; London shared the Army's preference for Lyons to Dundas, and Newcastle constantly urged Raglan forward, little knowing his enormous difficulties. Lyons himself (courageously supported by Graham's bother Charles) proved that a Naval bombardment of the fortifications was useless, but Newcastle protested to Graham that Dundas's 'incapacity might cause a great disaster', secretly urged Raglan to persuade Lyons to disobey any orders which might imperil the Army and asked Aberdeen for support. Graham, in attendance at Balmoral, resented the slight; he agreed with some of the attacks on Dundas and would prefer Lyons, but could not consent to Dundas's immediate recall (although he had long supported Lyons, whom he had selected, against the over-cautious Dundas). By the autumn he was secretly communicating with Lyons, as Dundas's successor.[20] As the Crimean winter drew on, the Army which had triumphed at Balaclava and Inkerman was starting to rot, freeze and starve. Neither the excited public nor the divided Cabinet approved of Dundas (who retired in December) and Raglan. On 16 November Greville bitterly condemned 'those rash and impatient idiots, who were so full of misplaced confidence and who insisted on precipitating our armies on the Crimea and on any and every part of the Russian territory, without knowing anything of our means for such a contest'; and on the 23rd he wrote that 'half England was in mourning'.

The breakdown of the supply services and the dreadful conditions which Stafford and Florence Nightingale found at the base hospital at Scutari led to rising public indignation, and the Government barely held together, with Russell still talking of Reform and Palmerston swearing to oppose it. In December negotiations began at Vienna to end the war, but soon ran into difficulties. It was Lyons's duty, Graham wrote in January 1855, to 'proceed steadily in the prosecution of the war, regardless of negotiations which might be illusory'. He still maintained that 'everything turned on the fortune of war before Sebastopol'. The outlook for the New Year was, however, far from bright. 'Nothing can wear a gloomier aspect than affairs do at home and abroad', wrote Greville ' — the Government weak, unpopular, dispirited and divided [and] the army in the Crimea in a deplorable state . . .' *The Times* was now running a bitter campaign against the mismanagement of the war.

Parliament met on 23 January, and Roebuck instantly announced a motion for an inquiry into the conduct of the war. Most of the Cabinet stood by the responsible Ministers, Newcastle and Herbert, but Russell, now hostile, resigned. After a gloomy discussion, the entire Cabinet resolved to resign, but later obeyed the Queen's request to retain office 'for the purpose of meeting Mr. Roebuck's Motion'. The Peelites, 'viz. the Dukes of Newcastle and Argyll, Sir J. Graham, Mr. Gladstone and Mr. S. Herbert', the Queen recorded on the 25th, 'seemed to be very bitter against Lord John, and determined to oppose him should he form a Government, whilst they would be willing to support a Derby Government'. Graham had certainly changed his attitude since he had 'vehemently' supported Russell over Reform and had (in March 1854) 'devoted himself to Lord John, and went heart and soul with him'. The reason was Peelite resentment over Russell's 'treason' to Aberdeen.

Graham was ill during the Government's last days. After a long debate, early on 30 January Roebuck's motion was carried by 305 votes to 148, and Aberdeen carried his Government's resignation to the Queen that afternoon. Derby briefly tried to form an Administration and invited Palmerston, Gladstone and Herbert to strengthen him in the Commons. But Gladstone 'could not act without Lord Aberdeen's approval, nor would he willingly separate himself from Graham; if they joined, they must join in force'. When Palmerston withdrew his half-acceptance, Derby dropped the approach to the Peelites and gave up the task. After consulting Lansdowne, the Queen approached Russell, who also failed (because, Graham told him, of hostility roused by his 'rashness'). Finally, on 4 February the Queen reluctantly asked Palmerston to form a Ministry.[21]

Peelite loyalty to their leader remained strong enough for them to reject Palmerston's initial approaches. 'I am afraid there are difficulties in the way of my rendering you the assistance which you desire,' Graham told Palmerston. The group's policy was planned in his sick-room at the Admiralty; Greville believed that he had persuaded Gladstone. But Aberdeen eventually succeeded in making Graham, Gladstone and Herbert (with varying degrees of enthusiasm) accept office without him; lesser Peelites had already offered support. Indeed, Russell was soon complaining to Graham that the Peelites had taken too many posts. But Graham had retained the Admiralty only reluctantly, regretting the loss of Aberdeen and Newcastle and distrusting Palmerston. 'I pray that this sacrifice of personal feelings may not be made in vain,' he wrote to Baron Stockman, the Prince's tutor and adviser.[22]

V

The Court's rejoicing over Peelite support had scarcely subsided before further difficulties arose. Palmerston acted quickly on both foreign affairs and the Crimean army's troubles, but when Roebuck persisted with his demand for an inquiry he reluctantly accepted it. The Peelite Ministers felt that such an investigation would be directed against Aberdeen and Newcastle, and on the 21st Graham, Gladstone and Herbert resigned from the Cabinet. The old Whigs were delighted, being (noted the worried Greville) 'entirely indifferent to the consideration that the greater part of the brains of the Cabinet was gone out with these three'. Graham's last Ministerial action was the introduction of the Naval estimates on 16 February, when he defended the Navy's record. He was now subjected to public attacks by the incompetent Napier, who had been relieved of his command. And Clarendon thought that 'Gladstone acted upon a quirk, Sidney Herbert from sentiment and Graham from fear'. Graham himself told Claredon that 'he never took any decision from a sense of public duty with more pain', adding that

> It is not probable that we shall meet again in a Cabinet: my course is run; but I hope that you will sometimes remember me with esteem.

'We have lost our *three* best men — certainly from the purest and best of motives — but the result is *unfortunate*,' the Queen told the King of the Belgians.[23] After Graham had explained his belief that an inquiry would be 'unnecessary' and 'unjust' in the Commons on the 23rd, there were wide discussions about the propriety of his action. Personally, he had nothing to fear from the inquiry; his mistake, as he admitted, lay in not securing Palmerston's promise to oppose it, but (despite much gossip and speculation) his motives were pure.

Wood succeeded Graham and immediately solicited his advice; and Graham's friend Lewis followed Gladstone. Many, including Macaulay, Lord Cowley and the Naval chiefs, deeply regretted his departure from the Admiralty, but he kept in close touch with Naval affairs, not least because his son James Stanley was serving as a midshipman in Lyons's fleet. The Tsar's death and the succession of Alexander II raised hopes of peace in March, but the war dragged on, despite a long conference at Vienna. The Sevastopol investigation lasted from March to May and eventually blamed the late Cabinet and the Commissary-General for the army's breakdown. Later it was proved that the Treasury's refusal to buy extra forage was largely responsible. But the Navy had relatively few shortcomings in its supply position. In his evidence Graham pointed out that he was First Lord for twenty-six months and 'was not at his country residence six days during the whole of that time'; he had scarcely left London except on Naval business or to attend the Queen at Balmoral. Whatever deficiences there had been in the Naval war could not be ascribed to the hard-working head of the Admiralty. Napier, now M.P. for Southwark, bitterly attempted to blame Graham in the Commons, without success; but Graham suffered (as 'a naughty dirty boy' to *Punch*) for unjustly blaming opponents for the death of old Captain Christie, the inefficient transport officer at Balaclava.

The Peelite ex-Ministers took the 'Manchester school's' place on the second bench below the gangway, and with their seats seemed to inherit some of the Mancunians' pacifist notions. Gladstone in particular was disenchanted with the obsolete Ottoman tyranny and was willing to accept a compromise peace treaty by which Russia conceded most of the Allies' demands. Herbert protested in vain against associating too closely with Bright and Cobden, and Graham put his own views to Gladstone in June:

> I do not wish to be driven by the force even of circumstances into the ranks of the Opposition, which plays a reckless game without much skill and with still less honesty; but I am most desirous by every fair means to improve the chances of restoring peace . . .

In July he confessed that

> I have made many mistakes in public life, but perhaps the greatest I have ever made was consenting to join Palmerston . . . I have deeply regretted this error, it is the flaw in our case . . . [But] the grand object is to put an end to this war as soon as possible . . .

He and Gladstone had been prepared to support Milner Gibson's motion for renewed peace negotiations. 'Russia was ready to concede all that was necessary for our purpose in the East,' he told Herbert in July. 'The war is now continued because peace would have been the overthrow of the Palmerston Administration.' Russell himself, the British negotiator at Vienna, agreed that the terms proposed there might have led to peace, and resigned on 13 July. The sole pleasant news was the fall of Sevastopol on 8 September. Graham had agreed with the condemnation of Russell's 'crime' in hiding his pacific views. 'I am quite open to consider the course which we ought to take,' he told Aberdeen. 'It is contrary to my wish to give a vote of a vindictive character personally injurious to Lord John. I agree entirely . . . that our duty is to take the course which is most likely to ensure restoration of peace with the least delay.'[24] Henceforth, gouty and rapidly ageing, Graham determined to work for peace, to retain a seat in Parliament and to refuse any office. His regular talk of having reached the tired years of retirement had at last become true.

12

Finale

The Crimean War, which Palmerston reluctantly ended by the Treaty of Paris in March 1856, resulted in a wide withdrawal of Russian claims. And at home it provided an impetus to Radical attacks on the 'Establishment'. Dr. W. H. Russell's horrifying reports on military sufferings in *The Times* provoked condemnation of upper-class staff officers' 'incompetence, lethargy, aristocratic hauteur, official indifference, favour, routine, perverseness and stupidity'. Cobden even regretted 'the vote which changed Lord Derby's Government . . . for it had cost the country a hundred millions of treasure and between thirty and forty thousand good lives'.[1] But the Manchester pacifists gained little support; most Radicals supported the war, condemning only its shortage of triumphs. Palmerston, cynical and conservative in domestic affairs but still lively and popular at 72, seemed the man to win the war; and in the peace his magic appeal gave him a dominating position, which successive combinations of opponents failed to weaken.

I

Graham and his circle had earned considerable unpopularity by supporting peace moves; the *Quarterly Review* saw them as 'betrayers of the true interests of the Nation'. But the Peelites themselves were divided, as usual. When Graham, Herbert, Gladstone, Cardwell and St. Germans left the Ministry, Argyll, Canning and Lord Ernest Bruce had remained. Peelite influence was weakened, but Graham and his colleagues expected Palmerston's 'old concern' to fall without them and resented its apparent nepotism. On 28 April, however, Graham defended the

Government against Whiteside's attack on the surrender of Kars
in November. The peace dominated everything, and the Session
was uneventful after recent dramas. 'I never remember a more
barren and more annoying sitting,' Graham told Herbert in
August. 'No two people can agree about anything . . . and the
result is that an incompetent administration is all-powerful and
rules triumphant amidst the ruins of party. I fear that the peace
of Europe is hollow . . . and when the bellows is in the hands of
Palmerston, I know not where the extinguisher is to be found . . .
Affairs, when left alone, often settle themselves; but this is a
lesson which the experience of half a century does not teach all
aged ministers.'[2] Such fears made it vital to evolve some policy for
the now tiny Peelite group.

In May Graham and Herbert were worried about the effect on
Anglo–American relations of the illegal wartime recruiting of
American citizens by John Crampton, the Minister at Washing-
ton. The United States Government had requested Crampton's
recall in December and now ordered him to leave. Old opponents
of the controversial Foreign Enlistment Act soon raised the matter
in the Commons, and Thackeray thought that American opinion
was ready for war. Graham had never liked the enlistment of
incompetent foreigners, and though the Peelites could not
'condemn acts for which they were in part responsible', he would
'not be hustled into complicity with this American quarrel, of
which they stood entirely clear . . .' He told Herbert that

> My desire is not to overthrow Palmerston, but to keep him in the
> right course and to prevent his dangerous tendencies. But if he be
> determined to swagger and to attempt a course of bullying with
> the United States, I am not disposed to take a hand in this fatal
> game. I am rather prepared to resist him in that case to the utmost;
> and, in my opinion, his early overthrow would be a much less evil
> than the imminent danger of an American war . . .

Herbert agreed that Britain 'must end by knocking under', and
Gladstone 'made up his mind to speak and act in full concert with
Graham'; the trio 'stuck together, which seemed to be more than
any three of Derby's men now did'.[3] In July Palmerston was

persuaded to be conciliatory and various American disputes were gradually settled.

Naturally, Graham disliked 'the prospects of the country, which [he told Greville on 2 April] he considered very gloomy and full of danger, more particularly from the outrageous licence of the press . . .' He regretted 'the total destruction of parties and of party ties and connections' and maintained that 'there was not one man in the House of Commons who had ten followers, neither Gladstone, nor Disraeli, nor Palmerston. The Government went on because there was no organised opposition prepared and able to take its place . . .' He doubted whether Palmerston could survive, as most Whigs preferred Russell, and he thought that Gladstone, the ablest man in the House, would be unable to rally support for a Government of 'administrative reform'. If Palmerston fell, Clarendon would have the best chance of forming a Cabinet; Derby did not wish to act, though Disraeli was making overtures to Gladstone. Meanwhile, Graham found recent changes 'most alarming'; Peel had destroyed party, and patronage (formerly 'the great instrument of keeping parties together') was being abolished. 'The only hope of escaping from great perils was in that broad stratum of good sense and firmness' demonstrated during the war and in the acceptance of the peace. Such forebodings were now inevitable with Graham, but if some of his prophecies were eventually disproved his errors were not unique in a period of party confusion.

Russell's great policy for the Session was a national education scheme, with compulsory attendance, local rates, extended inspection and ratepayers' selection of teachers. On 10 April Graham opposed the plan as expensive, unnecessary, illiberal, anti-voluntaryist and likely to engender both religious rivalries and corruption. 'In a very able speech full of claptraps [Graham] made mincemeat of Johnny and his Education resolutions,' Granville told Canning; and Russell's hastily-modified proposals were rejected. After the high war-costs, Graham hoped for rigorous economy and opposed increased salaries for civil servants. And in July he attacked the Government's plan to create two life peers to assist with the Lords' appellate jurisdiction: 'he could not

u

conceive anything more painful than the position of a peer for
life, bearing a brand of dependence, a mark of inferiority, be-
longing to a class termed peers, but yet not *pares* . . .' The
Government was defeated. Graham also opposed the grant of
pensions to bishops and obtained a Bill providing that Gretna
marriages should require two weeks' domicile. But politics
provided little controversy. 'All party politics seemed to be
extinct' to Greville in September: 'the country cared about
nobody, desired no changes and only wished to go on and prosper
. . . Palmerston might remain minister as long as he lived, if he
did not commit any gross faults . . .'[4]

During the autumn the Peelites seriously examined their
position. 'Gladstone was over-active' and Cardwell wished to join
the Government, Graham told Aberdeen. Personally, he favoured
'a liberal policy', but denied that Palmerston was 'its legitimate
champion', believing that Gladstone was 'a more faithful
exponent', except on religion. Gladstone, fretting over his
'political isolation', thought an independent's duty 'would
probably be to put the present Minister out of his office', but
Graham opposed hasty decisions. Stuart-Wortley's secession to
the Government made Gladstone more eager for action and led
him again to consider joining Derby. Like Graham, he expected
from Palmerston 'a foreign policy keeping us in perpetual hot
water'. He sought means to avoid the scalding, but Graham, now
'ripened to decay', though unwilling to restrain him would not
join him: 'he could not give his confidence to Palmerston [but]
was not prepared to . . . join the band which surrounded
Disraeli'. When Gladstone denied any immediate intention of
joining the Derbyites and insisted on 'the general policy which
Peel in 1841 took office to support', Graham doubted whether
Derby would seriously accept it, believing that Peelite financial
ideas were more likely to be accepted by the Liberals (though
not under Palmerston). And when Derby proposed to communicate with Gladstone, Graham and Aberdeen warned their
friend against secret agreements. Such manœuvres reminded
Lord Morley of 'the chorus in Greek plays, sagely expostulating
with a hero bent on some dread deed of fate'.[5] The melancholic

chorus succeeded, and Gladstone did not move to the Conservative benches; but Athenian drama never contemplated a cast of nineteenth-century *prima donnas*.

By 1857 the last Peelites were united more by sentiment than by any coherent doctrine; only Palmerston ultimately prevented Graham from joining the Liberals, while Disraeli deterred Gladstone from aligning himself with the Conservatives. The divisions were demonstrated in Parliament, when Graham supported Locke King's Bill to extend the franchise to all occupiers of property worth £10 a year and Herbert and Gladstone opposed it, and when Graham and Herbert supported Gladstone's opposition to Lewis's Budget, which Cardwell supported. Meanwhile, Gladstone held discussions with Derby, feeling that the Peelites' isolation was 'a great evil' which increased 'that parliamentary disorganisation which so much clogged and weakened the working of [the] government'; he even 'denounced himself as a public nuisance'. On the other hand, Graham told Aberdeen that Herbert's 'leanings . . . were to the Liberal side, which in his humble judgment was the right bias'. But foreign affairs were to provide a unifying cause against Palmerston. Difficulties with Russia over the interpretation of the peace treaty had been settled and a campaign against Persia, fought from India without parliamentary sanction, had succeeded. In January Graham agreed with Herbert that 'Palmerston was still in the ascendant and . . . would not quail before a multitude of divided opponents'; but 'he had little doubt that John Russell would play him a slippery trick . . . and he regarded [Russell] as a more formidable adversary than Derby and Disraeli, "the Jew and the Jockey" . . .' As Herbert replied, 'with the exception of China, all the foreign questions were closed' and 'Parliament did not enter into the main questions of *how* they had been closed'.[6] But China provided the Opposition with its great opportunity.

The British dispute with the Chinese Emperor was typically Palmerstonian in its complexity. Previously Graham had hoped that Gladstonian finance might be the lethal weapon, 'but Palmerston barred the way, with his foreign broils and warlike

propensities, which, unfortunately, were congenial to the temper
and spirit of the nation'. The attack on the Budget, however, was
defeated on 24 February by 286 votes to 206, partly because of
Gladstone's vehemence. Now China provided greater hopes of
success. In October the Canton police had arrested the piratical
crew of the lorcha *Arrow*, a Chinese boat with an out-of-date
registration at Hong Kong. Sir John Bowring, a Radical
Imperialist, gained the seamen's release but was angered by
receiving Chinese condemnations instead of apologies and
ordered the bombardment of Canton. Here was a case to unite all
Palmerston's opponents, from Cobdenite pacifists and Gladstonian Christians to vengeful Russellites and bitter Tories.
During the debate on Cobden's motion strong speeches were
delivered by most leading politicians; Graham, 'for one, would
wash his hands of the innocent blood which, in his opinion, had
been shed'. On 3 March the Commons condemned the Government by 263 votes to 247, in 'a division doing more honour to the
House ... than any [Gladstone] ever remembered'. Palmerston
had warned the Court of the possibility of defeat, but the Queen,
expecting her ninth child, 'felt herself physically unable to go
through the anxiety of a Ministerial crisis' and would '*prefer any
other alternative*' to composing differences between 'the heterogeneous elements ... [of] the present Opposition'.[7] Palmerston
resolved to accept Disraeli's challenge to face the country. Some
opponents protested at being forced into an election and others
believed that Liberal-minded Britain would reject him. But
Greville sagely believed that Palmerston's appeal 'would not be
on the merits of the Canton case, but on his own political
existence ...'

Cobden (who had moved from the West Riding to Huddersfield
because, as Palmerston told the Queen, 'the line he took about the
late war had made him so unpopular ...') urged Graham to 'fight
the [election] on the Chinese question'. He thought that 'a great
principle was at stake: whether ... public servants should be
responsible to Parliament', and 'he was sure there was no safer
battleground than the Chinese business'. Peelites and Manchester
Radicals agreed in condemning warlike talk of Chinese 'bar-

barians'. 'Were the Chinese people to be judged by the purlieus
of Canton?' Herbert had asked, typically wondering whether 'the
British people [were] fairly represented by the rabble of
Shoreditch and Wapping'. Graham told Mounsey, his Carlisle
agent, that he had opposed the Government on county franchises,
the Budget and China, being 'true to his principles of Peace,
Retrenchment and Reform'. He denied collaborating with Derby:
he had rejected 'all secret combinations' and exercised his
'independent judgment in concert only with two or three
[Peelites] ... He had maintained an independent position ...
intrigued with no-one ... confederated with no-one. His approxi-
mation was more towards Lord John Russell than any other
parliamentary leader, but with him he had no understanding,
express or implied.' Nevertheless, he could not stand with the
Palmerstonian Ferguson.

Ferguson's friends initially dominated the Carlisle election and
three delegates threatened to arrange another Palmerstonian
candidature unless Graham joined them. Graham, urgently
requested by his friends to leave London at once, coldly refused
any pledge to support Palmerston, and Hayter could offer no
other candidate. Disgust with Palmerston's popularity almost led
Graham to retire. But instead he bravely told the Liberals in the
'Coffee House' that he would continue to oppose 'an unwise and
unworthy war' in China: 'Englishmen ought to fight their equals
... not to trample on their inferiors', and war simply deferred
Reform. The hostile crowd was gradually won over. Liberal
thoughts of inviting Poulett Thomson were dropped; Mounsey
stood firm; and Philip Howard, with 'disinterested magnanimity',
gave Graham support. Graham 'looked upon [Palmerston] as a
Tory of the deepest dye' and 'did not like the Liberal party to be
led by a high Tory ...' To many, such thoughts were tantamount
to supporting Chinese torturers, and Palmerstonians thrashed
Peelites and Cobdenites in many seats. But on 27 March the Tory
W. N. Hodgson and Graham were elected, with 529 and 502 votes
to Ferguson's 469.[8] This rare result was a considerable triumph
for Graham against the great defender of England's rights.

II

The elections not only weakened the Peelites but widened their differences. Herbert criticised Graham only for forcing a breach with the Carlisle Palmerstonians, while Gladstone thought he 'had undoubtedly inserted a certain amount of gap between [them]' by insisting on Reform. But even Gladstone derived 'exceeding pleasure' from Graham's 'most gallant, outspoken, energetic and apparently successful protest . . . [which] enthroned honesty and courage . . .' After the election Graham and Cobden discussed Bright's plan for a £10 county suffrage, household borough suffrage, the Ballot and a redistribution of seats. Graham considered the scheme 'the simplest, most practicable and the best', but still had 'grave and manifold' doubts over the Ballot, although 'the public voice in its favour might become irresistible'. But, as Greville noted, the Peelites had been routed: 'now the designation must fall to the ground . . . in one way or another there were no *Peelites* left'. 'The Peelite party was no more', declared *The Times*, 'because their ground was too narrow to stand on.' Even the trio of ex-leaders argued, as Aberdeen tried to persuade Gladstone that they were committed to Liberalism. While Gladstone supported retrenchment above all, Herbert thought that Graham 'looked to Reform as the weapon' to destroy the Government. In fact, 'Graham wished to turn out Palmerston to bring in Lord John; Gladstone wished to turn him out to bring in Lord Derby; and [Herbert] wished to keep him in.' The three friends, Herbert told Gladstone, were '*rari nantes*, and were not only broken up as a party . . . but the country intended them to be so broken up . . .' It was impossible to maintain any alliance, he suggested to Graham. Reform now seemed the vital issue to Herbert, who worried over the breach. Graham also would regret Gladstone's secession, as he did not consider anti-Palmerstonian Liberalism dead and thought it 'natural and decorous' for old colleagues to sit together unless divided on fundamental issues. 'The Peelites as a party are gone,' he wrote. 'Indeed I have never recognised their existence in that sense since the formation of Lord Aberdeen's Government . . . But though the Peelites have disappeared from the stage, yet you, Gladstone and I still linger on it.' The possibility of division was 'too painful for him to contemplate' and 'he would therefore do nothing which might seem to precipitate it . . .'[9]

Misery at the thought of a political separation was reinforced by other anxieties. Graham was increasingly concerned about his wife's health. And although Parliament was quiet from 30 April, satisfied with Palmerston's promise of Reform in 1858, there was some uneasiness in informed circles over Indian army unrest. The Meerut sepoys' mutiny on 10 May was not fully understood in Britain until late June. Thereafter, mid-Victorian Britain was horrified by reported atrocities, originally committed in defence of crumbling religious and social *mores* and later sometimes justified as legitimate nationalistic weapons.

As relatives of East India officials fretted and the Queen's husband rejoiced in the title of Prince Consort, Parliament examined another Bill to remove Jewish disabilities. On 10 July the Commons again passed the proposal, only to be opposed by the Lords. The Commons now faced a choice between reasserting its control on admissions and extending 'nonconformist' oath-taking. At a rally of Liberal Members under Edward Horsman, in the 'King's Head' in Palace Yard on the 16th, Graham pleaded for a moderate approach to the peers (which succeeded in 1858). Meanwhile, Gladstone hopelessly fought against the Divorce Bill: 'Graham was with them, much to [Gladstone's] delight and . . . surprise'. But as Gladstone grew apprehensive over his dying sister-in-law, Lady Lyttelton, Graham became gloomy about Fanny. In August the Grahams moved to Cowes, 'in the hope that [Fanny] might derive some benefit from sea air'. The change was in vain; Lady Graham died on 25 October.

Bereaved, ageing and periodically ill, Graham was no longer able to sustain a major position in a political world of fast-changing manœuvres. Croker, his former friend, had died in August. They had made their peace in 1853, when Graham confessed

I have committed many errors and I am conscious of many faults. I hope to be forgiven, as I am ready to forgive; and, on the whole, I have done my best.

Russell helped to ease his worries in September by soliciting his advice on a Reform Bill fully or partially disfranchising small boroughs and enfranchising county £10-ers and municipal voters. Graham generally agreed, but opposed equal constituencies (which 'would destroy the balance of interests') and still favoured separate representation for 'corporate and learned bodies'. When Russell wondered how to provide 'some mode of entrance for Liberal Tories and temperate Whigs, to keep the ship steady', Graham stressed his 'fancy franchises' and suggested cutting the disfranchisement: 'it was necessary to consider not only what was just and desirable but also what was possible and expedient without a violation of sound principle'. Both statesmen were concerned over India. 'Where was a fit military dictator to be found?' asked Graham; Russell was convinced that he did not exist among 'an imaginary body of merchants'.

As the many messages of condolence reached Netherby, Graham became more morose than ever. 'His wish was not to withdraw from public affairs', he told Russell, 'but not to be engrossed by them, and to moderate every passion by the recollection that with him the end was at hand.'[10] Fanny was buried at Whippingham, near the scenes of their honeymoon, and Graham retired to Netherby with his mourning family. Frederic had married Lady Jane St. Maur, eldest daughter of the 12th Duke of Somerset, in 1852, after serving in the Life Guards and as an attaché at Vienna. Malise Reginald, the second son, born in 1833, became Rector of Arthuret and married his cousin Sophia Musgrave. Mable Violet had become the 1st Countess of Feversham in 1851; James was a Naval commander; Constance was unmarried; and Helen was to marry Colonel Charles Baring in 1860. Graham's brothers were still alive to comfort him: Charles, now a Rear-Admiral, was to die in 1858, while George, a former Indian army major and since 1842 Registrar-General, survived until 1888.

Even his heartbreaking bereavement could not long keep Graham away from politics. On 12 November Palmerston and Lewis permitted the Bank of England to exceed the fiduciary note issue fixed in 1844, to halt a gathering financial crisis. Graham's 'crude opinions' were against such Government interference. 'I have always thought', he told Gladstone, 'that the Bank directors depart from their proper sphere when they consider the public interest instead of that of their proprietors. Let them attend to their own concerns, and let Parliament provide for the protection of the public . . . The Directors discount for profit without control from the Treasury, and when they are on the verge of insolvency, either from imprudence or false notions of providing for the public good, the law is violated by a *coup d'état* in their favour, but at the expense of the fixed standard of value, on which the money's worth of all property depends.' As for the Ottomans, Graham 'had no faith in "the integrity of Turkey". The Mahometan rule in Europe must soon come to an end'; and he supported 'a homogeneous Christian community of Roman origin' as 'the germ of an Eastern Christian Empire, which might in time take the place of the Moslem in Europe'. Gladstone 'cordially agreed in every word'. But the Government's action saved the financial situation.

In late November Bedford warned Greville that Russell was 'irritable . . . and disposed to wage war against the Government'. Lord John soon started to intrigue for power after the expected decline of Palmerston. 'India and Reform are . . . well worthy of your efforts,' he told Graham. '. . . On Reform there is little excitement, but a refusal of Reform, or a sham, would fan the flame.' From his sick-bed, Graham shared the hostility to 'Pam', but had no 'energy or spirit'. Recovery 'was a slow process when the spirit was broken', he told Gladstone, and he later confessed to Herbert that 'there was a sinking of energy and of heart from which he never should recover'. While Russell retained some contacts with Ministers, Graham wished 'to stand aloof from them'. Reform now seemed unlikely to bring down the Government, and by late December Graham considered that 'the future government of India was now the grand question'. But he could not join Russell in demanding a rapid reform of the dualism of Company and Government. 'I have crept into my shell', he explained in January 1858, 'and would gladly remain there.'[11]

III

Graham only slowly recovered from his illness. 'I have no fancy for making my appearance in the House of Commons on an early date,' he told Gladstone in January. 'My heart sinks within me when I think of a return to the strife of political warfare, yet I suppose that I must return.' Political prospects were gloomy, with the Liberals 'bought and sold' to Palmerston, and Derby's 'crew [unable to] man the ships.' But Graham kept in touch with his old friends. 'I dread the Indian Bill of the Government,' he wrote to Herbert. 'I am not prepared to hand over to Vernon Smith the fate of that tottering empire; and I am still less prepared to hand over the fortunes of England to "the Jockey and the Jew" . . .' He remained hostile to the Conservatives.

The scene changed rapidly. Palmerston was ageing, and his appointment of the disreputable Clanricarde to the Cabinet had shocked many observers. The Bill transferring Indian authority to the Government offended the Company. And when, on 14 January, the Italian nationalist Felice Orsini threw a British-made bomb at the Emperor, French passions rose dangerously against Britain for harbouring murderous revolutionaries. After receiving diplomatic protests, on 9 February Palmerston introduced the Conspiracy to Murder Bill, making such conspiracy a felony. Opposition rose quickly. Graham 'revolted at the idea of altering the law of England in obedience to the dictation of France and under threats from the praetorian guard of a usurper', but advised Russell not to oppose the Bill until public opinion had declared itself. The picture was 'alarming', with Britain under an untrustworthy Premier and France led by 'a most ambitious, false and daring tyrant'. Russell persisted in dividing the House and was easily defeated, but the publication of French despatches led Members to believe that Palmerston had yielded to France. Milner Gibson proposed to postpone the Bill until Count Walewski's message had been answered, and on the 19th the Government was beaten by 234 votes to 215. Two days later, defeated by a combination of Conservatives, Liberals, Radicals and Peelites, the Ministers resigned. Clarendon convinced the Prince that 'the whole move had been planned, and most dexterously, by Sir James Graham', and Derby, hastily summoned to the Palace and reluctantly accepting office, 'thought it was the work of Lord John Russell and Sir James Graham in the interest of the Radicals'.[12] Such was Graham's reputation that a subtle and crafty machination was almost inevitably ascribed to him.

Derby soon approached Gladstone, but the Peelite trio held aloof. Nevertheless, while openly favouring Russell, Graham preferred to let the Government continue rather than provoke a struggle over the Liberal leadership. 'I am not prepared to place Palmerston at the head of affairs', he bluntly informed Ellice, 'and, unless he and Lord John can come to some agreement, Derby for the present must be regarded as the least of two evils . . . We shall do no good while the two Kings of Brentford sit in the same House.' Consequently, he would tolerate Conservative rule. But by March, 'the Peelites were all verging towards a union with Lord John, some more, some less', Aberdeen told Bedford: 'Graham was devoted to him, Sidney Herbert and Cardwell perfectly well disposed . . . Newcastle gradually becoming so, and Gladstone . . . getting more friendly . . .'[13]

Indian atrocities had led to demands for reorganisation and (mainly from such Evangelical proselytisers as Shaftesbury) for vengeance. 'Clemency' Canning, the Governor-General since 1855, restrained some of the revenge, and both parties planned administrative reform. On 26 March Disraeli introduced Ellenborough's Bill in the Commons, where it 'was received with general aversion and contempt', because it proposed to grant representation on the new India Council to some large British constituencies and because the Council would neither check the Minister (as the Peelites wished) nor be composed entirely of experienced Indian administrators (as Palmerston hoped). Russell aided the Government by following Graham's suggestion of proceeding by 'resolutions, not [by] a Bill', a course accepted by Disraeli on 12 April. A Secretary of State replaced the President of the Board of Control; the Governor-General became a Viceroy; and a Council of State was established. Thus the

Company's powers and property passed to the Crown. Graham was reluctant to take everything from the merchants who had created the Indian empire and spoke up for the nomination of some directors to the Council, the prevention of patronage by giving the Council considerable independence, parliamentary control over the Minister and the retention of open competition for administrative appointments. The curious dichotomy of a partly-nominated executive and an open administration was not entirely accepted, but Graham had some influence on the ultimate compromise.

India provided further parliamentary troubles. On 3 March Canning uncharacteristically threatened confiscation and execution of Oudh landowners unless they immediately submitted. Ellenborough condemned this 'Proclamation of Oudh' on his own responsibility and allowed his censure to be made public, thus provoking protests. Despite Ellenborough's resignation on 11 May, the Palmerstonians sensed their opportunity. In the Lords, Shaftesbury's censure motion was defeated by only nine votes on the 14th. Simultaneously, Cardwell inaugurated a long debate in the Commons. Graham and his friends stood by Derby, and Disraeli even renewed his approaches to Graham and Gladstone, eventually offering them the Commons leadership and India or the Colonies respectively and urging Graham to announce that a defeat would cause a dissolution (a course reluctantly accepted by the Queen, on the understanding that it should not be used as a threat under her authority). On the 20th Graham denied any sympathy with the Ministry, admitted his support of Russell and insisted that 'the error of the proclamation was in its essence [and] the error of the despatch in its form and expression'. This speech, Disraeli told the Queen, 'produced a very great effect. No report gave a fair idea of it. The great country gentleman, the broad views, the fine classical allusions, the happiest all omitted, the massy style, contrasted remarkably with Sir Richard Bethell.' On the 21st Cardwell withdrew his motion.

His Government saved, Derby officially invited Gladstone to succeed Ellenborough, advising him to consult Aberdeen and Graham. Aberdeen opposed the move, but Graham was more understanding; he had announced his hostility to the Ministers because he 'wished it to be distinctly understood that any support which he gave to Lord Derby was in spite of his strong Liberal prepossessions, that he had ceased to have any personal or party objects and that he desired to wean himself from world affairs'. Graham 'could not listen for one moment to [Disraeli's] proposal to him, however generous and flattering'. But Gladstone could honourably join Derby; 'his honest Liberal tendencies would soon leaven the whole lump', and Graham would rejoice to see his talents employed. Gladstone, however, 'for a long time . . . in the odd position of one who thought well of both parties', sadly refused Derby's offer, fearing a breach with Peelite friends. Graham sincerely regretted this decision and pointed out that 'the reconstruction of the fossil remains of the old Peel party was a hopeless task', for 'it was decomposed into atoms and would be remembered only as a happy accident while it lasted'.[14] Most Peelites were so hostile to the Conservatives that Gladstone, the most earnestly desired ally, missed another opportunity.

Through the summer the gouty Graham fought to extend competitive entry in the Indian service, against the hostility of many politicians and, to some extent, of the Crown. He maintained close contact with Russell, who (Greville noted on 5 September) was 'busily employed in concocting a Reform Bill, which he had probably better leave alone'. He did not like Russell's drafts: 'abating the minority clause, he could not regard any new measure . . . as more safe, just and unobjectionable than the Bill introduced by [Russell and himself] on behalf of Lord Aberdeen's Administration. £10 for counties, £6 for cities and boroughs, with rating and residence respectively, were qualifications that would extend the popular power within limits which he considered sufficient.' But 'partial disfranchisement of the very small boroughs' would only provoke 'fresh demands and renewed agitation' and the omission of Ballot would undermine support; Russell had thought of taking only thirty Members from small boroughs. By late November, when the Ministry was preparing its own measure, Graham advised Russell not to move until Derby and Bright revealed their rival plans. In October, after consulting his (generally doubtful) friends, Gladstone had become Lord High Commissioner Extraordinary in the Ionian Islands. After Gladstone's departure, Graham corresponded in the winter on the Naval Reserve and the Indian Army.

Palmerston and Russell were still competing for the Whig–Liberal leadership, and in January 1859, after long cultivating Lord Stanley, Russell approached the Peelites. 'He wished [Graham and he] and Sidney Herbert and Lewis could come to an understanding to act together . . . on all matters relating both to expenditure and to Reform . . .' But Graham 'did not desire to form any new political combination, feeling that he had had his hour and the time for his departure was drawing near'. He told Ellice that 'the broken fragments of the old Whig party were so shattered that they could not be pieced together again', as 'the old stagers . . . disliked each other too much', while 'the youngsters . . . must look to Lord Stanley as their head'. He would join no group, being 'predetermined to be true to the principles of Lord Grey's measure'. To Herbert he pointed out that Russell had omitted foreign affairs from his proposal and that Bedford and Ellice's 'Whig reunion, embracing the houses of Devonshire, Sutherland, and Howard', was a fantasy: 'the day was gone by when a conclave of Dukes could sway a Parliament'. He favoured an extension of the suffrage but 'was disposed to resist subversion of the settlement of 1832'.[15] Graham consequently approached the new Session with greater independence than ever before.

Radical speeches by Bright roused both Russell and Graham. Bright would 'transfer power to the great towns and leave the land in a hopeless minority', complained Russell; and Graham agreed that he would oppose the Lords and make the Commons 'a mere creature of numbers, apart from property and intelligence'. The friends agreed on moderate reform of the 1832 Act, maintaining old balances, with some disfranchisement, an urban ratepaying and residential franchise and a compromise on redistribution. Disraeli's Bill of 28 February, lowering the county franchise to £10 and providing curious new qualifications in the towns, was too much for two Ministers, Walpole and Henley, who resigned; but it did not satisfy Russell and Graham. Russell demanded 'a greater extension of the suffrage in cities and boroughs', and on 28 March Graham warmly supported him, as 'the time had come when power must begin to descend to the working classes'. Early on 1 April, in a crowded House, the Government was defeated by 310 votes to 295. Three days later Derby announced a dissolution.[16]

IV

On 5 April Graham issued his address to the Carlisle electors, condemning Disraeli's Bill and the Ballot. He expected Hodgson to support Derby and young Wilfred Lawson to sympathise with Bright's Radicalism. 'Others may make larger professions,' he wrote: 'I can appeal to past services.' He naturally did not mention his current controversy with Aberdeen, who supported Austria against Lombard and Venetian nationalists even at the risk of fighting the French. Still far from well, he reached Carlisle only on the 20th, when he addressed crowds outside the town hall and in the 'Coffee House', attacking Derby over both Reform and alleged weakness in foreign affairs. 'Is not Graham's speech at Carlisle superlative?' Gladstone asked Herbert. 'I am rather sorry to add, however, that it is so in more senses than one . . .' Graham rested at home during the canvass, but on the 28th defied his doctor by appearing on the hustings, to deliver a masterly defence of his changed attitudes in a changing world. The result was a Liberal triumph: Graham and Lawson were elected, with 538 and 516 votes respectively, to Hodgson's 475. At a victory dinner on 8 May Graham quoted rumours of Government pledges amounting to bribes, but subsequently apologised when General Peel denied them.[17]

Carlisle had not followed the general trend: the Conservatives made nearly thirty gains, though the Government was still in a minority. Long discussions followed among Liberals, and by 26 May Greville thought that 'Palmerston and John Russell had made up all their differences and had come to a complete understanding and agreement on all points . . .' Graham had not conceived of such a possibility and even thought a union of

Derby and Palmerston 'the probable solution of existing differences'. But 'the question was how could 350 Liberals be brought to act together', and the problem would not be solved simply by Russell making arrangements with Palmerston. A Liberal Ministry would need Bright's support, and Graham also thought that the rival leaders should agree in advance on the Premiership. Russell hoped that Graham and Herbert would join him, and Palmerston gradually won over Gladstone to his Italian policy. But, as Herbert told Granville, the Liberals were now 'very independent in habits and feelings'. And Graham 'would have no more of [office] during the short remainder of his life'. Eventually, on 6 June Palmerston agreed to a meeting of Liberal M.P.s in Willis's Rooms. A two-party system was virtually restored when a majority of the 280 men present agreed to support the Marquess of Hartington's motion of censure. The debate on Hartington's amendment to the Address began next day, when Disraeli hotly attacked Graham, who retorted that he was 'the Red Indian of debate', cutting his way to power with a tomahawk. Graham 'had a first-rate dressing, to [Gathorne Hardy's] great joy'. Early on the 11th the Government was defeated by 323 votes to 310. Derby resigned and, after a fruitless attempt by Granville to form a Ministry, the Queen sent for Palmerston.

The new Government represented many shades of Liberalism, although Palmerston would offer Bright no more than a Privy Councillorship (to which the Queen refused her consent) and Cobden rejected the Board of Trade. 'Its composition', thought Greville, 'was curiously, and might prove fatally, like that which Aberdeen formed in 1852, of a very Peelite complexion, and only with a larger proportion of Radicals, though not enough, it was said, to satisfy their organs . . .' But by first approaching Granville, the Queen had forced 'the two dreadful old men' of Whiggery to come together. Campbell, Granville, Argyll, Lewis, Russell, Wood, the Duke of Somerset and Sir George Grey were joined by Milner Gibson and by Newcastle, Herbert, Gladstone, the Earl of Elgin and Cardwell (amid some Whiggish grumbling about Peelite greed). Palmerston thanked Graham 'very heartily and sincerely for the kind and friendly assistance' given to mutual friends, and Graham praised Palmerston's 'forgiving temper and exemplary fairness' in forming a comprehensive Cabinet. Gladstone's acceptance of the Chancellorship of the Exchequer after supporting Derby against Hartington was the most surprising move; but he later explained that 'his friends were enlisted, or . . . would enlist: Sir James Graham indeed declining office, but taking his position in the party'. Despite his old hostility to Palmerston, Graham could certainly approve of a Ministry containing so many friends, including the Peelites and his heir's father-in-law. The Government's 'glories . . . were not dazzling', he told Aberdeen in August, but he could take an avuncular pleasure in the success of Gladstone and Herbert.[18]

Home life at Netherby became increasingly attractive. 'I am here doing the patriarch,' Graham wrote to Aberdeen in September from the company of his children and grandchildren. 'As phantoms vanish and as sad experience teaches the truth that all on earth is vanity, we naturally cling more and more to home and learn the happiness of the chimney corner.' While the Franco–Italian campaign against the Austrians ended with the armistice of Villafranca on 7 July and provoked discussion in the chanceries, the elder statesman was content in Cumberland. 'I am occupied with my railroad [he had turned the first sod of the Carlisle and Silloth line on 31 August 1855] and with my woods', he told Aberdeen's son, Arthur Gordon, in December, 'and I quite realise the enjoyment which attends the "*sollicitae jucunda oblivia vitae*". I almost shrink from plunging into the stream again . . .' But, as Graham expected, he 'took to the collar' when 'he heard the crack of the whip', and by January 1860 he was pointing out the unreasonableness of Cobden trying to convert France to Free Trade while the Government simultaneously armed against France.

Although ill health prevented some activities, after Parliament opened on 24 January Graham resumed many political interests. He had long grown out of his youthful enthusiasm for Italian nationalism, strongly distrusted Imperial France, doubted the foreign policies of a Palmerstonian Ministry and would never offend Aberdeen, who favoured the Hapsburgs as a bulwark of the

x

European settlement of 1815. Consequently, in March he declined
Russell's invitation to move an amendment to A. W. Kinglake's
motion condemning the French annexation of Nice and Savoy. 'I
have ceased to take a prominent part in public affairs', he explained, 'and both on public and private grounds this is not the
occasion which I am willing to choose for a return to active
service.' But he was interested in the controversy between
Gladstone and Herbert (the War Secretary) over defence costs.
Herbert had warned Graham in November that he would propose
'a heavy bill [and] did not know how Gladstone would stand the
demands made on him by [Somerset, the First Lord] and himself'.
Steamships, he insisted, made it unsafe to rely on the Navy alone,
and he proposed to increase the Army and militia. Despite
Gladstone's protests, the Cabinet generally favoured increased
military expenditure, even with increased income taxation.

Graham tried to prevent a rupture between his friends,
agreeing with Herbert and Aberdeen that further reduction of the
militia 'would be perfect madness' but urging a clear restatement
of the estimates. When Herbert failed to convert Gladstone he
tendered his resignation, which was not accepted; and Graham
urged the Ministers 'either to compromise or to break'.[19] When the
Cabinet accepted a compromise, Graham advised the disappointed Gladstone. 'Stick together in the Cabinet as long and as
firmly as possible', he wrote, 'but avoid borrowing [for defence],
and in preference risk additional taxation.' And when Gladstone
reluctantly compromised his Free Trade Budget, after long
struggles over the paper duty, by planning a loan for coastal
fortifications, Graham found the plan 'very objectionable'
financially and acceptable only as a means of keeping Gladstone
in office. 'Never at any time of his life had [Gladstone] had such a
sense of mental and moral exhaustion.' Graham, equally tired,
rejoiced that Gladstone retained the Chancellorship, being
'certain that a rupture would have been injurious to all parties
concerned . . .'[20]

Although counselling his friends, Graham's actions were mainly
off the central stage. But weakness did not prevent him from all
action. In March a petition against the Carlisle election was

considered by a Select Committee under J. M. Cobbett. On the 27th Graham vigorously rebutted charges of bribery and treating. He had spent about £269 on four elections and 'had not the slightest intention of paying one farthing beyond it'. He had not canvassed:[21]

> I do not think that since 1852 I have asked four persons for their votes; at the last election I was very ill . . . with great pain and difficulty I addressed the constituency in the Market Place [and] then went home and was confined to my bed for two days, and with great difficulty appeared at the nomination. I never at the last election asked a single man for his vote, except by that public appeal . . .

Next day Cobbett, R. W. Crawford and Hartington resolved (against Lord Robert Montagu and Colonel Pakenham) that Graham and Lawson were duly elected.

On 25 August Graham saw his daughter Helen married to Colonel Baring and then, suffering from sciatica, returned home for the harvest. Melancholy news of old friends and associates regularly grieved him. 'Friends drop so fast around me', he had told Cardwell in 1859, 'that I am almost tempted sometimes to say "I'd join the Party who repose without". It is better far than any Party which I see surviving.' Macaulay had died in December 1859 and Aberdeen followed a year later, when Graham braved a long, cold journey to act as a pallbearer. A sense of duty, despite increasing heart trouble, made him serve conscientiously on committees on the War Office and Admiralty and in January 1861 to accept the chairmanship of a committee on public business. And honesty led him to confess in May 1860 that his predictions on past factory legislation had been disproved: by voting for the Bleaching and Dye-Works Bill he 'endeavoured to make some amends'. He gave advice to many Ministers on constitutional precedents and lectured Gladstone on the impropriety of soliciting outside help in reducing the military estimates. In response to Mrs. Gladstone's appeals, he supported the Budget. And in July 1861 he tearfully bade farewell to his executor, the recently-ennobled Herbert, bound for a continental cure from which he soon returned to die.

After attending Herbert's funeral Graham returned home, again ill. Gentle exercise and reading Motley were his recreations; the county agricultural dinner in September would be too much for his 'health and spirits', although visits from Arthur Gordon and Sir Roundell Palmer delighted him during the warm autumn. But in October he was again bed-ridden and suffering. On the 25th, surrounded by his relations, he died, exactly four years after his wife.[22]

V

Old friends naturally mourned Graham. Lady Herbert recalled that 'he was [Herbert's] truest friend and counsellor', and Gladstone remembered him as 'an invaluable adviser', endowed with 'extraordinary powers ... high moral gifts and Christian graces ...' His 'death was unexpected' by Lewis, despite Graham's prophecies. 'His importance and usefulness as a politician were not equal to his ability both as a reasoner and a speaker,' Lewis told Clarendon. 'Nobody discussed a subject in private better than he did.' The Prince Consort was less sympathetic. 'Politically [Graham] was used up,' he told Stockmar, 'especially as he had not the courage to undertake the part which, from his position and experience, devolved on him, of moderator and arbitrator amid the complications of every-day policy ... His loss, important as he was, will therefore be scarcely felt in the country as a loss.'[23]

Such different immediate reactions to Graham's death represented the variety of views on his career, both during his life and afterwards. In 1849 Clarendon 'was struck with [Graham's] great sagacity and at the same time with a pusillanimity which went far to neutralise that sagacity' and Greville 'had remarked this himself, and that his judgment was often blinded by his fears'. Russell thought in 1850 that 'Graham was always rather too much disposed to be running before what he thought was public opinion'. Three years later Granville considered that 'of the whole Cabinet ... Aberdeen had the most pluck, Gladstone a great deal, and Graham ... the least'. Guizot told Torrens in 1862 that

I saw in [Graham] an eminent representative of a class of man whom I much esteem, though I think them too irresolute in their ideas and conduct and rather too complaisant to the popular humour. He was one of those Liberal Conservatives who, while defending public order and authority, knew how to comprehend and to concede at a suitable time demands made, whether rightly or not, by public opinion, either enlightened or led away by impulse. Such men would not save the Government or institutions of their country in days of revolution; but they serve it usefully in times of law and order, and help it to make without shock considerable progress. They are skilful pilots when you have but to follow the current; but they are far from fit to hold the helm when you must struggle against the storm.

During the Ministerial crisis of early 1851 Gladstone hoped that Graham would lead an independent Peelite party, 'but it soon appeared that, unconsciously I think more than consciously, he was set upon the object of avoiding the responsibility either of taking the government with the Peel squadron or of letting in Stanley and his friends'. Yet for over twenty years Gladstone had 'more spontaneous recourse to him for advice ['on administrative questions'] than to all other colleagues together'. Gladstone's biographer, Lord Morley, had 'heard nobody use warmer language of commendation about [Graham] than Mr. Bright. But nature had not made him for a post of chief command.' When the Peelites left Palmerston's Government in 1855, Delane maintained in *The Times* that[24]

Although no-one contests the brilliant oratorical powers of Mr. Gladstone or the administrative abilities of Sir James Graham, we do not hesitate to express our conviction that the Ministry may be strengthened rather than weakened by their withdrawal from office.

Wise elder statesman or cowardly temporiser; bullying second-line Minister or courageous minority leader; defender of a Whiggish 'Conservative Interest' or constant appeaser of Radicalism; the hack of currently-successful party alignments or the consistent defender of a liberal conservatism — such were the roles variously ascribed to Graham. He was always a man of many

faces; and even those who knew him well disagreed over many of
his characteristics. Gladstone maintained in 1879 that Graham's
apparent asperity was unreal: 'he had never known [a leading
politician] . . . more distinguished . . . by the charitableness and
therefore in the highest sense the Christian character of his
judgment upon the motives and acts of men'. Other standard
views were also challenged by assorted contemporaries. Graham
has often been regarded as a lesser Peel; but Dr. Chalmers
thought differently. 'Sir Robert's extreme caution and coldness
operate as a damper on a man's spirits', he wrote in 1839, 'whereas
Sir James is a fine, hearty, honest, outspeaking Englishman, of
great good feeling and practical sense withal.' It must be admitted
that Chalmers's view was virtually unique — and was almost
certainly changed by subsequent events in the Scottish Church.

As Home Secretary, with responsibility for maintaining public
order and the obligation to be the scapegoat over the letter-
opening affair, Graham was widely condemned. One prisoner, the
Tory Oastler, constantly denounced him, asking whether any
Minister 'had made and broken so many promises as he had', on
the Poor Law and many other topics. But an imprisoned Radical,
G. J. Holyoake, regarded Graham as 'his friend, as no Home
Secretary since had befriended any similar prisoner'. Holyoake
never forgot Graham's generous protection of a secularist from
the vindictiveness of religious-minded justices and his permission
to write articles. He told Lawson that he 'cherished grateful
memories of his uncle for his generous interference on two
occasions when he was a prisoner, with no other friend in
authority save himself'. Lawson reported that Graham was consoled by such a message, fearing that 'he would only be
remembered as the Home Secretary who opened Mazzini's
letters'. And Holyoake insisted that 'there has been no Home
Secretary in my time who had shown the same regard for the
self-respect and rights of unpopular prisoners as [Graham]
showed towards me'.[25] Even prisoners did not agree.

One of the principal attacks on Graham by contemporary
politicians rested on the assumption that changes of party
allegiance involved changes of principle. Graham understood the

suspicions provoked by his party switches and by his retreat on such themes as the 'finality' of the Reform Act. He took some care to explain his position in the Reform debate of March 1859. 'The authors of the Bill of 1832 held out the assurance to the Sovereign and to Parliament that . . . they hoped it would be accepted as a final settlement,' he admitted:

> He had clung to it in that sense, but he found . . . that finality was a position which was no longer tenable . . . [Derby's] measure was framed on an entire misconception of that which, if well understood, was Conservative in its Character. What were the real dangers of extreme democratic changes in this country ? [Disraeli] declared that identity of suffrage was the keystone of the measure. There was then identity of suffrage, electoral districts not equal but less unequal, and voting papers. [Graham] contended that these three outlines had a direct tendency to raise the apprehensions of those who supported what were called Conservative principles . . .

Graham 'had stated that the operation and object of the Bill of 1832 was to transfer power to the middle classes'. But

> he felt that it was a most dangerous doctrine to hold that the humbler classes . . . did not take a real and deep interest in this question . . . He was speaking in a strictly Conservative sense, when he held that it was infinitely more safe to make timely concessions to reasonable demands than pertinaciously to stand upon extreme right and make no concession. He did not believe the demands of the working classes for the franchise could be longer refused with safety.

When Carlisle electors murmured of his 'change of opinion', Graham could fairly retort that within his half-century of active life

> all has changed around me. I have seen the face of nature change, . . . morasses converted into dry ground, . . . desert wastes in this country made to team with golden harvests, . . . grass supplanting heather, . . . night turned into day in our cities and dwellings by the aid of gas, . . . time and distance all but annihilated by the locomotive power of steam, by sea and land . . . [and] the electric telegraph conveying from zone to zone the intercourse of man . . . I have seen mighty monarchies fall; I have seen Republics founded

on their ruins crumble into dust. I have seem military despotism grow up and wither. And shall man, frail man, amidst all these changes of nature and of polity, alone stand immovable, unaltered in his opinions and feelings? I say that if a man is to refuse to yield to the pressure of the times and of the circumstances in which his lot is cast ... [he] may be fit for a lunatic asylum, but I say he does not possess the true recommendations for any deliberative assembly in the world.

The argument, while unacceptable to strict party members, was at least reasonable for a man born during the swelling tide of the Industrial Revolution and speaking in a Britain which had become the Workshop of the World.

If he had no permanent party loyalties, Graham could certainly play a partisan role. His ability to envisage long-term strategic manœuvres and to organise factional tactics was often important. On the Dublin by-election of 1842 he wrote to Peel that

the Government must enter the lists forcibly and give to the Conservative candidate the full measure of their support and influence. If the antagonist be a Repealer, I think that every man receiving the pay of the Crown should be required to vote in favour of the Government candidate: if Morpeth be brought forward, then I would use against him *exactly* the same degree of pressure and of influence which he himself applied at the last election ...

Graham had too often accepted patronage entirely to condemn its exercise at elections. But in office he exercised Governmental powers of appointment honestly, and he regularly supported the principles of entry by competition and promotion by ability in official positions. He opposed many forms of political corruption and cynically expected others to extend it: in any complicated Irish Bill, he counselled, 'look for the patronage clause and ... you will find the key of the measure'. Yet there was some truth in Whig protests about Peelite lust for power after 1850; and Graham always supported his own family's interests.[26]

Graham's political philosophy was neither brave nor dramatic. 'Every day teaches us more and more that in politics long-sighted views are generally fallacious,' he wrote in 1849. 'He is the successful statesman who seizes opportunities as they arise, and bends them to his purpose and to his will. The current of events may be directed, it cannot be turned.' Throughout his life Graham was tormented by doubts and fears. 'He entertained a great dread of the violence of the working-classes [and] often expressed this' to Le Marchant.[27] Popular movements aroused both his hostility and his apprehensions: if they were comparatively weak they must be repressed — and if they were strong they should be met by some compromise. But Graham's dislike of agitations and his general approval of the theoretic 'laws' of the political economists did not lead him to use *laissez-faire* as an excuse for inaction. His years as Peel's Home Secretary were a period of intense activity; indeed, throughout his life, Graham worked extremely hard to master the details of major current problems and to modernise traditional administrative hierarchies. The human, personal interests which endeared Radicals of all sorts, from the Tory Oastler to the socialistic Julian Harney, to public rallies and to later biographers never appealed to Graham. He disdained demagogic persuasion; he saw no easy, popular way of solving the world's problems; and he was almost Benthamite in his passion for honest and efficient administration. As both Home Secretary and First Lord of the Admiralty he was responsible for important parts of that administrative revolution which adjusted Britain's social organisation to the needs created by rapid industrialisation.

Graham was connected with many of the greatest events of his time. He had helped to plan the conservatism of the Reform Act and had taken a prominent part in arranging the provisions of the New Poor Law. 'It was *our* support of the Poor Law that enabled the Government to pass it without fearful resistance,' Peel reminded Croker in 1838:

> It was *our* co-operation in practically working the Law, in becoming Guardians, Chairmen of Unions, &c., that has reconciled, where it is reconciled, the rural population to it. The defender of the Poor Law on the Poor Law Committee was Sir James Graham, not the Government.

After Peel's death, Graham was the most prominent Peelite commoner, exercising considerable influence over the strange political situation of the 1850s, always hoping to maintain and extend Peel's principles. Throughout his life he disliked old-style Toryism, even as a Conservative Minister; and his hostility was important in deciding mid-century alignments. Some early principles perhaps owed something to a reaction against paternal ideas; Graham associated with Harriette Wilson while his father supported the Church Missionary Society and the Society for the Suppression of Vice,[28] and broke with Pittite Toryism to become a Whig. In his liberal social and economic views, however, he remained consistent, as he did in his desire for peace. Above all, his contribution to the remodelling of Victorian Britain rested on administrative reform: the modernisation of Cumbrian local government, the overhaul of Admiralty organisation, the great Peelite reforms of the 1840s, the demand for competitive entry to the Civil Service in the 'fifties. And if he was prepared to retire (but only to prepared positions) before seemingly overwhelming opposition, he was also willing to make courageous stands on matters of high principle — over the Irish Church in 1834, the Corn Laws in 1846, 'Papal Aggression' in 1851 and war in 1856 and 1857.

Through most of his career Graham earned the hostility of the Press. He was sensitive enought to be hurt, but he generally chose to ignore such opposition. 'I have some experience of the attacks of malignant editors, and I have learned that it is wise to bear injustices with patience and to falsify groundless accusations by conduct which will bear the test of adverse scrutiny,' he told Sir William Napier in 1844. When Alexander Somerville was doubtfully reported to have attacked Graham over the release of his seaman brother in 1832, the Radical editor Samuel Smith (who had publicised Somerville's monstrous military flogging) insisted that H. Fairburn 'had better not bring a serious charge against Sir James Graham on Somerville's authority — or rather, on the authority of anything he may be reported to have said'. Few editors shared such views, and many printed biting attacks on Graham. Somerville himself lived to praise Graham as 'a spirited agriculturalist' who had performed virtual miracles by draining and cultivating poor, wet land. Throughout his life, Graham was a practical agriculturalist of some importance. He supported the Royal Agricultural Society's *Journal* as 'an authentic record of practical experiments [for] by multiplying facts and proofs of this description agriculture would be treated as a science'.[29]

As the generally hostile *Times* recorded in its obituary notice, Graham's 'strength lay in his power of work and power of argument. The celebrity of the Peelites for administrative ability was largely based on the effectiveness of Graham.' He was, as G. M. Young wrote in a much later edition, 'after O'Connell perhaps the most powerful debater in the House . . . [and] might have been Prime Minister had he set his course that way'. There was, indeed, no particular quality which Graham lacked that debarred him from the Premiership. He was both abler and wealthier than several nineteenth-century First Ministers. He was hard-working, honest and capable of great generosity to friends and lethal invective to opponents. His 'trimming' was more apparent than real. His unpopularity, his occasional unfairness and his self-admitted errors of judgement were no worse than those of other contemporary politicians. A personal, psychological factor, more than any public disability, prevented him from achieving the highest prize. Fundamentally, behind the cold haughtiness displayed in public, he was a modest and sensitive man, lacking the egoistic certainties entertained by some of his friends. 'Sir James, who was thought to have some haughtiness in his manner,' Gladstone declared in 1879, 'was undoubtedly one of the humblest men that I have ever known in public life, or perhaps out of public life.' Gladstone's first great biographer wrote that 'the more he studied that generation, the more did he incline to put Sir James Graham in the very front for sagacity, pure sense of public duty, and for moral depth of character, all in combination'. Graham's major 'wart', to contemporaries and biographers alike, was his very mastery of politics. He never sought public acclaim by some Palmerstonian or Disraelian melodrama, or to rouse what people might think were their consciences by stage-managed Cobdenite or Gladstonian appeals to 'morality'. In his cool, impersonal way, he was impressed and convinced primarily by the logic of events. He was 'very much opposed to the discussion of abstract questions of extreme right', he told Colonel Phipps in 1855:[30]

In our mixed form of government the machine would soon be brought to a standstill if they were insisted on; and more than half of the matters of state, as well as of society, are best adjusted by compromise and mutual forbearance.

Politics, particularly in the 1850s, was based on compromise; but compromise as a principle did not appeal to the partisans of each hopefully-manœuvring group any more than its dramatic inadequacies attracted most subsequent historians.

Graham rarely joined in Victorian high society's life in London *salons* and rounds of country-house parties. As an assiduous Minister and Parliamentarian, he walked home from the Palace of Westminster late at night and refreshed himself only by brief holidays on the Isle of Wight; and when his political and financial situation allowed him to return to the beloved Netherby, he sought lonely relaxation with his books and shooting Solway wildfowl, occasionally accompanied by some of his doting children. His youngest daughter remembered him as a generous, indulgent father; behind the cold mask, relations and associates insisted, was a kindly, rather nervous old gentleman, whose idea of duty had impelled him to overtask his rheumatic frame for many years. The Oxford dandy, the amatuer diplomat and the glamorous candidate for Parliament had served in many fields in later life. On the front stage, he had helped to plan the classic Reform Act, the emancipation of Negro slaves, the Poor Law, the rise of the new Conservatism, the administrative revolution, the reaction to possible revolution, the abolition of mercantilist economic policies and the whole political scene of mid-Victorian Britain. He had worked within self-imposed rules; he made mistakes which he both admitted and regretted; he sometimes appeared to be harsh, legalistic and timid. But he was an important force in the creation of Victorian Britain.[31] The boy who travelled to Westminster School by stage-coach and finally returned to Netherby by railway express had not only witnessed the greatest changes in British history; he had also played an essential role in moulding and forming and controlling the changes; and therein lay his claim to historical recognition.

Notes

PREFACE

1. D. H. Elletson, *Maryannery* (1959), 110, 123; 'Runnymede' letter to Lord Normanby, 11 Feb. 1837 [B. Disraeli, ed. W. Hutcheon, *Whigs and Whiggism* (1913), 359]; B. Disraeli, *Coningsby* (1844; 1948 ed.), 213, 105–6; K. Marx in *New York Daily Tribune*, 21 Aug. 1852 [K. Marx, F. Engels, *On Britain* (Moscow, 1953), 355].

2. J. W. Croker to J. C. Herries, 15 Aug. 1853 [Edward Herries, *Memoir of the Public Life of the Right Hon. John Charles Herries* (1880), ii. 279].

3. G. Hardy's diary, 21 Feb. 1845 [A. E. Gathorne-Hardy, *Gathorne Hardy, First Earl of Cranbrook, A Memoir* (1910), i. 56–57].

4. See W. R. Brock, *Lord Liverpool and Liberal Toryism* (Cambridge, 1941), and D. G. Southgate, *The Most English Minister: The Policies and Politics of Palmerston* (1966), *passim*.

5. S. J. Reid, *Life and Letters of the First Earl of Durham, 1792–1840* (1906), i. 235.

6. Graham to Lord Lyndhurst, 21 Aug., to Sir Henry Hardinge, 1 Sept., to Lord Wharncliffe, 2 Sept. 1842.

7. Graham to Kay-Shuttleworth, Aug. 1842 [Frank Smith, *The Life and Work of Sir James Kay-Shuttleworth* (1923), 139].

8. R. H. Mottram, 'Town Life', in G. M. Young (ed.), *Early Victorian England, 1830–1865* (Oxford, 1951), i. 196.

9. Graham to Croker, 11 Dec. 1844 [quoted in Norman Gash, *Reaction and Reconstruction in English Politics, 1832–1852* (Oxford, 1965), 116 n. 2].

10. Gervas Huxley, *Lady Elizabeth and the Grosvenors. Life in a Whig Family, 1822–1839* (Oxford, 1965), 98.

11. Mrs. Hardcastle, *Life of Lord Campbell* (1881), i. 467.

12. [Sir] Edward Baines, *Letter to the Right Honourable Lord Wharncliffe . . . on Sir James Graham's Bill . . .* (1843), 9, and *The Social, Educational and Religious State of the Manufacturing Districts . . .* (1843), 11.

13. George W. Sandys, *A Letter to the Right Honourable Sir James R. G. Graham . . .* (1843), 3.

14. James C. Evans, *Letter to Sir James Graham, Bart., on the Education Clauses of the Factory Bill* (1843), 3.

15. Graham to Lord Granville Somerset, 17 Dec. 1836, and to Peel, 15 Nov. 1837.

16. Graham to Lord Macdonald, 3 Feb. 1832 (Bosville–Macdonald MSS. in the East Riding Record Office).

CHAPTER 1

1. The following account is principally based on Graham's letters to his father, some of which are partially quoted in C. S. Parker, *Life and Letters of Sir James Graham* (1907), i. *passim*.

2. See C. D. Yonge, *The Life of Arthur, Duke of Wellington* (1891), 207–20; H. R. Clinton, *The War in the Peninsula* (1878), ch. 8; G. R. Gleig, *The Life of Arthur, Duke of Wellington* (1911 ed.), ch. 18; on Russell's visit, see G. W. E. Russell, *Collections and Recollections* (1903), 24–25.

3. See R. M. Johnston, 'Lord William Bentinck and Murat' (*English Historical Review*, xix. 74, April 1904); Mrs. F. Best, 'Lord William Bentinck in Sicily, 1811–12' (ibid., xlii. 167, July 1927); Elizabeth Wiskemann, 'Lord William Bentinck, Precursor of the Risorgimento' (*History Today*, ii. 7, July 1952).

4. Henry Lonsdale, *The Worthies of Cumberland, II: Sir J. R. G. Graham, Bart., of Netherby* (1868), 22 n.; T. M. Torrens, *The Life and Times of the Right Honourable Sir James R. G. Graham* (1863), i. 77–78.

5. Graham to Aberdeen, 26 Jan., Aberdeen to Graham, 18 Feb. 1814.

6. Graham to Bentinck, 7 March 1814. See John Rosselli, *Lord William Bentinck and the British Occupation of Sicily, 1811–1814* (Cambridge, 1956), 132–4, appendix B, ii.

7. Lonsdale, op. cit., ii. 16; Parker, op. cit., i. 6. See Ford K. Brown, *Fathers of the Victorians. The Age of Wilberforce* (Cambridge, 1961), 282, 359, 429, on Sir James's support of Evangelical societies.

8. H. Lonsdale, *Worthies . . . I: J. C. Curwen, William Blamire* (1867), 209–11.

9. See Brian Bonsall, *Sir James Lowther and Cumberland and Westmorland Elections, 1754–1775* (Manchester, 1960); A. S. Turberville, *The House of Lords in the Age of Reform, 1784–1837* (1958), 247; R. S. Ferguson, *The Cumberland and Westmorland M.P.s . . . 1660–1867* (1871), i. 126 et seq.; Sir Lewis Namier and John Brooke, *The House of Commons, 1754–1790* (1964), i. 242–5.

CHAPTER 2

1. The following account is mainly based on *The Hull Advertiser and Exchange Gazette*, 6, 13, 20, 27 June, 4, 11, 18, 25 July; *The Rockingham and Hull Weekly Advertiser*, 27 June, 4 July 1818; *A Copy of the Poll . . . in the Town of Kingston-upon-Hull* (Hull, 1818). Benjamin Tate, a local printer, published most of the election literature in *Kingston Wit, Humour and Satire. An Impartial Record of the Spirit of Party* (Hull, 1818). A less accurate account is given in W. A. Gunnell, *Sketches of Hull Celebrities* (1876). On the 18th-century background, see Namier and Brooke, op. cit., i. 434–5.

2. G. H. Jennings, *An Anecdotal History of the British Parliament* (1880 ed.), 252; Torrens, op. cit., i. 113–15. This period of Graham's political career is detailed in A. B. Erickson, *The Political Career of Sir James Graham* (Oxford, 1952), 34 et seq.

3. Arthur Aspinall (ed.), *Three Early Nineteenth Century Diaries* (1952), 288–9.

4. Graham and Hobhouse were members of the Select Vestry of St. George's, Hanover Square, 'by far the best-governed parish in the Metropolitan area' [S. and B. Webb, *The Parish and The County* (1963 reprint), 241]. Hobhouse later thought Graham 'a reformer who will go all lengths with me' (Hobhouse to Place, 23 March 1830).

5. J. Hobson Matthews, *The History of the Parishes of St. Ives, Lelant, Towednack and Zennor* (1892), 358, 497, 503–4. See also Namier and Brooke, op. cit., i. 237–8, on the borough's previous history, and J. H. Philbin, *Parliamentary Representation, 1832, England and Wales* (New Haven, 1965), 34, on subsequent elections.

6. For an individual Whig's eye-witness account of the Queen's proceedings, see John Gore (ed.), *Creevey* (1949 reprint), 183–216. See also Frances Hawes, *Henry Brougham* (1957), 115–61.

7. Diary of John Lewis Mallet, quoted in Torrens, op. cit., i. 141; Lonsdale, op. cit., ii. 28.

8. Matthews, op. cit., 359–60, 504. James Halse was elected Tory M.P. for the borough in 1826.

9. Lonsdale, op. cit., i. 217–83; David Spring, *The English Landed Estate in the Nineteenth Century: Its Administration* (Baltimore, 1963), 165–7; *D.N.B.*, ii (1908), 654–6.

10. Lonsdale, op. cit., iii. 201–92, 189–200; ii. 44–45.

11. Ferguson, op. cit., 190, 198–213; W. Parson, W. White, *History, Directory and Gazetteer of the Counties of Cumberland and Westmorland . . .* (Leeds, 1829), 126–7, 184; W. W. Bean, *The Parliamentary Representation of the Six Northern Counties . . .* (Hull, 1890), 34–35, 70–72; Namier and Brooke, op. cit., i. 245–8.

12. Lonsdale, op. cit., ii. 75–88. See also S. and B. Webb, *The Parish and The County* (1963 reprint), 507, and *Statutory Authorities for Special Purposes* (1963 reprint), 385.

CHAPTER 3

1. John Burke, *A Genealogical and Heraldic Dictionary of the Peerage and Baronetage of the British Empire* (1845 ed.), 448, 697.

2. Torrens, op. cit., i. 1–25; Lonsdale, op. cit., ii. 6 et seq.; Parker, op. cit., i. 2 et seq.; Burke, op. cit., 449–50; T. H. B. Graham, 'The Debatable Land' (*Trans. Cumberland and Westmorland Antiquarian and Archaeological Society*, xiv. 143 et seq.).

3. *The Gentleman's Magazine*, LV. ii (Nov. 1785), 843–5; Torrens, op. cit., i. 25–33; Parson and White, op. cit., 45–56, 432.

4. Ibid., 403–12, 431–2; William Dickinson, 'On the Farming of Cumberland' (*Journal of the Royal Agricultural Society of England*, xiii,

1852); cf. J. Bailey, G. Culley, *General View of the Agriculture of the County of Cumberland* (1794).

5. Torrens, op. cit., i. 148 et seq.; Dickinson, loc. cit.; Arvel B. Erickson, 'Sir James Graham, Agricultural Reformer' (*Agricultural History*, xxiv, 1950, 170–4); David Spring, 'A Great Agricultural Estate: Netherby under Sir James Graham, 1820–1845' (ibid., xxix, 1955, 73–81); Lonsdale, op. cit., ii. 29–30.

6. Parson and White, op. cit., 406; Lonsdale, op. cit., ii. 16; Spring, 'Netherby', loc. cit.; William Vinard to Graham, 20 Dec. 1822.

7. Lonsdale, op. cit., ii. 31, 34–35, 40; Torrens, op. cit., i. 154–8. See R. Trow-Smith, *A History of British Livestock Husbandry, 1700–1900* (1959), 112–14; Lord Ernle, *English Farming, Past and Present* (1961 ed.), 180.

8. Erickson, Dickinson, loc. cit.; Lonsdale, op. cit., ii. 35–39; Parker, op. cit., i. 57–58; Sir J. R. G. Graham, 'On the Deanston Frequent Drain System' (*Jour. R. Ag. Soc. of Eng.*, i, 1840).

9. Mrs. Elizabeth Sheldon, who had a life interest in the estate, was the widow of Graham's uncle Charles. Of Graham's sisters, Elizabeth Frances died in 1810, Elizabeth Anne married the Rev. William Waddilove in 1816, Caroline married Wilfrid Lawson in 1821, Harriet Anne married Frederick Madan in 1832 and Charlotte married Sir George Musgrave in 1828.

10. Sir J. R. G. Graham, *Corn and Currency, in an Address to the Land Owners* (1826), 10, 11, 58–68, 99 et seq., 113.

11. *Quarterly Review*, xxv (1826); *Westminster Review*, vi (1826); G. D. H. and M. Cole (eds.), *Rural Rides . . . By William Cobbett* (1930), ii. 394–5, 426–7, 442–3, 464, 467.

12. *Parliamentary Papers*, 1874, lxxii: 'Return of Owners of Land, 1873' [C. 1097: 1875], i: Cumberland section, 13; John Bateman, *The Great Landowners of Great Britain and Ireland* (1879 ed.), 184; *Parl. Papers*, 1895, xvii: 'Royal Commission on Agriculture. England. Report . . . on . . . Cumberland' [C. 7915: 1895], 26–27, 35.

CHAPTER 4

1. Bean, op. cit., 35–42; Ferguson, op. cit., i. 206–ii. 250 *et passim*; *Annual Register* (1826), chronicle, 94–95; *Carlisle Patriot, Carlisle Journal*, 10, 17 June 1826. The poll figures vary in different accounts.

2. See Arthur Aspinall, *The Formation of Canning's Ministry*, Camden Soc. 3rd ser., lix (1937), *passim*; 'The Coalition Ministries of 1827', *Eng. Hist. Rev.*, xlii (1927), 201–26, 533–59; 'The Last of the Canningites', ibid., l (1935), 639–67; 'The Canningite Party', *Trans. R. Hist. Soc.*, 4th ser., xvii (1934), 177–226.

3. *Carlisle Patriot*, 17 Jan., *Carlisle Journal*, 17, 24 Jan. 1829.

4. Francis Bamford and the Duke of Wellington (eds.), *The Journal of Mrs. Arbuthnot, 1820–1832* (1950), ii. 196–9; Gore, op. cit., 305 et seq.; the Marquess of Anglesey, *One Leg* (1963 ed.), ch. 10.

5. Lonsdale, op. cit., ii, ch. 6; Graham to Brougham, 7 Sept. 1830

[quoted in Arthur Aspinall, *Politics and the Press, c. 1780–1850* (1949), 281].

6. Bamford and Wellington, op. cit., ii. 290, 293.

7. Torrens, op. cit., i. 242–9, 252–73; Parker, op. cit., i. 74–80; Erickson, op. cit., 66–72; cf. Norman Gash, *Mr. Secretary Peel* (1961), 613–14; J. R. M. Butler, *The Passing of the Great Reform Bill* (1964 ed.), 69.

8. Bamford and Wellington, op. cit., ii. 370. On Graham's support for Althorp see Sir Denis Le Marchant, *Memoir of . . . Viscount Althorp* (1876), 246.

9. *Carlisle Journal*, 31 July, 7, 14 Aug. 1830. Professor Norman Gash has shown ['English Reform and French Revolution in the General Election of 1830', in *Essays Presented to Sir Lewis Namier* (1956), 258–88] that the events in France influenced few British elections.

10. To Huskisson's proposal of an alliance in June, Grey had written that 'he had no indisposition towards [him] and his friends, but that on the contrary he was quite ready to act with them when the occasion should offer' [G. M. Trevelyan, *Lord Grey of the Reform Bill* (1929 ed.), 218].

11. Despite Huskisson's friendly correspondence, as late as 7 Sept. Graham asked Brougham about rumours that Huskisson might commit 'political suicide' by supporting the Duke's 'tottering fortunes'. On the 2nd he had told Brougham that Wellington, 'would not scruple' to adopt Whig measures to save his Ministry.

12. *The Times*, 17 Sept.; Mrs. Arbuthnot, 26 Sept. (Bamford and Wellington, op. cit., ii. 386); Creevey to Miss Ord, 19 Sept. (Gore, op. cit., 317); C. C. F. Greville (ed. Henry Reeve), *A Journal of the Reigns of King George IV and King William IV*, ii. (1875), 48; Brougham to Graham, 17 Sept.; Warrender to Graham, 21 Sept.; Mrs. Emily Huskisson to Graham, n.d., 1830. After some discussion with the varied Opposition groups, Grey told Princess Lieven on 2 July that 'if the new elections did not turn out very favourably to [Wellington] . . . and if he could not get some more efficient assistance in the House of Commons, . . . it was not possible that the present Administration should continue' [Guy Le Strange (ed.), *Correspondence of Princess Lieven and Earl Grey* (1890), ii. 20].

13. Butler, op. cit., 96–97, 100; A. A. W. Ramsay, *Sir Robert Peel* (1928), 135–6; Bishop of Carlisle to Graham, 4 Oct.; Graham to Rooke, 15 Oct.; Brougham to Graham, 1 Nov.; Graham to Brougham, 2 Nov. 1830. Grey had hoped that Russell might propose the Reform motion and resented Brougham's claim to the honour.

14. Bamford and Wellington, op. cit., ii. 389–96; Gash, op. cit., 644–6; Sir H. L. Lytton, *Life of Viscount Palmerston* (1871), i. 363–4; C. S. Parker, *Sir Robert Peel* (1899), ii. 163–6; E. Ashley, *Life of Palmerston* (1876), i. 213.

15. H. Brougham, *The Life and Times of Lord Brougham* (1871), iii. 58; Greville, op. cit., ii. 71; S. Smith to Countess Grey, 21 Nov. 1830 (Lady Holland and Mrs. Austin, *A Memoir of the Reverend Sydney Smith*

(1855), ii. 310–11). See also Carlos Flick, 'The Fall of Wellington's Government' (*Journal of Modern History*, xxxvii. 1, March 1965, 65–71).

CHAPTER 5

1. Greville, op. cit., ii. 90–91; Bamford and Wellington, op. cit. ii. 417; Graham to Rooke, 15 Oct. 1830; Sir T. Wemyss Reid, *The Life, Letters and Friendships of R. M. Milnes* (1890), i. 95.

2. For varied accounts, see S. J. Reid, op. cit., i. 235–6; L. Cooper, *Radical Jack* (1959), 100–1; Spencer Walpole, *The Life of Lord John Russell* (1889), i. 165; Butler, op. cit., 159–60, 172–3; Lord Broughton, *Recollections of a Long Life* (1910), iv. 178; D. G. Southgate, *The Passing of the Whigs, 1832–1886* (1962), 12–13; Hawes, op. cit., 225; Arthur Aspinall, *Brougham and the Whig Party* (1939), 189; Brougham, op. cit., iii. 68, 93.

3. Gore, op. cit., 319. See Graham's memories, recorded in 1851 (Graham to J. A. Roebuck, 4 Jan. 1851, in Parker, op. cit. i. 114–22).

4. Graham to Grey, 21, Western to Graham, 26 Dec. 1830; Earl Grey (ed.), *Correspondence of William IV and Earl Grey* (2 vols., 1867), *passim*; Graham to Grey, 18 Jan. 1831.

5. Greville, op. cit., ii. 110; Palmerston to Graham, 31 Jan. 1831; Graham to Grey, 29 Dec. 1830, and to Stanley, 6 Jan.; Stanley to Graham, 31 Jan. 1831.

6. Greville, op. cit., ii. 116–17; Graham to Grey, 17 Feb.; Stanley to Graham, 27 Feb.; Russell to Graham, March; Greville, op. cit., ii. 125–6, described Graham's speech as 'a total failure'.

7. See Butler, op. cit., 203 et seq.; Parker, op. cit., i. 105 et seq.; Grey, op. cit., i. 225 et seq.; Anglesey to Graham, 24 April 1831; Michael Joyce, *My Friend H* (1948), 216.

8. Graham to Browne, 7 April; Torrens, op. cit., i. 373–6; Lonsdale, op. cit., ii. 106–8; Parker, op. cit., i. 111; Graham to the Rev. E. Stanley, 11 April 1831.

9. *Carlisle Journal*, 30 April, 7 May 1831; Lonsdale, op. cit., i. 243, ii. 108–10; Torrens, op. cit., i. 376–83; Grey to Graham, 2, 10, Graham to Grey, 5 May 1831; *1831 Cumberland Election. The Poll for the Knights of the Shire . . .* (Cockermouth, 1831), *passim*; Bamford and Wellington, op. cit., ii. 421.

10. Galloway to Graham, 25, Graham to Stanley, 23 May 1831; see Turberville, op. cit., 110, 474.

11. Graham to Grey, 30, Howick to C. Grey, 28 May (Butler, op. cit., 230), Graham to Stanley, 31, Wilson to Graham, 30 May, 1 June, Graham to Wilson, 30 May, Richmond to Graham, 2, 3 June 1831; Greville, op. cit., ii. 145.

12. Graham to Grey, 5, to Stanley, 6, Stanley to Graham, 8 June, Graham to B. Earle, 1 July, to J. I. Carew, 15, to Grey, 25 Aug. 1831.

13. Butler, op. cit., 255; Graham to Grey, 17, 27 June 1831.

14. See Gore, op. cit., 331–7; Turberville, op. cit., ch. 12; Greville, ii. 202 et seq.; Grey, i. 363–6, ii. 58 et seq.; Butler, op. cit., chs. 7–9;

Southgate, *Whigs*, ch. 1, and *Most English Minister*, 82 et seq.; Parker, op. cit., i, ch. 6; Reid, op. cit., i. 270 et seq.; Brougham, op. cit., iii, *passim*; Le Marchant, op. cit., *passim*; Duke of Wellington (ed.), *Despatches . . . of the Duke of Wellington*, 3rd ser. viii (1880), *passim*. Professor Gash, *Reaction and Reconstruction*, 57, points out that the Whigs gradually created nearly 70 peers between 1830 and 1852, to the Conservatives' 9.

15. Graham to Grey, 30 Nov.; Duchess of Kent to Graham, 9, 19 Dec.; Sir G. O. Trevelyan, *The Life and Letters of Lord Macaulay* (1959 ed.), 174; Graham to Grey, 31 Dec. 1830, and 5, 6, 7, 18 Jan. 1831.

16. Graham to Grey, 15, 25, 29 Jan., 2, 4 Feb., 7 June; the King to Graham, 24, Grey to Graham, 25 Sept.; Graham to Grey, Sept. 1831.

17. Graham to Grey, 24 Jan. 1831; Sir W. L. Clowes, *The Royal Navy* (1903), vi. 190–1.

18. See Erickson, op. cit., 95 et seq.; C. J. Bartlett, *Great Britain and Sea Power 1815–1853* (Oxford, 1963), 9 et seq.; Parker, op. cit., ch. 7; Graham to Grey, 27 July, 28 Aug., 1 Sept., Graham to Stanley, 11 June 1831; Graham to Grey, 20 Sept., Grey to Graham, 21, 22 Sept., Graham to Grey, 26, 27 Sept., Grey to Graham, 28, 30 Sept., 4 Oct., Graham to Stanley, 5, 18 Nov., to Grey, 15 Nov. 1832 (most of these letters are partly quoted by Parker); Greville, op. cit., ii. 364.

19. Graham to Grey, 23 Dec. 1832, 2 Aug. 1833, to Parker, 31 Aug. 1832, to Grey, 5 June 1834.

20. Graham to Grey, April, 28 July 1831; Parker, op. cit., i. 147, 165–8; *The Extraordinary Black Book* (1831), 181–2, 447. [The editor was 'somewhat at a loss to discover (Graham's) claims' to the Admiralty and found him vague on Reform and wrong on currency, but praised his abilities and 'liberal and enlightened' sentiments.]

CHAPTER 6

1. Anglesey to Graham, 30 July, Graham's reply, 4 Aug.; Anglesey to Grey, 19 Dec., to Melbourne, 28 Oct. 1831 (see Anglesey, op. cit., 259, 263); Graham to Anglesey, 9 July, 21 Aug., Anglesey to Graham, 6 Oct., Grey to Graham, 3 Nov., Graham to Stanley, 3 Nov., Grey to Graham, 8 Nov., Graham to Grey, 13 Nov., Richmond to Graham, 11 Nov. 1832.

2. Torrens, op. cit., i. 315–21; Graham to Stanley, 18, 19, Stanley's reply, 21 Nov. 1832; W. D. Jones, *Lord Derby and Victorian Conservatism* (Oxford, 1956), 36; Greville, op. cit., ii. 363–6; Anglesey, op. cit., 264–76.

3. Littleton to Graham, 30 Sept., Graham to Littleton, 19 Oct., Ellice to Graham, 7 Feb. 1833. See Southgate, *Whigs*, 44 et seq.; Sir E. L. Woodward, *The Age of Reform 1815–1870* (1949 reprint), 330 et seq.

4. Greville, op. cit., ii. 105, iii. 59–65; Graham to Grey, 13 Feb. 1834; *Annual Register* (1834), 17–18. Graham later told Stanley (18 Jan. 1835) that 'that vote was the most painful one I ever gave, because it was in opposition to you . . .'.

5. Lord Russell, *Recollections and Suggestions, 1813–1873* (1875), 120–1; Parker, op. cit., i. 186–9; *Annual Register* (1834), 42; Brougham to Graham, 7 May; Ashley, op. cit., i. 205; Brougham, n.d., Palmerston o Graham, 26 May 1834; Greville, op. cit., iii. 86–87; Graham's 'Minutes of the occurrences at the Levée ...', 27 May (Parker, i. 190–2); cf. Jones, op. cit., 44–45; George Saintsbury, *The Earl of Derby* 1892), 38–40; Angus Macintyre, *The Liberator* (1965), 131–2 and cf. ibid., 129, 156.

6. Greville, op. cit., iii. 88–93; W. J. Fitzpatrick, *Correspondence of Daniel O'Connell* (1888), i. 439; Brougham, op. cit., iii. 248; Lord Stanley, 1, Goodenough, 9 June 1834, to Graham.

7. Graham to Lord Stanley, 4, to Lord W. Bentinck, 12 June 1834; Parker, op. cit., i. 194 et seq.

8. Trevelyan, op. cit., 230; Greville, op. cit., iii. 93; Parker, op. cit., i. 205–6.

9. Graham to H. Howard, 13 Dec. 1834, 2 Jan. 1835; address, 16 Dec.; Carlisle to Graham, 24 Dec. 1834; Lonsdale, op. cit., ii. 121–9; Torrens, op. cit., ii. 15–29; *Speech of the Right Hon. Sir J. R. G. Graham, on being Nominated ... at Carlisle, on Monday, January 12, 1835* (Carlisle, 1835), 3–17. Graham considerably changed his views on religious reform during the 1830s.

10. Graham to Lansdowne, 28 April 1827; Stanley to Graham, 21 Jan. 1835; *Carlisle Patriot*, 17 Jan. 1835.

11. Graham to Stanley, 18, 23, Stanley to Graham, 21, 30, 31 Jan. 1835. See G. Kitson Clark, *Peel and the Conservative Party* (1964 ed.), 248–51; D. W. J. Johnson, 'Sir James Graham and the "Derby Dilly"' (*University of Birmingham Historical Journal*, iv. 1, 1953, 66–80).

12. Lonsdale, op. cit., ii. 134; Torrens, op. cit., ii. 72–73; Greville, op. cit., iii. 282, 332, 334, 336.

13. Graham to Hardinge, 22 Jan. (quoted by Erickson, op. cit., 130, n. 6), to Peel, 12 Feb. 1836; Torrens, op. cit., ii. 77; Macintyre, op. cit., 192, 241–2, 249–56.

14. *Parl. Papers*, 1836, viii.; see F. M. L. Thompson, *English Landed Society in the Nineteenth Century* (1963), 197, 233–5; Lonsdale, op. cit., ii. 135; *Annual Register* (1836), 223. Graham had also sat on the 1833 Committee (*Parl. Papers*, 1833, v.).

15. Trevelyan, op. cit., 251; Torrens, op. cit., ii. 92–97.

16. Graham to Stanley, 30 Aug. 1836.

17. Greville, op. cit., iii. 394; Graham to Lord G. Somerset, 17 Dec., to Peel, 11 Dec. 1836.

18. *The Times*, 20 April 1837; Erickson, op. cit., 135, 137; Torrens, op. cit., ii. 112–13; Jennings, op. cit., 252–3; Lonsdale, op. cit., ii. 138–42.

CHAPTER 7

1. C. C. F. Greville (ed. Henry Reeve), *A Journal of the Reign of Queen Victoria from 1837 to 1852* (1885), i. 5–6, 9–10; Graham to Stanley, 7 July; *Morning Chronicle*, 3 July; Lonsdale, op. cit., ii. 143–53; Torrens,

op. cit., ii. 114–17; *Carlisle Patriot, Carlisle Journal,* 7, 14 July 1837; Ferguson, op. cit., ii. 268.

2. Aspinall, *Brougham,* 241.

3. Lonsdale, op. cit., ii. 153–60; Torrens, op. cit., ii. 117–25; *Carlisle Patriot,* 4, 12 Aug. 1837; Norman Gash, *Politics in the Age of Peel* (1953), 132, 142; Erickson, op. cit., 137–8. Graham described the 'popular violence and intimidation' to Peel (Parker, *Peel,* ii. 348–50).

4. Gash, *Politics,* 224, 201; Lonsdale, op. cit., ii. 162–5; Torrens, op. cit., ii. 123, 126–31; Lord G. Bentinck to Graham, 12 Jan. 1838; Aspinall, *Press,* 367–8; Philbin, op. cit., 263–5. Falmouth was expensive (see Gash, *Politics,* 449–52).

5. Peel to Graham, 21 Nov., Graham to Stanley, 12 Dec. 1837.

6. Graham to Lord Tavistock, 29 Aug. 1838. This was part of a long correspondence in which Tavistock sought to defend Russell's attitudes; see Parker, op. cit., i. 265 et seq.

7. Graham to Sir H. Hardinge, 17, 21, Hardinge to Graham, 19, 20, 22, 23, 26, 27, Spencer to Graham and Charlemont, 20 Jan. 1838.

8. Tavistock to Graham, 21, Russell to Tavistock, 19, Graham to Tavistock, 23, Tavistock to Graham, 28 Nov., Graham to Stanley, 9 Dec. 1838.

9. Graham to Stanley, 21 Oct., 4 Nov. 1838. Before Stanley the Rectors had been Lord Jeffrey (1820), Sir James Mackintosh (1822), Brougham (1824), Thomas Campbell (1826), Lansdowne (1829) and Lord Cockburn (1831).

10. Stanley to Graham, 8, D. MacFarlane to Graham, J. F. Morier to Graham, 15, Graham to Morier, 16, to Stanley, 18 Nov. 1838. The *Glasgow Herald,* 16 Nov., gave 282 votes to 207.

11. Hamilton, 19, Goodenough, Canning, 30 Nov., Peel, 5 Dec. 1838, to Graham.

12. Morier to Graham, 15 Nov.; Graham to Stanley, 9 Dec. 1838; *Speech of the Right Honourable Sir James Graham at Glasgow* (Carlisle, 1838); *Glasgow Herald,* 24 Dec. 1838. On Auchterarder see Robert Buchanan, *The Ten Years' Conflict* (Glasgow, 1852), i. ch. 8.

13. Stanley, Alderson, 26 Dec. 1838, and Wharncliffe, 1, Hardinge, 12, Peel, 16 Jan. 1839, to Graham.

14. Graham to Stanley, 28 Dec. 1838, and 14, to Peel, 29, Peel to Graham, 16 Jan. 1839.

15. Graham to Peel, 29 Jan. 1839.

16. Peel to Arbuthnot, 24 Jan. (Parker, *Peel,* ii. 377); Graham to Jackson, 23 Jan., to Minto, 16, 20 Feb. 1839.

17. Norman McCord, *The Anti-Corn Law League, 1838–1846* (1958), ch. 1; Torrens, op. cit., ii. 149–56.

18. Graham to Stanley, 22, 26 March 1839; Greville, *Victoria,* i. 176–8, 180–90, 193, 196.

19. Parker, *Peel,* ii. 388–407; L. J. Jennings (ed.), *The Croker Papers* (1884), ii. 342–7, 356. Graham suspected that the Whigs had a hand in the Queen's decision (Graham to Peel, 9 May), but thought that Peel was entirely right in refusing to give way (letter to Peel, 13 May). On

the 7th the Queen had 'talked [to Melbourne] of her great dislike to some of these people — Sir H. Hardinge — Graham — Peel' [Lord Esher, *The Girlhood of Queen Victoria* (1912), ii. 162]. In June she 'liked Stanley . . . a little better [than Peel], but Graham not at all' (ibid., 205). Her hostility to Graham apparently arose from his physical similarity to her mother's unpleasant secretary, Sir John Conroy (Lady Longford, *Victoria R.I.* (1965 ed.), 110). See A. C. Benson and Lord Esher, *The Letters of Queen Victoria* (1908), i. 160–71.

20. For a succinct account of the controversy, see G. F. A. Best, 'The Religious Difficulties of National Education in England, 1800–70' (*Cambridge Hist. Jour.*, xii. 2, 1956).

21. Greville, *Victoria*, i. 213–15; Graham to Arbuthnot, 1 June 1839.

22. Arbuthnot to Graham, 2 June, Graham to Arbuthnot, 3 June, Arbuthnot to Graham, 5, 6 June 1839.

23. Graham to Stanley, 5 June, Stanley to Graham, 6 June, Graham to Stanley, 6, 7 June 1839.

24. Graham to Arbuthnot, 7 Aug. 1839.

25. Lord Morley, *The Life of W.E. Gladstone* (1903), i. 177; Gladstone to Graham, 5, 7 Aug., Graham to Cawdor, 18 Sept.; Greville, *Victoria*, i. 235–6, 242; Stanley to Graham, 2, Graham to Stanley, 6 Oct. 1839.

26. Graham to Stanley, 25 Nov. 1839.

27. Peel to Arbuthnot, 20 Dec. (Parker, *Peel*, ii. 425); Graham to Peel, 18, to Stanley, 24 Dec. 1839; Greville, *Victoria*, i. 253. See also Kitson Clark, op. cit., 449 et seq. Graham replied to Wellington's comments, again urging Peel to grasp the opportunity (Graham to Peel, 26 Dec. 1839), but Wellington still insisted that much could be gained by delay (Parker, *Peel*, ii. 431).

28. On *Stockdale* v. *Hansard*, see Sir C. G. Robertson, *Select Statutes, Cases and Documents* (1949 ed.), 524–33, and on the Sheriff of Middlesex, ibid., 533–5; Graham to Arbuthnot, 26 Jan., to Stanley, 8 Feb. 1840.

29. Graham to Arbuthnot, 28 Feb. 1840. Peel brilliantly supported Graham's opposition to the grant of a pension to Sir John Newport, and the Government was defeated by 240 votes to 212.

30. Graham to Arbuthnot, 1, Arbuthnot to Graham, 10, 12, 13 June, 8 July; Ellenborough to Graham, 5, Graham to Arbuthnot, 9, 27, Arbuthnot to Graham, 12 July, 6, 7 Sept. 1840; Trevelyan, op. cit., 390–2. Dr. Kitson Clark (op. cit., 459) points out that Graham's fears of a rift reflected 'his lack of experience of Conservative affairs'. See Graham to Peel, 9, 14 June 1840 (Parker, *Peel*, ii. 438–46); cf. Macintyre, op. cit., 256–61.

31. Gash, *Politics*, 399.

32. Graham to Peel, 17 Jan.; Greville, *Victoria*, i. 373–7, ii. 1 et seq.; Graham to Arbuthnot, 24 March, 3 May 1841. See Southgate, *Whigs*, 118–21.

CHAPTER 8

1. See Betty Kemp, 'The General Election of 1841' (*History*, n.s., xxxvii. 2, June 1952); Gash, *Politics*, 224–7; Torrens, op. cit., ii. 200. One

estimate [*Ann. Reg.* (1841), 147] gave the Conservatives 78 gains and the Liberals 38, making their totals 368 and 292; cf. Greville, *Victoria*, ii. 22.

2. Graham to Peel, 1 Aug., to Stanley, 2 Aug.; Arbuthnot to Graham, 4 Aug., reply 6 Aug. See Parker, *Peel*, ii. 490 et seq. Peel corresponded with Goulburn, Graham, Stanley, Ripon, Gladstone, Ashburton and Herries. Graham opposed Gladstone's proposal of a House Tax as 'more difficult to carry than an Income Tax' (Graham to Peel, 14 Nov. 1841). Russell told Lansdowne on 12 November that Peel's 'reserve [on the Corn Law] had led him into great difficulty'; he would offend either the squires or the manufacturers [G. P. Gooch, *The Later Correspondence of Lord John Russell* (1925), i. 50].

3. Greville, *Victoria*, ii. 63–66; Asa Briggs, *The Age of Improvement* (1959), 330–1.

4. *The Ten Hours Factory Question. A Report Addressed to the Short Time Committees of the West Riding of Yorkshire* (1842), 15–22.

5. See Norman Gash, 'Ashley and the Conservative Party in 1842' (*English Hist. Rev.*, liii. 212, Oct. 1938); *Fleet Papers*, 18, 25 Sept., 16, 23 Oct., 27 Nov., 11, 18 Dec. 1841.

6. See F. C. Mather, *Public Order in the Age of the Chartists* (Manchester, 1959), 43–44; Greville, *Victoria*, ii. 68–69, 77–80; McCord, op. cit., 108 et seq.

7. Greville, *Victoria*, ii. 83–86; Graham to de Grey, 7 Feb. 1842. Richmond had refused Buckingham's post.

8. Graham to de Grey, 10 Feb., 8 March 1842.

9. Torrens, op. cit., ii. 206–7; Graham to de Grey, 16 March 1842; Greville, *Victoria*, ii. 87. Greville (ibid., ii. 92) considered on the 20th that 'the general feeling in the country is . . . not yet known'. Herries had told Graham on the 2nd that he opposed the concession to Ireland, which had long enjoyed tax remissions.

10. Graham to Peel, 30 Dec. 1842.

11. Peel to Graham, 5, to Arbuthnot, 29 Sept. 1841. See G. Kitson Clark, 'Hunger and Politics in 1842' (*Journal of Modern History*, xxv. 4, Dec. 1953, 355–74), and A. G. Rose, 'The Plug Riots of 1842 in Lancashire and Cheshire' (*Trans. Lancs. and Cheshire Antiquarian Soc.*, lxvii., 1957, 75–112); Mark Hovell, *The Chartist Movement* (Manchester, 1943 ed.), 259–67.

12. Peel, 13, Graham, 15, 16, 17, 18, 19, 20 Aug., to the Queen; Graham to Peel, 25, 26, 30 Aug.; Benson and Esher, op. cit., i. 422 et seq.; Parker, *Peel*, ii. 538 et seq., *Graham*, i. 320, et seq.; Graham to Powis, 27 July, to Galloway, 26 Aug. 1842.

13. Mather, op. cit., *passim*; Wellington to Graham, 21 Aug.; Graham to Lord Dartmouth, 13, to Peel, 24 July, to Lyttelton, 8 Aug. 1842. While not entirely agreeing with Wellington's advice on suppressing the riots, Graham organised many arrests: 'you must whop these fellows without loss of time,' he told William Beckett of Leeds on 17 Aug.

14. Graham to Sir T. Arbuthnot, Talbot, 24, Croker, 20 Aug., 1 Sept., Townley Parker, 24 Aug. 1842.

15. Peel to Croker, 21 Feb., 27 July 1842 (Jennings, op. cit., ii. 380 et seq.).

16. Graham to Croker, 1 Sept., to Peel, 24 Aug., 1, 8 Sept., 22 Nov., 12 Oct., to Croker, 1, 4, 5 Dec.; Peel to Croker, 4 Dec. 1842 (Jennings, op. cit., ii. 392–3); Croker to Graham, 28 Jan. 1843. See *Quarterly Review*, lxxi., Dec. 1842; F. C. Mather, 'The Government and the Chartists', in Asa Briggs (ed.), *Chartist Studies* (1959), 385–94, 401–5, and *Chartism* (Historical Association pamphlet, 1965), 28.

17. Graham to Brougham, 21, to Powis, 30, to Kay-Shuttleworth, 30 Aug., to Peel, 1, Peel to Graham, 11 Sept. 1842.

18. Lord Ashley, 'Reply to the Short Time Committee of Lancashire', 26 Sept. 1842; Brougham to Graham, 21, Graham to Brougham, 24 Oct. 1841; Graham to Peel, 18 June, Peel to Graham, 9, Graham to Peel, 17 Sept. 1842.

19. See M. W. Thomas, *The Early Factory Legislation* (Leigh-on-Sea, 1948), chs. 5, 11, 12; Graham to Peel, 21 Dec., to the Bishop of London, 27 Dec. 1842; Lord Ashley, *Moral and Religious Education of the Working Classes* (1843), *passim*; J. T. Ward, 'A Lost Opportunity in Education: 1843' (*Researches and Studies*, 20: 1959).

20. Ashley to Graham, 1, Graham to Ashley, 4 March 1843; Graham to R. Burgess, 22 Nov. 1842, and to G. R. Gleig, 6, to Horatio Powys, 17 March 1843.

21. Graham to Stanley, to Gladstone, 25, Ashley to Graham, 28 March, Graham to the Bishop of London, 20, to Peel, 13, Ashley to Graham, 26 April; Ashley to Peel, 17, Peel to Ashley, 16 June 1843 (Parker, *Peel*, ii. 560–2). See J. T. Ward, *The Factory Movement, 1830–1855* (1962), 258–68; Frank Smith, op. cit., 140–51.

22. See J. R. H. Moorman, *A History of the Church in England* (1954 ed.), 347 et seq.; G. F. A. Best, *Temporal Pillars* (Cambridge, 1964), 239 et seq.; Graham to Peel, 17 Sept., Peel to Graham, 22 Dec. 1842. After much ministerial discussion, Peel merely allowed the Church Commissioners to borrow from Queen Anne's Bounty for the endowment of new churches in 'populous parishes'.

23. Chalmers to Graham, 6 Jan. 1840; Graham to Peel, 11 Dec. 1836; Chalmers to Graham, 6 June 1839. See Robert Buchanan, *The Ten Years' Conflict* (Glasgow, 1849 ed.), i. chs. 6, 8; William Hanna, *Memoirs of the Life and Writings of Thomas Chalmers* (Edinburgh, 1852), iv. 91–174; W. M. Hetherington, *History of the Church of Scotland* (Edinburgh, 1852 ed.), ii., *passim*.

24. Gladstone to Graham, 5, Graham to Gladstone, 8 Dec.; Wellington to Peel, 18, 23, Dec. (Parker, *Peel*, ii. 418, 429); Arbuthnot to Graham, 10, Graham to Arbuthnot, 13, to Peel, 18 Dec. 1839.

25. Graham to Colquhoun, 25, Peel to Graham, 29, to Wellington, 26, Graham to Chalmers, 30 Dec. 1839; Peel to Graham, 4, Chalmers to Graham, 6 Jan.; Graham to Peel, 2 Sept. 1840. See Parker, *Peel*, ii. 467–74; Hanna, op. cit., iv. 120–1, 212–13, 279 *et passim*.

26. The Home Office was responsible for Scottish affairs until the Scottish Secretaryship was created in 1885.

27. Rae to Graham, 16 Sept.; Graham to Muir, 25 Oct., to Agnew, 26 Nov.; Peel to Graham, 17 Oct.; Graham memorandum, 15 Oct. 1841 (Parker, *Peel*, iii. 77–78). See Parker, *Graham*, i. ch. 17, and *Peel*, iii. ch. 3; Erickson, op. cit., 197–210; Torrens, op. cit., ii. 228–33.

28. Graham to Peel, 2, 3 Jan., 26, 30 Dec. 1842; *The Times*, 14 Jan. 1843; *Ann. Reg.* (1843), 463–70. See also Peel's explanations to the Queen (Benson and Esher, op. cit., i. 447–8); Hanna, op. cit., iv. 320.

29. Graham memorandum, 27 Jan., to Rae, 9 April, to Peel, 7 May 1843. See Hanna, op. cit., iv. 335–43; Thomas Brown, *Annals of the Disruption* (Edinburgh, 1877 ed.), chs. 7, 9. Aberdeen's Bill, thought Greville (*Victoria*, ii. 207) 'did no sort of good and only seemed to drag the House of Lords through the dirt'; it was introduced only on 13 July.

30. Graham to Arbuthnot, 13 Dec. 1839. See E. C. S. Wade, G. G. Phillips, *Constitutional Law* (1936 ed.), 472; Torrens, op. cit., ii. 233; Parker, *Peel*, i. 396.

31. Lord Ashley's diary, 11 May, 16 June, 8 July 1843, and 2, 4, 6, 16, 18 March 1844 [Edwin Hodder, *The Life and Work of the Seventh Earl of Shaftesbury*, K.G. (1887 ed.), 245–8, 257, 291, 294–5]. Peel told the Queen on 19 March that his Government opposed Ashley's proposal because 'it exposed the manufacturers of this Country to a very formidable competition with those of other countries, in which labour is not restricted, . . . must lead at a very early period to a great reduction in wages [and] . . . would incur great risk of serious injury to our commerce' (Parker, *Peel*, iii. 147–8).

32. Ashley's diary, 19–27 March (Hodder, op. cit., 296–8); Greville, *Victoria*, ii. 236–7; Ashburton to Croker, 7 April 1844 (Jennings, op. cit., iii. 17–18).

33. *The Times*, 10, Ashley to Graham, 17 April; Ashley's diary, 14–16 May (Hodder, op. cit., 303); Greville *Victoria*, ii. 242; see Thomas, op. cit., 201–22; Ward, op. cit., 283–99.

34. S. and B. Webb, *English Poor Law History*, pt. 2, i. (1963 reprint), 170–9; W. B. Ferrand, *The Great Mott Question* (1844); *The Times*, 10, 11, 23, 24–27, *Leeds Intelligencer*, 13, *Standard*, 24–27, *Morning Post*, 24–27, 30 April 1844; Torrens, op. cit., ii. 350–8. On Ferrand, see J. T. Ward, 'Young England' (*History Today*, xvi. 2, Feb. 1966).

35. S. and B. Webb, *English Poor Law History*, pt. 2, ii. (1963 reprint), 1030–5; Peel to Arbuthnot, 30 Oct. 1842 (Parker, *Peel*, ii. 532). Graham had granted small sums to Paisley, together with exhortations on local action (Erickson, op. cit., 160–2). See also A. A. Cormack, *Poor Relief in Scotland* (Aberdeen, 1923), especially ch. 13, and, on the Andover case, Webbs, op. cit., pt. 2, i. 179–82.

36. Peel to Graham, 12 Oct., 18, 22 Nov.; Graham to Peel, 13 Oct., 20 Nov., 10 Dec.; Peel to Graham, 2 Sept. 1842; Hodder, op. cit., 224–32; Erickson, op. cit., 219–20; David Roberts, *Victorian Origins of the British Welfare State* (New Haven, 1960), 60–61.

37. *Fleet Papers*, 19 Feb., 28 May, 26 Nov. 1842. See also Cecil Driver, *Tory Radical. The Life of Richard Oastler* (New York, 1946), *passim.*

CHAPTER 9

1. Gladstone note, 6 Sept. 1897 (Morley, op. cit., i. 114). Gladstone always expressed 'enormous admiration' for Graham [Lord Morley, *Recollections* (1918), ii.71].

2. Peel memoir, 1846 (Parker, *Peel*, iii. 376); Graham to Peel, 9 Jan. 1848; *Punch*, i. (1841), 54.

3. *Fleet Papers*, 10 Dec. 1842; Mather, op. cit., 202–3, 218–24; Parker, *Graham*, i. ch. 19; Greville, *Victoria*, ii. 272; T. H. Duncombe, *Life and Correspondence of T. S. Duncombe* (1868), i. 314–40; Croker to Graham, 16 July 1844; Brougham to Graham, 21, 22 Feb. 1845; Parker, *Graham*, i. 447.

4. Benson and Esher, op. cit., i. 455–9, 468–9; Greville, *Victoria*, ii. 141–4; Parker, *Peel*, ii. 552–5; On the 'separate system' of isolation — 'perhaps the most momentous official decision in English prison history' — and the dietaries, see S. and B. Webb, *English Prisons Under Local Government* (1963 reprint), 114, 134–7. Graham to Brougham, 16 Oct. 1841, to the Queen, 13 May 1845.

5. Edwin Chadwick, *Report on the Sanitary Condition of the Labouring Population of Great Britain*, ed. M. W. Flinn (Edinburgh, 1965), 46, 68, 116–17; Erickson, op. cit., 243–55; S. E. Finer, *The Life and Times of Sir Edwin Chadwick* (1952), 209 et seq.; Torrens, op. cit., ii. 396–8. Lonsdale (op. cit., ii. 205) recalled that as secretary to the Edinburgh medical faculties he 'always found [Graham] highly regardful of the interests of the profession. He presented a marked contrast to his predecessor, the Marquess of Normanby.'

6. See Mather, in Briggs, op. cit., 390–3, 403; David Williams, *The Rebecca Riots. A Study in Agrarian Discontent* (Cardiff, 1955), *passim*; Graham to Peel, 21, to Wharncliffe, 26 Dec. 1843. Graham reorganised Welsh road administrations [S. and B. Webb, *The Story of the King's Highway* (1963 reprint), 217–20; Williams, op. cit., 281–3]. On the problems of maintaining public order, see Mather, op. cit., *passim*.

7. Graham to Peel, 3 Dec., Gladstone to Graham, 30 Nov. 1843. 'With respect to Young England', Graham told Croker on 22 Aug., 'the puppets are moved by Disraeli, who is the ablest man among them: I consider him unprincipled and disappointed . . . they will return to the crib after prancing, capering and snorting, but a crack or two of the whip well applied may hasten and ensure their return. Disraeli alone is mischievous; and with him I have no desire to keep terms. . . .'

8. Fitzpatrick, op. cit., ii. 257–8; Graham to Peel, 6 Nov., 21 Oct.; Peel to Graham, 6 Dec.; de Grey to Graham, 29 Dec. 1841.

9. Stanley to Peel, 30 Nov. 1841 (Parker, *Peel*, iii. 35–36); Eliot to Peel, 15 July (ibid., 38), Peel to Graham, 16 July, Graham to Peel, 17 July, to Eliot, 16 Sept., to de Grey, 9 Nov., to Eliot, 15 Nov., to Peel, 17 Oct., to Stanley, 21 Nov., to Peel, 15 Dec., Peel to Graham, 15 Dec. 1842. See Kevin B. Nowlan, *The Politics of Repeal* (1965), 20–34, and, for an excellent brief survey of the background, R. B. McDowell, 'Ireland on the Eve of the Famine', in R. D. Edwards and T. D. Williams (eds.),

The Great Famine (Dublin, 1962 ed.), 3–86.

10. De Grey to Peel, 6 May (Parker, *Peel*, iii. 46); Graham to de Grey, 24 April, to Peel, 5, 7 May, to de Grey, 8, 9, 20, 21 May, to Peel, 18 June, 15, 17 July, Peel to Graham, 16 July; de Grey to Peel, 18 Aug. (Parker, *Peel*, iii. 56); Graham to Peel, 5 Sept., to Stanley, 16 July, to Peel, 23 Sept. 1843. See Macintyre, op. cit., 268–70. On 6 June Lord Malmesbury recorded a report that Stanley and Graham 'had resigned on account of Sir Robert Peel having given up some clauses in the Irish Arms Bill, but no one seemed to believe there was any truth in the rumour, though there certainly had been a disagreement . . .' [Earl of Malmesbury, *Memoirs of an Ex-Minister* (1855), 107].

11. Graham to Peel, 2, 6 Sept., 17 Oct., 26 Sept., to Stanley, 4, 10 Oct., to Eliot, 14, 20 Oct., to Peel, 25, 28 Oct., 29 Nov. 1843. See Parker, *Graham*, i. ch. 16, 18, and *Peel*, iii. ch. 2; Greville, *Victoria*, ii. 188–92, 194–200, 204, 206, 210–11, 214–15, gives varied views on the arrest and forthcoming trial.

12. Peel to Graham, 19 Oct. 1843; Peel memoranda, 11, 17 Feb. (Parker, *Peel*, iii. 101–3, 105–7); Stanley to Peel, 18 Feb. (ibid., 107); Graham, 12, Gladstone, 14 April 1844 (ibid., 110–11). Greville (*Victoria*, ii. 197) recorded on 10 Sept. 1843 that Bedford was 'quite convinced that Peel's *do-nothing policy* had been wise, but that Lord John [Russell] was not pleased when he told him so'.

13. Greville, *Victoria*, ii. 205; Graham to de Grey, 8, 9, 25 Jan., to Stanley, 4 Feb. 1844; Greville, ii. 218–21, 228; W. F. Monypenny, *The Life of Benjamin Disraeli* (1912), ii. 173–8, 188–94; Graham to Disraeli, 21 Dec. 1843. See Nowlan, op. cit., 70–71; Macintyre, op. cit., 271–2, 276, 280–2.

14. Eliot to Peel, 7 May; Parker, *Peel*, iii. 111–20; Graham to Peel, 17 Sept.; Peel to Lord Heytesbury, 17 Oct. 1844 (Parker, *Peel*, iii. 122). See Nowlan, ch. 3, *passim*. Peel and Heytesbury employed Isaac Butt to attack Federalism in the *Morning Herald*, and on 14 Oct. Graham persuaded Croker to attack it in the December *Quarterly Review* (Jennings, op. cit., iii. 20–21).

15. Peel to Graham, 7, Graham to Peel, 13 April, to Lyndhurst, Heytesbury and Peel, 2 Sept.; Greville, *Victoria*, ii. 254–7; Peel to Graham, 26, 28 Sept., 4 Oct., 6 Dec.; Parker, *Peel*, iii. 126–33; Graham to Peel, 3, to Wellington, 9 Oct., to Croker, 15 Sept. 1844.

16. Graham to Anson, 13 July 1845; Greville, *Victoria*, ii. 256. 'I am hardly able to stagger on under the load of business and of care which oppresses me,' Graham told Croker on 24 May 1845. See also Torrens, op. cit., ii. 398–402.

17. Graham to Heytesbury, 30, memorandum, 16 Nov., to Peel, 10, 23 Dec. 1844; Parker, *Peel*, iii. 164–9; Morley, *Gladstone*, i. 270–9. Graham told Peel that 'it is always difficult through the haze of words to catch a distant glimpse of Gladstone's meaning. . . . [His] omission to seal such a letter was unfortunate, but . . . I doubt whether there is a postmaster in England who . . . would understand one word of it' (Graham to Peel, 4 Jan. 1845).

18. Greville, *Victoria*, ii. 278; Monypenny, op. cit., ii. 323–30; Parker, *Graham*, ii. 8–9; Torrens, op. cit., ii. 361–81.

19. Greville, *Victoria*, ii. 280; Graham to Croker, 22 March, Peel to Croker, 22 April (Jennings, op. cit., iii. 31–32); Graham to Heytesbury, 12 April 1845.

20. Graham to Heytesbury, 10, to Stanley, 24 May, to Heytesbury, 10 Aug. 1845. See Nowlan, op. cit., 83–92; Torrens, op. cit., ii. 381–91.

21. Peel to Graham, 26 March, 8 July, 22, 26 Aug., Graham to Heytesbury, 27 Aug., to Peel, 8, 30 Sept., 2 Oct., Peel to Graham, 5 Oct. 1845. Wellington was again pressing for coercion.

22. Stanley to Graham, 12, Graham to Peel, 15 Aug., 28 Sept., 6, 10, 13 Oct., Peel to Graham, 13, 15 Oct., Graham to Peel, 15, 17, 27 Oct. 1845. See Jones, op. cit., 108–10; Cecil Woodham-Smith, *The Great Hunger. Ireland, 1845–9* (1962), 39–43; Edwards and Williams, op. cit., *passim*; Nowlan, op. cit., 93–94. Anti-Corn Law Leaguers carefully watched the weather during the summer [Archibald Prentice, *History of the Anti-Corn Law League* (1853), ii. 357, 379; McCord, op. cit., ch. 8].

23. Peel to Graham, 26 July 1842; Croker to Peel, n.d. (Jennings, op. cit., iii. 11).

24. Earl Stanhope, E. Cardwell (eds.), *The Memoirs of Sir Robert Peel* (1857), ii. 148 et seq.; Parker, *Peel*, iii. 225–32; Lord Stanmore, *Sidney Herbert* (1906), i. 42–47; Greville, *Victoria*, ii. 301; Peel to Graham, 7 Nov., Stanley to Peel, 3 Nov. 1845.

25. Parker, *Graham*, ii. 24–25, and *Peel*, iii. 231–55, 283–9; Jones, op. cit., 111–15; Graham to Herbert, 19, to Peel, Stanley to Peel, 29 Nov. See Benson, Esher, op. cit., ii. 48–67; Greville, *Victoria*, ii. 309–44, 349–50, 359–61; Graham to Fremantle, 18, Russell to Graham, 20, Peel to Graham, Graham to Peel, 22, 23 Dec. 1845.

26. Greville, *Victoria*, ii. 292–4; Graham to Peel, 16 Aug., 27 Oct., 31 Dec. 1845; Stanmore, op. cit., i. 70–73; Woodham-Smith, op. cit., 60–61; T. P. O'Neill, 'The Organisation and Administration of Relief, 1845–52', in Edwards, Williams, op. cit., 209–59; Graham to Heytesbury, 6 Jan., 10 Feb. 3, 13, 25, 27 April 1846; Torrens, op. cit., ii. 448–57. On Trevelyan see Jenifer Hart, 'Sir Charles Trevelyan at the Treasury' (*English Hist. Rev.*, lxxv. 294, Jan. 1960, 92–110).

27. Graham to Croker, 18 Feb., to Heytesbury, 11, 20 June; Prince Albert's memorandum, 6 July (Benson, Esher, op. cit., ii. 85); Greville, *Victoria*, ii. 357, 363–6, 374, 379, 381, 384, 389–91, 401; Morley, *Gladstone*, i. 296; Croker to Graham, 3 April 1846, 23 Sept. 1847; Parker, *Peel*, iii. 376, 369–70; Graham to Peel, 1, 2, Peel to Graham, 3 July, Graham to Peel, 4 July, to Rooke, 4 Sept. 1846.

CHAPTER 10

1. Duchess of Northumberland to Arbuthnot, 8 June 1846 (Parker, *Peel*, iii. 352); Colquhoun to Torrens, Nov. 1862 (Torrens, op. cit., ii. 483); Hobhouse to Graham, 6 Aug. 1846; Greville, *Victoria*, ii. 427; Gladstone memorandum, 12 July 1846 (Morley, *Gladstone*, i. 295–6).

2. Peel analysed the votes on 27 Feb. as 'Government, 112; Whigs and Radicals, 227; Protectionists, 231; Whig Protectionists, 11' (Peel to the Queen, 28 Feb., in Parker, *Peel*, iii. 342); Graham to Peel, 31 Aug., 4 Sept., Peel to Graham, 2, Graham to Peel, 26 Sept., 20 Nov., Peel to Graham, 22 Nov., Graham to Peel, 1, 9, Peel to Graham, 16 Dec. 1846. Charles Wood had feared that Graham, 'a bitter opponent, excellent tactician &c.', might be given a peerage and weaken the Ministry in the Lords (Walpole, op. cit., i. 427).

3. Peel to the King of the Belgians, 27 Jan. 1847 (Parker, *Peel*, iii. 479); Graham to Sandars, 17 Sept. 1846; Torrens, op. cit., ii. 486–98. See J. B. Conacher, 'Peel and the Peelites, 1846–50' (*English Hist. Rev.*, lxxiii. 288, July 1958).

4. Greville, *Victoria*, iii. 51, 87–93; Torrens, op. cit., ii. 498–503; Russell to Ellice, 16 June (Parker, *Graham*, ii. 57–58); Graham to Londonderry, 10 Feb. 1847; Palmerston to Sulivan, 31 Dec. 1852 (Southgate, *Most English Minister*, 315); on Ripon see Gash, *Politics*, 220–3; Graham to Peel, 22 July 1847. Graham signified his independence in the Commons: '[he] sits under his old pillar and never comes down to Peel's bench, even for personal communications, seems to keep himself aloof from everybody and to hold himself free to act according to circumstances', Palmerston told Normanby on 23 April, 'but as yet he is not considered as the head of any party' (Ashley, op. cit., i. 22).

5. Clarendon to Graham, 21, Lewis to Graham, 24 May, Langdale to Graham, 24 April, Graham to Lewis, 13 Oct. (Parker, *Graham*, ii. 54–60); Greville, *Victoria*, iii. 107–8, 124–5 (and cf. ibid., 94); Morley, *Gladstone*, i. 351. Graham had often played some part in discussions on colonial policy, for instance on the New Zealand Company in 1845, on Canadian agriculture in 1842, on the penal settlements in 1842 and 1845 and on India. See W. P. Morrell, *British Colonial Policy in the Age of Peel and Russell* (1966 impr.), 120–3, 177–8, 388, 392.

6. Peel to Graham, 2, 12 Jan. 1848, 3 April 1847; Graham to Peel, 15 Jan. 1848; Greville, *Victoria*, iii. 123–4, 127–8.

7. Graham to Jarnac, 8 March, to Peel, 30 April 1848; Greville, *Victoria*, iii. 129, 146–8.

8. Greville, *Victoria*, iii. 160–4, 175–6, 186–8, 195–6, 199, 201, 205; Graham to Lewis, 22 April 1848. Graham attended committees on Scottish entails four times, Lunatic Asylums three times, Railway Bills four times, public business five times, the Ecclesiastical Commission nine times, Commercial Distress twenty-five times and Army and Navy expenditure thirty-six times in 1848 (Torrens, op. cit., ii. 516–17).

9. Graham to Peel, 25 Sept. 1848, 12, 16 Jan. 1849; Walpole, op. cit., ii. 97–98; Greville, *Victoria*, iii. 259–60, 262–3; Parker, *Graham*, ii. 76–78.

10. Greville, *Victoria*, iii. 264–5; Lady Londonderry, *Frances Anne* (1958), 206; Graham to Londonderry, 20, to Peel, 21, Peel to Graham, 20 Jan. 1849.

11. Lincoln to Peel, 27 Jan. (Parker, *Peel*, iii. 503); Greville, *Victoria*, iii. 265–6, 269–70, 281; Torrens, op. cit., ii. 517–19; Nowlan, op. cit., 221–2; Morley, *Gladstone*, i. 351–3; Graham to Peel, 10 March 1849.

Disraeli replied to Graham's speech of 23 April with the question 'Progress where? . . . to Paradise, or . . . to the devil?' (See Monypenny and Buckle, op. cit., iii. 204–205.)

12. Greville, *Victoria*, iii. 297–340; Graham to Peel, 27 Oct. 1849; Parker, *Peel*, iii. 518–21.

13. Peel to Graham, 24 July, 15, 17, 27 Nov., 6, 19 Dec., Graham to Peel, 14, 22 Nov., 8, 23, 28 Dec. 1849; Greville, *Victoria*, iii. 294.

14. Londonderry to Graham and reply, 18 Feb., Lewis to Graham, 24 Jan. 1850; Monypenny, Buckle, op. cit., iii. 242; Morley, *Gladstone*, i. 587; Lady Londonderry (ed.), *Letters from Benjamin Disraeli to Frances Anne, Marchioness of Londonderry* (1938), 100; Greville, *Victoria*, iii. 319–20; Parker, *Graham*, ii. 97–103.

15. Graham to Peel, 31 March, 3, 5, 7 April, Peel to Graham, 2, 4, 6 April, Aberdeen to Peel, 4 April 1850 (Parker, *Peel*, iii. 539–40); Greville, *Victoria*, iii. 321; Morley, *Gladstone*, i. 355–6.

16. Greville, *Victoria*, iii. 321–2, 341–60; Disraeli to Lady Londonderry, 21 March (Monypenny, Buckle, op. cit., iii. 246; see ibid., 255–263); Parker, *Peel*, iii. 541–6, *Graham*, ii. 104–11; Southgate, *Most English Minister*, 263–78; Londonderry, 28 June, Prince Consort to Graham, 3 July, Graham to Lady Peel, 24 Dec. 1850.

17. Torrens, op. cit., ii. 528–32; Greville, *Victoria*, iii. 338–40, 360; Graham to J. Sandars, 16 July 1850. See Southgate, *Whigs*, 229.

18. Graham to Howard, 23 Nov., to Herbert, 1 Dec. 1850. See Benson, Esher, op. cit., ii. 272–3; W. Ward, *Life and Times of Cardinal Wiseman* (1897), i. 625 et seq.; Walpole, op. cit., ii. 120–1; Monypenny, Buckle, op. cit., iii. 266–73; Greville, *Victoria*, iii. 366–7; Parker, *Graham*, ii. 111–15; Morley, *Gladstone*, i. 378–87, 407–10; Stanmore, op. cit., i. 131; Lady Frances Balfour, *Life of George, 4th Earl of Aberdeen* (1922), 160; T. C. Edwards, 'Papal Aggression: 1851' (*History Today*, i. 12, Dec. 1951, 42–49); Southgate, *Whigs*, 190–2.

19. Disraeli to Londonderry, 29 Dec. 1850, to Stanley, 21, to Londonderry, 29, Graham to Londonderry, 31 Jan. 1851. See Monypenny, Buckle, op. cit., iii. 273–8; Parker, *Graham*, ii. 120–4; Lady Londonderry, op. cit., 240–1; Benson, Esher, op. cit., ii. 287.

20. G. M. Trevelyan, *The Life of John Bright* (1913), 192–5; Cobden to Bright, 22 Nov. 1850, to Joseph Sturge, 19 Feb. 1851 [Lord Morley, *The Life of Richard Cobden* (1910 ed.), 549–51]; Morley, *Gladstone*, i. 385–7; Monypenny, Buckle, op. cit., iii. 281–2; Stanmore, op. cit., i. 131 et seq.; *Orange and Protestant Banner*, July 1855.

21. Memorandum by the Queen, 17 Feb. 1851 (Benson, Esher, op. cit., ii. 286–8).

22. Le Marchant, op. cit., 292, n. 2; Disraeli to Lady Londonderry, 27 March 1851 (Lady Londonderry, op. cit., 241).

23. Memoranda by Prince Albert, 22 Feb.–3 March; Russell to Aberdeen and Graham, 22, 24, Graham and Aberdeen to Russell, 24, 25 Feb.; Ellenborough, 21, Newcastle, 23, Carlisle, 26 Feb., de Grey, 1 March, to Graham. Benson, Esher, op. cit., ii. 288–315; Greville, *Victoria*, iii. 378–90; Walpole, op. cit., ii. 124–8; Asa Briggs, *1851*

(Historical Association pamphlet, 1951) and *Victorian People* (Penguin ed., 1965), ch. 2; G. H. L. Le May, 'The Ministerial Crisis of 1851' (*History Today*, i. 6, June 1951, 52–58); Stanmore, op. cit., i. 140–2; Torrens, op. cit., ii. 539–43; Monypenny, Buckle, op. cit., iii. 284–96; O. W. Hewett, *And Mr. Fortescue* (1958), 9, 10 [quoting the diary of Chichester Fortescue, who admired Graham's speeches on 28 Feb. and 20 March]; Malmesbury, op. cit., 203–6 [who recorded on 25 Feb. that Graham had 'asked (Russell) for Lord Clarendon and six Cabinet places, which were hard terms'].

24. Greville, *Victoria*, iii. 391–406; Monypenny, Buckle, op. cit., iii. 297–8, 303–8.

25. Russell to Graham, 12, Graham to Russell, 20 Sept. 1851; Greville, *Victoria*, iii. 410–13, 439; Torrens, op. cit., ii. 544–6; Parker, *Graham*, ii. 132–5; Walpole, op. cit., ii. 130; *Punch*, xx. 107.

26. Hardinge to Graham, 30 Oct., Graham to Bouverie, 19, to Lewis, 30 Nov. 1851; Torrens, op. cit., ii. 546–51; Greville, *Victoria*, iii. 413–42; Benson, Esher, op. cit., ii. 324–31, 340–55; Southgate, *Most English Minister*, 285–93; Ashley, op. cit., i. 307.

27. Graham to Greville, 5 Dec., Greville to Graham, 22, 23, 29 Dec., Graham to Aberdeen, 25 Dec. 1851, to Lewis, 2 Jan., to Lady Graham, 8, 9, 10 Jan., Russell to Graham, 14 Jan., Graham to Russell, 15 Jan.; the Queen to Russell, 15 Jan. (Benson, Esher, op. cit., ii. 359–60); Parker, *Graham*, ii. 141–52; Greville, *Victoria*, iii. 435–40; Bright to Cobden, 3 Jan. 1852 (Trevelyan, *Bright*, 198).

28. Benson, Esher, op. cit., ii. 363, 367–77; Southgate, *Most English Minister*, 309; Greville, *Victoria*, iii. 447–51; Monypenny, Buckle, op. cit., iii. 341–76.

29. De Grey to Graham, 1 March 1851; E. B. Roche to Graham, 9 Jan., Graham to Gladstone, 11, 29 March, Gladstone to Graham, 30 March, Graham to Mounsey, 27 Jan., 11 April; *Carlisle Journal*, 5, 9 July 1852; Morley, *Gladstone*, i. 420–1; Torrens, op. cit., ii. 554–9; Ferguson, op. cit., ii. 276.

30. Greville, *Victoria*, iii. 464–5, 468–9; Roebuck to Graham, 20, Graham to Roebuck, 21 July 1852.

CHAPTER 11

1. Molesworth to Delane, 13 Jan. 1852 [A. I. Desant, *J. T. Delane . . . Life and Correspondence* (1908), i. 129]; Monypenny, Buckle, op. cit., iii. 379; Morley, *Gladstone*, i. 428; Southgate, *Whigs*, 240.

2. Frank Eyck, *The Prince Consort. A Political Biography* (1959), 149, 175–80, 185, 193; Duchess of Argyll (ed.), *George Douglas, 8th Duke of Argyll . . . Autobiography and Memoirs* (1906), i. 379–80; Reid, *Milnes*, i. 473; J. Pope-Hennessy, *Monckton Milnes. The Flight of Youth* (1951), 19–20; Trevelyan, *Macaulay*, 512–13.

3. Memorandum by Prince Albert, 26 Feb. (Eyck, op. cit., 193); Graham to Russell, 17, 22, 26, Russell to Graham, 19, 23, 24 July 1852; Greville, *Victoria*, iii. 468–70. In October Greville [pt. iii, i. (1887)

(hereafter referred to as *Victoria,* iv.), 2–3] noted that Graham was 'heart and soul with Lord John' and still believed that Palmerston would join Derby. Greville used the term 'Liberal party' presumably to cover all non-Tories except some Radicals, Irishmen and individual 'independents'.

4. Graham to Dunfermline, 5, 11 Aug.; the Queen to Derby, 14 March (Benson, Esher, op. cit., ii. 381); Graham to Aberdeen, 5, 6 Aug., to Russell, 25 June, to Ellice, 17 Aug., to Aberdeen, 25 Aug., 15 Sept.; Herbert to Gladstone, 30 March 1852 (Stanmore, op. cit., i. 149); Walpole, op. cit., ii. 152–4; Parker, *Graham,* ii. 170–5; Greville, *Victoria,* iii. 471; Morley, *Gladstone,* i. 417–20.

5. Graham to Gladstone, 29, Herbert to Mrs. Herbert, 31 March 1852 (Stanmore, op. cit., i. 151); Morley, *Gladstone,* i. 423; Greville, *Victoria,* iii. 473–4; cf. Benson, Esher, op. cit., ii. 383.

6. Russell to Graham, 25 Aug., Graham to Russell, 1, 24, to Aberdeen, 29 Sept., 9 Oct., Aberdeen to Graham, 27 Sept., 8, 12 Oct. 1852.

7. Russell to Graham, 23, Herbert to Aberdeen, 22 Oct. (Stanmore, op. cit., i. 162–4); Graham to Russell, 1 Nov.; Disraeli to the Queen, 15 March (Benson, Esher, op. cit., ii. 382); Lewis to Graham, 25 Oct., Graham to Russell, 30 Oct. 1852. See Greville, *Victoria,* iv. 4–5.

8. Russell to Graham, 25 Aug., 2 Nov.; Graham to Russell, 1 Sept., to Lewis, 2 Nov.; Aberdeen to Graham, 27 Sept.; Herbert to Aberdeen, 22 Oct. 1852 (Stanmore, op. cit., i. 164).

9. Graham to Lady Graham, 12, to Russell, 16, to Gladstone, 20 Nov. 1852. See Southgate, *Whigs,* 236–9, *Most English Minister,* 313; Walpole, op. cit., ii. 158–9; Monypenny, Buckle, op. cit., iii. 407–22; Morley, *Gladstone,* i. 433–5; Parker, *Graham,* ii. 185–8; Greville, *Victoria,* iv. 6–9, 11–13.

10. Monypenny, Buckle, op. cit., iii. 425–9; Benson, Esher, op. cit., ii. 406–13; Greville, *Victoria,* iv. 13–15. Baron Stockmar advised the Queen, after consulting Aberdeen, Graham and Cobden in November — and misunderstanding Graham's comments (Eyck, op. cit., 199–201).

11. Prince Albert's memoranda, 19, 22, 28, the Queen to Aberdeen; 23, and memorandum, 25 Dec. (Benson, Esher, op. cit., ii. 413–28), Graham's journal, 17–30 Dec. 1852 (Parker, *Graham,* ii. 190–203); Southgate, *Whigs,* 238–48; Walpole, op. cit., ii. 160–8; Morley, *Gladstone,* i. 443–50; Greville, *Victoria,* iv. 15–29. Graham had told Bright on 18 December that he favoured Radical representation in the Cabinet, and Hayter actually apologised 'in some sort' to Bright and Cobden for their omission (Bright's diary, 22 Dec. 1852, in Trevelyan, *Bright,* 208–9). Argyll later recalled (on 9 Dec. 1889) that 'Lincoln could not bear Lord John; Graham was suspicious; Palmerston was contemptuous' [Lord Edmond Fitzmaurice, *The Life of . . . [the] Second Earl Granville* (1905), i. 81].

12. *Carlisle Journal,* 1 Jan.; Torrens, op. cit., ii. 560; Graham to Lewis, 5 Jan. 1853; Monypenny, Buckle, op. cit., iii. 484–7; Argyll, op. cit., i. 559; Greville, *Victoria,* iv. 23, 41, 45. Malmesbury (op. cit., 300–1) recorded on 20 March Napoleon III's strong objections to attacks by

Graham and Wood: 'Their excuses are nonsense. One of three things: either they are fools, which is not the case, or they really felt what they said, which, being Cabinet Ministers, is very serious for me, or they abused me to please their audience, which is still worse, as it would imply that the English people are hostile to me . . .'. Several writers have confused Graham's and Wood's constituencies (Carlisle and Halifax respectively).

13. Greville, *Victoria*, iv. 21, 52–56; Erickson, op. cit., 332–3; Bartlett, op. cit., 290, 299–300 *et passim*; Benson, Esher, op. cit., ii. 437, 441–5; Sir Herbert Maxwell, *The Life and Letters of . . . [the] 4th Earl of Clarendon* (1913), ii. 3, 6–8.

14. Morley, *Gladstone*, i. 458–75; Greville, *Victoria*, iv. 59–62; cf. ibid., 73: 'Tom Baring, however, told me he thought Gladstone had made some great mistakes and that Graham would have been a better Chancellor; but this I much doubt. Popularity is very necessary . . . and Graham would never have been so persuasive with the House as Gladstone.'

15. Greville, *Victoria*, iv. 63–64; Benson, Esher, op. cit., ii. 447.

16. Palmerston to Graham, 29, 31 May, Graham to Palmerston, 1 June, to Clarendon, 9 May 1853; Greville, *Victoria*, iv. 64–65, 67. Conversation with Soviet historians leads me to deduce that they would contest this interpretation.

17. Stratford to Graham, 20 June, Graham to Stratford, 8 July, to Clarendon, 18, to Seymour, 4, Seymour to Graham, 18 Aug., Clarendon to Graham, 27, Graham to Clarendon, 25, 3 Sept. 1853; Parker, *Graham*, ii. 221–4; Maxwell, op. cit., ii. 16–17, 19; Greville, *Victoria*, iv. 69–89. Aberdeen later considered that there was a strong case against Stratford (Benson, Esher, op. cit., ii. 456). Cf. John Martineau, *The Life of Henry Pelham, 5th Duke of Newcastle* (1908), 124–9; S. Lane-Poole, *Life of . . . Lord Stratford de Redcliffe* (1888), ii., *passim*.

18. Maxwell, op. cit., ii. 30; Greville, *Victoria*, iv. 92–102; Morley, *Gladstone*, i. 481–2; Aberdeen to Graham, 8, Prince Consort's memoranda, 10, 16 Oct. 1853 (Benson, Esher, op. cit., ii. 454–8).

19. Graham to Dunfermline, 2 Jan., Russell to Graham, 24, Graham to Russell, 25, 27 Nov. 1853; Greville, *Victoria*, iv. 104, 106–19; Benson, Esher, op. cit., ii. 465–72; Maxwell, op. cit., ii. 31–36; Ashley, op. cit., ii. 21; Martineau, op. cit., 129–31. Russell pressed his increasingly unpopular Bill during 1854, backed by Aberdeen and Graham, until persuaded to withdraw it in April.

20. Graham to Gladstone, 4 Jan.; Greville, *Victoria*, iv. 123; Graham to Lyons, 2 July, to Russell, 7 Nov.; Lyons to Graham, 18 Oct. Newcastle to Graham, 5 Oct., Graham to Gladstone, 6 Oct., to Aberdeen, 7 Oct. 1854; Parker, *Graham*, ii. 230–60; Martineau, op. cit, 139–72. See Christopher Hibbert, *The Destruction of Lord Raglan* (1961). *passim*; Erickson, op. cit., 336–52. Graham delivered an uncharacteristic speech at a Reform Club dinner for Napier in March, rivalling any Palmerstonian in his brash bellicosity and shocking many observers (Trevelyan, *Bright*, 233–4; Greville, *Victoria*, iv. 145–6).

z

21. Graham to Lyons, 12, 19 Jan. 1855; see Greville, *Victoria*, iv. 199–201, 218, 229–31, 242–3; Martineau, op. cit., 253; Stanmore, op. cit., i. 325; Maxwell, op. cit., ii. 55–56; Morley, *Gladstone*, i. 521–3, 526; Benson, Esher, op. cit., iii. 72–97. See Asa Briggs, *Victorian People* (Penguin ed., 1965), ch. 3.

22. Graham to Palmerston, 5, to Stockmar, 6 Feb. 1855; Greville, *Victoria*, iv. 238–40; Morley, *Gladstone*, i. 532–6; Benson, Esher, op. cit., iii. 97–104; Parker, *Graham*, ii. 263–4.

23. Graham to Clarendon, 22 Feb. 1855; Southgate, *Most English Minister*, 359–62; Greville, *Victoria*, iv. 243, 245–6; Benson, Esher, op. cit., iii. 109–10; Maxwell, op. cit., ii. 69; Parker, *Graham*, ii. 266–72; Torrens, op. cit., ii. 609–10, 612–21; Martineau, op. cit., 253–8.

24. Graham to Gladstone, 2 June, 7 July, to Aberdeen, 12 July 1855; Morley, *Gladstone*, i. 544–9; Stanmore, op. cit., i. 424–51. In 1854 Bernal Osborne, Graham's Secretary at the Admiralty, told Chichester Fortescue that he was 'a wonderful fellow for work, trusts no-one. "I know he doesn't trust me", said B.O.' (Hewett, op. cit., 60). On 3 May Granville had prophesied to Argyll that 'Grey, Herbert, Gladstone, Graham, Bright, and possibly Ellenborough, aided by the pressure of the war budget, will soon make a peace party, strong enough to take away all appearance of unanimity in the country for a war in which the religious feelings and the material interests of the nation are not concerned' (Fitzmaurice, op. cit., i. 107–8).

CHAPTER 12

1. *The Times*, 23 Dec. 1854; Morley, *Cobden*, 615. (The actual figures were over 22,000 men and over £50,000,000.)

2. *Quarterly Review*, xcviii. 254; Southgate, *Whigs*, 280–5; Torrens, op. cit., ii. 623–4; Graham to Herbert, 10 Aug. 1856.

3. Herbert to Graham, 16, 22 May, Graham to Herbert, 21 May, Gladstone to Herbert, 12 July 1856 (Stanmore, op. cit., ii. 47–48); Greville, *Victoria*, v. 47–49; Southgate, *Most English Minister*, 390–3.

4. Greville, *Victoria*, v. 40–43, 55; Granville to Canning, 11 April 1856 (Fitzmaurice, op. cit., i. 176); Erickson, op. cit., 372–5; Torrens, op. cit., ii. 626–7.

5. Graham to Aberdeen, 11, to Gladstone, 15, 22 Nov., 1, 3, 6, 16, 27 Dec., to Herbert, 16, 30 Nov., 16 Dec., to Newcastle, 23 Nov., Gladstone to Graham, 10, 21, 29 Nov., 2, 4, 15 Dec. 1856; Morley, *Gladstone*, i. 551–6.

6. Morley, *Gladstone*, i. 558–62; Graham to Aberdeen, 20 Jan., to Herbert, 29 Jan., Herbert to Graham, 27 Jan. 1857.

7. Graham to Gladstone, 6 Dec. 1856; Southgate, *Most English Minister*, 421–5; Prince Albert to Palmerston, 3 March, and Benson, Esher, op. cit., iii. 225–9; Gladstone's diary, 3 March 1857 (Morley, *Gladstone*, i. 364); see Morley, *Cobden*, 651–5.

8. Greville, *Victoria*, v. 95–96; Benson, Esher, op. cit., iii. 226; Cobden to Graham, 16, Graham to Mounsey, 6, to Howard, 17, *Carellis*

Journal, 20, 27 March, 3 April 1857; Stanmore, op. cit., ii. 74, 79–81; Lonsdale, op. cit., ii. 261–71; Ferguson, op. cit., ii. 277. Torrens (ii. 636), Parker (ii. 305) and Erickson (379) asserted that Graham headed the poll.

9. Herbert to Graham, 15 March, 14 April, to Aberdeen, 12 April, to Gladstone, 13 April; Gladstone to Herbert, 22 March; Cobden to Graham, 24, Graham to Cobden, 26, to Herbert, 15 April, 1857; Greville, *Victoria*, v. 105; Morley, *Gladstone*, i. 565–7; Stanmore, op. cit., ii. 85–95. 'The Peelites are smashed as a party, which is good . . .', Granville told Canning, on 8 April. 'Graham has made the most Radical speech which has yet been made . . .' (Fitzmaurice, op. cit., i. 228).

10. Torrens, op. cit., ii. 636–9; Morley, *Gladstone*, i. 567–73; Graham to Gladstone, 21 Aug. 1857, to Croker, 20 Oct. 1853; Russell to Graham, 3, 16 Sept., Graham to Russell, 11, 22 Sept., 28 Oct. 1857.

11. Greville, *Victoria*, v. 133–5; Gladstone to Graham, 24, 26 Nov., Graham to Gladstone, 25 Nov., 19 Dec.; Russell to Graham, 13, Graham to Russell, 16, 23, 27 Dec. 1857, and 9, 13, 15, 24 Jan., to Herbert, 21 Jan. 1858.

12. Graham to Gladstone, 26 Jan., 3 Feb., to Herbert, to Cardwell, 21 Jan., to Russell, 4 Feb.; Prince Albert's memorandum, 21 Feb. 1858 (Benson, Esher, op. cit., iii. 266–8); Southgate, *Most English Minister*, 438–40.

13. Graham to Russell, 2, to Aberdeen, 31 March, to Ellice, 5 April 1858; Morley, *Gladstone*, i. 576–81; Jones, op. cit., 237–8; Greville, *Victoria*, v. 181.

14. Michael Maclagan, *Clemency Canning* (1962), ch. 8; Greville, *Victoria*, v. 182, 191–8; G. E. Buckle, *The Life of Benjamin Disraeli*, iv. (1916), 127–33, 140–62; Hodder, op. cit., 544–50; Benson, Esher, op. cit., iii. 282–95; Morley, *Gladstone*, i. 583–91; Stanmore, op. cit., ii. 115; Graham to Russell, 17 Jan., Disraeli to Graham, 16, 17, 18 May; Gladstone to Graham, 23, 26 May, Graham to Gladstone, 25, 27 May, to Aberdeen, 28 May 1858. On 10 May Herbert had told Gladstone that Graham was 'undecided', but that Aberdeen expected him to support Cardwell (Stanmore, op. cit., ii. 114). Fortescue thought that t'hared of Palmerston probably decided his course' (Hewett, op. cit. 130). See also Sir Philip Magnus, *Gladstone. A Biography* (1963 ed.), 132–4. Recording Derby's offer of a Cabinet post to Graham, Malmesbury noted on 17 May that Graham had refused, 'saying he is too old and broken in health to accept, and that his sympathies were always with Lord John' (Malmesbury, op. cit., 436).

15. Graham to Gladstone, 27, 31, to Russell, 29, to Prince Albert, 30 July (Parker, *Graham*, ii. 354–8); Benson, Esher, op. cit., iii. 297; Graham to Russell, 1 Sept., 27 Nov., to Cardwell, 24, to Lord Stanley, 28 Nov. 1858; Russell to Graham, 3 Jan., to Ellice, 7 Jan., to Herbert, 9 Jan. 1859. Herbert agreed that the Whigs were 'incurable in their superstitions about ducal houses' (Stanmore, op. cit., ii. 165).

16. Russell to Graham, 19, Graham to Russell, 21 Jan. 1859; Torrens, op. cit., ii. 646–53; Parker, *Graham*, ii. 369–78; Greville, *Victoria*, v. 226–32, 234–40.

17. Torrens, op. cit., ii. 653–60; Parker, *Graham*, ii. 379–81; Gladstone to Herbert, 23 April (Stanmore, op. cit., ii. 178); Ferguson, op. cit., ii. 277; *The Times*, 30, *Carlisle Journal*, 29 April, 6 May, *Morning Herald*, 11, *The Times*, 17 May 1859.

18. Greville, *Victoria*, v. 247–54; Southgate, *Most English Minister*, 455–7, and *Whigs*, 293–5; Stanmore, op. cit., ii. 180–201; Benson, Esher, op. cit., iii. 340–50; Morley, *Gladstone*, i. 621–8; Graham to Russell, 9, 17, 18, 24 May; Palmerston to Graham, 29, Graham to Palmerston, 30 June, to Aberdeen, 15 Aug. 1859. See also Trevelyan, *Bright*, 281–3; Morley, *Cobden*, 690–700; Gathorne-Hardy, op. cit., i. 133.

19. Graham to Aberdeen, 2 Sept., to Gordon, 12 Dec. 1859 (Parker, *Graham*, ii. 392); M. F. Barbey, 'From Carlisle to Silloth' (*The Railway Magazine*, ci. 646, Feb. 1955, 92–96, 120); Torrens, op. cit., ii. 639–40; Graham to Gladstone, 18 Jan., to Russell, 7 March 1860; Herbert to Graham, 13 Nov. 1859, and 8, 12, 28 April, Graham to Herbert, 2, 4, 10, 14, 29 April 1860. See Stanmore, op. cit., ii. 208–69.

20. Morley, *Gladstone*, ii. 26–36, 42–48; Stanmore, op. cit., ii. 277–93; Graham to Gladstone, 2 June, 15, 23 July, Gladstone to Graham, 22 July 1860.

21. *Minutes of Evidence taken before the Select Committee on the Carlisle Election Petition* . . . (1860), 45.

22. Graham to Cardwell, 16 Jan. 1859; Parker, *Graham*, ii. 402–15. 458–63; Torrens, op. cit., ii. 661–72; Ward, op. cit., 403; Hodder, op. cit., 375–6; Stanmore, op. cit., 436–41; Georgina Battiscombe, *Mrs, Gladstone* (1956), 121–2.

23. Lady Herbert, 28, Gladstone, 26 Oct., to Mrs. Baring (Parker, *Graham*, ii. 442–4); Lewis to Clarendon, 27 Oct. (Maxwell, op. cit., ii. 244); Prince Consort to Stockmar, 28 Oct. 1861 [Theodore Martin, *The Life of His Royal Highness the Prince Consort* (1880), v. 407]. 'In politics the Prince regarded him as too much of a partisan, and too covetous of popularity to be entitled to take a leading rank as a statesman; but . . . ability and experience . . . gave him great weight in council . . .' (ibid., v. 407).

24. Greville, *Victoria*, iii. 284, 339, iv. 66; Guizot to Torrens, 27 Sept. 1862 (Torrens, op. cit., iii. 519–20); Morley, *Gladstone*, i. 407–8; Desant, op. cit., i. 205; *The Times*, 16 Feb. 1855.

25. Parker, *Graham*, ii. 444–5; Chalmers' diary, 9 July 1839 (Hanna, op. cit., iv. 121); *Fleet Papers*, 21 Jan., 11, 18, 25 Feb., 6, 13 May, 17, 24 June, 8, 22, 29 July, 26 Aug. 1843; G. J. Holyoake, *Sixty Years of an Agitator's Life* (1906 ed.), 153–4, 173–5.

26. Torrens, op. cit., ii. 646–53, 655–6; Graham to Peel, 1 Jan. 1842; R. B. McDowell, *The Irish Administration, 1801–1914* (1964), 281. Graham's brother George was his private secretary at the Admiralty and Home Office and in 1842 became Registrar-General, on Graham's nomination (Parker, *Graham*, ii. 440; Roberts, op. cit., 163).

27. Graham to Sandars, 22 Nov. 1849; Le Marchant, op. cit., 292, n. 2.

28. Peel to Croker, 13 Dec. 1838 (Jennings, op. cit., ii. 337); F. K. Brown, op. cit., 282, 429.

29. Graham to Napier, 12 March 1844; S. Smith to H. Fairburn, n.d (in the possession of Mr. Godfrey Meynell); Alexander Somerville, *The Autobiography of a Working Man* (ed. John Carswell; 1951 ed.), *passim*, and *The Whistler at the Plough and Free Trade* (Manchester, 1852), 204; *Journ. R. Agric. Soc.*, i. (1839). Graham maintained that 'skill in agriculture does not so much consist in the discovery of principles of universal application, as in the adaptation of acknowledged principles to local circumstances'.

30. *The Times*, 26 Oct. 1861, 11 May 1937 [G. M. Young, *Victorian Studies* (1962), 15]; Parker, *Graham*, ii. 444; Morley to Sir W. Lawson, 24 Aug. 1899 (ibid., 435); Graham to Phipps, 20 April 1855 (ibid., 436).

31. Parker, *Graham*, ii. ch. 20; H. W. C. Davis, *The Age of Grey and Peel* (Oxford, 1964 reprint), 241–2; see Mandell Creighton's notice in *The Dictionary of National Biography*, viii. (1908), 328–32.

Index

Index of Authors

PRINTED IN GREAT BRITAIN BY ROBERT MACLEHOSE AND CO. LTD
THE UNIVERSITY PRESS, GLASGOW